Migration & Integration 8

Herausgeber:

Mathias Czaika, Lydia Rössl,
Thomas Pfeffer, Friedrich Altenburg

Mathias Czaika, Lydia Rössl,
Thomas Pfeffer, Friedrich Altenburg
(Hg.)

Migration & Integration 8

Dialog zwischen Politik, Wissenschaft und Praxis

EUROPA
INTEGRATION
ÄUSSERES
BUNDESMINISTERIUM
REPUBLIK ÖSTERREICH

Dieses Projekt wird durch den AMIF und das Bundesministerium für Europa, Integration und Äußeres kofinanziert.

Die in der Publikation geäußerten Ansichten liegen in der Verantwortung der Autor/inn/en und geben nicht notwendigerweise die Meinung der Donau-Universität Krems wieder.

Verlag: Edition Donau-Universität Krems
Herstellung: tredition GmbH, Halenreie 40-44, 22359 Hamburg
ISBN Taschenbuch: 978-3-903150-56-0
ISBN e-Book: 978-3-903150-57-7

Kontakt:
Department für Migration und Globalisierung
Donau-Universität Krems
www.donau-uni.ac.at/mig
migration@donau-uni.ac.at

Satz: Thomas Pfeffer
Umschlaggestaltung: Gudrun Mittendrein

Zitiervorschlag: Mathias Czaika, Lydia Rössl, Thomas Pfeffer, Friedrich Altenburg (Hg.) (2019) Migration & Integration 8. Dialog zwischen Politik, Wissenschaft und Praxis. Reihe DialogForum Integration. Krems (Edition Donau-Universität Krems).

Inhaltsverzeichnis

PRAXISBERICHTE

Einleitung

Lydia Rössl, Mathias Czaika

Die Veranstaltung „DialogForum Migration & Integration" blickt auf inzwischen elf Jahre der Vernetzung und des Dialogs zwischen Politik, Wissenschaft und Praxis zurück. Das DialogForum macht es sich zur Aufgabe einen Rahmen für unterschiedliche AkteurInnen als Vortragende, DiskutantInnen, ImpulsgeberInnen sowie TeilnehmerInnen aus der Wissenschaft, öffentlichen Verwaltung, Politik und Zivilgesellschaft für einen offenen und konstruktiven Austausch zu Themen zu bieten, die offensichtlich, manchmal aber auch über Umwege, in einem Zusammenhang mit Migration und Integration stehen. Die Herausforderungen hierbei sind vielfältig, dazu zählen eine Brücke zwischen Theorie und Praxis herzustellen und, im Sinne von Capacity Building und Lösungsorientierung, Instrumente zu fördern, die die Entwicklung nachhaltiger Strategien für Zusammenarbeit und gegenseitiges Verständnis unterstützen; auf die Dynamiken und andauernden Veränderungen internationaler und nationaler Migrations- und Integrationsprozessen einzugehen; sowie die Analyse damit verbundener gesellschaftlicher, politischer, institutioneller und wissenschaftlicher Herausforderungen

Das DialogForum hat sich 2019 in der Wahl der Themen, Beiträgen und Diskussionen der Komplexität und der Vielfalt an Widersprüchen in der Wissenschaft und Gesellschaft, zwischen Fakten und politischen Konstrukten sowie Ideal, Handlungsempfehlung und Praxis gewidmet. Die Schwerpunkte des DialogForums 2019 zeichneten sich durch eine hohe Aktualität aus, dazu gehören Themen wie die Mobilität von Hochqualifizierten; Selbstständigkeit von MigrantInnen; Rückkehrmigration im Spannungsfeld zwischen (Un-)Freiwilligkeit und (Re-)Integration; sowie Fragen hinsichtlich der Herausforderungen und Gestaltung eines postmigrantischen Wandels zu Einwanderungsgesellschaften. Diese Themen werden in diesem Tagungsband mit Bezug auf die wissenschaftliche Perspektive und bestehende Forschungsergebnisse abgehandelt. Die vielfältigen offenen Frage- und Problemstellungen, die in diesen komplexen Themenfeldern auftreten, werden durch Perspektiven und Beispielen aus der Praxis vertieft.

Der erste Abschnitt dieses Tagungsbandes befasst sich mit der Mobilität von Hochqualifizierten. Studien zeigen die vielfältigen Vorteile der Zuwanderung von hochqualifizierten ArbeitnehmerInnen in Bezug auf das Wirtschaftswachstum, Innovation und Wettbewerbsfähigkeit (Czaika, 2017). Die Mobilität von Hochqualifizierten steigt, der Bedarf und Wettbewerb auf nationalstaatlicher Ebene und unter (internationalen) Unternehmen wird sich in den nächsten Jahren voraussichtlich weiterhin verschärfen (Boeri et al., 2012). Unterschiedliche Maßnahmenpakete, Anreizsystem und vielfältige Visavarianten illustrieren das bestehende Bewusstsein zu dieser Entwicklung (Czaika, 2017), zeitgleich bedingt eine zunehmend restriktive Zuwanderungspolitik in vielen europäischen Ländern das Risiko, dass Zuwanderung auch für Hochqualifizierte zunehmend unattraktiver wird (Amelie & Strøm-Olsen, 2019).

Die Beiträge zu der Mobilität von Hochqualifizierten umfassen und verbinden Themen aus der Politik, der Wirtschaft und Unternehmertum. Ausgehend von der Makroebene analysiert Mathias Czaika in seinem Artikel *High-skilled Migration Policies* inwiefern die Gestaltung und Umsetzung von Migration policies Einfluss auf die Möglichkeiten der Mobilität von Hochqualifizierten haben, und welche Implikationen dies wiederum auf europäischer, nationalstaatlicher bis zur individuellen Ebene daraus resultieren. Auch Sascha Krannich beschäftigt sich mit Einwanderungspolitiken für hochqualifizierte MigrantInnen und vergleicht das Vorgehen in Kanada, Australien, Neuseeland, Großbritannien und Österreich. Er legt hierbei besonderes Augenmerk auf die dort geltenden länderspezifischen Punktesysteme und beschäftigt sich mit deren Vor- und Nachteilen. Washika Haak-Saheem adressiert in ihrem Beitrag die Chancen, welche sich aus transnationaler Mobilität von Hochqualifizierten für multinationale Unternehmen eröffnen. Sie diskutiert Zusammenhänge von Mobilität, Entwicklung, Innovation und Unternehmenserfolg, als auch die vielfältigen Herausforderungen, Ziele und Strategien im Bereich des Personalmanagements bei der Rekrutierung von hochqualifizierten MitarbeiterInnen.

Auch der Weg in die Selbstständigkeit und der Trend zu Start-ups werden stark mit Innovation und einen Gewinn für Wirtschaft und Gesellschaft verbunden. In diesem Zusammenhang findet zunehmend das Thema 'Migrant Entrepreneuship' und die Möglichkeiten der Unternehmensgründung für MigrantInnen über Ländergrenzen hinweg Beachtung in Politik und Wissenschaft. In Widerspruch hierzu stehen nicht nur komplexe länderspezifische Regulierungen und Beschränkungen von Mobilität, sondern auch die umfassenden und belegten Schwierigkeiten von MigrantInnen und insbesondere anerkannten Geflüchteten, sich am Arbeitsmarkt – und dies nicht nur in Österreich - ihrer Qualifikation entsprechend zu integrieren (Bock-Schappelwein & Huber, 2016). Studien zeigen, dass Geflüchtete zwar im Vergleich mit ArbeitsmigrantInnen im Durchschnitt geringer qualifiziert sind, allerdings etwa gleich gute Qualifikationen wie andere MigrantInnen vorweisen können, die nicht vorrangig aus Arbeitsmotiven migriert sind (Bock-Schappelwein & Huber, 2016).

Der übergeordnete Titel dieses Abschnitts des Tagungsbandes *„Selbstständigkeit von Migranten und Migrantinnen als Integrationsmotor?"* soll hierbei als eine Aufforderung zu einer kritischen Diskussion und Generierung weiterführender Fragestellungen verstanden werden. In einem einführenden Beitrag beschreibt Gudrun Biffl die Charakteristika und Rahmenbedingungen von ‚migrant entrepreneurship' und unterstreicht hierbei die Komplexität dieses aktuell intensiv diskutierten Themas. Hierbei werden nicht nur der Zusammenhang zwischen migrantischem Unternehmertum und Integration kritisch betrachtet, sondern auch die mögliche Rolle von migrant entrepreneurship als Vernetzungsinstrument für Wirtschaft, Wissen und Innovation im Globalisierungszeitalter angesprochen. Monder Ram ruft in seinem Artikel *The Centre for Ethnic Minority Entrepreneurship: A Vehicle for Criti-*

cal Engagement zu einer Erweiterung der kritischen Forschung und der Wissensgenerierung zu migrant entrepreneurship auf, um eine nachhaltige Gestaltung europa-
weiter Maßnahmen in diesem Bereich zu ermöglichen. Er stellt in diesem Kontext
das Centre for Research in Ethnic Minority Entrepreneurship (CREME) an der As-
ton Universität vor und betont die Bedeutung der Verschränkung theoretischen und
praktischen Wissens sowie Erfahrungen im Sinne eines Ansatzes des 'critical engagement'. Alexander Spiegelfeld und Ave Lauren behandeln anhand der Länderbei-
spiele Österreich und Estland Migrationswege für Drittstaatsangehörige, die eine
Aufenthaltserlaubnis in Österreich und Estland beantragen wollen, um ein Start-up
zu gründen. Der Artikel beschreibt die Strategien beider Länder zur Gewinnung und
Bindung Drittstaatsangehöriger, die innovative Unternehmungen planen, sowie be-
währte Verfahren und Herausforderungen im Zusammenhang mit diesen Maßnahmen.

Auch Rückkehrmigration, ob nun auf freiwilliger und unfreiwilliger Basis, wird
im öffentlichen Diskurs häufig in einem engen Zusammenhang mit einem wirtschaftlichen und gesellschaftlichen Mehrwert – in diesem Fall für die RückkehrerInnen und dem jeweiligen Herkunftsland – gebracht. Mögliche Vorteile sind hierbei, dass MigrantInnen, falls sie Zugang zum Arbeitsmarkt hatten und eine entsprechende Arbeitsstelle besetzen konnten, Ersparnisse erwirtschaften konnten und
diese wieder in ihrem Herkunftsland investieren, z.B. in Form einer Unternehmensgründung. Sie können im Ausland erworbene Fähigkeiten, neue Ideen und Zugänge
wirtschaftlich und politisch in ihrem Herkunftsland einbringen und somit zu der
Entwicklung des Landes beitragen. Investitionen dieser Art von RückkehrerInnen
zeigen sich von einer Vielzahl weiterer Faktoren abhängig, wie bürokratische Hürden, dass angeeignete Fähigkeiten tatsächlich den Bedarf des Arbeitsmarkts im Herkunftsland entsprechen, oder auch eine Offenheit gegenüber neuer Ideen und An-
sätzen besteht. Nicht zuletzt waren nicht alle RückkehrerInnen - im Sinne einer Erweiterung von Finanzen und Fähigkeiten - im Ausland 'erfolgreich'. Im Falle von
nicht anerkannten Geflüchteten kann dies auf Basis eines in vielen Ländern fehlen-
den Arbeitsmarktzuganges nahezu ausgeschlossen werden. Die verfügbaren Daten
zur Rückkehrmigration zeigen allerdings Forschungsbedarf auf, dies wird auch im
letzten Abschnitt dieses Tagungsbandes anhand einiger Forschungsvorhaben adressiert.

Amparo González-Ferrer, Inmaculada Serrano und Adrien Vandenbunder schaffen in ihrem Artikel eine Übersicht zu der umfassenden konzeptionellen Diskussion
über Rückkehr und zirkuläre Migration sowie ihre forschungsbezogenen und politischen Implikationen. Nach der Vorstellung der bestehenden Definitionen und der
Diskussion ihrer Vor- und Nachteile für statistische Messungen und politische Be-
wertungen, wird die in den TEMPER-Umfragen 2017/18 unter zurückgekehrten
MigrantInnen und Nicht-MigrantInnen in Argentinien, Rumänien, Senegal und der
Ukraine angenommene Definition erläutert und auf vorläufige Ergebnisse aus den
Umfragen eingegangen.

Im Anschluss befassen sich Özge Bilgili und Sonja Fransen unter dem Titel *Return, Reintegration and the Role of State* vertiefend mit der Rolle des Aufnahmestaats bei der Reintegration von rückkehrenden MigrantInnen. Auf der Basis von weltweiten Beispielen von Rückkehr- und Reintegrationsprozessen betonen die Autorinnen die Bedeutung eines guten Verständnisses für die Heterogenität unter RückkehrerInnen und ihren Erfahrungen unter Berücksichtigung von Dimensionen wie sozialem Zusammenhalt und sozioökonomische Ungleichheit.

Marieke van Houte als auch Andrea Götzelmann-Rosado gehen in ihren Beiträgen auf das konkrete Beispiel Afghanistan ein. Marieke van Houte nimmt eine kritische Perspektive auf die Erfolge von Rückführungsprogramme ein und bezieht sich hierbei auf die Ergebnisse und Analyse ihrer Feldforschung von 2012 unter 35 afghanischen RückkehrerInnen und deren gelebten Erfahrungen. Die Autorin stellt den Begriff der nachhaltigen Reintegration in Frage. Andrea Götzelmann-Rosado befasst sich mit Projekt RE-START II, das von der Internationalen Organisation für Migration (IOM) durchgeführt wird und Unterstützung bei der freiwilligen Rückkehr und Reintegration von aus Österreich zurückkehrenden AfghanInnen bietet. Sie analysiert die demographischen Daten und Rückmeldungen der im Projekt Involvierten und beleuchtet deren Rückkehrmotive sowie Realitäten.

Auch das Idealbild einer postmigrantischen Integration (und weiterführend einer postmigrantischen Gesellschaft), die sich laut Naika Foroutan (2015) durch die Möglichkeiten von Anerkennung, Chancengleichheit und Teilhabe in einer vielfältigen Gesellschaft definiert, steht in einem harten Gegensatz zu den politischen und gesellschaftlichen Trends verstärkter Regulierungen, Grenzziehungen und Abgrenzungen. Die postmigrantische Gesellschaft und die Erweiterung des Verständnisses von Integration im Sinne einer postmigrantischen Integration werden von Rainer Bauböck und Ernst Fürlinger aus unterschiedlichen Perspektiven angesprochen.

Rainer Bauböck illustriert in seinem Beitrag die Vielfalt und Komplexität des Zugangs zu Staatsbürgerschaft und dem Wahlrecht in Österreich im internationalen Vergleich. Seine Ausführungen zeigen auf, wie rechtliche und nationalstaatliche Konstrukte in einem Widerspruch zu dem Anspruch einer postmigrantischen Integration darstellen, wie sie Foroutan (2015) definiert. Auch Ernst Fürlinger geht in seinem Artikel auf globale politische und wirtschaftliche Entwicklungen seit den 1990er Jahren ein, die Bestrebungen nach einer postmigrantischen Gesellschaft erschweren, wenn nicht unmöglich machen. Er bezieht sich hierbei unter anderem auf den Begriff und Verständnis der ‚Hyperglobalisierung' von Dani Rodrik (2011) und kritische Überlegungen von Andreas Reckwitz (2019), wie eine faire und sozial sowie ökologisch verträgliche Form der wirtschaftlichen Globalisierung erreicht werden kann.

Der letzte Abschnitt dieses Tagungsbandes bietet einen Einblick in offene Forschungsfragen und damit verbundene Forschungsvorhaben mit einem Fokus auf die Rückkehrmigration. Friedrich Altenburg zieht das Beispiel von Bosnien und Herzegowina heran. Er hinterfragt, auf welche Weise die Rückkehr nach konfliktbedingter Flucht zu einer integrativen Gesellschaft und zur Wiederherstellung von Frieden und Stabilität beitragen kann. Der Autor zeigt hierbei die Gegensätze der

theoretischen Zielsetzungen des Friedensabkommens von Dayton als richtungswei-
sendes politisches Dokument mit starken Bezug zu der Bedeutung von Rückkehrmigration, und den tatsächlichen Rückkehrprozessen auf, die von ethnischen Span-
nungen, sozialer Ungleichheit und damit einhergehenden Konflikten charakterisiert
waren. Auch Hakan Kilic und Gudrun Biffl sprechen in ihrem Beitrag freiwillige
Rückkehrmigration und die Rolle der Politik und Strategien der Türkei an, um hochqualifizierte MigrantInnen und deren Nachkommen zur Rückwanderung zu moti-
vieren. Zu den Zielsetzungen zählen die Diversifikation der Arbeitskräfte und wirt-
schaftliches Wachstumspotenzial zu verbessern.

Im Gegensatz zur freiwilligen Rückkehrmigration steht die Vertreibung von
mehr als einer halben Million afghanischer Flüchtlinge im Jahr 2016 aus Pakistan,
die dadurch zu einer Rückkehr nach Afghanistan gezwungen waren und sich in hohem Ausmaß in und im Umfeld von Kabul niederließen. Ali Ahmad Safi geht in
seinem Beitrag auf die Lebenssituation und Erfahrungen der RückkehrerInnen, mit
den Herausforderungen der (Re-)Integration und Reintegrationsprogrammen, soziale Ausgrenzung und Arbeitslosigkeit in zwei informellen Siedlungen in Ostafgha-
nistan ein.

Margarita Fourer adressiert in ihrer Forschung die Bedeutung der lokalen Auf-
nahmebevölkerung und der Rahmenbedingungen, die auf einer Makroebene beeinflusst werden können. Sie behandelt exemplarisch die vom Europäischen Rat vor-
geschlagenen Ausschiffungsregelungen, die sich an dem australischen Modell ori-
entieren. Auf Basis einer Analyse des australischen Modells geht sie vertiefend auf
mögliche Konsequenzen einer realen oder vermeintlichen Benachteiligung der Aufnahmegesellschaft ein und weist auf die Bedeutung entsprechender Unterstützungs-
leistungen hin, die Information, Partizipation, Kapazitätenaufbau und Integrations-
prozesse gewährleisten.

Im finalen Abschnitt wird ein Einblick in die Praxis und ‚Good Practice' Projek-
ten am Beispiel der Mobilität von Hochqualifizierten gegeben. Der Beitrag von
Christiane Schnetzer fokussiert auf die Herausforderungen und Rahmenbedingungen von Expats, um unter kulturell und sozio-strukturell unterschiedlichen Voraussetzungen erfolgreich sein zu können. Im Sinne einer Lösungsorientierung stellt sie
den „Erweiterten Selbstmanagement-Fragenkatalog" (Schnetzer, 2015) vor, der einer Einschätzung und Reflexion der Selbstmanagementfähigkeiten diesen soll.

In dieser Hinsicht hat sich das DialogForum des Jahres 2019 nicht nur dem Auf-
zeigen bestehender Komplexitäten und Widersprüchen gewidmet, sondern auch einen Raum für die Formulierung offener Fragen in Theorie und Praxis, sowie von
Forschungs- und Handlungsbedarf zur Verfügung gestellt. Dieser Raum versteht
sich hierbei als ortsunabhängig, und soll in den Begegnungen und der Vernetzung
der TeilnehmerInnen eine nachhaltige und dynamische Fortsetzung finden.

Auch 2020 soll dieses inhaltlich weitgefächerte Programm, das nur durch die
finanzielle Förderung durch den Asyl-, Migrations- und Integrationsfonds, das
BMEIA und das BMBWF möglich wurde, weitergeführt werden. Wir laden Sie
herzlich ein, auch im kommenden Jahr Ihr Wissen und Ihre Erfahrungen einzubrin-
gen und Teil des Dialogs zu sein.

Literatur

Maria Amelie und Nicolai Strøm-Olsen (2019): Startups Migrants. Frekk Forlag.

Julia Bock-Schappelwein und Peter Huber (2016): Zur Arbeitsmarktintegration von Asylsuchenden in Österreich. In: WIFO-Monatsberichte, 2016, 89(3), S. 157-169.

Tito Boeri (2012): Introduction. In: Tito Boeri, Herbert Brücker, Frédéric Docquier, und Hillel Rapoport (Hg.): Brain Drain and Brain Gain. The Global Competition to Attract High-Skilled Migrants. S. 1 – 14. Oxford University Press.

Mathias Czaika (2017): „Global Competition for Talent": Eine migrationspolitische Herausforderung. In: Friedrich Altenburg, Anna Faustmann, Thomas Pfeffer, Isabella Skrivanek (Hg.): Migration und Globalisierung in Zeiten des Umbruchs. S. 83-99. Edition Donau-Universität Krems.

Naika Foroutan (2015): Konviviale Integration in postmigrantischen Gesellschaften In: Adloff, F. / Volker M. H. (Hrsg.): Konvivialismus. Eine Debatte. S. 205 - 216. Transcript.

Andreas Reckwitz (2019): Das Ende der Illusionen. Politik, Ökonomie und Kultur in der Spätmoderne. Edition Suhrkamp.

Dani Rodrik (2011): The Globalization Paradox: Democracy and the Future of the World Economy. W.W. Norton.

Schnetzer, Christiane (2015): Einfluss und Entwicklung des Selbstmanagements im Rahmen beruflicher Auslandseinsätze. Master Thesis, Donau-Universität Krems.

Jackline Wahba (2015): Who benefits from return migration to developing countries? https://wol.iza.org/uploads/articles/123/pdfs/who-benefits-from-return-migration-to-developing-countries.pdf?v=1. Doi: 10.1518 5/ i z aw o l.12 3. Accessed 28th November 2019.

MOBILITÄT VON HOCHQUALIFIZIERTEN: POLITIKEN, REKRUTIERUNG, INTEGRATION AM ARBEITSPLATZ

High-skilled Migration Policies

Mathias Czaika

Abstract

Immigration policies are increasingly designed to attract and select high-skilled workers from abroad. This chapter provides an overview of skill-selective and attracting migration policies and policy instruments and a brief assessment of their effectiveness. While points-based and other supply-side systems often increase both the absolute numbers of high-skill migrants and the skill composition of international labour flows, demand-driven systems are generally rather deterring for international talent. The broader immigration policy package that combines explicit skill-attracting migration policies with other migration-relevant public policies determines the overall attractiveness of a destination for international talent seem more relevant and effective in supporting employers in recruiting highly skilled labour.

Introduction[1]

European immigration is increasingly characterised by ambivalence between relatively liberal, albeit selective, immigration regulations vis-à-vis skilled foreign workers and rather restrictive measures with regard to low-skilled migration from non-European third countries. The immigration of low-skilled migrants and workers, especially if they come from poorer, ethnically and culturally more distanced non-European countries, is increasingly perceived as a problem that requires massive restrictions of various kinds, whereas qualified people and migrants find largely positive resonance and support in most political and public circles. In the context of general concerns about national identity and socio-cultural change as a result of increasing ethnic-religious diversity, the importance of skilled immigration for ensuring economic sustainability is currently rather subordinate. This is fatal as the intensity of a global competition for the best "hands and minds" continues to accelerate. It is not only European economies that have developed a growing need and demand for skilled labour, but also other highly developed economies, and increasingly also middle-income and low-income developing countries are establishing policies and strategies to either retain their talent, or attract new talent from abroad.

It is politically acknowledged that countries, rapidly transforming to "knowledge-based" economies, are under increasing pressure to develop strategies that are suitable for attracting, selecting and retaining highly qualified workers

---

[1]   This chapter is mostly based on a German version published in Altenburg, F. et al. (2018).

(Doomernik et al., 2009, OECD, 2008). Numerous empirical studies have illustrated that the immigration of skilled workers can make a significant contribution to economic growth, public finances, and the overall competitiveness and innovation of the host economy. As a result, the global competition for skilled workers continues to intensify and a steadily increasing number of states, companies and other actors are competing for the *"best and brightest"* (Boeri et al., 2012, Kapur and McHale, 2005).

Highly qualified employees and well-trained people play a key role in almost all private and public sectors because of their knowledge, experience and expertise. They are often referred to as *"knowledge workers"* (DTI, 2002) whose day-to-day work is characterised by creative thinking, research and development (Davenport, 2005). However, a uniform definition of a highly qualified migrant has not yet been established, which is why often the level of education (tertiary), the level of income (varied, e.g. top quintile of wage earners) or the type of occupation (top three categories of the ISCO classification system[2]) are used to define a high-skilled migrant (Parsons et al. 2018). In any case, qualified workers are seen as a valuable contribution to any economy. Particularly in the knowledge- and innovation-driven knowledge economies of the 21st century, "brain workers" are seen as an essential component or even a prerequisite for securing long-term economic growth and prosperity.

The global market for highly qualified work

Over the last half century, a widespread increase in the global supply of qualified labour is attributable to growing interest in (higher) education and to massive private and public investment in primary, secondary and tertiary education capacities. Education nourishes the aspiration for more and better education and thus creates a continuously growing number of people who strive for more, better and more differentiated education and qualifications. A rising *"return on human capital investment"* in the form of increased productivity and corresponding remunerations is an important driving force behind this development (Czaika 2018a).

Education nourishes also the desire for a "good life" and provides for the knowledge of how and, in particular, where this quality of (professional) life can be achieved. An increasingly mobile and skilled workforce is an expression of an aspirations-driven process. Rising educational levels however also require of qualified and highly specialised workers to be (internationally) mobile. Therefore, the general increase in human capital stocks and the associated expansion of professional demands on the "good life" in combination with a geographical concentration of high-

---

[2]   The top three categories of the ten classes of the international standard classification of occupations (ISCO-08) comprise managers, senior officials and legislators (ISCO-1), professionals (ISCO-2), and technicians and associate professionals (ISCO-3).

quality employment opportunities – especially in some economic metropoles of various OECD and non-OECD countries – promotes the international mobility of (highly) qualified people. At a global scale, highly trained, mostly tertiary educated people have a migration propensity that is significantly higher than of less formally educated people, and a so-called "mobility gap" between tertiary and secondary educated people seems to be widening (Czaika 2018a). This mobility gap is an expression and consequence of differences in aspirations and opportunities between highly qualified and educated people and those who have enjoyed less formal education.

On the demand side of this global market for (highly) skilled labour, we observe companies and employers expressing a growing need for specialized knowledge, skills, and expertise. Most developed and emerging economies are experiencing a supply gap in certain sectors and occupations that cannot be adequately met by the domestic supply of highly skilled labour. Such structural bottlenecks in certain skill segments or occupations may even increase in the future due to a further differentiation of qualification requirements, which is why qualification- and skill-specific immigration is often regarded as a means of overcoming these occupational bottlenecks.

Internationally, the demand for skilled labour has been rising steadily for decades, so that in many OECD countries highly qualified, tertiary educated workers will represent the majority of immigrants in the near future (Czaika 2018a). The ongoing transformation of economic and labour market structures and the transition to knowledge-based economies strengthens the demand of companies for highly specialized and diversified qualification structure of labour supply that cannot be domestically reproduced to the necessary extent, at least not in the short term.

This trend will further intensify the international competition for the scarce resource of human capital. Demographic, economic and technological transitions in combination with internationally operating agencies and companies as well as the harmonisation of education systems have created the preconditions for the emergence of an international or even global labour market for highly qualified workers. This dynamically globalizing labour market is characterized by a reciprocal selection process between the "scarce" supply of qualified skilled workers and the demand of recruiting states and companies with a need for skilled workers with specialized knowledge and skills (Chiswick, 2011). As a consequence of this mutual selection process, highly qualified workers can increasingly choose between several job offers in their employment decisions: If the attractiveness of a particular job, company or city, region or country is perceived as insufficient, many skilled workers can opt for more attractive alternative offers. This flexibility of internationally mobile, highly-qualified workers and the rapidly changing skill needs of competing countries and enterprises challenge them to continuously adapt their recruitment strategies and offers to the needs in order to increase their ability to attract and retain highly-qualified workers.

This trend reflects a *globalisation of occupational skill shortages,* which does not only concern the highly-skilled, but also medium- and even some low-skilled occupations that are increasingly in high demand, usually in relation to specific occupations, sectors, regions or time periods. While an increasing number of countries face similar labour market challenges and are therefore engaging in a competition for talent, national recruitment strategies and regulations for admitting and (re-)integrating skilled workers from abroad often differ significantly according to the respective occupations, national needs, and strategic priorities of national migration policies.

Attracting, selecting, admitting and integrating skilled foreign labour

State-led recruitment of foreign labour involves various challenges. A fundamental challenge in matching demand and supply of skilled foreign labour in response to perceived labour shortages, for instance, is the accurate identification and anticipation of national – or in some occupations rather regional – shortages. Forecasting short-, medium- and long-term skill and occupational shortages requires prediction of economic cycles and structural changes as well as business, wage, or technological developments and innovations.

Another challenge is the development of a recruitment mechanism that is effective in attracting and selecting the right "types" of foreign workers and the adaption of tools to monitor and respond to altering immigration flows and shortages in a timely manner. Furthermore, most countries find it challenging to attract immigrants to the regions where they were most needed and to ensure that credentials of the immigrants are accepted on the domestic country labour market.

Therefore, over the past two decades, the OECD and, to a lesser extent, non-OECD governments have taken measures to redesign their migration policy regimes in order to attract and select (highly-)skilled migrants to alleviate the often short-term, cyclical, shortage of skilled labour and to fill structural supply gaps in certain sectors, such as health, ICT or the so-called STEM (science, technology, engineering and mathematics) subjects.

In principle, a general distinction can be made between demand-side and supply-side policy approaches (cf. Figure 1). The former, for instance, requires a job offer before obtaining a work and residence permit, whereas this is not fundamentally necessary in the case of a supply-side recruitment and selection policy. Rather, access to the labour market is granted through an examination of individual qualifications and other personal characteristics, which are often determined by multiple-criteria points-based systems (e.g.in Canada, Australia and New Zealand). However, many countries also use mixed or hybrid forms, which include short-, medium- and long-term strategies with varying degrees of priority and intensity in order to acquire international know-how, knowledge and human capital (cf. Abella, 2006, Czaika and Parsons 2017).

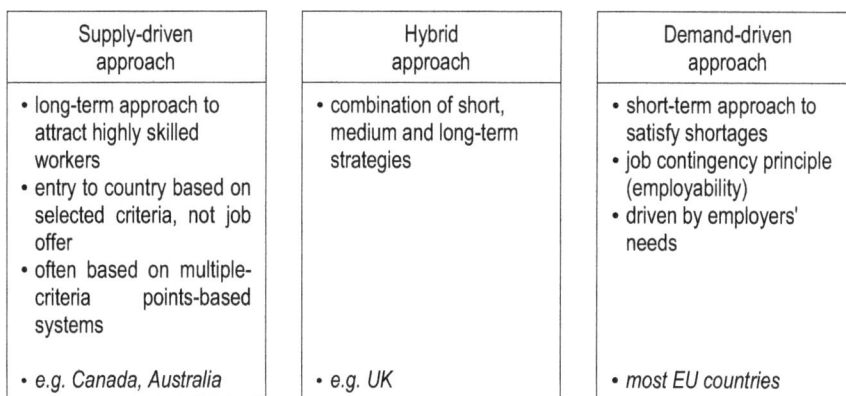

Supply-driven approach	Hybrid approach	Demand-driven approach
• long-term approach to attract highly skilled workers • entry to country based on selected criteria, not job offer • often based on multiple-criteria points-based systems	• combination of short, medium and long-term strategies	• short-term approach to satisfy shortages • job contingency principle (employability) • driven by employers' needs
• *e.g. Canada, Australia*	• *e.g. UK*	• *most EU countries*

Figure 1 Dominant policy approaches for attracting and selecting highly qualified migrants

Source: ICMPD (2019)

Demand-side policy strategies

A demand-side labour migration policy responds directly to the current labour market situation and is rather short-termed in nature and is mostly influenced by corresponding economic and employment cycles. Employers' needs are the driving force, as this policy approach is first and foremost about the rapid closure of a mostly very specific gap in labour supply. A basic principle for a demand-driven admission policy of foreign workers is the employability of the migrant worker, which is to be ensured by a sponsoring on part of the employer. A demand-driven recruitment and selection process is usually initiated by the employing companies themselves, and employers usually play an active role in recruiting and promoting foreign skilled workers to qualify for temporary or permanent work and residence permits. This job contingency principle is intended to guarantee the employability and skill-adequate incorporation of foreign employees in the domestic labour market. Obviously, while prioritising employability and ‚matched‘ admission of foreign workers to address short-term labour market shortages, the requirement of a job offer, and sometimes, of a labour market audit can also deter (highly) skilled immigrants. This is particularly the case if, despite the qualifications of the potential immigrant, there are no direct labour market bottlenecks (no shortage occupations) in the specific sector (Czaika and Parsons, 2017). Most European immigration systems (including the EU Blue Card and also the Austrian Red-White-Red Card) as well as the temporary US work visas (H1B) are based on the principle of job offers.

The granting of a work permit by the employer often requires a regional, national or even Europe-wide labour market examination to ensure that no "equivalent" domestic workers are available. However, the bureaucratic burden of appropriate labour market tests can be considerable. Many countries therefore operate with so-called sector-specific or occupation-specific shortage lists, which normally replace an individual-specific labour market review for each applicants. Shortage lists accelerate recruitment processes, especially when entire occupational sectors are affected by a high demand for labour. However, the sometimes dubious stringency of the underlying analysis for determining a shortage of skilled labour and the corresponding labour demand is frequently criticised (cf. Sumption 2013).

States sometimes also recruit qualified workers on the basis of bilateral or multilateral agreements and provide mostly temporary, but often also permanent labour and residence rights for this purpose. Other policy strategies often aim to attract international investors and companies. This rather indirect recruitment strategy enables qualified workers to obtain work and residence permits on the basis of an internal posting of qualified personnel (expatriation, intra-company transfers).

Supply-side policy strategies

A small but growing number of countries are pursuing a rather long-term human capital approach, which seeks to accumulate human capital independently of immediate cyclical demand for skilled labour in order to strengthen long-term capacities for knowledge production and innovation. Highly mobile and sought-after knowledge workers, once attracted for immigration, often gain direct or at least rapid access to unlimited residence rights and citizenship without necessarily having a job offer in the pocket. In these rather supply-driven and long-term migration policy strategies, human capital is assessed on an individual basis, usually as part of a points-based system in which foreign applicants accumulate credits on the basis of their qualifications, age, work experience, language skills and earning potential. Job offers are generally not necessary, although applicants who have a job before entering the country often receive additional points for it. Canada (since 1967) and Australia (since 1989) are pioneers of these points-based systems, which are generally regarded as relatively effective in attracting (highly) qualified migrants (Facchini and Lodigiani, 2014, Czaika and Parsons, 2017). More recently, however, these systems have also shown that in some cases they select applicants who do not address directly existing labour market shortages and who cannot be placed on the labour market for a longer period of time despite high qualifications (Aydemir, 2013). Most countries that have implemented points-based systems are therefore increasingly aiming to combine supply- and demand-side elements in so-called hybrid labour recruitment systems in order to ensure that the objectives of human capital accumulation and employability are both met.

Such more long-term human capital strategies often include measures aimed at foreign students and graduates of post-graduate education as 'semi-finished' human capital (Khadria, 2001) and an investment in a country's future. This policy approach aims at the permanent recruitment and integration of these partially or completely domestically trained workers, who are not only professionally educated but also socio-culturally educated and thus considered to be socially and economically

Legal measures		
Tool	*Advantages*	*Disadvantages and Risks*
Labour Market Tests	• Ensure that jobs are offered locally; • Demonstrate lack of local supply; • Ensure that employers effectively attempt to recruit locally before looking abroad; • Employers understand job search techniques.	• Further lengthens the process of deciding whether to allow the use of a migrant worker; • May be applied unevenly by different officials and regions (quality assurance and fairness of assessments); • Conflicting views between a PES and employers on availability, suitability or willingness of candidates on the unemployment register to fill vacancies; • Easy to distort (job description); • Often no standardised testing within country, PES may not actually be real location for matching; • Beyond nominal listings, difficult to enforce; • Requires administrative machinery to be effective, which imposes delays and costs.
Occupational shortage lists	• Tighter and more consistent than individual decentralised labour market tests carried out across various offices; • Easy to explain to the public; • Signal that labour migration is focused on specific occupations; • Mirror for demand; • Can be combined with other tools such as labour market test;	• Complicated to develop (methodological constraints); • Difficult to assess experience component; • Subject to interest group lobbying; • Frequency of revision affects responsiveness to demand; • Not appropriate for all occupations.
Quotas	• Clear reference framework; • Legal framework: Measures to balance interests (labour demand/public concerns); • Human resource development: Quotas for highly skilled workers may be part of the human resource development strategy	• Bureaucracy/lack of flexibility: Labour market needs are difficult to identify and hardly predictable over a medium time period; • Difficult matching: difficult to match skilled migrant workers with jobs in quota-specified sectors and employers; • Distinguishing level of skills: Quotas can define a corresponding type of skills but cannot ensure a certain level of skills; • Labour market competition: definition of skill-based quotas may result in undesired competition between migrant workers and native workers in certain labour market segments; • Adjustment of labour markets: Labour migration quotas may slow down the adjustment of labour markets (e.g., regarding wages and conditions) to suitable domestic workers.
Salary thresholds	• When based on binding job offers, salary thresholds guarantee jobs upon arrival; • Most salary threshold models require employer commitment in form of concrete job offers. As one of the results, workers have jobs upon arrival; • Reduce administrative burdens, in particular when they are used as alternatives (and not as complements) to other eligibility criteria.	• Thresholds may be too high (deterrent); • Thresholds may be too low to be attractive; • Thresholds may serve as barriers for medium skills in shortage occupations; • Thresholds may serve as barriers for young migrants.

Job Search Visa / Residence Permit	• Retaining a supply side option with limited time duration helps overcome the barriers of matching from abroad; • Chance to become proficient in the local language and environment.	• Selection criteria difficult to identify and need to be revised based on practice; • Matching and skills verification can be difficult; • Few may qualify; need to manage return of unsuccessful migrant job seekers.
Points-Based Systems	• Transparency, flexibility and adjustability to changing economic needs and evidence on integration outcomes of immigrants; • Control over the immigration mix, i.e. immigrants with differing structural characteristics; • PBSs often widely accepted by the public.	• Relatively high administrative costs (creating and adjusting, examining applicant qualifications); • Methodological problems in identifying labour shortages by occupation and industry; • Time lag between receiving and processing labour-market data until when the immigration actually takes place; • Slow in reacting to unforeseen circumstances.
Employer Pre-Approval	• Incentive for companies to hire from abroad; • Ease of procedures for employers; • Standard of labour market regulations maintained; • For high-volume employers, less administrative burden for authorities.	• Relevant only for medium-sized to large companies. • Need to regularly inspect continued adherence to labour market regulations and enforcement of migrant workers' rights (risk of exploitation)
'Road to Permanency' rights	• Provides a "trial period" for integration; • Clear trajectory for migrants may serve as part of attractive package; • Allows both the migrant and the host country a test period to "try before buy".	• State of limbo can delay family reunification; • Potentially less attractive in global competition for talent, since some countries offer immediate permanency rights; • Increases administrative complexity (managing status changes).
Employer Portability Rights	• Strengthening migrant workers' rights; • Migrants less vulnerable to unsatisfactory working conditions or exploitation; • Migrants may feel that they can make the most of their (temporary) visa; • May increase the efficiency of the labour market, as migrants would move on to better paying jobs once their lack of information has caught up.	• Employers have less incentive to invest time in sponsorship process; • Minimum contract duration requirements can reduce this issue.

Support for employers

Tool	Advantages	Disadvantages and Risks
Job Fairs	• Bridge the gap between potential migrants and employers with face to face meetings; • Government implementation: especially beneficial to small and medium size companies (SMEs) – lack of resources.	• Cost compared to limited impact may be too high – if there is no specific target group; • Relies on participation of employers and potential immigrants alike – risk factors if not well-designed.
Online Matching Tools	• Higher outreach compared to face-to-face job fairs; • Concrete impact; • Can bring information and various tools together in one place; • Support to companies with limited resources.	• Relies on usage of employers and potential immigrants alike – risk factors if not well-designed; • Involvement of employers and industry associations in the development; • Needs to be regularly maintained and advertised.

Cross-cutting		
Tool	Advantages	Disadvantages and Risks
Information Activities	• Crucial for any activity; • Bring information and various tools together in one place; • Support for companies with limited resources – learn about possibilities; • Immigrants learn about opportunities; • Concrete impact.	• Cost, depending on scale and duration; • Relies on participation of employers and potential immigrants alike – risk factors if not well-designed; • Involvement of employers and industry associations in the development; • Needs to be regularly maintained and advertised ("dead" websites/channels can be damaging); • Possible negative perception as "promotion of immigration" (if there is no wide-spread consensus)
Attracting and retaining international students	• Smooth transition from education to work: graduates are familiar with institutions, workplace culture and language of the host country; • Students are of prime workforce age, smaller risk of skills discounting than migrants qualified abroad; • Early career recruitment is strategy with highest pay-off in terms of socio-economic integration outcomes; • Contribution to knowledge creation, innovation and economic performance in the host country.	• Insufficient language skills (ineffective integration support); • Lack of host country work experience (insufficient support from HEI, Public Services); • Employers hesitant to employ foreigners (deficient awareness raising/information activities); • Lack of professional networks; • Lack of job entry support and service accessibility (insufficient support from HEI, Public Services); • Legal barriers, incoherent policies; • Labour market substitution.
Bilateral agreements	• Reduce costs, ensure quality and quantity for specific sector or occupation, incorporate development objectives, reduce overstay; • Help achieve a flow of labour that meets the needs of employers and industrial sectors; • Achieve foreign policy, cultural and social objectives; • Increase youth mobility; • Ensure access to overseas labour markets workers.	• Unfair to privilege specific countries, employer preference may be for other nationalities not covered, or specific groups; • May be signed without regard to real labour market demands; • For circular programme, first movers are prime beneficiaries; • High administrative oversight costs.

Figure 2 Migration Policy toolbox

Source: ICMPD (2019)

well "integrable". Most Western countries therefore offer job search visas, which should enable university graduates to find adequate employment within a certain period of time. Within this period (usually between 6 and 24 months), foreign graduates should be given the opportunity to meet the criteria for regular highly qualified employment.

In principle, what exact migration policy strategy a country pursues and by what design of the immigration regime is mostly determined by historical-institutional tradition and influenced by the economic goals and the weight of often competing political actors and interest groups. Migration policy is increasingly negotiated and shaped in complex political-economic contexts in which the interests and preferences of politicians and voters, employers, trade unions and other politically active groups compete with each other. This competition results in country-specific rules, regulations and measures that are increasingly characterized by a high degree of complexity (Czaika and de Haas 2013).

International emulation of the most effective policies for attracting and selecting (highly) skilled workers has only just begun. Migration policy competition, which is likely to intensify in the future, has produced a toolbox of multiple innovative policy instruments and measures in recent years that can be understood as part of a broader *"immigration package"* (Papademetriou et al., 2008) (Figure 2). It has been shown to be unlikely that a single migration policy measure per se will make a country more or less attractive to (highly) skilled migrants. Rather, the concept of the immigration package illustrates the importance of the entire range of migration and integration policy instruments in combination with the provision of other public goods and services (Papademetriou et al., 2008, Papademetriou and Sumption, 2013, Tuccio 2019).

Evolution and effectiveness of labour migration policies

A study by Czaika and Parsons (2017) on migration policy developments in 19 OECD countries[3] between 2000 and 2012 illustrates the relative spread of the above-mentioned policy strategies and instruments. For example, three-quarters of these 19 highly developed countries use 'job contingency' systems, while about half use additional demand-oriented policy instruments such as shortage lists and labour market tests. Ten countries also use numerical ceilings (quotas). Point-based systems are used in six countries. The most rapidly spreading policy instrument is the visa for post-graduate job search. In 2000, none of the 19 countries surveyed had used such an instrument, while ten years later almost half of the countries surveyed had introduced corresponding measures designed to give foreign graduates the opportunity to stay.

In addition to the selection instruments mentioned above, immigration packages usually contain additional elements that are intended to increase the attractiveness of the recruiting countries. For example, the prospect of a permanent right of residence, which is necessary for long-term (career) planning, is an important incentive for potential foreign workers to immigrate. (Highly) qualified migrants are therefore offered a permanent residence permit immediately or after a certain period of time. This right is normally also granted to family members of qualified migrant workers, even if individual countries only allow this after a certain period of time (e.g. Korea or Romania). For most (highly) qualified migrants, the immediate right to family reunification is an indispensable prerequisite for immigration, the absence of which has an immensely negative impact on the attractiveness of a location. More than 80

---

[3]   These countries are: Australia, Canada, Czech Republic, Denmark, Finland, Germany, Israel, Japan, Korea, New Zealand, Norway, Poland, Portugal, Romania, Slovakia, Sweden, Switzerland, the UK, the US.

percent of the 19 OECD countries surveyed therefore, offer immediate family reunification rights. Similarly, the provision of work permits for family members is seen as an important factor in the successful recruitment of (highly) skilled migrants. Such attractiveness provisions for family members of (highly) skilled migrants have gained considerable popularity in recent years. Furthermore, more and more countries are using financial incentives, such as tax exemptions and financial allowances, to attract or retain internationally (highly) qualified workers. Over the past decade, the number of countries that have implemented such financial incentive systems has increased significantly (Czaika and Parsons 2017).

Interestingly, the global financial and economic crisis starting in 2007/08, and which has not yet been overcome in many countries, has had only an insignificant impact on demand for (highly) skilled labour and international migration flows, despite its generally negative impact on the overall state of labour markets. Migration flows of (highly) skilled labour, as well as migration policy strategies, appear to be relatively independent of such economic fluctuations. At the very least, this resilience of corresponding policy measures can be seen in the context of the global economic and financial crisis after 2007 (Czaika and Parsons 2018). Despite some readjustments and minor adjustments, such as labour shortage lists or individual revaluations in points-based immigration systems, there have been no significant policy reversals in most countries. The demand for high-quality labour has tended to increase in a growing number of professions, and both governments and cities and enterprises are becoming more and more active demand-side actors in the globalised human capital market.

As mentioned, another trend has been the increased targeting of foreign students and graduates by demand-side actors. Investment in so-called 'semi-finished' human capital is often seen as an effective policy option for the long-term accumulation of human capital. The recruitment of 'high potentials' at an early stage in their careers is seen as an efficient strategy, since this group has relatively low integration and absorption costs, especially if they have been trained domestically, and therefore normally achieve the best results of all immigrants on the labour market (OECD 2008). As a result, many countries have recognised that generous provision of visas for study and employment is a useful and sustainable policy strategy, even in times of economic crisis.

Many countries have also signed bilateral and multilateral agreements to regulate social security, double taxation and the recognition of foreign qualifications and diplomas. These agreements are intended to facilitate the transition and integration of (highly) qualified migrants into the labour market. Agreements regulating the recognition of foreign qualifications have attracted the greatest political attention in the past ten years. As a rule, these agreements are aimed at specific occupations and/or subject areas and, often initiated by professional associations, regulate the quality and comparability of teaching content and courses of study in order to ensure equivalence with domestic courses of study. Empirical studies show that such agreements can effectively promote the mobility of both skilled and unskilled workers (Czaika and Parsons, 2017). Furthermore, international tax treaties aim to avoid double taxation of income from wages and capital, among other things. Although it is generally assumed that such agreements promote mobility, empirical findings suggest that they have a very limited effect (Czaika and Parsons, 2017). Finally, social security agreements aim to regulate rights with regard to the equal treatment of foreign benefits, such as the transferability of pension benefits, disability benefits, payments to widowed or caring relatives or unemployment benefits. These highly complex legal issues are increasingly being coordinated internationally and tend to have a positive effect on the willingness to migrate.

Czaika and Parsons (2017) are investigating the effectiveness of various migration policy instruments on the migration flows of highly qualified immigrants in 10 (of the previously mentioned 19) OECD countries. We find that points-based systems are generally more effective in recruiting and selecting highly skilled migrants than demand-side systems, where the immigration process is initiated by employer sponsorship and complemented by a labour market test or skills shortage list. Other, more financial incentive instruments, such as tax relief or allowances, often lead to better effects. Furthermore, offers that grant immediate permanent residence status are very attractive and effective for highly qualified workers.

Overall, however, the question of whether, and under what conditions, certain migration policy instruments achieve their intended effects can only be answered provisionally and requires further large-scale empirical research. Since, in recent years, public and policy debates on the 'right' migration policy have focused heavily on the immigration of low-skilled workers and asylum seekers or irregular migrants, much less research and public attention has been devoted to the migration and recruitment of the (highly) skilled. This effectiveness of recruitment and selection instruments, for which a systematic investigation is only just beginning, can be described as quite ambivalent on the basis of the data available so far. The design of effective, i.e. target-oriented policy measures requires a special understanding of the peculiarities of this specific, globally integrating labour market. Solid knowledge of the fundamental and specific drivers and dynamics of international skilled migration is therefore an essential prerequisite for the development of a realistic and effective migration policy aimed at influencing the mobility and migration behaviour of this target group in an intended direction (Czaika and de Haas 2013).

Policies that are based on simple assumptions such as that highly qualified people are primarily looking for higher wages and can therefore be recruited through liberal ('open door') policies, for example in combination with tax breaks, are not necessarily successful. The recruiting efforts in the form of a quasi-'open door' or 'red carpet' immigration regulations for highly qualified persons, which are practised in many countries, have not always produced the desired results, since the effectiveness of these programmes is often assessed as quite inconsistent.

Migration decisions are far from deterministic but rather depend on a complex mix of preferences and ideas about 'the good life' and career goals and aspirations that change over time. An effective migration policy that aims to attract the best 'hands and minds' is based on a comprehensive knowledge of the often diverse migration motives that depend on the employment sector and life situation. A well-designed migration policy promotes migration options, i.e. it offers people with sought-after skills and qualifications, occupations, age, experience, education, and sometimes also social and cultural backgrounds the necessary opportunities to migrate temporarily, circularly or permanently. Highly qualified and often internationally mobile workers in high demand, perceive immigration regulations and offers as incentive structures and usually opt for the most attractive 'total immigration package'.

Of course, these immigration packages contain more than just entry and residence regulations (Papadimitriou and Sumption 2013). Empirical evidence suggests that although migration policy measures influence migration processes, the magnitude of these effects is limited compared to other policy measures and structural determinants. Thus, labour market regulations, housing, education, taxation and social security provisions - i.e. measures that are not primarily focused on migration itself - are part of a much broader immigration package. As a result, designing effective and efficient migration and recruitment strategies requires a comprehensive and integrated assessment and coordination of all migration-related policies. This also applies to policies whose main purpose is not the recruitment and selection of highly qualified migrants.

Therefore, from a policy-making perspective, the problem of ineffectiveness of individual policies is often that migration policies are too narrowly defined and designed and do not take into account other economic, social and cultural policy areas. In order to increase the effectiveness of recruitment strategies, coherent 'whole-of-government' immigration strategies must be developed that are embedded in the economic, social and political structures and transformations of the country and the general context of international migration processes and dynamics. In a world where more and more countries and enterprises are competing for foreign labour, policy packages aimed at enhancing the overall attractiveness of a location must provide opportunities for migrant workers to find good employment and secure, pleasant living conditions.

Furthermore, it is increasingly recognised that the influx of skilled labour can be self-perpetuating by creating positive externalities in terms of a conducive professional environment. Recruitment of complementary expertise and skills can increase the productivity of all workers (and also of capital employed) and consequently attract further skilled foreign labour (Peri and Sparber, 2009). Highly qualified immigration and its positive externalities can trigger a migration dynamic both within and between individual occupational groups and occupational networks (Beine et al., 2011). Skill-based recruitment and immigration strategies that only react to existing demand gaps can therefore be largely ineffective, at least in the short term, if (i) corresponding complementarities between occupational groups and (ii) long-term career and retention prospects for this internationally highly mobile group of highly qualified individuals are not taken into account. Internationally mobile professionals respond to the existence of a 'critical mass' of other professionals that are collectively creating an attractive environment for a 'creative class' (Florida 2002).

Thus, migration trajectories and dynamics of highly qualified workers are individually path-dependent and self-reinforcing, which implies that professional and socio-culturally attractive places and environments are self-recreating (Czaika and Toma 2017, Florida 2003, 2006). Metropolitan areas normally function here as nodes of a globally networked human capital systems. Scientific, technical or management expertise is produced and reproduced at these nodes (Khadria 2003). In such a system, urban metropolises are important gravitational centres in which professional and cultural diversity can produce a fertile basis for social, economic and technical innovation. As a result, cities and regional clusters themselves become important attractors of the internationally mobile group of highly qualified people (Ozgen et al. 2014). The role of skill-attracting policies implemented at regional and local (city) levels has not yet been full recognised.

Conclusions

Numerous studies have shown that the immigration of highly skilled workers can make a significant contribution to economic growth, public finances, and the overall competitiveness and innovation of the host economy (Worldbank 2017). Only those societies and economies that create an open, conflict-free environment for migrants, attractive professional conditions and opportunities for employees, and a positive economic climate for employers, will not be left behind in an intensifying global competition for highly qualified work. In this context, countries in different parts of the world are trying to develop measures to recruit urgently needed human capital internationally or to keep their own 'talents' in the country. Particularly in the past two decades migration policy activities have intensified and appropriate instruments and best practices have been established for recruiting and selecting highly qualified workers. Even if the general demand for skilled workers continues unabated, the issue of immigration remains a highly controversial one in many parts of the world. However, despite increasingly restrictive policy measures and xenophobic public debates against 'unwanted' low-skilled workers, more liberal views and policy approaches regarding urgently needed human capital have become entrenched. Despite some controversies in the public debate, most Western countries, but also numerous non-Western countries, have made increased efforts to recruit international talent and retain it in the domestic labour market.

The overarching objectives of these recruitment efforts are diverse and not always fully compatible. These include, for example, the saturation of very specific and often short-term labour market shortages, the acquisition of highly qualified human capital as a stimulus for national innovation systems, or the cushioning of demographic transition and the associated safeguarding of the sustainability of social systems. It is foreseeable that these reasons for the implementation of skill-attractive migration policy packages will increase in the course of the next decade, as a reversal of this trend seems unlikely due to the increasing structural demand for highly qualified work in Europe and most countries of the world. 'Crisis-resilient' labour migration flows and respective migration policy strategies are partly associated with a trend towards 'hybrid' immigration systems, which combine both demand and supply-side measures in order to balance the diversity and with regard to the quantitative as well as qualitative composition of the immigrant working population.

References

Abella, M. (2006) Global competition for skilled workers and consequences. In: Kuptsch, C. and Pang, E. F. (eds.) Competing for global talent. Geneva: International Labour Office-International Institute for Labour Studies and Singapore Management University.

Aydemir, A. (2013) Skill-based immigrant selection and labor market outcomes by visa category. In: Constant, A. F. & Zimmermann, K. F. (eds.) International Handbook on the Economics of Migration (Chapter 23): 432-452. Cheltenham: Edward Elgar.

Beine, M., Docquier, F. & Özden, C. (2011) Diasporas. Journal of Development Economics. 95 (1), 30–41.

Biffl, G. & Pfeffer, T. (2013) Recognition of qualifications of citizens of another EU Member State. In: FEANI News. The European Engineers Publication, Issue 11, June 2013, pp 19-26

Boeri, T. (2012) Introduction. In: Boeri, T., Brücker, H., Docquier, F. & Rapoport, H. (eds.) Brain Drain and Brain Gain: The Global Competition to Attract High-skilled Migrants. Oxford: Oxford University Press.

Chiswick, B. R. (2011) High-skilled Immigration in a Global Labor Market. Washington, D.C.: American Enterprise Institute Press.

Czaika, M. (2018a) High-Skilled Migration: Introduction and Synopsis, in: Czaika, M. (ed) High-Skilled Migration: Drivers and Policies, Oxford University Press

Czaika, M. (2018b) Conclusion, in: Czaika, M. (ed) High-Skilled Migration: Drivers and Policies, Oxford University Press

Czaika, M. & de Haas, H. (2013) The Effectiveness of Immigration Policies. Population and Development Review. 39 (3), 487–508.

Czaika, M. & Parsons, C. (2017) The gravity of high-skilled migration policies. Demography. 54 (2), 603–630.

Czaika, M. & Parsons, C. (2018) High-skilled migration in times of global economic crisis, in: Czaika, M. (ed) High-Skilled Migration: Drivers and Policies, Oxford University Press

Czaika, M. & Toma, S. (2017) International academic mobility across space and time. The case of Indian academics. Forthcoming Population Space and Place.

Davenport, T. H. (2005) Thinking For A Living: How to Get Better Performance and Results From Knowledge Workers. Boston: Harvard Business School Press.

Doomernik, J., Koslowski, R. & Thränhardt, D. (2009) The Battle for the Brains: Why Immigration Policy Is Not Enough to Attract the Highly Skilled. Brussels Forum Paper Series. Washington, D.C.: German Marshall Fund of the United States.

DTI (2002) Knowledge Migrants: The Motivations and Experiences of Professionals in the UK on Work Permits. London: Department of Trade and Industry.

Facchini, G. & Lodigiani, E. (2014) Attracting Skilled Immigrants: An Overview of Recent Policy Developments in Advanced Countries. National Institute Economic Review. 229 (1), R3–R21.

Florida, R. (2002) The rise of the creative class. Vol. 9. New York: Basic books.

Florida, R. (2003) Cities and the creative class. City & Community. 2 (1), 3–19.

Florida, R. (2006). The flight of the creative class: The new global competition for talent. Liberal Education, 92(3), 22-29.

ICMPD (2019) Labour Migration Policies in Poland, unpublished report

Kapur, D. & McHale, J. (2005) Give us your best and brightest: the global hunt for talent and its impact on the developing world. Washington, D.C.: Center for Global Development.

Khadria, B. (2001) Shifting Paradigms of Globalization: the Twenty First Century Transition towards Generics in Skilled Labour Migration from India. International Migration. 39 (5), 45–71.

OECD (2008) A Profile of Immigrant Populations in the 21st Century: Data from OECD Countries. Paris: OECD.

Ozgen, C., Peters, C., Niebuhr, A., Nijkamp, P. & Poot, J. (2014) Does Cultural Diversity of Migrant Employees Affect Innovation? International Migration Review. 48, 377–416.

Papademetriou, D. G., Somerville, W. & Tanaka, H. (2008) Talent in the 21st-Century Economy. Washington, D.C.: Migration Policy Institute.

Papademetriou, D. G. & Sumption, M. (2013) Attracting and Selecting from the Global Talent Pool – Policy Challenges. Washington, D.C.: Migration Policy Institute.

Parsons, C. R., Rojon, S., Rose, L., & Samanani, F. (2018). High skilled migration through the lens of policy. Migration Studies.

Peri, G. & Sparber, C. (2009) Task Specialization, Immigration, and Wages. American Economic Journal: Applied Economics. 1 (3), 135–169.

Sumption, M. (2013) The Elusive Idea of Labor-Market 'Shortages' and the U.S. Approach to Employment-Based Immigration Policy. In: Fix, M., Papademetriou, D. G. & Sumption, M. (eds.) Immigrants in a Changing Labor Market. Washington, DC: Migration Policy Institute.

Tuccio, M. (2019), "Measuring and assessing talent attractiveness in OECD countries", OECD Social, Employment and Migration Working Papers, No. 229, OECD Publishing, Paris, https://doi.org/10.1787/b4e677ca-en.

Worldbank (2017) Moving for Prosperity: Global Migration and Labor Markets, World Bank Policy Report, Washington, DC: Worldbank

Einwanderungspolitik für hochqualifizierte Migranten im internationalen Vergleich. Kanada, Australien, Neuseeland, Großbritannien und Österreich

Sascha Krannich

Zusammenfassung[1]

Der vorliegende Aufsatz untersucht und vergleicht die verschiedenen Einwanderungspolitiken für hochqualifizierte Migranten in Kanada, Australien, Neuseeland, Großbritannien und Österreich, insbesondere in Bezug auf die dort geltenden Punktesysteme. Der Vergleich macht die grundsätzlichen Vor- und Nachteile von Punktesystemen deutlich. Während ein Punktesystem einerseits für mehr Einheitlichkeit, Transparenz und Flexibilität bei der staatlichen Steuerung von hochqualifizierten Arbeitsmigranten sorgen kann, kann es andererseits aber auch Fehlallokationen auf dem heimischen Arbeitsmarkt sowie eine ineffektive Verwaltung der Bewerbungen verursachen. Letztendlich kommt es auf die konkrete Ausgestaltung eines Punktesystems an, die von den jeweiligen sozialen und ökonomischen Verhältnissen im Land abhängig gemacht werden sollte.

Einleitung

Hochqualifizierte Migrantinnen und Migranten[2] können als „erwünschte" und weltweit stark umworbene Fachkräfte – insbesondere Akademiker im MINT-Bereich (Mathematik, Informatik, Naturwissenschaft und Technik) – angesehen werden, von denen sich die Einwanderungsländer entscheidende Beiträge zur Entwicklung der heimischen Wirtschaft und somit zur Entwicklung des gesamten Landes versprechen. Für viele Länder des Globalen Nordens ist die Zuwanderung von Hochqualifizierten zudem auch vor dem Hintergrund des demographischen Wandels und des damit einhergehenden Fachkräftemangels entscheidend. Deshalb

---

[1] Dieser Aufsatz basiert auf den Ergebnissen zweier Studien zu Einwanderungsregelungen in Deutschland und im internationalen Vergleich, die ich zusammen mit Uwe Hunger (Universität Münster) im Auftrag der Friedrich-Ebert-Stiftung in den Jahren 2015 und 2017 durchgeführt habe.

[2] Im Folgenden soll aus Gründen der Vereinfachung und Lesbarkeit nur die männliche Form benutzt werden, jedoch sind natürlich immer beide Geschlechter gemeint.

werden hochqualifizierte Migranten mit gezielten Maßnahmen angeworben, die die Einwanderung und Integration erleichtern soll. Nur um ein paar Beispiele zu nennen: Die USA führten Visa-Erleichterungen für Hochqualifizierte bereits in den 1980er Jahren ein, die sich dann im H-1B-Visum speziell für Hochqualifizierte in den 1990er manifestierten.[3] Auch die Einführung der EU-Blue Card zielte darauf ab, die Europäische Union für hochqualifizierte Migranten aus Drittstaaten attraktiver zu machen. Zudem ergriffen auch die einzelnen EU-Mitgliedsländer Maßnahmen, die in diese Richtung führen sollen. So hat Deutschland in den letzten 15 Jahren eine Reihe von Gesetzen und Verordnungen verabschiedet, die mehr Zuwanderung von Hochqualifizierten ermöglichen sollen (Krannich 2018, S. 36). Dazu gehört auch die Regelung, dass hochqualifizierte Akademiker mit Qualifikationen, die von der Wirtschaft nachgefragt werden, ohne konkrete Arbeitsplatzzusage für sechs Monate zur Arbeitsplatzsuche nach Deutschland einreisen dürfen (vgl. Hunger/Krannich 2017). Frankreich erleichterte Hochqualifizierten aus Drittstaaten den Aufenthalt mit der Einführung des Titels „Compétences et Talents" (Kane 2019, S. 167). Und selbst das jahrhundertelang isolierte Japan, das nach wie vor eine der restriktivsten Einwanderungspolitiken der Welt praktiziert, führt schrittweise Einwanderungserleichterungen für hochqualifizierte Migranten ein (vgl. Rochel 2018). Dieser Wettbewerb um die „besten Köpfe" wird auch als „Global Race for Talents" (Münz 2014) bezeichnet.

Um die Zuwanderung von hochqualifizierten Migranten effizienter steuern zu können, wurde in den letzten Jahren in einigen Einwanderungsländern des Globalen Nordens auch die mögliche Einführung bzw. die Neugestaltung eines Punktesystems diskutiert, darunter auch die USA, Deutschland und Japan (Hunger/Krannich 2018). Unter einem Punktesystem versteht man die Auswahl von Zuwanderern nach bestimmten Kriterien (wie Alter, Qualifikation, Berufserfahrung etc.), für die jeweils Punkte vergeben werden. Wenn ein potentieller Zuwanderer genügend Punkte gesammelt hat, wird er für eine Zuwanderung in das betreffende Einwanderungsland zugelassen.

Andere Einwanderungsländer haben schon seit längerer Zeit ein Punktesystem zur Steuerung der Arbeitsmigration eingeführt. Allen voran Kanada, das als erstes Einwanderungsland ein Punktesystem bereits im Jahr 1967 einführte. Weitere Länder sind u.a. Australien, Neuseeland, Großbritannien und Österreich.[4] Dabei werden in diesen Ländern die unterschiedlichen Konzipierungen und Anwendungen des Punktesystems zum Teil sehr positiv bewertet (vgl. Buchanan et al. 2013; Hawthorne 2011, 2014), die auch Anregungen und Modelle für die mögliche Einführungen in weiteren Ländern liefern könnten. Im Folgenden sollen daher die unterschiedlichen Punktesysteme in diesen fünf Ländern miteinander verglichen

---

[3]   Zur Einwanderungs- und Integrationspolitik der USA vgl. auch Martin (2014) und Krannich (2017).

[4]   Zudem haben auch andere Länder Punktesysteme in unterschiedlicher Ausgestaltung in den letzten Jahren eingeführt (und teilweise wieder abgeschafft), darunter Dänemark, Niederlande und Tschechien.

und abschließend die grundsätzlichen Vor- und Nachteile eines Punktesystems diskutiert werden.

Methode

Die Studie basiert im Wesentlichen auf zwei Untersuchungsschritten: erstens auf einer Literatur- und Dokumentenanalyse der einschlägigen Literatur sowie der Gesetzes- und Verfahrensvorschriften zur Einwanderung in Kanada, Australien, Neuseeland, Großbritannien und Österreich[5] sowie zweitens auf der Durchführung von Experteninterviews.[6] Bei den fünf untersuchten Ländern handelt es sich um die Länder, die ein Punktesystem zur Steuerung der ökonomischen Zuwanderung zuerst eingeführt haben und somit über die längsten Erfahrungen mit diesem System verfügen. Zudem sind alle fünf Länder Einwanderungsländer, die über ähnliche soziale und wirtschaftliche Strukturen verfügen, und zudem eine hohe Nachfrage nach hochqualifizierten Fachkräften aufweisen.

Die Analyse der Punktesysteme in Kanada, Australien, Neuseeland, Großbritannien und Österreich basiert auf einer klassischen ländervergleichenden Politikfeldanalyse (Policy Analysis) (vgl. Schubert 1999), in deren Rahmen die Unterschiede und Gemeinsamkeiten der Inhalte und Formen von Punktesystemen als Steuerungsinstrument für Einwanderung aufgezeigt werden. Dabei werden die Policy Outputs, d.h. die gesetzlichen Regelungen und Leitlinien zu den Punktesystemen, und die Policy Outcomes, die Implementierung und Wirkung der Punktesysteme in Bezug auf die Auswahl von Arbeitsmigranten, insbesondere hochqualifizierte Migranten, im Politikfeld „Zuwanderungssteuerung" für die Länder dargestellt. Die Analyse erfolgt vorwiegend anhand folgender Dimensionen: Zugrunde gelegte Kriterien und Gewichtung innerhalb des Punktesystems, Bedeutung der Arbeitsplatzzusage, Regelungen für Mangelberufe, Art des Bewerbungsverfahrens

---

[5] Bei der Literatur- und Dokumentenanalyse stand vor allem die Auseinandersetzung mit den Einwanderungsregelungen zu Erwerbs- und Ausbildungszwecken und den Steuerungsmöglichkeiten von Arbeitsmigration im Allgemeinen und zu den konkreten Punktesystemen in den Vergleichsländern im Mittelpunkt. Dabei lieferten insbesondere die offiziellen Onlineangebote der für die Einwanderung zuständigen Ministerien und Behörden umfangreiche und aktuelle Informationen bzgl. der Kriterien und Gewichtungen der Punktesysteme sowie über den Antrags- und Bewerbungsprozess im Rahmen der Punktesysteme. In Kanada war dies vor allem das CIC (Citizenship and Immigration Canada), in Australien das Department of Immigration and Border Protection und das Department of Immigration and Citizenship, in Neuseeland das Immigration New Zealand, in Großbritannien das UK Visas and Immigration sowie in Österreich die Migrationsplattform der österreichischen Bundesregierung.

[6] Die Experteninterviews wurden durchgeführt, um die Analyse abzusichern und offene Fragen in den jeweiligen Ländern zu klären und einen Einblick in die Einwanderungspolitik aus der Perspektive des jeweiligen Landes zu bekommen. Insgesamt wurden 14 Experteninterviews durchgeführt.

auf der einen Seite (Policy Output) sowie Effektivität und Wirkung der Punktesysteme auf der anderen Seite (Policy Outcomes).

Punktesysteme in Kanada, Australien, Neuseeland, Großbritannien und Österreich

Kanada

Kanada führte, wie bereits erwähnt, 1967 als erstes Land weltweit ein Punktesystem zur Steuerung der Arbeitsmigration ein. Dabei war das Punktesystem lange Zeit als rein humankapital- bzw. angebotsorientiertes Modell konzipiert, bei dem die tatsächliche Nachfrage auf dem heimischen Arbeitsmarkt nur in zweiter Linie Beachtung fand. So wurde nur über ein festgelegtes Kontingent der jährliche allgemeine Rahmen der Arbeitszuwanderung festgelegt, eine konkrete Arbeitsplatzzusage musste im kanadischen System jedoch lange Zeit nicht vorgelegt werden. Viele der (hochqualifizierten) Einwanderer gingen somit erst nach ihrer Ankunft in Kanada auf Arbeitssuche. Ein Problem bestand darin, dass viele von ihnen entweder überhaupt keinen Arbeitsplatz fanden oder nur einen unterhalb ihrer eigentlichen Qualifikation (Schmidtke 2008, 2014). Im Jahr 2001 galt dies etwa für über ein Drittel aller Einwanderer, die durch ein Punktesystem in Kanada ausgewählt wurden (Birrell et al. 2006, S. 192). Als abschreckendendes Beispiel galt hierbei der „Akademiker als Taxifahrer" (Thränhardt 2014, S. 5). Auch gab es lange Bearbeitungszeiten im Bewerbungsverfahren. So entstand ein Ungleichgewicht zwischen der Anzahl freier Plätze im Jahresplan und der tatsächlichen Bewerberanzahl, die in dem jeweiligen Jahr nach Kanada kommen wollten (Interview mit Maia Welbourne, Citizenship and Immigration Canada, 2015). Teilweise kam es dabei zu mehrjährigen Wartezeiten (Interview mit Lesleyanne Hawthorne, Melbourne University, September 2015).

Jedoch hat sich das kanadische System in den letzten Jahren stark verändert, indem schrittweise Elemente eingebaut wurden, die verstärkt auch Aspekte der Arbeitsmarktnachfrage berücksichtigen (vgl. Kaulisch 2012, Bauder et al. 2014, S. 4). Konkret wurde neben dem Kriterium einer Einladung von einer Regionalverwaltung auch das Kriterium einer Arbeitsplatzzusage durch ein kanadisches Unternehmen in das System aufgenommen, das inzwischen auch sehr hoch bewertet wird. Im sogenannten „Express Entry"-Verfahren macht die Arbeitsplatzzusage mittlerweile die Hälfte aller möglichen Punkte aus. Neben der Arbeitsplatzzusage spielen noch folgende Kriterien eine Rolle: Sprachkenntnisse (1), berufliche Qualifikationen (2), Berufserfahrung (3), Alter (4) sowie Erfahrungen und Qualifikationen des Lebens- oder Ehepartners (5). Insgesamt muss der Bewerber mindestens zwei Drittel aller möglichen Punkte erreichen, um sich für ein kanadisches Arbeitsvisum zu qualifizieren (vgl. Tabelle 1). Das Kontingent im Rahmen des Punktesystems beträgt 51.000 Zuwanderer pro Jahr.

Punktevergabekriterien für hochqualifizierte Arbeitskräfte	Punktegewichtung
Englisch- oder Französischkenntnisse	Maximale Punktzahl: 28
Berufliche Qualifikationen und Fähigkeiten	Maximale Punktzahl: 25
Berufserfahrung	Maximale Punktzahl: 15
Alter	Maximale Punktzahl: 12
Arbeitsangebot in Kanada	Maximale Punktzahl: 10
Erfahrungen und Qualifikationen des Lebens- oder Ehepartners	Maximale Punktzahl: 10
Maximalpunktzahl	**100**
Mindestpunktzahl	**67**

Tabelle 1: Punktekriterien und -gewichtung für hochqualifizierte Arbeits-kräfte im Rahmen des kanadischen Punktesystems

Quelle: Citizenship and Immigration Canada (CIC) 2015; eigene Übersetzung.

Obwohl es noch zu früh ist, die Effektivität und Wirkungen des überarbeiteten Punktesystems im Rahmen des Express-Entry-Systems grundsätzlich zu bewerten, gibt es schon erste Zahlen, die auf eine Optimierung des Systems schließen lassen. So wurden laut dem kanadischen Einwanderungsministerium allein im ersten Quartal 2017 24.652 Arbeitskräfte über das Online-Punktesystem angeworben, die größtenteils bereits einen Arbeitsplatz haben (CIC 2017). Damit wurde bereits zu Beginn des Jahres fast die Hälfte des gesamten Jahreskontingents ausgeschöpft. Um noch mehr hochqualifizierte Bewerber für den kanadischen Arbeitsmarkt zu gewinnen, versucht sich Kanada als lebenswertes Land im Ausland zu vermarkten und sein Punktesystem intensiv zu bewerben. Insgesamt kann man festhalten, dass es Kanada zunächst geschafft hat, durch die Neuregelungen des Punktesystems und die Einführung des Online-Bewerbungsverfahrens den Gap zwischen der Form der Anwerbung von auf dem kanadischen Arbeitsmarkt nachgefragten Mig-ranten (Policy Output) und der tatsächlichen Auswahl von Arbeitsmigranten durch das Punktesystem (Policy Outcome) deutlich zu verringern.

Australien

In Australien wurde das Punktesystem im Jahr 1979 eingeführt. Es war damals das zweite seiner Art nach dem kanadischen Modell. Im Rahmen des Punktesystems können sich ausschließlich hochqualifizierte Arbeitskräfte bewerben. Hierfür ist ein jährliches Kontingent von insgesamt 44.000 vorgesehen. Die Bewerber wer-den nach den Kriterien Alter (1), Englischkenntnisse (2), Berufserfahrungen (3), Bildungsstand (4) und Studienabschlüsse in Australien (5) bewertet. Dabei sind die Kriterien relativ gleichmäßig gewichtet, wobei das Alter etwas hervorgehoben ist. Hier können bis zu 30 Punkte erreicht werden. Für die anderen Kriterien wer-den jeweils bis zu 20 Punkte vergeben. Insgesamt muss die Mindestpunktzahl von 65 erreicht werden, um ein Arbeitsvisum zu erhalten (vgl. Tabelle 2). Eine Ar-beitsplatzzusage spielt im australischen Punktesystem keine Rolle.

Punktevergabekriterien für hochqualifizierte Arbeitskräfte	Punktegewichtung
Alter	Maximale Punktzahl: 30
Englischkenntnisse	Maximale Punktzahl: 20
Berufserfahrungen (in den letzten 10 Jahren)	Maximale Punktzahl: 20
Bildungsstand	Maximale Punktzahl: 20
Weitere Faktoren	Maximale Punktzahl: 20
Nominierung/Förderung (nur für Visa subclasses 190 und 489)	Maximale Punktzahl: 5
Maximalpunktzahl	**110 (bzw. 115)**
Mindestpunktzahl	**67**

Tabelle 2: Punktekriterien und -gewichtung für hochqualifizierte Arbeitskräfte im Rahmen des australischen Punktesystems

Quelle: Department of Immigration and Citizenship 2015; eigene Übersetzung.

Wie in Kanada gab es auch am australischen Punktesystem Kritik, und es wurde seit seiner Einführung mehrfach reformiert. Vor allem wurde bemängelt, dass das Punktesystem zu unflexibel sei und zu langsam auf Veränderungen auf dem Arbeitsmarkt reagieren würde (Murray 2011, S. 19). Dies war etwa zu Beginn der 2000er Jahre der Fall, als im Rahmen des Punktesystems weiterhin viele IT-Spezialisten zugelassen wurden, obwohl die Nachfrage auf dem australischen Arbeitsmarkt bereits merklich abgeebbt war. Die Folge war, dass, wie in Kanada, viele Zuwanderer keinen Job fanden und arbeitslos wurden. Zwischen 2001 und 2004 stieg z.B. die Arbeitslosenquote unter IT-Kräften auf über 30% an (vgl. Murray 2011, S 22). Auch gab es, ähnlich wie in Kanada, Probleme mit der Bearbeitungszeit der Visaanträge.

Um die Auswahl der Bewerber im Rahmen des Punktesystems effektiver zu gestalten und stärker an die Bedürfnisse der australischen Wirtschaft anzupassen, wurde im Jahr 2012 eine Reihe von Reformen durchgeführt. Im Zentrum stand dabei die Einführung des Online-Bewerbungsprogramm „SkillSelect", mit dem das Bewerbungs- und Antragsverfahren deutlich schneller und günstiger gemacht wurde (Department of Immigration and Border Protection 2015). Heute müssen Bewerber nur noch ein Formular online ausfüllen, das sogenannte „Expression of Interest" (EOI), in dem die beruflichen Fähigkeiten und Erfahrungen aufgelistet werden, die schon vor der Einreise von australischen Unternehmen eingesehen werden können, sodass möglichst frühzeitig ein Kontakt zwischen Bewerber und Unternehmen hergestellt werden kann.

Darüber hinaus wurde eine sogenannte Mangelberufsliste eingeführt. In dieser Liste werden die von australischen Unternehmen nachgefragten Arbeitskräfte jährlich nach Priorität geordnet (Department of Immigration and Citizenship 2015). Zudem wurden in den letzten Jahren die Sprachanforderungen erhöht, die Qualifikationen und Berufserfahrungen strenger überprüft und das Mindestausmaß an „Sponsorship" durch australische Unternehmen und Bundesstaaten bzw. Territorien finanziell aufgestockt, um die Arbeitsmarktfähigkeit der Bewerber zu verbessern. Die Mangelberufliste und das SkillSelect-Programm wurden dabei unter Einbeziehung von Vertretern der Wirtschaft, der Bildungsinstitutionen und internationalen Studierendenvertretungen, sowie der Bundesstaaten und Kommunen entwickelt (Department of Immigration and Citizenship 2015).

Das australische Punktesystem hat sich damit als durchaus effektiv und anpassungsfähig erwiesen. Seit der großen Reform 2012 wird es regelmäßig durch ein wissenschaftliches Begleitteam evaluiert und kontinuierlich überarbeitet. Das Kontingent von 44.000 wurde in den letzten Jahren regelmäßig ausgeschöpft. Im Zeitraum von 2008 bis 2014 entfielen die meisten der rund 340.000 Bewerbungen im Punktesystem auf IT-Fachkräfte (39.000 Bewerbungen), Ingenieurberufen (27.000), Mediziner (5.500) und Wissenschaftlern (4.000) (Hawthorne 2014, S. 10). Die Verbesserung des Auswahlsystems zeigt sich auch darin, dass in den letzten Jahren über 80% der Bewerber innerhalb von sechs Monaten einen Arbeitsplatz in Australien gefunden haben. Bei hochqualifizierten Migranten gibt es nahezu keine Arbeitslosigkeit (unter 0,5%) und ihr Durchschnittsverdienst liegt bei ca. 75.000 australischen Dollars pro Jahr (Buchanan et al. 2013, S. 11), was deutlich über dem Landesdurchschnitt liegt.

Neuseeland

Neuseeland führte das Punktesystem als drittes Land weltweit, nach Kanada und Australien, im Jahr 1991 ein. Ähnlich wie in Australien erfolgt die Auswahl über fünf Kriterien, allerdings spielt hier die Arbeitsplatzzusage eine Rolle. Neben dem Arbeitsplatzstatus (1) sind Alter (2), Familienmitglieder in Neuseeland (3), Berufserfahrung (4) und berufliche Qualifikationen und Fähigkeiten (5) die anderen Kriterien. Im Vergleich zu Kanada und Australien gestaltet sich die Punktevergabe deutlich komplexer und umfangreicher, weil der Antragsteller in vielen Kategorien Zusatzpunkte erhalten kann (vgl. Tabelle 3). Die maximale erreichbare Punktzahl beträgt 350 Punkte, wobei „nur" eine Mindestpunktzahl von 100 Punkten erlangt werden muss, um in das Visasystem aufgenommen zu werden. Dabei ist eine Arbeitsplatzzusage nicht zwingend notwendig, sie wird aber innerhalb des Punktesystems besonders berücksichtigt, sowohl beim Antragsteller selbst, als auch für den Ehe- oder Lebenspartner. Demnach kann der Antragsteller 50 Punkte für eine Arbeitsplatzzusage erhalten, was bereits die Hälfte aller notwendigen Punkte ausmacht. Gegenwärtig gibt es im Rahmen des Punktesystems ein Kontingent von 26.000 Hochqualifizierten pro Jahr, das jedes Jahr fast vollständig ausgeschöpft wird.

Wie in Kanada und Australien ergaben sich auch in Neuseeland ernsthafte Probleme bei der Umsetzung des Punktesystems. Als größtes Problem stellte sich dabei, ähnlich wie in Kanada, die lange Bearbeitungszeit heraus.

Um diesen Problemen Herr zu werden, wurde im Jahr 2003 das Online-Bewerbungssystem eingeführt, das das erste seiner Art im Rahmen des Punktesystems war und später von Australien und Kanada übernommen wurde. Die langen Wartezeiten werden nun dadurch verkürzt, dass Bewerber, die nicht direkt einreisen nach spätestens drei Monaten aus dem Onlinepool gelöscht werden und sich danach wieder neu bewerben müssen (Immigration New Zealand 2015). Dass das gegenwärtige Punktesystem seit dem Jahr 2003 nicht mehr wesentlich modifiziert

Punktevergabekriterien für hochqualifizierte Arbeitskräfte	Punktegewichtung
Alter	Maximale Punktzahl: 30
Familienmitglieder	Maximale Punktzahl: 10
Arbeitsplatzstatus	Maximale Punktzahl: 110
	(davon 50 für Arbeitsplatzzusage in Neuseeland)
Berufserfahrung	Maximale Punktzahl: 75
Berufliche Qualifikationen	Maximale Punktzahl: 125
Maximalpunktzahl	**350**
Mindestpunktzahl	**100**

Tabelle 3: Punktekriterien und -gewichtung für hochqualifizierte Arbeitskräfte im Rahmen des neuseeländischen Punktesystems

Quelle: Immigration New Zealand 2015; eigene Übersetzung.

wurde, ist auch ein Indiz dafür, dass es seither effizient funktioniert und positiv bewertet wird (Interview mit Richard Bedford, University of Waikato, 2015). Überhaupt wird es als sehr erfolgreich beschrieben (vgl. Bedford 2006, Hawthorne 2011 und 2014). Hochqualifizierte Migranten weisen durchweg eine gute Arbeitsmarktperformance auf, d.h. die meisten von ihnen konnten schnell einen geeigneten Beruf finden, der relativ gut bezahlt wird (Immigration New Zealand 2015). Umgekehrt konnten durch hochqualifizierte Einwanderer viele Lücken im neuseeländischen Arbeitsmarkt geschlossen werden (Hawthorne 2014, S. 15).

Großbritannien

Im Jahr 2008 führte Großbritannien ein Punktesystem für verschiedene Zuwanderergruppen ein. Neben hochqualifizierten Migranten auch für Geringqualifizierte, Unternehmer, Familienmitglieder und Studierende. Diese Gruppen werden in 5 Ebenen ausgewählt (hochqualifizierte Migranten in Ebene 2).[7] Im Unterschied zu den Einwanderungspunktesystemen in Kanada, Australien und Neuseeland, können die Bewerber in Großbritannien nur einwandern, wenn sie eine Arbeitsplatzzusage von einem britischen Unternehmen nachweisen können und dazu eine festgeschriebene Punktzahl von 70 vorweisen können. Dabei können sie fehlende Punkte nicht durch gesammelte Punkte in anderen Kriterien (wie z.B. Alter oder Berufserfahrung) ausgleichen. Die 70 Punkte kann man ausschließlich nur über die folgenden vier Kriterien erreichen: Ein Arbeitsplatzangebot bzw. Empfehlungsschreiben eines britischen Unternehmens an die zuständige britische Behörde (sogenanntes Sponsoring), wofür 30 Punkte vergeben werden; Nachweis eines

---

[7] Die 5 Auswahlebenen sind: Investor_innen, Unternehmer_innen und „Exceptional Talents" (einzigartige Talente) (Auswahlebene 1); hochqualifizierte Arbeitskräfte mit einem Arbeitsplatzangebot in Großbritannien (Auswahlebene 2); geringqualifizierte Arbeitskräfte (Auswahlebene 3), wobei diese Ebene zur Zeit nicht genutzt wird, weil die Arbeitsmarktnachfrage nach geringqualifizierten Fachkräften gegenwärtig und auf absehbare Zeit vollständig aus dem EU-Ausland abgedeckt wird; internationale Studierende in Großbritannien (Auswahlebene 4) und temporäre Arbeitskräfte (Auswahlebene 5).

Punktevergabekriterien	Punktegewichtung
Hochqualifizierte Arbeitskräfte mit Arbeitsplatzangebot (allgemeine Arbeitskräfte, unternehmensinterne Transfers, Sportler und Geistliche)	Punktzahl: 70
Sponsoring-Förderung	30
Mindesteinkommen von 20.800 Pfund	20
Englischkenntnisse	10
Lebensunterhalt (945 Pfund einmalig)	10

Tabelle 4: Punktekriterien und -gewichtung für hochqualifizierte Arbeitskräfte im Rahmen des britischen Punktesystems

Quelle: UK Visas and Immigration (2015); eigene Übersetzung.

Mindesteinkommens in Höhe von £ 20.800 (20 Punkte), ausreichende Englisch-kenntnisse (10 Punkte) und einmalig nachgewiesene Ersparnisse für den Lebens-unterhalt in Höhe von £ 945 (10 Punkte) (vgl. Tabelle 4).

Regelungen für Mangelberufe und Engpässe in bestimmten Sektoren werden jedes Jahr in einer Liste von der britischen Regierung mit Unterstützung des Migration Advisory Committees (MAC) zusammengestellt.[8] Bewerber müssen sich, ähnlich wie in Neuseeland, online über die offizielle UK Government-Homepage bewerben. Dort werden die einzelnen Auswahlkriterien im Rahmen des Punkte-systems abgefragt und die erreichten Punkte dem Bewerber sofort mitgeteilt. Die Bearbeitungszeit wird auf der Homepage der britischen Regierung mit offiziell drei Wochen angegeben (UK Government 2019), was aber in der Regel nicht eingehalten werden kann und in einigen Fällen auch mehrere Monate dauern kann (Interview mit Martin Ruhs, Oxford University, September 2015).

Grundsätzlich wird das britische Punktesystem recht gut bewertet. Allerdings ist zu betonen, dass es sich hierbei eigentlich um kein Punktesystem im engeren Sinne handelt, da es sich jeweils um Ausschlusskriterien handelt und die Punkte-vergabe, wie oben dargestellt, nicht kumulativ erfolgt. So muss z.B. jeder Bewer-ber (außer Studierende) eine Arbeitsplatzzusage vorweisen, um einwandern zu können. Dies sorgt allerdings auch für eine optimale Arbeitsmarktallokation, das heißt, es gibt so gut wie keine Arbeitslosigkeit infolge der Einwanderung über das „Punktesystem". Auch die Beratungs- und Evaluationsfunktion des MAC wird überwiegend positiv bewertet. In den meisten Fällen werden Handlungsempfeh-lungen, die vom MAC ausgesprochen werden, auch tatsächlich von der Regierung umgesetzt. Das liegt auch daran, dass die Regierung das MAC direkt für eine Problemlösung konsultiert. In der Regel braucht das MAC nicht länger als drei Monate, um eine Anfrage zu beantworten. Der Lösungsvorschlag wird auch veröf-fentlicht, so dass es der Regierung erschwert wird, Vorschläge einfach abzulehnen (Martin/Ruhs 2014, S. 29).

Demgegenüber beschweren sich Unternehmen über die hohen bürokratischen Hürden. Um eine ausländische Arbeitskraft einstellen zu können, müssen sie erst

---

[8] Auf der Liste für das Jahr 2018 standen Mangelberufe wie Führungskräfte in der Energie-wirtschaft, Elektroingenieure, Physikwissenschaftler oder Softwareprogrammierer (UK Government 2019).

einmal einen Antrag auf Zulassung bei der UK Border Authority (UKBA) stellen. Dafür müssen sie zahlreiche Unterlagen einreichen und eine hohe Gebühr zahlen. Zudem kann die UKBA, die Zulassung jeder Zeit zurückziehen, selbst wenn der Arbeitnehmer bereits im Land ist. Dies kann enorme Kosten für das Unternehmen verursachen (Interview mit Martin Ruhs, Oxford University, September 2015).

Österreich

Österreich führte im Jahr 2011 parallel zur EU-Blue Card die sogenannte Rot-Weiß-Rot-Karte (RWR-Karte) für hochqualifizierte Migranten ein.[9] Die RWR-Karte basiert in Teilen auf einem Punktesystem nach britischem Vorbild und löste das bis dahin bestehende Quotensystem ab. Dabei teilt die RWR-Karte die hoch-qualifizierten Migranten aus Nicht-EU-Staaten in folgende Bewerbergruppen ein: 1. besonders hochqualifizierte Fachkräfte, 2. Fachkräfte in Mangelberufen, 3. sonstige Schlüsselkräfte und 4. Start-up-Gründer. Potenzielle Arbeitsmigranten können sich über einen dieser vier Kanäle für ein Arbeitsvisum in Österreich be-werben. Die Arbeitsvisa werden dabei – nach unterschiedlichen Kriterien – zu-nächst für 24 Monate vergeben. Nach Ablauf der 24 Monate können sich die RWR-Kartenbesitzer für eine sog. RWR-Karte plus bewerben, die dann zu einem unbeschränkten Arbeitsmarktzugang berechtigt. Zudem gilt die RWR-Karte plus auch für Familienmitglieder. Bei der neuen RWR-Karte werden zudem nicht mehr jährliche Höchstgrenzen (Quoten) für die Vergabe der Arbeitsvisa festgelegt, vielmehr richtet sich die Vergabe nur noch nach den Bewerberzahlen und der tatsächlichen Nachfrage auf dem österreichischen Arbeitsmarkt. Für jede dieser vier Bewerbergruppen gelten unterschiedliche Kriterien und Gewichtungen im Rahmen des Punktesystems. Die umfangreichste Punkteregelung gilt für beson-ders hochqualifizierte Arbeitskräfte.[10]

Besonders hochqualifizierte Arbeitskräfte müssen insgesamt mindestens 70 von maximal 100 Punkten erreichen. Diese 70 Punkte werden nach folgenden 5 Kate-gorien vergeben: berufliche Qualifikation, Berufserfahrung, Sprachkenntnisse, Alter und Studienabschlüsse in Österreich (vgl. Tabelle 5). Dabei gibt es die meis-ten Punkte für Bildungsabschlüsse und Kenntnisse im MINT-Bereich sowie für wissenschaftliche und Managementberufe.

Demnach benötigen hochqualifizierte Arbeitskräfte zunächst keine Arbeits-platzzusage, wenn sie sich für ein Visum zur Arbeitssuche bewerben, sondern müssen ausschließlich die oben genannten Kriterien im Punktesystem erfüllen. Nachdem der Bewerber die Mindestpunktzahl erfüllt und einen Nachweis über

---

[9]   Die RWR-Karte wird auch als „Dachmarke" (Faßmann 2013, S. 2) bezeichnet, weil sie verschiedene Gruppen von Fachkräften im Rahmen eines Punktesystems anspricht und unter-schiedliche Zuzugs- und Aufenthaltsoptionen eröffnet.

[10] Aufgrund der besonderen Fragestellung dieses Aufsatzes wird hierbei nur die Bewerbergrup-pe der besonders hochqualifizierten Fachkräfte dargestellt und diskutiert.

Punktevergabekriterien	Punktegewichtung
Berufliche Qualifikationen und Fähigkeiten	Maximale Punktzahl: 40
Berufserfahrung	Maximale Punktzahl: 20
Sprachkenntnisse	Maximale Punktzahl: 10
Alter	Maximale Punktzahl: 20
Studium in Österreich	Maximale Punktzahl: 10
Maximalpunktzahl	**100**
Mindestpunktzahl	**70**

Tabelle 5: Punktekriterien und -gewichtung für besonders hochqualifizierte Fachkräfte im Rahmen des österreichischen Punktesystems

Quelle: Migrationsplattform der österreichischen Bundesregierung (2019).

alle erforderlichen Qualifikationen erbracht hat, kann er einen Antrag für ein sechsmonatiges Visum bei der zuständigen österreichischen Botschaft stellen und zur Arbeitssuche nach Österreich einreisen. Nachdem eine entsprechende Beschäftigung gefunden wurde, kann die RWR-Karte für zwei Jahre erteilt werden (Migrationsplattform der österreichischen Bundesregierung 2019).[11]

Die Rot-Weiß-Rot-Karte ist nicht unumstritten in Österreich. Kritikpunkte von Experten sind insbesondere die Höhe des Mindesteinkommens, die Bindung an einen bestimmten Arbeitgeber, der Nachweis von Deutschkenntnissen und die Notwendigkeit eines Arbeitsvertrages. In den österreichischen Medien wird häufig berichtet, dass die Regierung das ursprüngliche Ziel von 8.000 RWR-Karten pro Jahr deutlich verfehlt habe. Tatsächlich wurden in den ersten vier Jahren insgesamt auch nur 7.572 RWR-Karten ausgestellt, wovon 418 an Hochqualifizierte gingen (Salzburger Nachrichten 2015). Dabei betont die österreichische Wirtschaftskammer, dass die kursierende Zielmarke von 8.000 RWR-Karten pro Jahr niemals von offiziellen Stellen ausgegeben wurde, da dies viel zu hoch sei. Vielmehr könne seit der Einführung des Punktesystems ein Anstieg der hochqualifizierten Einwanderung nach Österreich beobachtet werden, nämlich insgesamt 1.800 Karten pro Jahr (Interview mit Margit Kreuzhuber, Wirtschaftskammer Österreich, September 2015). Auf der anderen Seite gebe es aber auch Probleme mit der RWR-Karte. Hier werden vor allem bürokratische Hürden genannt. Zudem wurde angeregt, die RWR-Karte auch für etwas ältere und geringer qualifizierte Arbeitskräfte zugänglich zu machen (Interviews mit österreichischen Experten, September 2015).

---

[11] Demgegenüber müssen Fachkräfte in Mangelberufen und sonstige Schlüsselarbeiter aus Drittstaaten immer eine Arbeitsplatzzusage vorweisen, um eine RWR-Karte zu erhalten. Start-up-Gründer müssen mindestens ein Kapital von € 50.000 für die geplante Unternehmensgründung nachweisen können (Migrationsplattform der österreichischen Bundesregierung 2019).

Zusammenfassung und Diskussion

Wie der Vergleich von fünf verschiedenen Punktesystemen zur Einwanderungsre-
gelung von hochqualifizierten Migranten gezeigt hat, gibt es eine Reihe von Un-
terschieden sowohl was die Auswahlbedingungen als auch die gewährten Rechte
angeht. Vielfach hängen die Effektivität und der Erfolg eines Systems von der
konkreten Ausgestaltung ab. Interessant ist zu sehen, dass es im Verlauf der Jahr-
zehnte auch zu vielen Veränderungen und Anpassungen gekommen ist, was für
eine gewisse Lernfähigkeit dieses Systems spricht. So hat z.b. Kanada eine höhere
Gewichtung der Arbeitsplatzzusage im neuen „Express Entry"-Verfahren eingeführt, bei dem ein Jobangebot von einem kanadischen Unternehmen die Hälfte
aller möglichen Punkte bringt. Hintergrund war eine hohe Arbeitslosigkeit unter
Neuzugewanderten. Die Beispiele Australien und Neuseeland zeigen jedoch, dass
dies nicht zwingend der Fall sein muss. Hier geschieht die Arbeitszuwanderung
über das Punktesystem ohne bzw. mit einer geringeren Bewertung der Arbeitsplatzzusage und dennoch liegt die Beschäftigungsquote bei Hochqualifizierten in
beiden Ländern bei nahezu 100%. Im Hinblick auf den Policy Outcome kann
festgehalten werden, dass Kanada, Australien und Neuseeland ihre jährlichen
Kontingente regelmäßig ausschöpfen, was für die Attraktivität dieser Länder für
internationale Arbeitskräfte spricht. Alle drei Länder richten ihre jährliche Kon-
tingentierung an den jeweiligen Bedürfnissen der nationalen Wirtschaft aus: In
Kanada liegt das Kontingent demnach bei 51.000, in Australien bei 44.000 und in
Neuseeland bei 26.000 Arbeitskräften pro Jahr. Großbritannien und Österreich
haben keine Kontingente im Rahmen ihrer Punktesysteme eingeführt, was auch an
der bisher geringeren Nachfrage von hochqualifizierten Migranten aus Nicht-EU-
Ländern liegt. Als sehr positiv hat sich zudem die Einführung eines Online-
Bewerbungssystems herausgestellt, das in allen Ländern in den letzten Jahren
optimiert wurde.

Dennoch wurden grundsätzlich Vor- und Nachteile eines Punktesystems durch
den Vergleich deutlich. Auf der Habenseite stehen sicher die drei zentralen Vorteile des Punktesystems: Einheitlichkeit, Transparenz und Flexibilität. Alle darge-
stellten Fälle haben deutlich gemacht, dass die Einführung eines Punktesystems zu
einer wesentlichen Vereinheitlichung und somit auch einer Vereinfachung der
oftmals komplexen und unübersichtlichen Einwanderungsregelungen beigetragen
haben. Punktesysteme bestechen also durch eine einheitliche und übersichtliche
Darstellung der Einwanderungspolitik nach außen. Auch haben die Punktesysteme
in den Untersuchungsländern zu mehr Transparenz geführt, weil sowohl die Bewerber als auch die Unternehmen und politische Entscheidungsträger überblicken
können, welche Kriterien für die Einwanderung gelten. Dies ist auch für potentiel-
le Einwanderer von Vorteil, weil man besser einschätzen kann, welche Anforderungen gelten und wie realistisch die jeweiligen Einwanderungchancen sind.
Bewerber können, falls sie den Anforderungen des Punktesystems noch nicht
entsprechen, dadurch motiviert werden, zusätzliche Qualifikationen, wie z. B.
Sprachkenntnisse, zu erwerben, um die notwendige Punktzahl zur Einwanderung

zu erreichen. Schließlich liegt eine weitere Stärke des Punktesystems in seiner Flexibilität, d.h. der ständigen Anpassungsfähigkeit an neue ökonomische und politische Gegebenheiten, ohne dass es gleich zu einer Gesetzesänderung kommen muss. So kann z.B. in Zeiten wirtschaftlicher Hochkonjunktur und einer hohen Nachfrage nach ausländischen Arbeitskräften die Mindestpunktzahl herabgesetzt werden, damit mehr Bewerber zugelassen werden können. Umgekehrt kann die Mindestpunktzahl in Zeiten ökonomischer Rezession, wenn die Nachfrage nach ausländischen Arbeitskräften nachlässt, wieder hochgesetzt werden und zudem auch die Arbeitsplatzzusage von einem inländischen Unternehmen höher gewichtet werden, um Arbeitslosigkeit zu vermeiden.

Die Risiken bestehen auf der anderen Seite vor allem in einer ineffektiven Verwaltung der Bewerbungen und einer möglichen Fehlallokation am Arbeitsmarkt. Im Mittelpunkt dieser Kritik steht vor allem die Befürchtung, dass Arbeitskräfte, die ohne einen Arbeitsvertrag ins Land kommen (wie dies lange Zeit in Kanada der Fall war) arbeitslos oder nicht ihrer Qualifikation entsprechend auf dem Arbeitsmarkt eingesetzt werden. Daher hat die Frage einer Arbeitsplatzzusage in den meisten Ländern, die mit einem Punktesystem operieren, eine hohe Priorität bekommen und viele Länder sind inzwischen auch dazu übergegangen, eine Arbeitsplatzzusage als Kriterium einzuführen (wie in Großbritannien und Österreich) bzw. sie sehr hoch in dem Punktesystem zu bewerten (wie in Kanada). Allerdings hat der vorhergehende Vergleich auch gezeigt, dass sich das Risiko einer migrationsinduzierten Arbeitslosigkeit mit einer hohen Bewertung einer Arbeitsplatzzusage sowie einem effizienten (Online-)Bewerbungssystem durchaus abmildern lässt. Letztendlich kommt es auf die konkrete Ausgestaltung eines Punktesystems an, die von den jeweiligen sozialen und ökonomischen Verhältnissen im Land abhängig gemacht werden sollte.

Literatur

Bauder, Harald / Lenard, Patti / Straehle, Christine (2014) Lessons from Canada and Germany – Immigration and Integration Experiences Compared. IMISCO – Comparative Migration Studies, University Press, Amsterdam: 1-7.

Bedford, Richard (2006) Skilled Migration Policy in Australia and New Zealand: Similarities and Differences. In: Birrell, Bob / Hawthorne, Lesleyanne / Richardson, Sue (Hrsg.) Evaluation of the General Skilled Migration Categories, Commonwealth of Australia, Canberra: 24-48.

Birrell, Bob / Hawthorne, Lesleyanne / Richardson, Sue (2006) Evaluation of the General Skilled Migration Categories. Commonwealth of Australia, Canberra.

Buchanan, Kelly / Ahmad, Tariq / Feikert-Ahalt, Clare (2013) Points-Based Immigration Systems – Australia, Canada, United Kingdom. The Law Library of Congress, Global Legal Research Center. http://www.loc.gov/law/help/points-based-immigration/. Gesehen 22.11.2017.

CIC [Citizenship and Immigration Canada] (2015) Help Centre. http://www.cic.gc.ca/english/helpcentre/glossary.asp#points. Gesehen 23.11.2017.

CIC [Citizenship and Immigration Canada] (2017) Changes to Canada's Express Entry CRS Coming in June. https://www.cicnews.com/2017/03/slight-changes-canada-expressentry-immigration-system-coming-june-039007.html. Gesehen 22.11.2017.

Department of Immigration and Border Protection (2015) SkillSelect. http://www. border.gov.au/Trav/Work/Skil. Gesehen 23.2017.

Department of Immigration and Citizenship (2015) Department of Immigration and Citizenship 2015: Additional Results from the Continuous Survey of Australia's Migrants. http://www.immi.gov.au/media/publications/research/_pdf/csam-additionalresults.pdf. Gesehen 22.11.2017.

Faßmann, Heinz (2013) Die Rot-Weiß-Rot-Karte in Österreich. Inhalt, Implementierung, Wirksamkeit. Gütersloh: Bertelsmann Stiftung.

Hawthorne, Lesleyanne (2011) Competing for Skills: Migration Policies and Trends in New Zealand and Australia, IMSED Research (International Migration, Settlement, and Employment Dynamics), Service of the Department of Labour.

Hawthorne, Lesleyanne (2014) A Comparison of Skilled Migration Policy: Australia, Canada and New Zealand. http://sites.nationalacademies.org/cs/groups/pgasite/documents/webpage/pga_152512.pdf. Gesehen 20.11.2017.

Hunger, Uwe / Krannich, Sascha (2015) Einwanderungsregelungen im Vergleich – Was Deutschland von anderen Ländern lernen kann. WISO Diskurs, Wirtschafts- und Sozialpolitik, Friedrich-Ebert-Stiftung, Bad Godesberg.

Hunger, Uwe / Krannich, Sascha (2017) Einwanderung neu gestalten – transparent, attraktiv, einfach. WISO Diskurs, Wirtschafts- und Sozialpolitik, Friedrich-Ebert-Stiftung, Bad Godesberg.

Hunger, Uwe / Krannich, Sascha (2018) Vor- und Nachteile einer punktebasierten Zuwanderungssteuerung für den Arbeitsmarkt. Lehren aus einem internationalen Vergleich der Zuwanderungsregelungen klassischer Einwanderungsländer. In: Zeitschrift für Vergleichende Politikwissenschaft, 1: 229-243.

Immigration New Zealand (2015) Skilled Migrant Category. http://www.immigration.govt.nz/migrant/stream/work/skilledmigrant/. Gesehen 22.11.2017.

Kane, Marie-Isabel (2019) Deutschland und Frankreich im globalen Wettbewerb um Talente. Zwischen europäischer Harmonisierung und nationaler Kompetenzwahrung. Lit-Verlag, Münster.

Kaulisch, Thomas (2012) Australien – Migrationspolitik als Wachstumsmotor. Friedrich-Ebert-Stiftung, Internationale Politikanalyse. http://library.fes.de/pdf-files/id/ipa/09365.pdf. Gesehen 22.11.2015.

Kolb, Holger (2008) Punktesystem, Einwanderungsplanwirtschaft und marktwirtschaftliche Alternativen oder: Was kann Deutschland von Kanada lernen?. In: Bendel, Petra / Kreienbrink, Axel (Hrsg.) Kanada und Deutschland: Migration und Integration im Vergleich. Bundesamt für Migration und Flüchtlinge – Schriftenreihe Migration, Flüchtlinge und Integration, Nürnberg: 56-77.

Krannich, Sascha (2017) The Reconquest of Paradise? How Indigenous Migrants Construct Community in the United States and Mexico, Lit-Verlag, Münster.

Krannich, Sascha (2018) Wie ein kohärentes Zuwanderungs- und Integrationsgesetz aussehen könnte. In: Neue Gesellschaft/Frankfurter Hefte, 9: 35-40.

Martin, Philip (2014) The United States. In: Hollifield, James / Martin, Philip / Orrenius, Pia (Hrsg.) Controlling Immigration. A Global Perspective, third edition, University Press, Stanford: 47-77.

Martin, Philip / Ruhs, Martin (2014) Independent Commissions and Labour Migration: The British MAC. In: Migration Letters, 11, 1: 23 - 32.

Migrationsplattform der österreichischen Bundesregierung (2019) Punkterechner. https://www.migration.gv.at/de/service-und-links/punkterechner/. Gesehen 20.09.2019.

Münz, Rainer (2014) The Global Race for Talent: Europe's Migration Chal-lenge, Bruegel Policy Brief, 2. http://bruegel.org/wp-content/uploads/imported/publications/pb_2014_02_. pdf. Gesehen 16.01.2016.

Murray, Alasdair (2011) Britain's Points Based Migration System. CentreForum. http://www.centreforum.org/assets/pubs/points-based-system.pdf. Gesehen 22.6.2015.

Rochel, Johan (2018) Protecting Japan from immigrants? An ethical challenge to security-based justification in immigration policy. Contemporary Japan, 30, 2: 164-188.

Salzburger Nachrichten (2015) Rot-Weiß-Rote Karte – Es kommen zu wenig qualifizierte Zuwanderer. http://www.pressreader.com/austria/salzburger-nachrichten/20150807/2815651744 80989/TextView. Gesehen 12.8.2015.

Schmidtke, Oliver (2008) Die Einwanderungspolitik Kanadas – beispielgebend für Deutschland?. In: Thränhardt, Dietrich (Hrsg.) Entwicklung und Migration, Berlin: Lit-Verlag, Berlin: 51-78.

Schmidtke, Oliver (2014) Beyond National Models? Governing Migration and Integration at the Regional and Local Levels in Canada and Germany. IMISCO – Comparative Migration Studies, University Press, Amsterdam: 77-99.

Schubert, Klaus (1999) Politikfeldanalyse, Leske und Budrich, Opladen.

Thränhardt, Dietrich (2014) Steps toward Universalism in Immigration Policies: Canada and Germany. RCIS Working Paper, 2, Toronto.

UK Government (2019) Visas Immigration. https://www.gov.uk/browse/visas-immigration/work-visas. Gesehen 07.09.2015.

UK Visas and Immigration (2015) Points-based Calculator. https://www.points. homeoffice. gov.uk/gui-migrant-jsf/SelfAssessment/SelfAssessment.faces. Gesehen 06.09.2015.

Rekrutierung und transnationale Mobilität von Hochqualifizierten in multinationale Unternehmen: Herausforderungen, Ziele, Strategien

Washika Haak-Saheem

Zusammenfassung

Hochqualifizierte Mitarbeiter spielen eine zentrale Rolle in der heutigen wissensbasierten internationalen Betriebswirtschafts- und Personalmanagementlehre. Insbesondere in den Bereichen der Innovation, sowie der Forschung und Entwicklung ist der Beitrag dieser Talente zur Wettbewerbsfähigkeit von Unternehmen nicht mehr wegzudenken. Vor dem Hintergrund einer zunehmenden Globalisierung der Märkte kommt der Entwicklung und Umsetzung einer internationalen Personalstrategie eine Schlüsselrolle im Rahmen der Unternehmensstrategie zu. Nahezu jedes Problem im internationalen Management ist letztendlich auf Mitarbeiter zurückzuführen, sei es, dass es durch sie verursacht wurde, sei es, dass es durch sie zu lösen ist. Aus diesem Grunde stellt der richtige Mitarbeiter zur richtigen Zeit am richtigen Ort den wesentlichen Erfolgsfaktor im internationalen Geschäft dar. Obwohl die MNUs (multinationalen Unternehmen) vom globalen Talentpool profitiert haben, ist das Phänomen transnationale Mobilität in der internationalen betriebswirtschaftlichen Forschung weitgehen unberücksichtigt geblieben. Das internationale Personalmanagement hat sich überwiegend mit dem Konzept der traditionellen Auslandsentsendungen von Mitarbeitern beschäftigt, bei dem Führungs- und Fachkräfte aus dem Mutterkonzern ins ausländische Tochterunternehmen für eine befristete Zeit entsendet wurden. Die zunehmende globale Migration von hochqualifizierten Individuen und die damit verbundenen Veränderungen im Bereich des Personalmanagements werden nahezu gänzlich vernachlässigt.

Der vorliegende Beitrag skizziert zunächst die grundsätzliche Bedeutung der globalen Mobilität von Hochqualifizierten in der internationalen Betriebswirtschaftslehre und des Personalmanagements und geht anschließend detaillierter auf relevanten Rekrutierungsmaßnahmen der MNUs ein.

Einleitung

Die Zahl der Migranten mit einem tertiären Bildungsabschluss ist in den Jahren 1990-2010 etwa um 130 Prozent gestiegen (Kerr, Kerr, Ozden, & Parsons, 2016).

Die Mehrheit dieser Migranten ziehen von ihren weniger entwickelten Heimat-
ländern in die westlichen Industriestaaten, wie die USA, Kanada, Australien oder
Deutschland. Die Gründe, die zur Migration dieser hochqualifizierten Personen führen, sind von unterschiedlicher Natur. Die Motivation zur Migration reicht von Arbeitslosigkeit und Mangel an Karrieremöglichkeiten im Heimatland bis zu Wettbewerbsvorteilen im Gastland, wie die institutionelle Stabilität oder bessere Lebens-
und Bildungsqualität. Neben diesen Motiven spielt das Vorhandensein relevanter
Industrien in den Gastländern eine wesentliche Rolle. Die geographische Lage und
der Entwicklungsstand des Gastlandes bieten Zugang zu finanziellem und physi-
schem Kapital, Technologie und komplementären Institutionen, die die Qualität der
potentiellen Arbeitsplätze beeinflussen. Es ist davon auszugehen, dass die Industriestaaten weiterhin an Attraktivität gewinnen.

Trotz dieser weltweiten Entwicklung neigen MNUs dazu, die Einbindung von
Migranten in die Belegschaft als „Black Box" zu betrachten, die kaum oder gar
keinen Einfluss auf die Internationalisierungsinitiativen des Unternehmens haben.
Die Besonderheiten beim Management von hochqualifizierten Migranten in ausgewählten personalwirtschaftlichen Feldern, wie etwa der Rekrutierung, werden oft
nicht berücksichtigt. Stattdessen fokussieren MNUs nach wie vor auf die mit Aus-
landseinsätzen verbundenen Spezifika, wie beispielsweise die kulturelle Anpassung
oder Reintegration von Entsendeten (Expatriates).

Obwohl die Bedeutung des Humankapitals auf theoretischer Ebene anerkannt
wird, bedeutet das starke wirtschaftliche Erbe des internationalen Managements,
dass die Tendenz besteht, dem Finanz- und Wissenskapital oder klassischen Auslandsentsendungen mehr Aufmerksamkeit zu schenken. Es wird davon ausgegangen, dass sich die Personalrekrutierung leicht verlagern lässt, mögliche Engpässe
bei der Gewinnung und Bindung qualifizierter, effizienter und produktiver Arbeitskräfte werden kaum berücksichtigt. Vor allem wird die Qualität des verfügbaren
Personals auf dem Arbeitsmarkt weitgehend ignoriert. Dies spiegelt zum Teil die
empirischen Herausforderungen wider, die sich auch mit quantitativen Studien be-
legen lassen, dass es nur begrenzte Möglichkeiten gibt, die Vielfalt und Qualität der
Humanressourcen innerhalb und außerhalb des Personalbestandes des MNUs ein-
zuschätzen. Da der Qualitätsaspekt des Humankapitals ignoriert wird, besteht außerdem die Tendenz, auch den relativen Mangel an Fach- und Führungskräften zu
ignorieren. Unter der Annahme, dass das Angebot an verschiedenen Arbeitnehmern
an jedem Standort ähnlich ist, ignorieren MNUs eine zentrale Herausforderung, der
Manager gegenüberstehen.

Mit der zunehmenden Anzahl der globalen Migranten müssen sich Unternehmen
diesen veränderten Marktbedingungen stellen. Die gestiegene Mobilität von Arbeitskräften und damit die zunehmend internationale Karriereorientierung von Individuen hat einen wesentlichen Einfluss auf die Rekrutierungspraktiken von
MNUs (Lanvin und Evans, 2016). Die daraus resultierende Diversität der Belegschaft kann als eine Chance, aber zugleich auch als eine unternehmerische Herausforderung angesehen werden. Kleinere und große MNUs müssen sich den verän-

derten Bedingungen anpassen, da der Zugang zu globalen Arbeitsmärkten einen immer stärkeren Beitrag zur Wettbewerbsfähigkeit dieser Unternehmen leistet. Während effiziente Personalmanagementpraktiken in MNUs eine wichtige Rolle spielen, ist die Rekrutierung von hochqualifizierten Mitarbeitern, die über ein gewisses Maß an internationaler Mobilität verfügen, von großer Bedeutung. Trotz des unumstrittenen Stellenwertes dieser Individuen im internationalen Wettbewerb gibt es in der Betriebswirtschaftslehre keine einheitliche Begriffsdefinition, die sich mit dem Phänomen globale Migration auseinandersetzt.

Globale Migration:
Die Suche nach einer betriebswirtschaftlichen Begriffsdefinition

Angesichts der immer größeren Aufmerksamkeit, die dem internationalen Management von hochqualifizierten Mitarbeitern gewidmet wird, ist leicht anzunehmen, dass das Konzept des „hochqualifizierten Migranten" klar definierter ist. Dies ist jedoch bei weitem nicht der Fall, und der Begriff „hochqualifizierter Migrant" ist bis dato ein eher nebulöses Konstrukt in der Betriebswirtschaftslehre. Die Globale Kommission für internationale Migration der Vereinigten Nationen (2005) berichtet, dass die traditionelle Unterscheidung zwischen qualifizierten und ungelernten Arbeitskräften in gewisser Hinsicht nicht hilfreich sei und schlägt stattdessen den Begriff der „essentiellen Arbeitnehmer" vor. Dieser Vorschlag ist jedoch nicht vereinbar mit der Gestaltung spezifischer Strategien der MNUs.

Auch die Europäische Kommission verwendet ihre eigene Typologie. Sie bezeichnet eine Person, die als Manager, Führungskraft, oder Techniker oder ähnliches qualifiziert ist und sich innerhalb der internen Arbeitsmärkte transnationaler Unternehmen oder über internationale Arbeitsmärkte eine Beschäftigung suchen als „hochqualifizierten Migranten". Im EU-Kontext wird ein Drittstaatsangehöriger, der eine Beschäftigung in einem EU-Mitgliedstaat sucht und über die erforderliche angemessene und spezifische Kompetenz verfügt, wie einen höheren Bildungsabschluss als hochqualifizierter Migrant bezeichnet (Das Europäische Migrationsnetzwerk, 2012).

Die zunehmende Globalisierung von Handelsbeziehungen hat zu zirkulären Migrationsmustern geführt, die wiederum neue Karriereentwicklungen ermöglichten. Internationale Mobilität, Auslandsentsendungen und selbstinitiierte Auswanderung werden als Phänomene in der internationalen Betriebswirtschaftslehre intensiv diskutiert (siehe z.B. Briscoe, Tarique, und Schuler, 2012; Brewster, Vernon, Sparrow und Houldsworth, 2016). Allerdings ist eine einheitliche Begriffsdefinition zur Beschreibung wesentlicher Formen der internationalen Mobilität nicht vorhanden. Ein wachsendes Forschungsgebiet untersucht das Phänomen der internationalen Mobilität und der grenzüberschreitenden Karriereentwicklung aus der Perspektive hochqualifizierter Individuen und des Personalmanagements (Hajro, Stahl,

	Internationale Migranten (IMs)	Selbst-initiierte Mobilität (SIEs)	Auslandsentsendungen (AIEs)
Geographische Herkunft und Zielland	Typischerweise von Entwicklungs- oder Schwellenländern in Industrieländer	Typischerweise von Entwicklungs-/Schwellen- in Industrieländern, oft auch nur in ein "attraktiveres" Land	Typischerweise vom Hauptstandort des Arbeitgebers (in der Regel einem Industriestaat) in ein ausländisches Tochterunternehmen (weltweit)
Zeithorizont	Absicht, auf unbestimmte Zeit (manchmal dauerhaft) zu bleiben	Absicht, sich nicht dauerhaft niederzulassen, obwohl Aufenthalte länger sein können (mehr als 10 Jahre)	Absicht ist vorübergehender, klar befristeter Aufenthalt
Motivation und Individuelle Handlungsmächtigkeit	Selbstverantwortlich für eigene Mobilität, manchmal erzwungen. Vielzahl unterschiedlicher Motive möglich: politische, wirtschaftliche, gesellschaftliche, familiäre oder persönliche Gründe	Selbstverantwortlich für die eigene Mobilität. In erster Linie motiviert durch Karriereentwicklung, Lebensqualität oder familiäre Gründe	Entsendung durch den Arbeitgeber. In erster Linie motiviert durch Karriereentwicklungsziele, finanzielle Anreize und Beitrag zu organisatorischen Zielen
Verwundbarkeit, Status und Macht	Sicherung der eigenen Beschäftigung. Lokaler Arbeitsvertrag. Oft unterbeschäftigt, in prekären Beschäftigungsverhältnissen, hohe Wahrscheinlichkeit von Diskriminierung	Sicherung der eigenen Beschäftigung. Lokaler Arbeitsvertrag. MNUs sind häufig der lokale Arbeitgeber	Gesicherte Beschäftigung durch den Arbeitgeber im Herkunftsland (MNU). Internationaler (grenzüberschreitender) Arbeitsvertrag
Unterstützung durch den potentiellen Arbeitgeber	Selbstfinanziert. Keine organisatorische Unterstützung. Karriereentscheidungen sind selbstgesteuert, aber oft durch Regelungen im Gastland eingeschränkt	Selbstfinanziert. Keine organisatorische Unterstützung. Karriereentscheidungen sind selbstgesteuert	Finanziert durch Arbeitgeber. Organisatorische Unterstützung verfügbar. Karriereschritte werden durch die Organisation erleichtert
Wissenschaftlich häufig untersuchte Ergebnisse in der Personengruppe	Akkulturation/Integration	Individuelle- und Karriereentwicklung	Anpassung und Leistung

Abbildung 1 Konzeptionelle Herangehensweise

Quelle: Angelehnt an Hajro, Zilinskaite & Stahl, 2017

Clegg und Lazarova, 2019). Abbildung 1 zeigt die unterschiedlichen Ansätze in der internationalen Betriebswirtschafts- und Personalmanagementlehre, die sich mit den unterschiedlichen Formen globaler Mobilität befassen.

Wie Abbildung 1 zeigt, unterscheidet die gegenwärtige Forschung zwischen traditionelle Auslandsentsendungen (assigned expatriates, AIEs), der selbstinitiierte Umzug ins Ausland (self-initiated expatriates, SIEs) und die internationale Migration (IMs). Diese Unterscheidung spielt eine herausragende Rolle innerhalb der Personalmanagementpraktiken von MNUs. Während MNUs seit einigen Jahrzenten bereits mit der Entsendung und dem Management von AIEs vertraut sind und entsprechende Praktiken entwickelt haben, um ihre global mobile Führungs- und Fachkräfte zur Generierung von Wettbewerbsvorteilen optimal einzusetzen, stoßen sie häufig an ihre Grenzen, wenn es um die Rekrutierung von qualifiziertem Personal auf internationalen Arbeitsmärkten geht. Insbesondere fehlen den MNUs Personalmanagementkompetenzen, die auf die Bedürfnisse von Migranten ausgerichtet sind.

Die Bedeutung von ‚globalen Talenten' und die Nachfrage nach Kompetenzen auf globalen Arbeitsmärkten beeinflussen die Personalpolitik auf mehreren Ebenen. Ein wichtiges Ziel des Personalmanagements ist es, Anreizsysteme schaffen, um die Rekrutierung von hochqualifizierten Mitarbeitern zu ermöglichen. Unternehmen stehen aber oft vor der Herausforderung, diese Talente zu finden und für sich zu gewinnen. Dieser von McKinsey als „war for talent" (Beechler und Woodward, 2009) bezeichnete Wettbewerb verschärft sich durch die zunehmende Globalisierung immer mehr. Auch der wirtschaftliche Aufschwung in den sogenannten Schwellenmärkten, wie China oder Indien hat diesen Wettbewerb um hochqualifiziertes Personal verstärkt (McGregor und Hamm, 2008).

Qualifizierte Mitarbeiter mit internationaler Erfahrung bringen multinational agierenden Unternehmen wertvolle Vorteile. Aus unterschiedlichen Gründen haben viele MNUs ihr Augenmerk auf internationale Personalrekrutierung gerichtet. Tendenziell wird der Markt für hochqualifizierte Mitarbeiter immer internationaler. Wie die Vereinigten Nationen berichtet leben und arbeiten zurzeit ca. 244 Million Menschen außerhalb ihrer Heimatländer (UN, 2017). Es ist davon auszugehen, dass transnationale Mobilität weiterhin ansteigt und immer deutlicher auch den europäischen Arbeitsmarkt und – in weiterer Folge – die Rekrutierungsmaßnahmen der MNUs in der EU beeinflussen wird. Die zunehmende Mobilität wird immer mehr zu standortunabhängigen Rekrutierungsmaßnahmen führen.

Die Schnittstelle zwischen internationalem Management und Personalmanagement

Es ist ein wichtiges Anliegen der internationalen Managementforschung, die Strategien und Praktiken der Unternehmen an unterschiedlichen Standorten besser zu verstehen. Gleichzeitig versucht die Forschung zum internationalen Personalmanagement die Herausforderungen und Unterschiede im Personalmanagement von

MNU zu verstehen. Dementsprechend würde man erwarten, dass sich diese beiden Forschungsrichtungen gegenseitig ergänzen und auf die Stärken des jeweils anderen bauen. Doch wird erst in Einzelfällen versucht, eine Verbindung zwischen internationalem Management und Personalmanagement herzustellen (Farndale, Scullion & Sparrow, 2010; Hajro et al., 2017; Welch & Björkman, 2015), zumeist sind beide Forschungsfelder nach wie vor voneinander abgegrenzt.

Die internationale Personalmanagementforschung vernachlässigt häufig die wirtschaftlichen Aspekte der Unternehmensentscheidungen. Es wird im Allgemeinen nicht untersucht, wie sich die Personalrekrutierung über den globalen Arbeitsmarkt mit anderen Funktionsbereichen im internationalen Umfeld überschneidet. In ähnlicher Weise vernachlässigt die internationale Betriebswirtschaftslehre die theoretischen und angewandten Erkenntnisse, die wichtige Aspekte der internationalen Personalmanagementliteratur liefern, wie die Bedeutung der Heterogenität von Individuen und der interkulturellen Dynamik. Die gegenseitige Befruchtung dieser Forschungsfelder gewinnt mit der zunehmenden globalen Mobilität vor allem von hochqualifizierten Führungs- und Fachkräften an Bedeutung.

Das Internationale Personalmanagement

Ein grundlegender Unterschied zwischen den Bereichen Personalmanagement und internationales Personalmanagement ist der Grad der Komplexität. Personalabteilungen sind grundsätzlich für die Rekrutierung, Einstellung, Ausbildung, Bezahlung, Entwicklung, Bewertung und Motivation der Belegschaft in einem Unternehmen verantwortlich. Allerdings nimmt die Komplexität dieser Aufgaben mit dem Grad der Internationalisierung des Unternehmens dramatisch zu. MNUs arbeiten nicht in einem Vakuum – sie arbeiten in mehreren nationalen Kontexten, jeder mit seinen eigenen institutionellen und kulturellen Merkmalen. Mitarbeiter, die in der zentralen Personalabteilung eines MNUs ansässig sind, müssen nicht nur über gutes Verständnis der Rekrutierungsstrategien in ihrem Heimatland verfügen, sondern auch über den operativen Kontext an internationalen Standorten, um die globale Personalstrategie ihres Unternehmens koordinieren zu können. Diese Komplexität kann durch kritische Wendepunkte, wie nationale oder globale Krisen oder veränderte Bedingungen auf dem Arbeitsmarkt, zunehmen. Das Management von Komplexität und von Risiken in Krisenzeiten ist zu einer Kernkompetenz von MNUs geworden, zu einer Kompetenz, zu der internationales Personalmanagement einen wesentlichen Beitrag leisten kann (Farndale, Horak, Phillips, Beamond, 2019). Vor dem Hintergrund der zunehmenden Globalisierung kommt der Entwicklung und Umsetzung einer internationalen Personalstrategie eine Schlüsselrolle im Rahmen der Unternehmensstrategie zu. Praktisch jedes Problem im internationalen Management ist letztlich auf Mitarbeiter zurückzuführen, sei es, dass es durch sie verursacht wurde, sei es, dass es durch sie zu lösen ist. Aus diesem Grund stellt der richtige Mitarbeiter zur richtigen Zeit am richtigen Ort einen wesentlichen Erfolgsfaktor im internationalen Geschäft dar.

Ein großer Teil der relevanten Forschung zum internationalen Personalmanagement hat sich tendenziell auf die Entsendung von Mitarbeitern ins Ausland konzentriert (Tung 1987; Mendenhall, Kuhlmann, Stahl und Osland, 2002; Yan, Zhu, & Hall, 2002). Neuere Forschungsansätze versuchen die vielfältigen Formen von transnationaler Mobilität zu verstehen.

Standortunabhängige Personalentscheidungen

Das Konzept der transnationalen Strategie wird häufig in Zusammenhang mit den internationalen Personalstrategien diskutiert (Kogut, 1985). Im Mittelpunkt solcher Diskussionen steht das Bestreben, Skaleneffekte (economies of scale), Verbundvorteile (economies of scope) und nationale Unterschiede gleichzeitig auszuschöpfen (Holtbrügge, 1996). Globalisierungs- und Lokalisierungsvorteile lassen sich dabei nicht mehr unternehmensweit einheitlich realisieren, sondern müssen für jedes Geschäftsfeld, jede Wertaktivität, jeden Unternehmungsprozeß und jede Internationalisierungsphase individuell geprüft werden. Des Weiteren ist der Transfer von Aktivitäten in internationalen Standorten oft von größeren unternehmerischen Freiheiten begünstigt (Streeck, 1998). Unter steigendem Druck der Orientierung am Shareholder Value konzentriert sich das Management auf kurzfristige Kostensenkungsstrategien, die häufig durch niedrige Löhne auf dem globalen Arbeitsmarkt realisierbar sind (Flecker 1998b).

In organisatorischer Hinsicht ist damit insbesondere der Aufbau integrierter Netzwerkstrukturen (Bartlett und Ghoshal 1990) bzw. der Übergang zu Heterarchien (Hedlund 1986) verbunden. Die Rolle der der Muttergesellschaft wandelt sich zunehmend, weg von der Rolle als zentrale Einheit zur direkten Steuerung und Kontrolle der ausländischen Tochtergesellschaften hin zu einer zunehmend moderierenden Rolle mit Zuständigkeit für die Kontextsteuerung dezentraler Entscheidungsprozesse.

Zugriff auf internationale Arbeitsmärkte

Jeder Zugriff auf ergiebige Arbeitsmärkte in anderen Regionen erweitert unmittelbar das Spektrum der Rekrutierungspotentiale. Besonders Unternehmen innerhalb der Europäischen Union werden über kurz oder lang ihre Personalpolitik anpassen, um nicht nur im jeweiligen Heimatland, sondern auch grenzüberschreitend nach optimal geeigneten Mitarbeiten zu suchen. Die gezielte Anwerbung ausländischer Fachkräfte wird in nächster Zukunft wesentlich wichtiger werden. Die Rekrutierung und Bindung solcher Mitarbeiter erfordert dann aber auch, dass ihnen attraktive Karriereaussichten geboten werden. Dieser Trend wird eventuell zu einer Machtasymmetrie auf internationalen und lokalen Arbeitsmärkte führen, die die bisherigen Unternehmensentscheidungen und -praktiken in Frage stellen könnten (Sengenberger, 1993). Neue Anreizsysteme auf dem europäischen Arbeitsmarkt sind aber von dringender Notwendigkeit, um die negativen Auswirkungen von lokalen Entwicklungen, wie dem wachsenden Fachkräftemangel, entgegenzuwirken.

Zwar führt die zunehmende Internationalisierung des Talentpools zu einer größeren Vielfalt, die maßgeblich zur Steigerung der Wettbewerbsfähigkeit in Unternehmen beitragen kann. Allerdings haben noch nicht alle MNUs die notwendigen Kompetenzen entwickelt, um die Vorteile dieser Diversität zu nutzen. Unternehmen müssen entsprechende Personalmanagementpraktiken und Unternehmenskultur entwickeln, um aus dem internationalen Talentpool erfolgreich rekrutieren zu können.

Zusammenfassend: die globale Mobilität von Hochqualifizierten hat die nationale und internationale Wettbewerbssituation der MNUs verändert, dies wirkt sich auf die internationalen Geschäftsaktivitäten vieler Organisationen aus. Die substanzielle und nachhaltige Rekrutierung von hochqualifiziertem Personal basiert nicht ausschließlich auf Fähigkeiten und Vermögenswerten potentieller Mitarbeiter im Heimatland. Migration als wichtige Ressource zur Entwicklung des Humankapitals in den Herkunfts- und Aufnahmeländern wird auch in den nächsten Jahrzehnten eine wichtige Rolle spielen. Daher ist es notwendig, dass internationale Wirtschafts- und Strategieforscher und Manager sich der laufenden multidisziplinären Debatte zu diesem Phänomen anschließen und die Generalisierbarkeit ihrer Rekrutierungspraktiken in ihrem Kontext neu bewerten.

Forschung und Entwicklung

Während in den 1990er Jahren die meisten MNUs aus dem deutschsprachigen Raum ihre Kapazitäten in der Forschung und Entwicklung (FuE) vor allem im Ausland ausgeweitet haben, verlagern in der Zwischenzeit ausländische Unternehmen ihre FuE zunehmend nach Europa (zum Beispiel nach Deutschland). Die Wahl des Standortes war früher vor allem von der Verfügbarkeit der relevanten Arbeitskräfte abhängig. Die aktuelle betriebswirtschaftliche Forschung untersucht internationales Personalmanagement aus unterschiedlichen Perspektiven, da die globale Mobilität die Konzentration auf standortgebundene Arbeitsmarktvorteile vermindert hat (siehe z.B. Cerdin und Brewster, 2014; Haak-Saheem und Brewster, 2017).

Es herrscht weitgehende Einigkeit darüber, dass dabei dem Aufbau, der Nutzung und der Erweiterung des organisatorischen Wissens eine zentrale Bedeutung zukommt (Gupta, und Govindarajan, 2000; Hedlund und Nonaka, 1993). Das Streben nach nachhaltiger Wettbewerbsfähigkeit hat sich unter anderem auf die Internationalisierung von Wissensgenerierung und -anwendung konzentriert. Organisatorisches Wissen kann als kontextuelle, zweckbezogene und verhaltensrelevante Vernetzung von Informationen aufgefasst werden, Wissen, das die Organisation zur Interpretation der für sie relevanten Realität entwickelt. Andere Studien, die sich mit globaler Mobilität befassen, finden in der Regel auf nationaler Ebene statt und diskutieren häufig „Brain Drain" oder „Skills Drain" (Schmitt und Soubeyran, 2006). Diese Forschungsrichtung hat sich öfter mit diesen Phänomenen auf organisatorischer und individueller Ebene befasst (Tung und Lazarova, 2006).

Ausblick

Die Rekrutierung von hochqualifizierten Migranten stellt ein vielversprechendes Thema für die zukünftige Forschung dar, die sich mit der Schnittstelle zwischen internationalem Management und Personalmanagement beschäftigt. Es ist davon auszugehen, dass das Fehlen einer besseren Verbindung größtenteils auf anhaltende theoretische Mängel zurückzuführen ist. Die grundlegenden Argumente, die für die Zusammenführung dieser beiden Forschungsbereiche sprechen, (Cooke, Veen & Wood, 2017; Buckley, Doh & Benischke 2017), beruhen überwiegend auf der Mobilität von humanem Kapital. Dies ist der Bereich, in dem der offensichtlichste Handlungsbedarf besteht. Die Entwicklung der Theorie muss nicht nur die Komplexität des Phänomens berücksichtigen, sondern auch ein Verständnis dafür entwickeln, wie Theoretiker und Praktiker diese Perspektiven und Herangehensweisen verstehen und anwenden. Die erfolgreiche Ausschöpfung heterogenen Ressourcen auf den internationalen Arbeitsmärkten ist auf die Kenntnisse in beiden Bereichen angewiesen. Akteure in der Politik, der Wirtschaft und der Wissenschaft können von dieser Zusammenführung profitieren und gesellschaftliche und wirtschaftliche Fragestellungen damit besser beantworten.

Referenzen

Beechler, S., & Woodward, I. C. (2009). The global "war for talent". Journal of international management, 15(3), 273-285.

Brewster, C., Vernon, G., Sparrow, P., & Houldsworth, E. (2016). International human resource management. Kogan Page Publishers.

Briscoe, D., Tarique, I., & Schuler, R. (2012). International human resource management: Policies and practices for multinational enterprises. Routledge.

Brookfield Global Relocation Services. (2014). Global relocation trends survey report. Woodridge, IL: Brookfield GRS.

Buckley, P.J., Doh, J.P. and Benischke, M.H. (2017). Towards a renaissance in international business research? Big questions, grand challenges, and the future of IB scholarship. Journal of International Business Studies, 48(9), 1045-1064.

Cerdin, J. L., & Brewster, C. (2014). Talent management and expatriation: Bridging two streams of research and practice. Journal of World Business, 49(2), 245-252.

Cooke, F.L., Veen, A. and Wood, G., (2017). What do we know about cross-country comparative studies in HRM? A critical review of literature in the period of 2000-2014. The International Journal of Human Resource Management, 28(1), 196-233.

Das Europäische Migrationsnetwerk (2012): https://publications.iom.int/system/files/pdf/intraeu_mobility_austria_de.pdf (Zugegriffen a, 08.09.2019).

Ec.Europa.https://ec.europa.eu/home-affairs/what-we-do/networks/european_migration_network/glossary_search/highly-qualified-migrant_en (Zugegriffen am 09.09.2019).

Farndale, E., Scullion, H., & Sparrow, P. (2010). The role of the corporate HR function in global talent management. Journal of world business, 45(2), 161-168.

Farndale, E., Horak, S., Phillips, J., & Beamond, M. (2019). Facing complexity, crisis, and risk: Opportunities and challenges in international human resource management. Thunderbird International Business Review, 61(3), 465-470.

Flecker, J. (1998b): „Einem indischen Ingenieur ist nichts zu schwer." Zu den Auswirkungen der Globalisierung(sdiskussion) auf die Arbeitsbeziehungen. In: Sallmutter, H. (Hg.): Wieviel Globalisierung verträgt unser Land? Zwänge und Alternativen. Wien: 47-66.

Ghoshal, S., & Bartlett, C. A. (1990). The multinational corporation as an interorganizational network. Academy of management review, 15(4), 603-626.

Gupta, A.K./ Govindarajan, V. (2000), Knowledge Flows Within Multinational Corporations, in: Strategic Management Journal, Vol. 21, 4, S. 473–496.

Haak-Saheem, W., & Brewster, C. (2017). 'Hidden' expatriates: international mobility in the United Arab Emirates as a challenge to current understanding of expatriation. Human Resource Management Journal, 27(3), 423-439.

Hajro, A., Zilinskaite, M., & Stahl, G. (2017). Acculturation of Highly-qualified Migrants: Individual Coping Strategies and Climate for Inclusion. In Academy of Management Proceedings (Vol. 2017, No. 1, p. 13666). Briarcliff Manor, NY 10510: Academy of Management.

Hajro, A., Stahl, G. K., Clegg, C. C., & Lazarova, M. B. (2019). Acculturation, coping, and integration success of international skilled migrants: An integrative review and multilevel framework. Human Resource Management Journal.

Hedlund, G. (1986). The hypermodern MNC—a heterarchy?. Human resource management, 25(1), 9-35.

Hedlund, G./Nonaka, I. (1993), Models of Knowledge Management in the West and Japan, in: Lorange, P. et al. (Hrsg.), Implementing Strategic Process, Change, Learning, and Cooperation, S. 117–144.

Holtbrügge, D. (1996), Perspektiven internationaler Unternehmenstätigkeit in der Postmoderne, in: Engelhard, J. (Hrsg.), Strategische Führung internationaler Unternehmen. Paradoxien, Strategien und Erfahrungen, S. 273–292.

Kogut, B. (1985), Designing Global Strategies: Profiting from Operational Flexibility, in: Sloan Management Review, Vol. 27, 1, S. 27–38.

Keller, B. (1997): Europäische Arbeits- und Sozialpolitik. München.

Lanvin B., Evans P. (Eds.) (2016). The Global Talent Competitiveness Index 2017. Talent and Technology 2017,INSEAD Fontainebleau, France.

McGregor, J., Hamm, S., 2008. Davos Special Report: managing the global workforce. BusinessWeek 34–43 (January 28).

Mendenhall, M. E., Kuhlmann, T. M., Stahl, G. K., & Osland, J. S. (2002). Employee development and expatriate assignments. The Blackwell handbook of cross-cultural management, 155-183.

Kerr, S. P., Kerr, W., Ozden, C., & Parsons, C. (2016). Global talent flows. The World Bank.

Pio, E., & Essers, C. (2014). Professional migrant women decentring otherness: A transnational perspective. British Journal of Management, 25(2), 252-265.

Schmitt, N., & Soubeyran, A. (2006). A simple model of brain circulation. Journal of International Economics, 69(2), 296-309.

Sengenberger, W. (1993): Labour Mobility and Western European Economic Integration. In: IIRA (Hg.): Economic and Political Changes in Europe: Implications on Industrial Relations. 3rd European Regional Congress, Bari-Naples/Italy 1991. Bari: 415-439.

Streeck, W. (1998): Industrielle Beziehungen in einer internationalisierten Wirtschaft, in: U. Beck (Hg.): Politik der Globalisierung, Frankfurt/M, S.169-202

Tung, R. L. (1987). Expatriate assignments: Enhancing success and minimizing failure. Academy of Management Perspectives, 1(2), 117-125.

Tung, R. L., & Lazarova, M. (2006). Brain drain versus brain gain: an exploratory study of ex-host country nationals in Central and East Europe. The International Journal of Human Resource Management, 17(11), 1853-1872.

United Nation (2005). International Migration Polcies. New York. Retrieved from: https://www.un.org/en/development/desa/population/publications/pdf/policy/international_migration_policies_data_booklet.pdf

United Nations (2017) International Migration Report. Highlights. United Nations, Department of Economic and Social Affairs, New York. Retrieved from: https://www.un.org/en/development/desa/population/migration/publications/migrationreport/docs/MigrationReport2017_Highlights.pdf

Welch, D., & Björkman, I. (2015). The place of international human resource management in international business. Management International Review, 55(3), 303-322.

Yan, A., Zhu, G., & Hall, D. T. (2002). International assignments for career building: A model of agency relationships and psychological contracts. Academy of Management Review, 27(3), 373-391.

SELBSTÄNDIGKEIT VON MIGRANTINNEN UND MIGRANTEN ALS INTEGRATIONSMOTOR

Charakteristika und Rahmenbedingungen von „Migrant Entrepreneurship"

Gudrun Biffl

Zusammenfassung

Das migrantische Unternehmertum gewinnt in weiten Teilen der westlichen Welt an Bedeutung. Dieser Beitrag geht den Hintergründen für diese Entwicklung nach. Zu Beginn des Beitrags wird ein Überblick über Begriffe und Organisationsstrukturen sowie Charakteristika des Unternehmertums von MigrantInnen gebracht. Darauf aufbauend wird auf die Wechselwirkung von institutionellen und gesellschaftlichen Rahmenbedingungen der Aufnahmeländer sowie auf ethnisch-kulturelle Traditionen der MigrantInnen, die einen Einfluss auf unternehmerisches Handeln haben, eingegangen Abgerundet wird der Beitrag mit einem Überblick über theoretische Ansätze zur Erklärung des ethnischen Unternehmertums.

Zur Einführung

In unserem Zeitalter der internationalen Wanderungen gewinnen die diversen Möglichkeiten der gesellschaftlichen und wirtschaftlichen Partizipation von MigrantInnen in der Politikgestaltung der Aufnahmeländer ebenso wie der der Herkunftsländer an Aufmerksamkeit. (Castles et al 2013; Santamaria-Alvarez et al. 2019) Das migrantische Unternehmertum spielt dabei eine zunehmend wichtige Rolle, nicht nur weil es ein möglicher Integrationsweg im Aufnahmeland ist, sondern auch weil es ein Instrument der Förderung der internationalen bzw. transnationalen wirtschaftlichen Vernetzung und Entwicklung sein kann. MigrantInnen können nämlich als Brückenbauer fungieren und über Geldüberweisungen und Investitionen ebenso wie Wissenstransfer das Unternehmertum auch im Herkunftsland fördern. In der Folge hat das Phänomen des grenzüberschreitenden Unternehmertums an Bedeutung gewonnen, unterstützt durch soziale und technologische Transformationen, insbesondere die Erleichterung der transnationalen Kommunikation und die Verringerung der Reise- und Transportkosten.

Anregungen, wie die Politik bei der Förderung des migrantischen Unternehmertums in Aufnahme- und Herkunftsregionen vorgehen kann, liefert ein diesbezüglicher „Policy Guide", der in Zusammenarbeit mit Einrichtungen der Vereinten Nationen (UNHCR und UNCTAD) und der Internationalen Organisation für Migrationen (IOM) 2018 erarbeitet und veröffentlicht wurde. (UNCTAD/IOM 2018) Innerhalb der EU liegt der Fokus auf der Förderung des Wachstums migrantischen

Unternehmertums über grenzüberschreitenden Wissenstransfer im Rahmen von Partner-Netzwerken.[1]

Wichtig ist bei jeder Förderung des migrantischen Unternehmertums, die Charakteristika von MigrantInnen ebenso wie die Rahmenbedingungen vor Ort vor Augen zu haben. Dabei sollte die individuelle Dimension nicht unberücksichtigt bleiben, die Wertehaltungen ebenso wie die Rolle der Familie und privater Netzwerke. Denn die individuellen Entfaltungsmöglichkeiten werden nicht nur von den rechtlichen, wirtschaftlichen, sozialen sowie kulturellen Rahmenbedingungen vor Ort beeinflusst, sondern auch von den Kompetenzen und Fähigkeiten des Einzelnen sowie dem Sozialstatus im Aufnahmeland, zum Teil auch dem im Herkunftsland. Migrantische Unternehmer kommen aus bestimmten sozialen und ethnisch-kulturellen Gruppierungen mit unterschiedlichen Wertehaltungen, Verhaltensmustern und Glaubenszugehörigkeiten. Diese Charakteristika haben einen Einfluss auf die sozialen und wirtschaftlichen (transnationalen) Netzwerke, die Denkschemata und Strategien der potenziellen UnternehmerInnen. Aber auch das Umfeld im Aufnahmeland ist zu berücksichtigen. Es ist oft von Misstrauen, Stereotypisierungen und auch Ablehnung geprägt, was nicht ohne Wirkung auf die Entscheidung für eine selbständige unternehmerische Aktivität im Aufnahmeland der MigrantInnen ist.

MigrantInnen, die unternehmerisch tätig werden wollen, müssen sich die Frage nach ihrem möglichen spezifischen Beitrag zu lokalen, nationalen oder internationalen Märkten, Produktionsmethoden und Technologien in den diversen Wirtschaftszweigen stellen, und ob sie eine Rolle in zum Teil transnationalen Wertschöpfungsketten übernehmen können. Migrantische Unternehmen haben in der Folge häufig andere unternehmerische Schwerpunkte als die eingesessenen Unternehmen. Dabei liegen die Unterschiede in den Kompetenzen und Fachqualifikationen der UnternehmerInnen ebenso begründet, wie in den verfügbaren Ressourcen. Zu denen gehören lokale, nationale und internationale Unternehmenspraktiken ebenso wie der Zugang zu Kapital, Business-Netzwerken und Technologien.

Zu bedenken ist auch, wie Berghoff und Spiekermann (2016) verdeutlichen, dass der unternehmerische Erfolg von MigrantInnen häufig den günstigen institutionellen Rahmenbedingungen vor Ort zugeschrieben wird und nicht den unternehmerischen Fähigkeiten, dem Durchhaltewillen und der Innovationskraft der MigrantInnen. So hatten Berghoff und Spiekermann zufolge deutsche UnternehmerInnen in den USA große Orientierungs- und Akkulturationsprobleme: „...*German immigrants, indeed, had immense difficulties with the patronage of the U.S. political machines, restrictive religious and moral codes, and nativist rejection and even violence.*" (S10, ebenda) Und doch gelten sie als eine unternehmerische Einwanderungsgruppe, die ihren Erfolg einer aufnahmewilligen und unterstützenden amerikanischen Gesellschaft schuldet. (ebd.)

Im Folgenden wird zunächst der Begriff der „Migrant Entrepreneurship" genauer durchleuchtet, indem auf die unterschiedlichen Begriffe und Organisationsstruktu-

---

[1]   Mehr dazu auf http://migrant-entrepreneurship.eu/

ren eingegangen wird. Darauf aufbauend wird dem Ausmaß und den Charakteristika des migrantischen Unternehmertums nachgegangen, gefolgt von der Rolle der institutionellen und gesellschaftlichen Rahmenbedingungen. In den verschiedenen Begriffen und Charakteristika spiegeln sich unterschiedliche Formen der strukturellen Inkorporation einer Einwanderungsgruppe. Dazu werden zumindest ansatzweise theoretische Erklärungsmuster angeführt.

Anzumerken ist zur Einleitung, dass die Forschung zu ‚Migrant Entrepreneurship" ihren Ausgangspunkt in den USA und Großbritannien genommen hat, womit eine bestimmte Begrifflichkeit eingeführt wurde, die mit den kontinental-europäischen Gegebenheiten und Termini nicht immer übereinstimmt. So setzte der wissenschaftliche Diskurs im angelsächsischen Raum auf ethnische Minderheiten während er in Europa vorwiegend auf MigrantInnen gerichtet ist. Darüber hinaus wird in Europa der Superdiversität der MigrantInnen besonderes Augenmerk geschenkt, die sich u.a. aus den verschiedenen Migrationsmodellen in der EU ergeben (siehe dazu Biffl 1996), sowie aus den unterschiedlichen Rechtsstati als Folge von Einwanderungsregelungen für spezifische Gruppen von Zuwanderern, die die Zugangsrechte zu unternehmerischem Unternehmertum beeinflussen. So stellen die Freizügigkeit der Arbeitskräfte und die Niederlassungsfreiheit innerhalb der EU andere Rahmenbedingungen für das Unternehmertum mobiler EU-BürgerInnen dar, als etwa die Familienzusammenführung von Drittstaatsangehörigen oder die humanitäre Zuwanderung und Niederlassung von Flüchtlingen. Auch ist der Fokus auf die transnationale Dimension des ethnischen Unternehmertums in Europa ausgeprägter als in den USA, nicht zuletzt, weil die EU eine verstärkte wirtschaftliche Vernetzung mit den typischen Herkunftsregionen der MigrantInnen in Europa anstrebt. Dabei kann die Diaspora eine wichtige Rolle spielen und potenziell auch den Charakter der Migrationen von einer primär auf Einwanderung gerichteten auf eine verstärkte zirkuläre Migration verschieben. (Vertovec 2006; Vershinina et al. 2019; Elo et al. 2018)

Begriffe, Definitionen und Organisationsmerkmale

Die Heterogenität der Business-Modelle und Strategien, die von Familienunternehmen über innovative Start-ups bis zu ethnischem Unternehmertum reichen, erschweren die Charakterisierung und damit Verallgemeinerung migrantischen Unternehmertums. Um einen besseren Überblick zu gewinnen, werden die verschiedenen Formen des migrantischen Unternehmertums in einen konzeptionellen Rahmen gestellt, der es ermöglicht, bestimmte Charakteristika in einen wirtschaftlichen und gesellschaftlichen Kontext ‚einzubetten'[2].

An den Beginn der Ausführungen sind die Begriffe ethnisches bzw. migrantisches Unternehmertum zu stellen. Von ethnischem Unternehmertum (ethnic entrepreneurship) wird gesprochen, wenn es eine enge Bindung zwischen dem ethnisch-

---

[2]   Dazu Barberis und Solano (2018).

kulturellen Hintergrund des Unternehmers und der lokalen ethnischen Community gibt, d.h. wenn der Unternehmer in der ethnischen Community aktiv ist und mit seinem wirtschaftlichen Handeln zur wirtschaftlichen Dynamik der Community beiträgt. Die Unternehmen können das traditionelle Handwerk beleben oder neu ausrichten ebenso wie hochwertige Dienstleistungen etwa im Informations- und Kommunikationstechnologie Bereich anbieten. Letzteres ist immer öfter als Folge der Höherqualifizierung der MigrantInnen und dem wirtschaftlichen Strukturwandel möglich. Ethnische Unternehmen schaffen Arbeitsplätze, insbesondere auch für vulnerable Personengruppen aus der eigenen ethnischen Community, etwa für Jugendliche und Frauen, und tragen damit zur Armutsbekämpfung in der Community bei. Bei ethnischem Unternehmertum geht es aber nicht nur um die Schaffung von Arbeitsplätzen, sondern auch um den sozialen Aufstieg von ethnischen Minderheiten, um die Förderung des Selbstvertrauens und der Selbsterhaltungsfähigkeit der MigrantInnen sowie den sozialen Zusammenhalt innerhalb der ethnischen Community. Damit kann ein wichtiger Beitrag zur Revitalisierung von heruntergekommenen Stadtteilen sowie zum Wirtschaftswachstum geleistet werden. Volery (2007) gibt einen umfassenden Einblick in die theoretische Untermauerung der Entwicklung von ethnischem Unternehmertum und weist auf seine integrationsfördernde Wirkung hin.

Ein besonderer Aspekt des ethnischen Unternehmertums betrifft ethnische Ökonomien (ethnic economy); darunter versteht man Betriebe oder Unternehmen, die von Einwanderern oder MigrantInnen aufgebaut oder geführt werden, und die komplementär zu ansässigen Unternehmen sind. Der Begriff stammt aus der Literatur zur Rolle von spezifischen ethnisch-kulturellen Minderheiten, die als Mittelsmänner fungieren. (Bonacich 1973) Bonacich führt als idealtypische Beispiele hierfür u.a. Juden in Europa, Chinesen in Südostasien, Parsen in Indien, Asiaten in Ostafrika, oder Japaner und Griechen in den USA an. Diese Minderheiten sind in der Sozialhierarchie eines Aufnahmelandes meist nicht am unteren Ende angesiedelt, sondern in der Mittelschicht. In der Forschungsliteratur ist die Theorie der „Middleman minorities" eine Inkorporationsstrategie bestimmter ethnischer Minderheiten. Dabei wird argumentiert, dass die Aufnahmegesellschaft gegenüber den Minderheiten aus Gründen ethnisch-kultureller (inklusive religiöser) Spezifika feindlich eingestellt ist. Das findet einen Niederschlag im Ausschluss dieser ethnisch-kulturellen Minderheiten von der Ausübung bestimmter Berufe oder Tätigkeiten oder zumindest zur Behinderung bzw. Diskriminierung bei der Ausübung dieser Berufe. Die Minderheit reagiert auf die Ausgrenzung und berufliche Marginalisierung mit der Bildung solidarischer, geschlossener Communities und der Entwicklung einer unternehmerischen Überlebensstrategie. Eine mögliche Funktion ist die Bildung einer Mittlerrolle zwischen bestimmten Gruppen der Aufnahmegesellschaft; dabei liegt der Schwerpunkt auf Händler, Makler, Pfandleiher, Bankiers/Financiers und ähnliche Berufe. Bestimmte ethnisch-kulturelle Minderheiten können sich auch als Mittelsmänner in hierarchisch strukturierten Gesellschaften etablieren, indem sie als wirtschaftliche und kommunikative Brücke zwischen ‚Eliten' und der ‚Masse' agieren, etwa zwischen Bauern und dem städtischen Bürgertum, oder der ‚Kolonialherrschaft' und den ‚Einheimischen'.

Eine besondere Untergruppe stellen ethnische Enklaven dar. Auf diese gehen Portes und Manning (2008/2014) ein. Sie entwickeln eine Theorie der Entstehung von ethnischen Enklaven (ethnic enclave), aufbauend auf Arbeitsmarktsegmentationstheorien, die empirisch anhand von spezifischen ethnischen Gruppen untermauert wird. Sie weisen nach, dass sich der soziale Zusammenhalt von ethnischen Gruppen wie den europäischen Juden und Japanern in den USA vor dem 2. Weltkrieg in der Bereitstellung von Wagnis-Kapital (venture capital) ebenso niederschlug wie in der vereinsmäßigen Organisation von Business - Co-operativen und der Förderung von Wertschöpfungsketten. Diese Vorgangsweise ermöglichte es den ethnischen UnternehmerInnen, die sich in den Mainstream der Wirtschaft und Gesellschaft nicht einbinden lassen wollten bzw. konnten, sich in Nischen zu etablieren. Diese Strategie ermöglichte es der ersten Generation Einwanderer ohne den mühevollen Weg der Akkulturation und Assimilation zu Wohlstand und sozialem Aufstieg zu gelangen. Portes und Manning zeigen aber auch auf, dass ethnische Enklaven nicht nur typisch für spezifische ethnisch-kulturelle Gruppen von MigrantInnen vor dem 1. Weltkrieg waren, sondern dass sie bis heute eine wichtige strukturelle Integrationsform für bestimmte ethnische Gruppen darstellen. In der US-Forschung gewann diesbezüglich das ethnische Unternehmertum von Koreanern, die sich in Kalifornien niedergelassen haben, und von Kubanern, die vorwiegend auf Florida und New York konzentriert sind, besonderes Augenmerk; in Europa lag der Fokus der Forschung in den traditionellen Gastarbeiterländern auf Italienern und Türken, in den vormaligen Kolonialländern auf Pakistani in Großbritannien, Algerier und Tunesier in Frankreich, und Surinamer, Indonesier und Chinesen in den Niederlanden. In jedem Fall wird ihr unternehmerischer Erfolg im Wesentlichen auf die soziale und finanzielle Unterstützung der eigenen ethnischen Gruppe zurückgeführt. Der Forschung zufolge ist das Herzstück jeder räumlich abgegrenzten, ethnischen Unternehmensenklave ein dichtes Netzwerk an Unternehmen in den unterschiedlichsten sich ergänzenden Bereichen, in denen prioritär Mitglieder der eigenen ethnischen Gruppe Beschäftigung finden. Sie bieten allerdings ihre Güter und Dienstleistungen nicht nur für den spezifischen ethnischen Konsumenten an, sondern auch für die Allgemeinheit.

Die Forschung zu den ethnischen Enklaven fokussiert einerseits auf biographische Faktoren, die für die Unternehmensgründung ausschlaggebend waren, andererseits auf die Löhne der in diesen Unternehmen beschäftigten ethnischen Minderheiten. Dabei wird vor allem der Lohnunterschied zwischen der ethnischen Gruppe, die in einem ethnischen Unternehmen beschäftigt ist, relativ zur Beschäftigung dieser Gruppe auf dem allgemeinen Arbeitsmarkt untersucht. Den Forschungserkenntnissen zufolge finden Neuankömmlinge nicht nur leichter einen Job in einem Unternehmen gleicher ethnischer Herkunft, sondern werden dort auch beim Einstieg tendenziell besser bezahlt, da ihre mitgebrachten Kompetenzen besser eingeschätzt werden können; darüber hinaus gibt es keine sprachlichen und verhaltensbedingten Kommunikationsprobleme. (Portes und Jensen 1989) Diese Erkenntnisse werden von Xie und Gough (2011) relativiert. Sie weisen nach, dass Neuzuwanderer in einer ethnischen Enklave zwar rascher eine Beschäftigung finden und auch besser bezahlt werden als Neuankömmlinge der ethnischen Minderheit, die in dem allgemeinen sekundären Arbeitsmarkt einsteigen: der erste Arbeitsmarkt steht ihnen nämlich meist mangels anerkannter Qualifikationen und Kommunikationsfähigkeiten in der Sprache des Aufnahmelandes nicht offen. Wenn die MigrantInnen jedoch mit der Dauer des Aufenthalts die Sprache der Aufnahmegesellschaft beherrschen, sich höher qualifiziert haben und darüber hinaus auch ein Verständnis für die Organisationsstrukturen und das generelle Arbeitsmarktverhalten der Aufnahmegesellschaft erworben haben, ist ein Wechsel in den freien Arbeitsmarkt meist mit einer deutlichen Einkommensverbesserung verbunden, d.h. sie können sich ökonomisch in der Aufnahmegesellschaft assimilieren. Zu ähnlichen Erkenntnissen kommen Brücker et al. (2018) für MigrantInnen in Deutschland.[3]

Ethnisches Business (ethnic business) ist ein weiterer Fachausdruck, bei dem es um jenen Teil der Wirtschaft bzw. der Unternehmen geht, der von ethnischen Gruppen oder MigrantInnen gegründet und geführt wird und der die spezifischen Bedürfnisse der MigrantInnen bzw. ethnischen Gruppen befriedigt, die vom nicht-ethnischen Markt nicht abgedeckt werden. Angesichts der regionalen Konzentrationen dieser Gruppen deckt das ethnische Business einen lokalen Bedarf ab und schafft Jobs für MigrantInnen aus derselben Herkunftsregion oder ethnischen Gruppe. Das ethnische Business bietet auf dem lokalen Markt meist keine innovativen Produkte und Dienstleistungen an. (Waldinger et al. 1990)

Eine völlig andere Dimension des ethnischen Unternehmertums spricht Immigrant Business an. Hierbei handelt es sich um UnternehmerInnen, die in speziellen Einwanderungsprogrammen zur Einwanderung eingeladen werden. Hier geht es einerseits um große Investoren, die nachweislich mit einer Niederlassung im Aufnahmeland eine bestimmte Geldmenge Investieren und/oder eine bestimmte Größenordnung von Arbeitsplätzen schaffen. Andererseits werden aber auch Unternehmensgründungen und Start-ups gefördert, die innovativ aber noch kleinbetrieblich strukturiert sind. Der Synthesebericht des europäischen Migrationsnetzwerkes zur Zulassung von Drittstaatsangehörigen zu Business-Zwecken zeigt, dass diese Form der unternehmerischen Tätigkeit sehr vielschichtig ist und viele Branchen und Unternehmensformen umfasst. (emn 2015)[4]

Minority Business wiederum ist eine Bezeichnung für Unternehmen, die sich zumindest zu 51% im Eigentum einer oder mehrerer ethnischer Minderheiten befinden, von ihnen geführt und kontrolliert werden.

In Europa spricht man von migrantischem Unternehmertum (migrant entrepreneurship), wenn MigrantInnen den Weg der selbständigen Erwerbstätigkeit wählen. Dieser wird Großteils als Reaktion auf eine empfundene oder tatsächliche Diskriminierung auf dem Arbeitsmarkt oder auf bestimmten Gütermärkten gesehen.[5] Hier

---

[3] Mehr zur Rolle der Anerkennung von im Ausland erworbenen Qualifikationen und dem Zugang zu reglementierten Berufen in Biffl (2019).

[4] Zu Österreich siehe Biffl (2014).

[5] Dazu Ebermann (2002).

können ethnische Enklaven als Pull-Faktoren fungieren. Die unternehmerische Tätigkeit kann ein Ausweg aus einer sozialen Isolation sein und den sozio-ökonomischen Status der Gruppe anheben und damit die soziale Partizipation erleichtern. Jedoch ist der Zugang zu Finanzkapital oft schwierig, insbesondere wenn Rücküberweisungen (remittances) ins Herkunftsland die Ressourcen der MigrantInnen im Aufnahmeland einschränken. Jedoch können auch alle anderen Formen des ‚ethnischen' Unternehmertums unter dem allgemeineren Terminus der MigrantInnen gefunden werden.

Ausmaß und Charakteristika des migrantischen Unternehmertums

Nach den langen Jahren des Wachstums international agierender Großbetriebe setzte in Europa ebenso wie in den USA in den 1970er Jahren eine Trendumkehr ein. Diese Entwicklung wurde von Schumacher (1973) mit seinem einflussreichen Werk „Small is Beautiful" wissenschaftlich argumentiert, wobei er die Grenzen des Gigantismus und der Ressourcenausbeutung aufzeigte und auf Klein- und Mittelbetriebe (KMU) für die Gestaltung eines nachhaltigen Wirtschaftens setzte. Die Restrukturierung der Wirtschaft und der Arbeitsmärkte resultierte u.a. aus der verstärkten Globalisierung der Märkte, die mit Outsourcing und Offshoring von Elementen einer vormals in Großbetrieben integrierten Wertschöpfungskette verbunden war. Das trug zur Schaffung bzw. dem Wachstum von KMUs bei, von denen viele ethnische Unternehmen waren. Die zunehmende Zahl von migrantischen UnternehmerInnen signalisierte nicht nur einen wirtschaftlichen Paradigmenwechsel, sondern auch den Wandel des Arbeitsmarktverhaltens vieler MigrantInnen, die nicht mehr in ausreichendem Maße als LohnarbeiterInnen in Großbetrieben eine Beschäftigung fanden. Dies galt für Gastarbeiter in Zentraleuropa ebenso wie für ethnische Minderheiten aus den vormaligen Kolonien in Frankreich, dem Vereinigten Königreich oder Holland. Sie waren überdurchschnittlich stark vom wirtschaftlichen und technologischen Strukturwandel der 1970er und 1980er Jahre betroffen und suchten alternative Erwerbsmöglichkeiten. Darüber hinaus stieg die Zahl der MigrantInnen infolge des Falls des Eisernen Vorhangs, verstärkter Fluchtzuwanderung - etwa im Gefolge des Zerfalls von Jugoslawien, sowie zunehmender Familien- und Bildungsmigration. Der starke Angebotsschub von migrantischen Arbeitskräften, der bis jetzt anhält, bewirkte in den diversen europäischen Ländern einen Ausbau von Förderprogrammen für Unternehmensgründungen sowie Änderungen in den rechtlichen Rahmenbedingungen zur Unterstützung von Unternehmensgründungen von MigrantInnen. (OECD 1991; IMES 2008; OECD 2013; EC 2016; OECD/EU 2017)

Der OECD (2011) zufolge unterscheidet sich der Anteil der migrantischen UnternehmerInnen an den im Ausland geborenen Beschäftigten kaum von dem im Inland Geborenen. Er lag 2007/08 in den OECD-Ländern zwischen 12,6% und 12%. Aus Abbildung 1 ist ersichtlich, dass sich die Selbständigenquoten zwischen

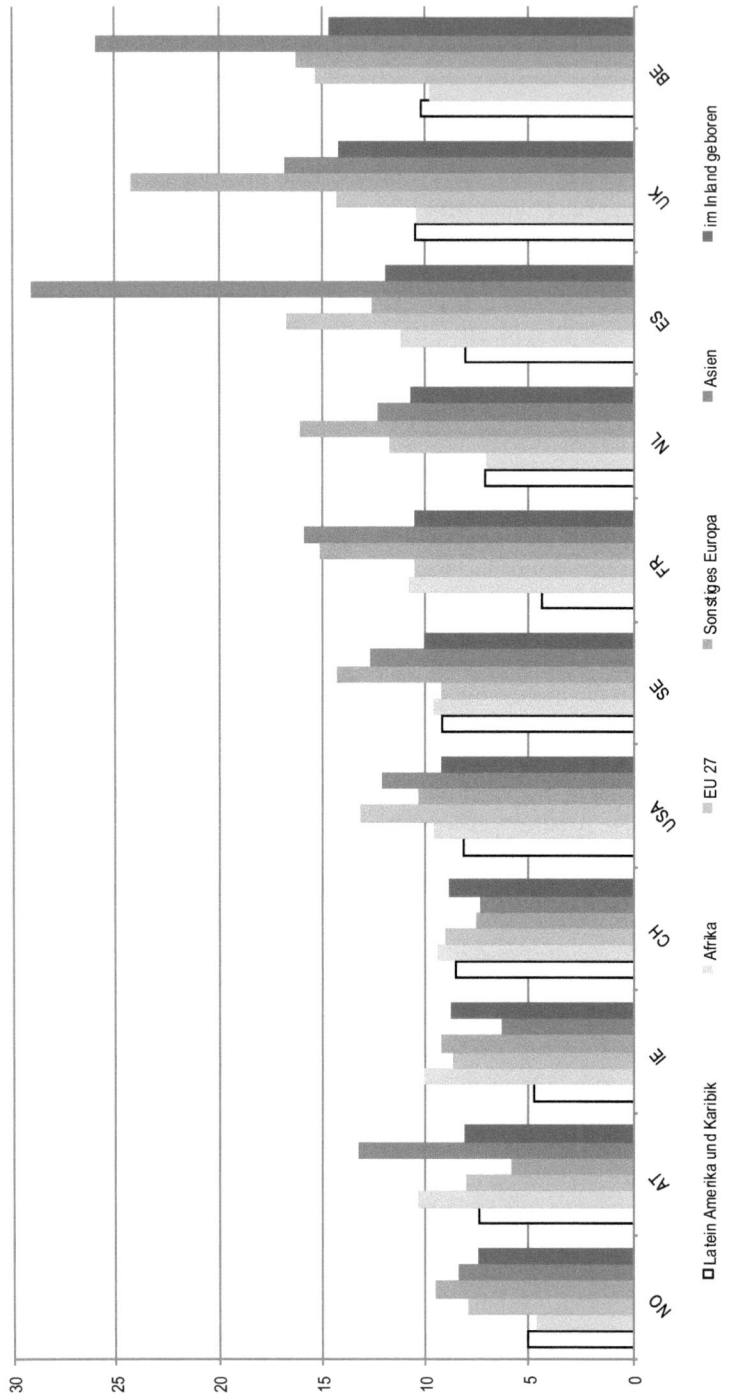

Abbildung 1 Selbständigenquoten nach Aufenthalts- und Herkunftsland: 2007-08 in %

Quelle: OECD 2011

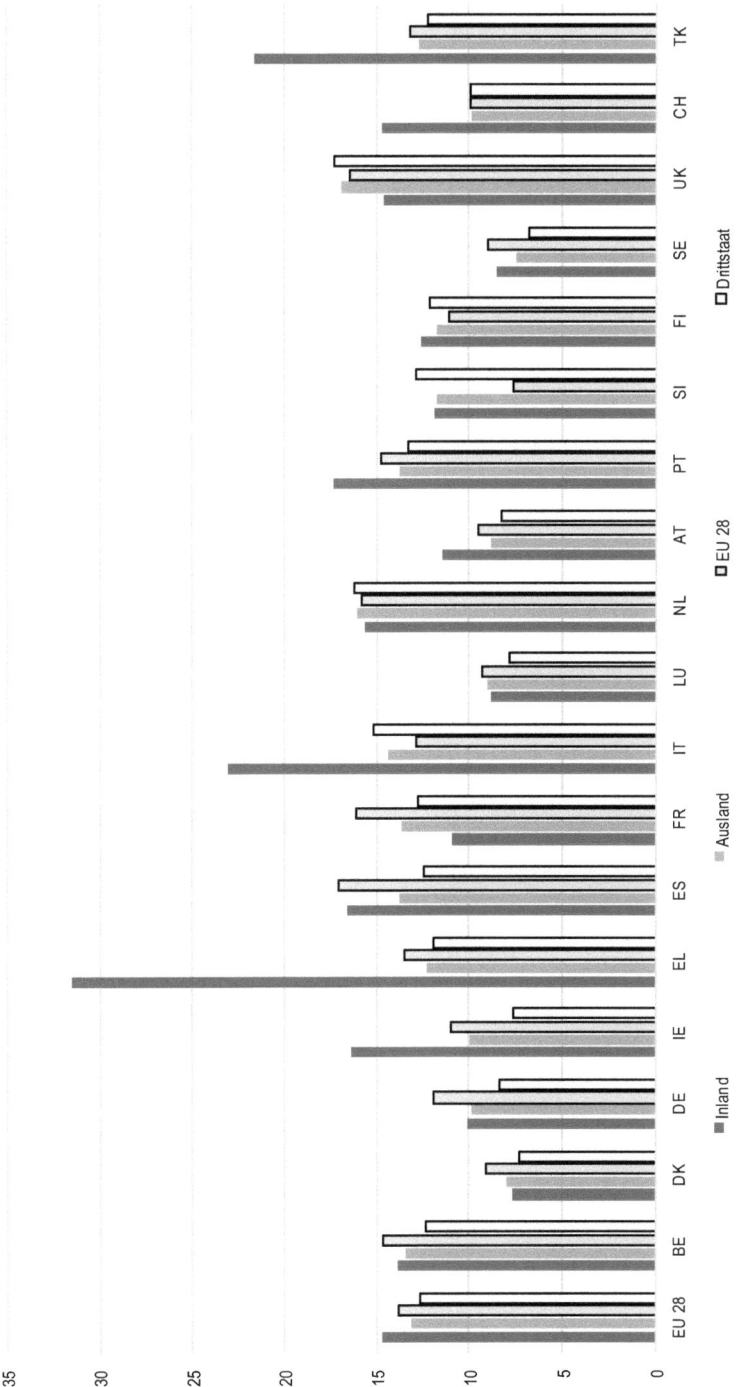

Abbildung 2 Selbständigenquoten in ausgewählten Ländern der EU-28 und der Türkei nach Geburtsregion: 2017 in %

Quelle: Eurostat

im Inland geboren   im Ausland geboren

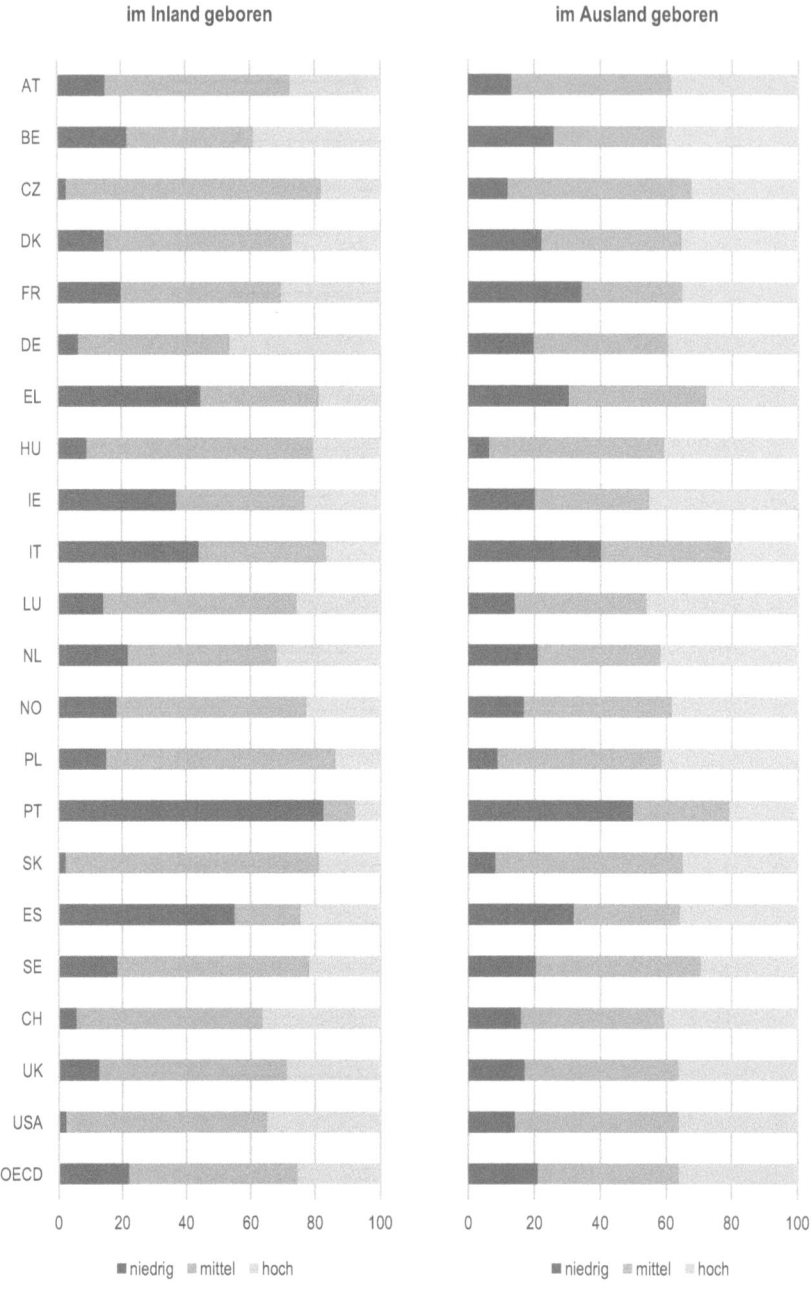

Abbildung 3 Qualifikationsstruktur der Selbständigen nach Geburtsland: 1998-2008

Quelle: OECD 2011

OECD-Ländern unterscheiden. In den meisten europäischen Ländern sowie in den USA lag der Anteil der Selbständigen unter den im Inland geborenen Erwerbstätigen im Jahr 2007/08 um die 10%. Ausnahmen waren das Vereinigte Königreich und Belgien mit einer etwas höheren Quote von knapp unter 15%. Jedoch gibt es wesentlich größere Unterschiede im Grad der Selbständigkeit zwischen MigrantInnen der verschiedenen Herkunftsländer. So sind die höchsten Quoten im Schnitt unter Asiatischen MigrantInnen zu finden, gefolgt von mobilen EuropäerInnen aus der EU-27 ebenso wie dem sonstigen Europa. Am geringsten waren im Schnitt Selbständigenquoten unter MigrantInnen aus Latein Amerika und der Karibik sowie aus Afrika, wobei es allerdings deutliche Niveauunterschiede zwischen den diversen Aufnahmeländern gab. Die Unterschiede im unternehmerischen Handeln zwischen den diversen Herkunftsländern haben einerseits mit Bildungs-, Qualifikations- und Vermögensunterschieden zu tun, andererseits mit gewissen traditionellen Verhaltensmustern. Es ist somit das Zusammenwirken von ethnisch-kulturellem Verhalten, das im Herkunftsland geprägt wird, und strukturellen Faktoren im Aufnahmeland wie rechtliche Rahmenbedingungen und Diskriminierung, die ein komplexes Bild ergeben, das Verallgemeinerungen zu migrantischem Unternehmertum nach Herkunfts- und Aufnahmeland erschweren.

In den letzten Jahren hat die selbständige Erwerbstätigkeit als Anteil an allen Erwerbstätigen in der EU noch zugenommen. So lag die Selbständigenquote in der EU-28 im Jahr 2017 bei 14,5%; sie war unter im Inland Geborenen mit 14,7% etwas höher als unter im Ausland geborenen Erwerbstätigen mit 13,1%. Sie war weiters unter Personen aus einem anderen EU-28 Mitgliedsland höher als unter Drittstaatsangehörigen (13,8% gegenüber 12,7%). Das kann als Hinweis dafür gelten, dass die institutionellen Rahmenbedingungen für mobile EU-BürgerInnen günstiger in Bezug auf selbständiges Unternehmertum sind als für Drittstaatsangehörige.

Zwischen den EU-Mitgliedsländern unterscheiden sich vor allem die Selbständigenquoten der Einheimischen. Sie sind in den südeuropäischen Ländern hoch und verringern sich auf dem Weg nordwärts. Dieses Süd-Nord-Gefälle der Selbständigenquoten entspricht in hohem Maße dem Muster der Wirtschaftskraft der Länder gemessen am BIP pro Kopf. Nicht nur einheimische Selbständige sondern auch migrantische sind in den Süd-Europäischen Ländern meist kleinbetrieblich strukturiert, verbunden mit einer vergleichsweise geringen Produktivität und Innovationsintensität.

Das länderspezifische Muster der Selbständigenquoten innerhalb der EU ist längerfristig relativ stabil, wie eine Auswertung der EU-weiten Arbeitskräfteerhebung von Hermes und Leicht (2010) für 2009 und Abbildung 2 für 2017 zeigen. So liegen in den nordischen und zentraleuropäischen Ländern die Selbständigenquoten der MigrantInnen meist geringfügig über den im Inland Geborenen. Im Gegensatz dazu sind die Selbständigenquoten der Einheimischen in den südeuropäischen Ländern zum Teil deutlich höher als unter den dort ansässigen MigrantInnen.

Die Selbständigenquote kann gewisse Anhaltspunkte für das Ausmaß des migrantischen Unternehmertums liefern; sie sagt aber nichts aus über die Bandbreite der Tätigkeiten und die Innovationskraft der Unternehmen. Es ist daher notwendig, an Hand der Qualifikationen bzw. des Bildungsgrades der Selbständigen, das Innovationspotenzial der UnternehmerInnen abzuschätzen. Die Auswertungen von Hermes und Leicht (2010:13) zeigen ebenso wie die Berechnungen der OECD (2011:149), dass der Anteil der Hochqualifizierten in der OECD im Schnitt unter den migrantischen UnternehmerInnen höher ist als unter den ansässigen Selbständigen (36% gegenüber 25% im Schnitt der Jahre 1998-2008, siehe Abbildung 3) Besonders hoch war der Anteil der Hochqualifizierten unter den MigrantInnen in den nordischen und zentraleuropäischen Ländern mit über 40%, während er in den meisten südeuropäischen Ländern mit rund 20% deutlich geringer war. Zwar lag der Schwerpunkt im Schnitt sowohl bei MigrantInnen als auch bei Einheimischen bei der mittleren Fachqualifikation, in manchen südeuropäischen Ländern hat jedoch der Großteil der langansässigen UnternehmerInnen eine einfache Qualifikation: Portugal mit 83%, gefolgt von Spanien mit 55% und Italien bzw. Griechenland mit 45%. In den südeuropäischen Ländern ist auch der Anteil der migrantischen UnternehmerInnen mit einfachen Qualifikationen überdurchschnittlich hoch (Portugal mit 50%, Italien mit 40%).

Dieses Muster legt nahe, dass das Unternehmertum in den südeuropäischen Ländern sowohl unter den Einheimischen als auch unter den MigrantInnen in hohem Maße von traditionellen kleinbetrieblichen Strukturen geprägt ist, die den lokalen Bedarf abdecken, während in den nordischen und zentraleuropäischen Ländern in stärkerem Maße skill-intensive hochqualifizierte Tätigkeiten mit hoher Innovationskraft das Bild des migrantischen Unternehmertums prägen.

Weiters sind Hermes und Leicht (2010) zufolge mobile EU-Selbständige im Schnitt höher qualifiziert als einheimische UnternehmerInnen – das gilt vor allem für Österreich und südeuropäische Länder. Nur in Deutschland, Belgien und Frankreich sind anteilsmäßig Einheimische in stärkerem Maße als EU-BürgerInnen hochqualifizierte UnternehmerInnen. Allgemein gilt, dass Drittstaatsangehörige seltener hochqualifizierte UnternehmerInnen sind. Das kann auf institutionelle Faktoren wie rechtliche Zugangsbarrieren und Schwierigkeiten in der Anerkennung mitgebrachter Qualifikationen zurückzuführen sein, aber auch auf eine im Schnitt schlechtere Qualifikationsstruktur der Drittstaatsangehörigen. Was die Branchenzugehörigkeit der migrantischen UnternehmerInnen anbelangt, so ist ebenfalls ein Nord-Süd-Unterschied zu beobachten. Während im Norden und in bestimmten zentraleuropäischen Ländern wie Deutschland, die Niederlande und Belgien sowie im Vereinigten Königreich und Irland ein überdurchschnittlich hoher Anteil der migrantischen UnternehmerInnen in unternehmensorientierten Diensten, dem Gesundheits- und Kultursektor sowie in sozialen Diensten aktiv ist, liegt der Schwerpunkt in den südeuropäischen Ländern im Handel, sowie im Hotel und Gastronomiebereich.

Studien der OECD zeigen, dass MigrantInnen in den meisten OECD-Ländern mit einer höheren Wahrscheinlichkeit als Personen der Aufnahmegesellschaft ein Unternehmen aufmachen, dass sie damit aber auch häufiger Schiffbruch erleiden. Die meisten migrantischen UnternehmerInnen sind mittleren Alters, aber tendenziell jünger als ansässige UnternehmerInnen. Sie sind im Schnitt älter als unselbständig beschäftigte MigrantInnen, da es offenbar einer gewissen Arbeitserfahrung im

Aufnahmeland bedarf, um sich auf das risikoreiche Terrain des selbständigen Unternehmertums einzulassen. Das zeigt sich auch an der im Schnitt längeren Aufenthaltsdauer der selbständigen MigrantInnen, die mehrheitlich über 10 Jahren liegt.

Migrantische UnternehmerInnen tragen mit ihrer Tätigkeit nicht nur zu ihrer eigenen materiellen Absicherung bei, sondern schaffen auch Arbeitsplätze für andere, erhöhen die Wertschöpfung, befriedigen Bedürfnisse der Aufnahmegesellschaft und verringern die Transaktionskosten des Handels mit den Herkunftsländern. Es ist daher nicht überraschend, dass die Förderung des ethnischen Unternehmertums zu einem eigenen Standbein der Europäischen Beschäftigungsstrategie geworden ist. Die Analyse von harmonisierten Statistiken der EU gewährt Einblicke in den Grad und die Vielfalt der wirtschaftlichen unternehmerischen Einbindungen verschiedener Gruppen von MigrantInnen in den unterschiedlichen EU-Mitgliedsländern. Die Daten zeigen, welche Formen und Schwerpunkte des migrantischen Unternehmertums es in den diversen EU-Ländern gibt und welche Personengruppen derzeit noch unterrepräsentiert sind. Letztere zu aktivieren bzw. in einen Dialog einzubinden ist das Ziel des jüngsten Berichts der OECD, der gemeinsam mit der EU herausgegeben wurde, und der den provokanten Titel „The Missing Entrepreneurs 2017" hat. (OECD/EU 2017) Die Untersuchungen zeigen, dass Frauen wesentlich seltener Unternehmerinnen sind als Männer, häufig weil sie nicht die notwendigen Qualifikationen haben, aber auch weil familiäre Verpflichtungen ihren Aktionsradius stark einschränken. Aber auch ältere Arbeitskräfte sowie Jugendliche sehen sich Barrieren unterschiedlicher Art gegenüber, die es zu identifizieren und zu überwinden gilt, wenn man ihre unternehmerischen Qualitäten fördern und dadurch den Grad ihrer sozialen und beruflichen Partizipation anheben will. Ein besonderes Augenmerk brauchen auch Flüchtlinge mit ihren spezifischen Herausforderungen. Dieser Gruppe, aber auch allen anderen Formen der Migration, wird in der Agenda 2030 der Vereinten Nationen gedacht, das unter dem Motto steht, niemanden zurückzulassen. (United Nations 2015)

Theoretische Erklärungsmuster und Rahmenbedingungen

Unterschiedliche Wissenschaftsdisziplinen haben einen Beitrag zu den theoretischen Erklärungsmustern des migrantischen Unternehmertums geliefert, allen voran die Soziologie, die Anthropologie, sowie ökonomische Arbeitsmarkttheorien. Soziologische Konzepte sehen im ethnischen oder migrantischen Unternehmertum primär eine Alternative zu schlechten Arbeitsbedingungen oder zu Arbeitslosigkeit, da sie mangels ausreichender Sprachkenntnisse und beruflicher Kompetenzen nicht in der Lage sind, eine zufriedenstellende Beschäftigung und Entlohnung auf dem offenen Arbeitsmarkt zu erhalten. Ihr komparativer Nachteil wird verstärkt, wenn sie arm sind, diskriminiert werden und wenig Wissen über lokale kulturelle und wirtschaftliche Verhaltensmuster haben. Dieser Theoriestrang kann zwar ein Verständnis für das Entstehen einer Bazar- oder Subsistenzselbständigkeit sowie einer ethnisch-kulturellen Nischenökonomie liefern, nicht jedoch die vielfältigen Formen von ethnischem Unternehmertum erklären. Auch Kulturtheorien sehen nur eine Seite des komplexen Phänomens, das ethnisches Unternehmertum umfasst. Letztere verweisen auf das Durchhaltevermögen bestimmter ethnischer Gruppen, auf ihre Risikobereitschaft, Sparsamkeit und die solidarische Unterstützung und Loyalität innerhalb bestimmter Communities. (Masurel et al 2004) Diese Charakteristika werden vor allem Asiaten zugeschrieben und sind ein wichtiger Erklärungsansatz für ihre hohen Selbständigenquoten relativ zu anderen ethnischen Gruppen. Dabei wird übersehen, dass auch andere Faktoren wie der Zugang zu Finanzkapital, berufliche Fähigkeiten, die lokalen Marktbedingungen, Genderrollen, institutionelle Strukturen, inter-ethnische Beziehungen und damit verbunden alternative Beschäftigungsmöglichkeiten eine Rolle bei der Entscheidung für eine unternehmerische Tätigkeit spielen. Ökonomische Theorien gehen auf einige dieser strukturellen Faktoren ein, ohne jedoch das komplexe Gefüge migrantischen Unternehmertums zur Gänze erklären zu können. Beide Theorieansätze bewegen sich auf der Mikro- oder Meso-Ebene der Analyse. Es fehlt jedoch die Makro-Ebene, in der die Unternehmen eingebettet sind, und die von institutionellen Regelmechanismen, Regierungspolitiken und wirtschaftlichen Entwicklungstrends geprägt wird. Diese Ergänzung des theoretischen Konstrukts liefert der ‚mixed-embeddedness' Zugang. Barberis und Solano (2018) schaffen einen Überblick über die diesbezügliche Forschung und sehen eine Weiterentwicklung der Theorie vor. Dabei stellt die Einbettung der ethnischen und migrantischen Unternehmen in eine lokale Wirtschaft eine Dimension des Spektrums der strukturellen Inkorporation dar, mit ihren spezifischen Rahmenbedingungen und Logiken. Hinzu kommt die eingangs erwähnte Super-Diversität der MigrantInnen in unseren von Mobilität geprägten globalisierten Gesellschaften als strukturierendes Merkmal, sowie der zunehmend transnationale Charakter des migrantischen Unternehmertums.

In Abbildung 4 wird, den Überlegungen von Barberis und Solano (2018) folgend, ein schematisches Konzept entworfen, das das Zusammenspiel von kulturalistischen und strukturalistischen Erklärungsansätzen darstellt und das in ein übergeordnetes Makro-System eingebettet ist. Letzteres wird von hoher Superdiversität im Sinne von Vertovec (2007) geprägt, und zwar sowohl auf der Angebotsseite, d.h. der migrantischen Unternehmerschaft, als auch auf der Nachfrageseite, d.h. den länderspezifischen institutionellen Rahmenbedingungen, die auch von der Migrationspolitik geprägt werden.

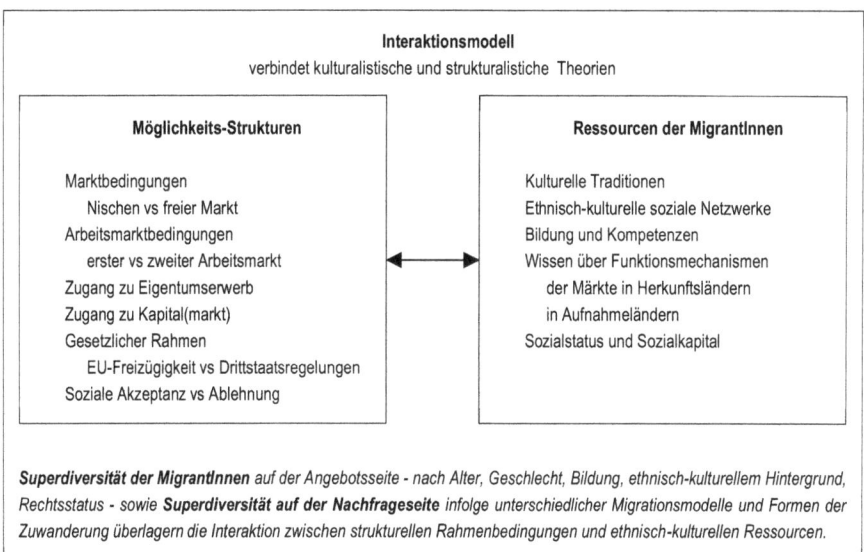

Abbildung 4 Schematische Darstellung der „Mixed ‚Embeddedness" des migrantischen Unternehmertums

Quelle: Eigene Darstellung, in Anlehnung an Barberis und Solano (2018)

Schlussfolgerungen und kritische Anmerkungen

Das migrantische Unternehmertum leistet nicht nur einen Beitrag zur Integration und Selbstentfaltung der MigrantInnen, sondern trägt auch zur Innovationskraft und der internationalen Wettbewerbsfähigkeit der Wirtschaft sowie transnationalen wirtschaftlichen Kooperationen bei. Es ist daher nicht überraschend, dass die Migrations- und Integrationspolitik den unternehmerisch denkenden und handelnden MigrantInnen zunehmend Aufmerksamkeit schenkt. Institutionelle Strukturen und Regelungen werden demzufolge auf ihre Unterstützungsfähigkeit des Unternehmertums untersucht bzw. soweit angepasst, dass sie die unternehmerische Entfaltungsmöglichkeit der MigrantInnen fördern. Für Unternehmensgründungen werden Möglichkeiten der Finanzierung etabliert, die von Mikrokrediten bis Venture Capital größeren Ausmaßes reichen, gegeben das Innovationspotenzial und die Größenordnung der Businesspläne. Auch die Bürokratie wird zusehends abgebaut, intermediäre Organisationen werden zur Unterstützung von JungunternehmerInnen geschaffen und Business Angels greifen den präsumtiven migrantischen UnternehmerInnen unter die Arme. Darüber hinaus wird überlegt, wie neue Formen von Arbeit wie die GIG-economy, die über online Plattformen organisiert werden, in ein Modell der nationalen bzw. internationalen sozialen Absicherung einzubinden sind. Das Spektrum dieser Tätigkeiten reicht von einfachen Tätigkeiten bis zu hochqualifizierter Freelance-Arbeit, von abhängiger Selbständigkeit und Ausbeutung bis zu kreativer Selbstentfaltung. Diese Entwicklung zeigt, dass das grenzüberschreitende migrantische Unternehmertum ein Bereich ist, der einem starken Wandel unterliegt und der institutionell mitzugestalten ist. Dabei ist darauf zu achten, dass Zugangserleichterungen zu Finanzkapital nicht dazu führen, dass der Pool an UnternehmerInnen auch auf jene Personen ausgeweitet wird, denen die notwendigen unternehmerischen Fähigkeiten fehlen. Das würde einen Anstieg des Scheiterns zur Folge haben, was sowohl Geldgeber von der Förderung abschrecken als auch das Selbstvertrauen der MigrantInnen untergraben könnte. Darüber hinaus ist davor zu warnen, MigrantInnen als Super-Entrepreneurs hochzustilisieren, die innovativer und erfolgreicher als VertreterInnen der einheimischen Bevölkerung sind. Dem widerspricht nämlich die Forschung, wie eine Erhebung von Unternehmensgründungen (start-ups) von MigrantInnen und Nicht-MigrantInnen in 69 Ländern zeigt, die vom GEM (Global Entrepreneurship Monitor) 2012 durchgeführt wurde. (Vorderwülbecke 2012) Ihr zufolge gibt es in den USA und Europa kaum einen Unterschied im Niveau und der Bandbreite der unternehmerischen Aktivitäten zwischen MigrantInnen und Nicht-MigrantInnen. Jedoch sind Unternehmensgründungsraten in wachstumsorientierten Bereichen unter MigrantInnen etwas höher. Es konnte aber kein Unterschied in der Innovationskraft der migrantischen gegenüber nationalen Unternehmen festgestellt werden, ebenso wenig war der wirtschaftliche Erfolg ausgeprägter. Eine Ausnahme ist allerdings der Handel mit den Herkunftsländern – hier sind MigrantInnen infolge ihrer transnationalen Netzwerke erfolgreicher. Das bedeutet, dass das migrantische Unternehmertum eine Variante der wirtschaftlichen Inkorporation von MigrantInnen ist, die allerdings als Folge der Superdiversität der MigrantInnen sehr komplex ist. Das legt nahe, dass die Unterstützungsmechanismen ebenfalls vielfältig sein sollten, dass aber vorrangig der Gleichbehandlung und der Bekämpfung von Diskriminierung Augenmerk geschenkt werden sollte.

Literatur

Barberis, Eduardo, Solano, Giacomo (2018). Mixed Embeddedness and Migrant Entrepreneurship: Hints on Past and Future Directions. An Introduction. Sociologica Vol. 12(2): S1-22.

Berghoff, Hartmut, Siekermann, Uwe (2016). Immigrant entrepreneurship as a challenge for historiography. In Hartmut Berghoff und Uwe Spiekermann (Hrsg.) Immigrant Entrepreneurship. The German-American Experience since 1700. Bulletin of the German Historical Institute, Supplement 12: 5-15; Washington, D.C.

Biffl, Gudrun (2019). Anschlussfähigkeit sicherstellen, Beschäftigungs- und Einkommenschancen verbessern. Daten und Fakten zur Anerkennung für Migration, Bildung und Arbeit. Magazin erwachsenenbildung.at. Ausgabe 37(09).

Biffl, Gudrun (2014). Admitting third country nationals for business purposes. Emn (European Migration Network) focused Study 2014, IOM. http://www.emn.at/wp-content/uploads/2017/01/EMN_Business_Study_2014_AT_EMN_NCP_final.pdf

Biffl, Gudrun (1996). Immigrant Labour Integration. In Günther Schmid, Jacqueline O'Reilly, Klaus Schömann (Hrsg.) International Handbook of Labour Market Policy and Evaluation. Chapter 18. Edward Elgar Publ.

Bonacich, Edna (1973). A Theory of Middleman Minorities. American Sociological Review Vol. 38: 583-594.

Brücker, Herbert, Glitz, Albrecht, Lerche, Adrian, Romiti, Agnese (2018): Occupational Recognition and Immigrant Labor Market Outcomes. SOEPpapers on Multidisciplinary Panel Data Research 1017, DIW Berlin.

Castles, Stephen, de Haas, Hein, Miller, Mark J. (2014). The Age of Migration: International Population Movements in the Modern World. Publ. Palgrave Macmillan, 5th edition (1st ed.1993).

Ebermann, Erwin (Hrsg.) (2007). Afrikaner in Wien. Zwischen Mystifizierung und Verteufelung. (3. Auflage, 1. Auflage 2002). Berlin-Münster-London: LIT Verlag.

Elo, Maria, Sandberg, Susanne, Servais, Per, Basco, Rodrigo, Discua Cruz, Allan, Riddle, Liesl, Täube, Florian (2018). Advancing the views on migrant and diaspora entrepreneurs in international entrepreneurship. Journal of International Entrepreneurship Nr. 16: S 119-133

European Commission (2016). Communication from the Commission to the European parliament, the Council, the European Economic and Social Committee and the Committee of the Regions. Action Plan on the integration of third country nationals. COM(2016)377final, Strasbourg.

European Migration Network (emn) 2015. Synthesis report - Admitting third-country nationals for business purposes. European Commission – Home Affairs.

Haberfellner, Regina unter Mitarbeit von Betz, Fritz, Böse, Martina, Riegler, Johanna (2000). „Ethnic Business": Integration vs. Segregation. Studie des ZSI (Zentrum für soziale Innovation), Wien.

Hermes, Kerstin, Leicht, René (2010). Scope and Characteristics of Immigrant Entrepreneurship in Europe. A Cross-National Comparison of European Countries. Universität Mannheim, Working Paper.

IMES (Institute for Migration and Ethnic Studies) (2008). Unternehmerische Vielfalt in einem geeinten Europa. Unternehmerische Initiative von ethnischen Minderheiten und Migranten. Prüfung und Auswertung guter Verfahren zur Förderung von Unternehmern aus ethnischen Minderheiten. Abschlussbericht einer von der Europäischen Kommission geförderten Studie der Universität Amsterdam. Ref. Ares (2014) 76605-15/01/2014.

Masurel, Enno, Nijkamp, Peter, Vindigni, Gabriella (2004). Breeding places for ethnic entrepreneurs: a comparative marketing approach. Entrepreneurship & Regional Development Vol. 16(1): S77–86.

OECD/EU (2017). The Missing Entrepreneurs 2017. Policies for Inclusive Entrepreneurship. OECD Publishing, Paris.

OECD (2013). The Missing Entrepreneurs. Policies for Inclusive Entrepreneurship in Europe. Paris

OECD (2011). Migrant Entrepreneurship in OECD Countries. In International Migration Outlook, Part II. Paris.

OECD (1991). Self-Employment among Immigrants in Selected OECD Countries. Paris.

Portes, Alejandro, Jensen Leif (1989). The enclave and the entrants: Patterns of ethnic enterprise in Miami before and after Mariel. American Sociological Review Nr. 54: S 929-949.

Portes, Alejandro, Manning, Robert D. (2014). The Immigrant enclave: theory and empirical examples, in David B. Grusky (Hrsg.) Social stratification: class, race, and gender in sociological perspective. 4th edition (2008 1st edition), Westview Press, Bloulder, Co.

Santamaria-Alvarez, Sandra M., Sarmiento-González, Maria A., Arango-Vieira, Luis C. (2019). Transnational migrant entrepreneur characteristics and the transnational business nexus. International Journal of Entrepreneurial Behavior & Research, Emerald Publ.

Schumacher, Ernst F. (1973). Small is beautiful. A study of economics as if people mattered. Blond & Briggs and HarperCollins.

UNCDAT/IOM (2018). Policy Guide on Entrepreneurship for Migrants and Refugees. https://unctad.org/en/PublicationsLibrary/diae2018d2_en.pdf

United Nations (2015). Transforming our World. The 2030 Agenda for Sustainable Development. https://sustainabledevelopment.un.org/post2015/transformingourworld/publication.

Vershinina, Natalia, Rodgers, Peter, MCAdam, Maura, Clinton, Eric (2019). Transnational entrepreneurship, gender and family business. Global Networks Nr.19 (2): S 238-260.

Vertovec, Steven (2007). Super-diversity and its implications. Ethnic and racial studies Vol.30(6): S 1024-1054.

Vertovec, Steven (2006). Migrant Transnationalism and Modes of Transformation. International Migration Review Vol. 38 (3): S 970-1001.

Volery, Thierry (2007). Ethnic entrepreneurship: A theoretical framework. In Léo-Paul Dana (Hrsg.) Handbook of Research on Ethnic Minority Entrepreneurship: A Co-evolutionary View on Resource Management. Cheltenham: Edward Elgar, S. 30-41.

Vorderwülbecke, Arne (2012). Global Entrepreneurship Monitor - 2012 Global Report, chapter Entrepreneurship and Migration, S 42–50. Global Entrepreneurship Consortium.

Waldinger, Roger, Aldrich, Howard, Ward, Robin (Hrsg.) (1990). Ethnic Entrepreneurs: Immigrant Business in Industrial Societies. Sage Publ., London.

Xie, Yu, Gough, Margaret (2011). Ethnic Enclaves and the Earnings of Immigrants. Demography Nr. 48(4): S 1293-1315.

The Centre for Ethnic Minority Entrepreneurship: A Vehicle for Critical Engagement

Monder Ram

Abstract

This paper is motivated by a concern that the proliferation of measures to support migrant businesses across Europe appear to be proceeding without recourse to an increasingly sophisticated and rich literature on the topic. The case of the Centre for Research in Ethnic Minority Entrepreneurship (CREME) – which forms the focus of the paper – offers modest grounds for optimism for critically-inclined scholars who want to 'make a difference' to the communities they seek to understand. Its creation, *modus operandi* and continuation represent a real-time attempt to promote change with practitioners whilst pursuing theoretically-informed research. The many shades of engagement that characterise CREME's work – from stakeholder consultation on conventional research projects to the creation of new ventures to support for migrant businesses – illustrates the contribution that the Centre's approach of 'critical engagement' can make to academic and practitioner domains.

Introduction

Self-employment often provides migrant[1] and ethnic minority communities with a job, a mechanism for survival in a context of racial inequality, and for some, a path to social mobility. Foreign-born migrants in the OECD countries and the EU28 are disproportionately represented in self-employment (OECD 2013; Eurostat 2017). Explaining why this is the case is staple fare for scholars of the phenomenon (for reviews, see Jones and Ram, 2007; Ram and Jones 2008); and they are joined in this endeavour by policy-makers keen to find solutions to challenges as diverse as innovation and societal integration (Ram et al. 2017). 'Mainstream' social scientists rarely venture into this academic sub-field, leaving the space to be filled either by

---

[1] The terminology used to describe businesses owned by immigrants, migrants and minority ethnic communities is contested and imprecise. For present purposes, we use the definition below, which is typical of the (implicit) approach of many studies: *"Ethnic minority entrepreneurs have been understood to be immigrants in the countries concerned or children or grandchildren of immigrants. Immigrants are defined as persons who have been born abroad. Irrespective of their nationality and irrespective of whether they are considered to be ethnic minorities in the countries concerned, immigrants also include the offspring of immigrants [...]"* (Smallbone, 2005:2)

'ethnic relations' scholars reflecting on the cultural distinctiveness of such enter-prises (see Rath 2000, for critique); or entrepreneurship specialists keen to enumer-ate and make comparisons with 'white'-owned businesses. Policymakers and prac-titioners involved in 'business support' – and innocent of the relevant research – often laud such businesses and view them in a positive light. For example, in the Action Plan for integrating third country nationals and the 2020 Entrepreneurship Action Plan, the European Commission portrays entrepreneurship as decent and sustainable employment for migrants. Some enthusiasts even celebrate the supposed innate entrepreneurial drive of particular ethnic groups (Gidoomal 1997), oblivious to powerful critiques that emphasise the political economy of migrant enterprise (Rath 2000; Jones & Ram 2007; Romero & Valdez 2016; Valdez 2011).

With few exceptions (Rath & Swagerman 2016; Ram et al. 2015), a noticeable bifurcation is emerging: the largely benign reporting of measures to support migrant businesses is developing in isolation from an increasingly critical and nuanced scholarly discourse (Jones & Ram 2007; Kloosterman 2010; Rath 2000; Ram et al. 2017; Romero& Valdez 2016; Villares 2016; Villares et al. 2017). Scholars and practitioners in this field rarely intermingle in a sustained way. We examine the implications of such an intermingling by reflecting on the experiences of a specialist migrant entrepreneurship research unit that was established to address scholarly *and* practitioner concerns. The Centre for Research in Ethnic Minority Entrepreneurship (CREME) in the United Kingdom (UK) was created in 2004 as a joint venture be-tween a Regional Development Agency aiming to encourage enterprise amongst *all* communities, and a group of researchers with a history of engagement with non-academic stakeholders. The Centre was conceived and designed as a vehicle for 'engaged scholarship' before Van de Ven (2007) coined the term and defined it thus: 'a participative form of research for obtaining the advice and perspectives of key stakeholders (researchers, users, clients, sponsors, and practitioners) to under-stand a complex social problem' (Van de Ven 2007, p. 10).

Our examination of CREME allows us to address the increasingly important is-sue of how social scientists can conduct research that is both 'critical' *and* relevant to practitioners. Van de Ven's (2007) approach to 'engaged scholarship' is one re-sponse. But it has been critiqued for its inattention to the underlying power relations of engaged research (Rouse and Woolnough 2018). McKelvey (2006) and Kieser and Leiner (2009) are sceptical of Van de Ven's belief that practitioners and aca-demics can produce genuinely collaborative research over a sustained period. Whitehouse and Richter (2018), whist sympathetic to engaged scholarship, identify tensions relating to identity, gaining and maintaining stakeholder engagement, and balancing and managing relationships within diverse research relationships. Our ap-proach is one of critical engagement. It is 'critical' in the realist sense that social science can reveal truths, albeit of a necessarily provisional and contested kind (Ed-wards 2015; Sayer 2000). 'Engagement' is the process whereby knowledge moves into action. We reflect on the tensions and commitments engendered by this ap-proach elsewhere (Edwards 2015; Ram et al., 2015). Our aim here is to reflect on how we attempt to navigate the boundaries of academic and practitioner domains.

The extent to which research can be critical and relevant is debated in the 'mainstream' business domains of management (Edwards 2015), 'Critical Management Studies' (Wickaert & Schaefer 2015) and industrial relations (Edwards 2015; 2017). One should also note the current agitation amongst some entrepreneurship scholars in favour of research that is meaningful beyond the narrow confines of academe (Frank & Landstrom 2016). More pertinently for the field of migration, proponents of 'critical race research' call for a new relationship between academic and extra-academic worlds in order to *widen the vision of what is possible and [to draw] together diverse constituencies for emancipatory ends'* (Bhattacharyya & Murji 2013, p. 1364). Serious assessment of the proliferating measures to support migrant entrepreneurs (Solano et al. 2019) is overdue, not least because, as the subtitle of a recent critical study (Rath & Swagerman 2016) reveals, such initiatives are 'sometimes ambitious, mostly absent, [and] rarely address structural features'. This has implications for migration scholars' interest in the extent to which self-employment facilitates or inhibits migrant integration (Ram & Jones 2008).

We examine a variety of initiatives from CREME – characterised by different levels of engagement - which aim to bring academic research to bear on the concerns of practitioners. Our objectives are threefold. First, we consider examples of CREME's work that share knowledge of ethnic minority firms with state agencies and a variety of non-academic stakeholders. They address key issues such as finance (Ram et al. 2003), accessing supply chains (Ram et al. 2007) and approaches to business support (Ram & Smallbone 2003a). Second, we reflect on a more direct form of engagement – (critical) action research - which involves sharing research with state agencies and altering their organisational practice (see Beckinsale & Ram 2006; Ram et al. 2015). Finally, we consider examples where CREME's activism with practitioners has resulted in the creation of social science inspired ventures. They include the establishment of an intermediary body to support minority firms to access supply chain opportunities in the corporate sector (Ram et al. 2007), a peer-support network for African-Caribbean entrepreneurs (Ram & Trehan 2010), and an ongoing initiative with civil society groups to support migrant businesses in disadvantaged areas (Mickiewicz et al. 2019).

Putting critical engagement to work

Before discussing CREME's interventions with practitioners, it is important to emphasise the interdisciplinary nature of the Centre's researchers (Monder Ram, Trevor Jones, Paul Edwards and various colleagues). Scholars have encouraged the field of migrant and ethnic minority entrepreneurship to widen its disciplinary gaze beyond the limiting confines of perspectives that focus on ethnic relations (Rath 2000). CREME's research draws on a range of disciplinary traditions. The political economy of migrant entrepreneurship, particularly the crucial role of the market, is a feature of Jones' work, who is a geographer (Jones et al. 2000). Ram (Ram et al.

2011) stresses the contested nature of the labour process in small firms, whilst pursing interventions that highlight the value of different forms of critical engagement (Ram et al. 2015). Edwards has made seminal contributions to critical studies on the employment relationship (Edwards 1986) and has recently elaborated key features of a critical approach to engaged research (2015; 2017). The Centre has added an explicit concern with the gendered nature of migrant entrepreneurship through its association with Maria Villares-Varela (2016; Vilarres et al. 2017). These contributions have complemented the influential mixed embeddedness perspective (Rath 2000; Kloosterman 2010), which by stressing the migrant entrepreneur's *economic* and social relationships, has encouraged more contextualised and balanced accounts of ethnic minority entrepreneurship.

The theoretical contributions of CREME researchers have implications for the field of migration, where assumptions about the role of migrant entrepreneurship are sometimes made without assessing the phenomenon in context. For example, the power of the *market* (associated with Jones; see Jones and Ram, 2007, for review) to shape and constrain migrant enterprise served as an important corrective to early studies that attributed the rapid proliferation of migrant-origin firms to dynamic motivation and family/community social capital (Werbner, 1990). Jones et al.'s (1989) counterpoint emphasised severe market pressures and an absence of labour market choice: the wave of self-employed South Asians in the UK, many of them displaced from manual labour, gravitated towards sectors with low entry thresholds, usually those requiring little start-up capital, specialised expertise, or formal credentials. This is equally true of new the new migrant self-employed (Jones et al., 2012). Jones et al. (2012) found that continuity prevailed over change, with the diversity of the migrants flattened by the demands of the market. Irrespective of geographical origins or personal characteristics, new migrant business owner followed a similar pattern to forerunners to survive in the system.

Integrating labour process analysis into studies of migrant firms is another feature of CREME's theoretical approach. Labour process theory has existed outside debates on migrants, which have focused on the labour market rather than the experience of work. Studies of migrant enterprise have also dwelt on the characteristics of the entrepreneur to the neglect of workers. Labour process analysis addresses how workers' capacity to work (labour power) is transformed into actual work effort, together with the social relations that govern this activity (Thompson & Smith 2009). Ram (1994) and colleagues (Edwards et al. 2016; Ram et al. 2007) have applied it to small and minority firms, with one key insight being the extent of informal negotiation around the effort bargain. Early studies suggested that intense product market competition would generate autocracy in the workplace (Hoel 1982). A range of later work (Ram 1994; Ram et al. 2007) found that this was empirically inaccurate, with evidence of informal bargaining and often close personal relationships. Reasons for this included economic dependency of employers on workers, close personal ties, and the moderating influence of familial and kin relationships on worker-manager conflict.

Edwards et al. (2006) have produced a model of small firm behaviour that draws together the market context of migrant firms, labour process analysis, and insights from mixed embeddedness. This framework that explains how external context and internal resources of small firms combine to shape behaviour. The framework was inductively derived from several studies (involving migrant entrepreneurs and their workers) that deployed ethnographic, case study and other qualitative methods (Edwards et al. 2006). It has been drawn on to explain in in-depth studies of practices like patch-working and multiple job-holding, which are designed to maximise the meagre returns from Low Valued Added (LVA) sectors (Edwards and Ram 2006). Alongside this are studies of survivalist cost-cutting through informal practices (Ram et al, 2007; Forthcoming). A more recent study used the framework to explain how new migrant firms mobilise their resources and pursue a range of market strategies (Edwards et al. 2016).

This interdisciplinary backdrop is an important feature of CREME's interactions with practitioners. Researchers in the Centre draw on social science concepts and approaches in their collaborations with policy actors. They are neither consultants nor detached academics. Rather, they occupy the role of 'enablers' (Olsen 1994), working with participants to bring critical knowledge to bear on organisational practice. The varied form that this role takes is summarised in Table 1 and discussed in more detail below.

Sharing knowledge with practitioners

CREME promotes awareness of ethnic minority firms by sustained study and engagement with non-academic stakeholders. It shares this knowledge with state agencies at a national (Ram & Smallbone 2003a) and local level (Ram et al. 2015). The Centre's wide-ranging policy-focused research is influenced by the 'Three M's Model' of US academic Timothy Bates (2011), and its own research. Bates argues that minority entrepreneurs need three ingredients to succeed: money, markets and management. Extensive research on minority communities in the USA led him to conclude that these resources – not ethnicity - are the key to entrepreneurial performance. Our projects with financial and supply chain intermediaries business support agencies' – 'money' and 'markets' and (indirectly) 'management' – are illustrative. They highlight a key feature of CREME's way of working, that is, to view the research report *'as a first and not the last step for researchers to engage in conversations with potential users, ... thereby gain[ing] a broader and deeper appreciation of the meaning of research findings'* (Van de Ven 2007, p. 26).

Access to finance has been cited as one of the most significant barriers facing migrant businesses (Bates 2011). CREME's research (Ram et al. 2002; 2003) and Fraser's important (2009) study on banks and migrant firms found no evidence of direct discrimination; but highlighted that the continuing *perception* of unfair treatment was a major issue for minority entrepreneurs and banks. Both studies recom-

Issue/study	Form of critical engagement	Outcome
Sharing Knowledge		
Access to finance Ram *et al.* (2002;2003)	Banking sector representatives involved in project steering group	- Recommendations to banking sector - Joint CREME/Bank workshops for migrant entrepreneurs - Long-term engagement with Banks
Supplier diversity Ram and Smallbone (2003a); Shah and Ram (2006)	National and local state agencies involvement in overseeing research	- Recommendations to national and local state agencies - Commissioned good practice guides for professional bodies - Creation of supply chain initiative (SDEM)
Business support for migrant businesses Ram *et al.* (2012)	Practitioner involvement in research design and data analysis	- Recommendations to local state agency - Long-term engagement with agency
Action Research		
ICT and migrant businesses Beckinsale and Ram (2006)	Collaboration with local state agencies, business and community groups	- ICT support for 20 migrant firms - Increase in 'mainstream' support by migrant businesses
New migrants and business support Ram et al. (2015)	Collaboration with local state agencies, migrant associations, researcher secondments	- 165 new migrant businesses engaged - Increase in new migrants using business support - Change in state agency practices
Activism: Creating New Ventures		
Supply chain intermediary Ram et al. (2007)	Creation of SDEM to promote supplier diversity with corporations	- Opening of corporate supply chains to minority firms - Actual contracts exchanged - Successful 'spin-out'
Peer to peer business support Ram and Trehan (2010)	Creation of peer mentoring support group with 8 African-Caribbean entrepreneurs	- Personal development of owners - Business growth - Support for community
Migrants and business support Ram et al. (2015)	Creation of cross-sector partnership to deliver support to migrant businesses	- Engagement and business support with 200+ firms - Novel cross sector partnership - Increase in 'mainstream' support by migrant businesses

Table 1: CREME's approach to critical engagement

mend engagement and knowledge exchange strategies to improve mutual understanding between banks and minority firms. As a review of ethnic minority and women-owned research noted (Carter et al. 2015, p. 52) *'Programmes of action learning and engaged scholarship may be expected to enable [ethnic minority firms] ... to appreciate the changing nature of modern bank lending with more objective systems and less scope for prejudice.'*

Following the Ram et al. (2002; 2003) and Fraser (2009) studies, CREME worked with individual Banks and their representative body – the British Bankers' Association [now UK Finance] – to devise practical ways of tackling the issue of perception. The Centre convened several workshops in partnership with the Banks' representative body on access to finance. Such events are a direct way of tackling the perception problem – that banks do not wish to lend to ethnic minority businesses – that undermine relationships between banks and minority businesses.

CREME also created a cross sector network to support migrant businesses, comprising corporations, banks, professional associations and academics.

The role that supplier diversity initiatives play in promoting ethnic minority business growth by facilitating linkages with public and private sector organisations is another important strand of CREME's research and knowledge exchange activities (Ram & Smallbone 2003b; Ram et al. 2007; 2011). The context for the topic is the importance of business diversification, for ethnic minority firms (or 'break-out'), which has been a recurring theme in the literature on migrant businesses (Engelen 2001; Ram & Jones 2008). Co-ethnic trading is a feature of minority businesses despite the limited scope for growth offered by this ethnic niche strategy. The result is a mass of ethnic small business owners trapped in a trading milieu with limited scope for significant business and income growth. Ram and Smallbone (2003b) examined the role that supplier diversity initiatives in the public and private sector could play in promoting the break-out of ethnic minority businesses. They reviewed several attempts by local authorities to improve the flow of procurement opportunities to ethnic minority firms (within the existing legislative constraints). They found that supplier diversity programmes were in the very early stages of development in the UK, particularly those concerned with increasing the access of migrant businesses to public and private sector contracts.

This lack of activity stands in contrast to the prevalence and success of supply chain initiatives in the US (Shah & Ram, 2006). CREME researchers (Shah & Ram, 2006) undertook a study tour of US multinationals; its findings prompted the Centre and the state agency that helped to launch CREME to establish its own supply chain intermediary – Supplier Development East Midlands (SDEM) – in 2004. We discuss this further in the section on activism.

Of key importance here is that the creation of SDEM led to sustained engagement with influential intermediaries who were gatekeepers of organisational practice in different domains, including the representative body for procurement profession (the Chartered Institute for Purchasing and Supply [CIPS]), the UK's Commission for Racial Equality (CRE, now Equalities and Human Rights Council) and the Migration Policy Group (MPG). CREME produced evidence-based guides for the membership of each of these bodies.

CREME researchers have examined the management of minority businesses (Bates' third 'M') in academic (Edwards et al. 2006) and policy-focused studies (Ram et al., 2017). The Centre has also exercised indirect influence on management by working with state agencies on business support for migrant firms (Ram & Smallbone 2003a; Ram et al. 2012; 2015). Our study (Ram et al. 2012) of migrant business support provision in the west Midlands region of UK is noteworthy for its careful use of Van de Ven's (2007) in all aspects of the research design (see Table 2). The project, which investigated how support agencies engaged with minority firms, had four stages, each of which involved close collaboration between research- ers and practitioners. The first stage, *problem formulation*, comprised discussions with a wide range of stakeholders involved in the provision of business support   to

Stage	Activity	Outcome
1. Problem formulation	Researcher-Practitioner interaction to establish nature of problem and engagement with minority businesses	Broadening of issue, incorporating wider spread of intermediaries
2.Intermediary classification	Deliberative process involving Researcher-Practitioner exchange of academic and experiential knowledge	Pragmatic classification of wide variety of actors supporting minority businesses
3. Qualitative interviews	Researcher interviews with ethnic minority business intermediaries	Insights into minority business support
4. Data Analysis	Exploration of key themes with practitioner involvement	Triangulated account of ethnic minority business support. Enhanced prospect of 'actionable knowledge'

Table 2: Critical engagement in action

Source: Methodological approach in Ram et al's 2012 study on the provision of minority business support

small firms in the region. Having agreed an approach to the research problem, the aim of the second stage was to *identify and classify relevant intermediaries.* The researchers interviewed representatives of intermediary organisations in the third stage (using interview schedules devised in consultation with practitioners). Researchers and practitioners discussed emerging findings and themes in the data analysis during the fourth and final stage. The participative approach allowed researchers and practitioners to share and interrogate each other's accounts, thus enhancing the prospect of the generation of actionable knowledge.

Action research

CREME frequently moves beyond knowledge sharing by collaborating with practitioners to interpret scientific research to accomplish practical tasks. This takes the form of 'action research', an approach first associated with the work of social psychologist Kurt Lewin in the 1940s. Action research has many variants (see Cassell & Johnson 2006, for discussion), but the approach we adopted defines it as *'the study of a social situation carried out by those involved in that situation in order to improve their practice and quality of their understanding'* (Winter & Munn-Giddings 2001, p. 8). It incorporates three key features: intent to take action on an organisational or policy issue; an explicit concern with theory formed from the characterisation or conceptualisation of the particular experience (this differentiates it from a pure consultancy intervention); a process of continual reflection (Eden & Huxham, 1995).

Beckinsale and Ram (2006) adopted an action research approach in a project that aimed to stimulate the adoption of information and communication technology (ICT) amongst migrant businesses in the North West region of the United Kingdom.

Evidence suggesting that migrant firms are less likely to use ICT than other small firms (Foley & Ram 2002; Allinson et al. 2004) prompted the initiative, which was located in Manchester's Chintatown and Rusholme (dominated by Pakistani restaurateurs and retailers). Three objectives were central to Beckinsale and Ram's intervention: the application and adaptation of existing models of ICT adoption; examining the distinctiveness of delivery issues regarding migrant businesses and a systematic application of an action research approach to policy evaluation. In terms of the first aim, the authors found that generalist models of ICT adoption had to be modified to meet the particular needs of Chinese- and Pakistani-owned firms operating in the catering and retail sectors. These tools had to be supplemented by culturally appropriate outreach activities (for example, the appointment of outreach workers with the trust of the local communities). Regarding the second objective, the championing of exemplar firms that were embedded in the community was a key feature of the initiative. This was an important spur to the involvement of locally based migrant businesses, which had not utilised formal sources of business support. We met the target of engaging 20 migrant firms, and many of these firms accessed other forms of business support. Finally, the process of continual reflection and formative evaluation showed how implementation could be improved by working closely with participants, and illuminates *'the nature of effects and impacts of policies and about how these effects are produced in the circumstances in which they are implemented'* (Sanderson 2002, p. 14).

Our second example (Ram et al. 2015) of action research involved CREME researchers and a state agency – SUPPAG – that wanted to improve the provision of business support for new migrant entrepreneurs. SUPPAG was a business support agency in the Midlands area of the UK. Its main responsibility was to provide business support for the region's small firms. SUPPAG had extensive links with businesses from established ethnic minority communities (Indians, Pakistanis and African Caribbeans), but little engagement with the growing number of new migrants (Eastern Europeans, Somalis, Iraqis and others). SUPPAG, like many metropolitan areas in the UK, was located in a region emblematic of 'superdiversity', defined as the arrival in significant numbers of *'new, small and scattered, multiple-origin, transnationally connected, socio-economically differentiated and legally stratified immigrants'* (Vertovec 2007, p. 1024). SUPPAG lacked knowledge of the dynamics of the new migrant business community in the region, their business support needs, and practical interventions aimed at such groups. Our role was to work with SUPPAG on each of these areas. The CREME team drew on the mixed embeddedness perspective to inform its intervention. A key outcome was the contextualisation of business support needs, as a SUPPAG officer explained:

"Before the project, most of our information on ethnic minority businesses came from specialist ethnic organisations. They tended to suggest that the key issues facing such businesses were ethnic issues ... What the research was saying was that these businesses faced business issues, not necessarily ethnic ones..." (SUPPAG officer, see Ram et al. 2015).

Evidence from the researchers' survey of 165 new migrant businesses - conducted as part of the project - highlighted the importance of understanding the *context* of owners' business support needs (rather than 'ethnicity-related' factors). The action research process provoked a constant re-assessment of how SUPPAG engaged with new migrant businesses. SUPPAG altered the way it promoted its services; started to develop relationships with a wider range of intermediaries (including those representing new communities); and intensified its efforts in areas where new migrant activity was identified. The success of the various engagement efforts that CREME supported during the project led to a substantial increase in the recorded number interactions with minority businesses. A SUPPAG officer suggested that:

> *"We would like to think that some of that is down to the contact that we have made with intermediaries. I don't think that we should underestimate the efforts of just two people [the CREME researchers] ... It increased awareness of the [our] brand ... With [researchers] out there on our behalf because of the research, and because they are talking about [SUPPAG] ... The ... referrals ... get back into the system..."* (SUPPAG officer, see Ram et al. 2015).

Activism: Creating New Ventures

CREME's activism with practitioners has extended beyond action research and involved the creation of new institutions to support migrant businesses. The Centre has established several social science inspired ventures since its inception. It founded 'Supplier Development East Midlands' (SDEM) in 2004: a novel initiative that brought together 20 leading corporations with minority businesses to promote supply chain relationships (Ram et al. 2007). Extensive research informed SDEM's development (Ram & Smallbone 2003b; Shah & Ram 2006). This revealed that supplier diversity was at an embryonic stage in the UK; few examples existed of robust and measurable supplier diversity initiatives in UK-based corporations; and there was no 'one best way' to implement supplier diversity. SDEM encouraged an approach sensitive to the particular circumstances of each of its members and recognised that progress towards the goal of supplier diversity would take a variety of forms. During the two-year pilot phase, corporate membership more than doubled; commercial contracts between corporations and minority businesses were exchanged, which were over five times the cost of the initiative; and there have been instances of minority businesses combining to bid for corporate sector contracts. SDEM was 'spun-out' in 2006 and operates to this day as 'Minority Supplier Development UK' (MSDUK).

CREME's activism led to the creation and maintenance of the 12/8 Group in 2003 (Ram & Trehan 2010). The 12/8 Group comprises 8 small African-Caribbean firms which offer peer-to-peer guidance in business development and community links. The decision to focus on African-Caribbean entrepreneurs arose from a realisation by CREME researchers and the local state agency that fewer African-Caribbeans run their own business compared with other minority groups. CREME consulted with local African-Caribbean entrepreneurs and, collectively, they agreed to start the 12/8 Group. Participants benefited in three ways from this ongoing initiative. First, the action learning sets held by the group encouraged individual reflection, which sometimes led to a re-evaluation of business goals. Second, business benefits included the sharing of resources (for example, human resource expertise). Finally, there were gains to the wider community as members often mentored aspiring entrepreneurs as part of their commitment to the group.

Our final example involves another ongoing project comprising a cross sector partnership to support migrant entrepreneurs in disadvantaged areas. Since 2008, CREME has undertaken a series of projects (Ram et al. 2008; Jones et al. 2014; Edwards et al. 2016) – using action research and more detached methods – to promote a theoretically-informed understanding of migrant businesses and their support needs. This research shows that the entrepreneurial potential of migrants is being hindered by a lack of guidance; exclusion from business support networks; and inadequate knowledge of how new migrant businesses operate. It also reveals a latent interest amongst entrepreneurs in using business support, and the important 'social' role of such enterprises (in providing employment, overcoming social isolation, and developing new services).

We shared these findings with a range of CREME's partners, including Citizens UK ([CUK], a civil society body that promotes community organising for social justice) a Bank (with an officer responsible for community engagement) and with the local business support agency. CREME and CUK also elicited the perspectives of migrant entrepreneurs in several listening campaigns with local entrepreneurs in three disadvantaged areas (the geographical focus of the eventual project). So the initial idea, which had been peer reviewed in the usual academic way, was now subject to the equally challenging form of review that is community engagement. In 2015, the state agency agreed to fund a cross sector partnership comprising CREME, CUK and the Bank. The proposal that secured the funding drew on CREME's research and the experiential outcomes from the listening campaigns. The partnership appointed a community organiser to engage local businesses. His interactions with local entrepreneurs proved crucial to building trust with communities often overlooked by those charged with supporting enterprise in the area. At the end of the first year of the project, 295 business owners had received support from the project. The overwhelming majority of these businesses had not engaged with 'mainstream' providers prior to the intervention. The project is also helping entrepreneurs to work together to address common problems (parking, anti-social behaviour); and CUK's expertise in supporting civil society is helping to bring these communities together so they can represent themselves more effectively.

Academics not associated with the project (Mickiewicz et al. 2019) drew attention to the importance of combining research-based insights with the perspectives of migrant entrepreneurs:

*"Recent research undertaken by the Centre for Research in Ethnic Minority En-
trepreneurship in partnership with Citizens UK and [the Bank] and funded by
the [state agency] demonstrates the importance of building an inclusive culture
of business support for old and new immigrant groups. Lessons point to the need
to understand the context for many immigrant entrepreneurs, the challenges it
creates for building sustainable business ventures, and ... the recognition that
connecting these businesses to wider business networks also means connecting
to the communities in which they operate."* (Mickiewicz et al. 2019, p 8)

Conclusions

This paper was motivated by a concern that the proliferation of measures to support
migrant businesses across Europe appear to be proceeding without recourse to an
increasingly sophisticated and rich literature on the topic. Practitioner initiatives are
based on an implicit 'deficit model', that is, they promote measures to remedy the
perceived shortcomings of migrants aspiring to become entrepreneurs. This explains the emphasis of 'agency-centric' interventions like language training, mentoring, and personal skills. Structural forces that continue to shape if not dictate the
context of migrant entrepreneurship - severe market competition, punitive regulations and endemic racism – are largely ignored (Jones et al. 2014; Rath & Swagerman 2016). Such lop-sidedness weakens the potential value of migrant business
support measures. Yet the invocation of migrant enterprise as a panacea for grand
societal challenges - accompanied by a profusion of policies and initiatives - feature
prominently in academic and practitioner domains.

The case of CREME offers modest grounds for optimism for critically inclined
scholars who want to 'make a difference' to the communities they seek to understand. Its creation, *modus operandi,* and continuation represent a real-time attempt
to promote change with practitioners whilst pursuing theoretically informed research. This is a challenging task, not least because social scientists often struggle
to translate complexities into programmes that have a direct influence on organisational practice (Vertovec 2007). Nonetheless, it is an urgent task if scholars of migrant entrepreneurship want to address the 'rigour' and 'relevance' challenge that
is a feature of other disciplines (Edwards 2015). Critical engagement offers a means
of addressing this challenge. The methodology involves the exploitation of scholarly and practitioner knowledge, a process that is likely to generate more useful
insights than either party working in isolation. Collaborating with practitioners in
this way is not necessarily an approach confined to action research. Critical engagement is valuable to different forms of social research, including basic social science
with advice of key stakeholders, collaborative co-production of knowledge with
stakeholders and design science to test an applied program (Van de Ven 2007). The
many shades of engagement that characterise CREME's work – from stakeholder
consultation on conventional research projects to CREME's activism in starting

new forms of institutional support for migrant businesses – illustrates the capacious nature of critical engagement.

Despite CREME's contribution to theoretically informed practitioner change, it is important not to overstate the potential of such programmes to alter radically the profound structural inequalities that beset migrant entrepreneurship. The SDEM supply chain initiative is a case in point. First, many of the corporate participants joined the initiative because of the so-called 'business case' of trading with minority suppliers. However, as the broader literature on diversity highlights, 'business case' arguments can work against, rather than for, an equalities agenda (Dickens 1999). Second, supplying large organisations can be very challenging for small firms and involve the ceding of control over their operations in important areas. Ram et al's (2011) study of knowledge-based migrant suppliers to large firms showed that engaging with corporations severely curtailed their ability to control their internal operations. Finally, following from the previous point, comparatively few migrant businesses will fulfil the often demanding criteria necessary to supply organisations in the corporate (and public) sector. In this and other initiatives, 'transforming recalcitrant structures' (Collier 1998, p. 464) that characterise migrant entrepreneurship will be a challenge.

We also acknowledge that our projects, whilst welcome by practitioner partners, have not been subject to formal independent evaluation in the conventional sense. Such evaluations are rare (Solano et al. 2019) and difficult to undertake for a variety of reasons including cost, difficulties in measurement and unclear objectives. Nonetheless, CREME initiatives have been subjected to scrutiny by external agencies. The Centre's work was cited as an exemplar in the Organisation for Economic and Cooperation and Development's (OECD) report on 'Inclusive Entrepreneurship' (2014, p.104). It was highlighted in the European Commission's 'Evaluation and Analysis of Good Practices in Promoting and Supporting Migrant Entrepreneurship' (2016); this report was based on independent assessors' view of examples of 'good practice'. A more recent publication for the European Commission (Solano et al. 2019) draws a similar conclusion.

CREME enters its 16th year with its most ambitious programme of research and knowledge exchange to date. It starts a major collaborative project on understanding and improving the productivity of microbusinesses owned by ethnic minority communities. Such firms rarely feature in contemporary debates and initiatives on productivity. The project exemplifies many of the features that characterise the Centre. It comprises an interdisciplinary group of academics interested in understanding what productivity actually means to owners and workers in microbusinesses. They combine with practitioner partners that include an award-winning social enterprise with a keen interest in promoting employability of migrants; a network representing Bangladeshi caterers; a national civil society alliance; and a music promotion company with a strong social mission to promote artists from deprived backgrounds. Together, this collaboration will create a business development intervention rooted in the concerns of (neglected) micro-businesses as well as scientific principles.

The Centre continues its interest in policy interventions by examining the evolution of measures to support migrant businesses in the UK (Roberts et al. 2019). This temporal analysis – comprising a novel and systematic assessment of parliamentary debates – casts light on the way the framing of debates and discourse on minority firms. There appears to be much in common with the 'deficit model' approach to migrant businesses noted earlier, and the panic-stricken and welfarist discourse that characterised the introduction – and continuation - of policies towards ethnic minority firms in the UK.

CREME also plans to contribute to the debates and practice on intersectional approaches to minority enterprise. Intersectional approaches (Villares-Varela 2016; Villares-Varela et al. 2017) acknowledge interdependent identities, such as gender, race and social class, rather than ethnic background alone. The complexity that attends this perspective can be difficult to translate into concrete programmes of business support. We aim to pursue this challenge in a major new project that builds on CREME's experience of developing supplier diversity initiatives. Leading companies are joining forces with CREME to boost supply chain opportunities for local firms from all backgrounds. We target the project at different kinds of minority-owned businesses i.e. those owned and managed by women (particularly women with children), people with limiting disabilities, lesbian, gay, bisexual, transgender (LGBT) people, ethnic minorities and young entrepreneurs. The three-year programme ensures that such firms get the support they need to take advantage of opportunities arising from opportunities in corporate supply chains.

The fifteen years since the founding of CREME has witnessed a dizzying degree of change in the way we understand ethnic minority enterprise, the range of stakeholders with an interest in the subject, and the positioning of minority business issues within the academy and different policy domains (migration, enterprise, employment and others). Who actually 'owns' the policy challenge of promoting migrant entrepreneurship is difficult to establish with any precision. This applies with particular force to austerity-blighted Britain, a country which – prior to the dismantling of public sector business support in 2010 - had a tradition of interesting policy experiments to encourage ethnic minority enterprise. The rich and diverse activities that characterise the Centre's work and its plans for the future provide a focal point against this uncertain context. They are crucial in helping CREME to make the case of diversity and entrepreneurship across a whole spectrum of institutions.

Acknowledgements

I would like to thank Gerardo Javier Arriaga Garcia, Paul Edwards, Andrew Maile, Richard Roberts, Giacomo Solano, Judy Scully and Maria Villares-Varela for their helpful comments on an earlier draft of this paper. I also appreciate the financial support of the ESRC in funding the time to develop this paper.

References

Allinson, G. Braidford, P. Grewer, N. Houston, M. Orange, R. Leigh Sear, R. and Stone, I. (2004), Ethnic Minority Businesses and ICT, Focus Group Research, Durham Business School for SBS.

Bhattacharyya, G. and Murji, K. (2013), Introduction: race critical public scholarship. Ethnic and Racial Studies, 36(9): 1359-1373.

Bates, T. (2011), Minority entrepreneurship. Foundations and Trends in Entrepreneurship, 7: 151-311.Bhattacharyya, G. and Murji, K. (2013), Introduction: race critical public scholarship. Ethnic and Racial Studies, 36(9): 1359-1373.

Beckinsale, M. Ram, M. and Theodorakopoulos, N. (2011), ICT adoption and ebusiness development: Understanding ICT adoption amongst ethnic minority businesses. International Small Business Journal, 29(3): 193-219.

Carter, S. Mwaura, M. Ram, M, Trehan, K. and Jones, T. (2015), Barriers to ethnic minority and women's enterprise: Existing evidence, policy tensions and unsettled questions. International Small Business Journal, 33(1): 49-69.

Cassell, C. and Johnson, P. (2006), Action research: Explaining the diversity. Human Relations, 59(6): 783-814.

Collier, A. (1998), Explanation and emancipation. In: M. Archer, R. Bhaskar, A. Collier, T. Lawson and A. Norrie (eds), Critical Realism: Essential Readings, London: Routledge, 444-72.

Dickens, L. (1999), Beyond the business case: a three-pronged approach to equality action. Human Resource Management Journal, 9(1): 9-11.

Edwards, P. (1986), Conflict at Work, Oxford: Blackwell.

Edwards, P. (2015), Industrial relations, critical social science and reform: 1, principles of engagement. Industrial Relations Journal, 46(3): 173-186.

Edwards, P. (2017), Making 'Critical Performativity' Concrete: Sumantra Ghoshal and Linkages between the Mainstream and the Critical. British Journal of Management, 28: 731–741.

Edwards, P. Ram, M. Sen Gupta, S. and Tsai, C. (2006), Institutionalized Action without Institutions: Negotiated Meanings in Small Firms. Organization, 13(5): 701-724.

Edwards, P. Ram, M. Jones, T. and Doldor, S. (2016), New migrant businesses and their workers: developing, but not transforming, the ethnic economy. Ethnic and Racial Studies, 39(9): 1587-1617.

Engelen, E. (2001), 'Breaking in' and 'breaking out': A Weberian approach to entrepreneurial opportunities. Journal of Ethnic and Migration Studies, 27(2): 203-223.

European Commission. (2016), Evaluation and Analysis of Good Practices in Promoting and Supporting Migrant Entrepreneurship. Brussels: European Commission.

Foley, P. and Ram, M. (2002), The Use of Online Technology by Ethnic Minority Businesses, DTI Small Business Service Research Report.

Frank, H. and Landstrom, H. (2016), What makes entrepreneurship research interesting? Reflections on strategies to overcome the rigour–relevance gap. Entrepreneurship and Regional Development, 28 (1-2): 51-75.

Fraser, S. (2009), Is there ethnic discrimination in the UK market for small business credit? International Small Business Journal, 27: 583–607.

Gidoomal, R. (1997), The UK Maharajahs' in the case of Indians. London: Nicholas Brealey Publishing.

Hoel, B. (1982), Contemporary clothing sweatshops. In West, J. (ed), Work, Women and the Labour Market, London: Routledge and Kegan Paul: 80-98.

Huxham, S. and Vangen, S. (2003), Researching Organisational Practice through Action Research: Case Studies and Design Choices. Organisational Research Methods, 6(3): 383-403.

Kieser, A. and Leiner, L. (2009), Why the rigour–relevance gap in management research is unbridgeable. Journal of Management Studies 49(3): 516–533.

Kloosterman, R. (2010), Matching opportunities with resources: a framework for analysing (migrant) entrepreneurship from a mixed embeddedness perspective. Entrepreneurship and Regional Development 22 (1): 25-45.

Kloosterman, R. Van Leun, J. and Rath, J. (1999), Mixed embeddedness: immigrant entrepreneurship and informal economic activities. International Journal of Urban and Regional Research 23: 252-66.

Jones, T. Ram, M. Edwards, P. Kisilinchev, A. and Muchenje, L. (2012), New migrant enterprise: novelty or historical continuity? Urban Studies, 49:1-18.

Jones. T, McEvoy, D. and Barrett, G. (2000), Market potential as a decisive influence on the performance of ethnic minority business. In Rath, J. (ed), Immigrant Businesses: the Economic, Political and Social Environment, Basingstoke UK, Macmillan.

Jones, T. and Ram, M. (2007), Re-embedding the ethnic business agenda. Work, Employment and Society, 21(3): 439-57.

Jones, T. Ram, M. Edwards, P. Kiselinchev, A. and Muchenje, L. (2014), Mixed embeddedness and new migrant enterprise in the UK. Entrepreneurship and Regional Development 26(5-6): 500-20.

Kloosterman, R. (2010), Matching opportunities with resources: a framework for analysing (migrant) entrepreneurship from a mixed embeddedness perspective. Entrepreneurship and Regional Development, 22 (1): 25-45.

McKelvey, B. (2006), Van de Ven and Johnson's 'engaged scholarship': Nice try, but... Academy of Management Review, 31(4): 822–829.

Mickiewicz, T. Hart, T. Nyakudya, F. and Theodorakopoulos, N. (2019), Ethnic pluralism, immigration and entrepreneurship. Regional Studies, 53(1): 80-94.

OECD. (2013), Self-employment rates of migrants. Entrepreneurship at a Glance 2013. Paris: OECD Publishing.

OECD. (2015), Inclusive Entrepreneurship in Europe Paris: OECD Publishing.

Olsen, W.K. (2010), Realist methodology: A review. In Olsen, W.K. (ed.), Realist Methodology. Volume 1. London: Sage, xix-xlvi.

Rath, J. (2000), Introduction to Rath, J. (ed), Immigrant Business: the Economic, Political and Social Environment. Basingstoke, UK, Macmillan.

Rath, J. and Swagerman, A. (2016), Promoting Ethnic Entrepreneurship in European Cities: Sometimes ambitious, mostly absent, rarely addressing structural features. International Migration Review, 54(1): 152-166

Ram, M. (1994), Managing to survive: Working lives in small firms. Blackwell Business.

Ram, M, and Smallbone, D. (2003a), Policies to support ethnic minority enterprise: The English experience. Entrepreneurship and Regional Development, 15(2): 151-166.

Ram, M. and Smallbone, D. (2003b), Supplier Diversity Initiatives and the Diversification of Ethnic Minority Businesses in the UK. Policy Studies, 24(4):187-204

Ram, M. Smallbone, D. and Deakins, D. (2002), The Finance and Business Support Needs of Ethnic Minority Firms in Britain. British Bankers Association Research Report

Ram, M. Edwards, P. and Jones, T. (2007), Staying underground - informal work, small firms, and employment regulation in the united kingdom. Work and Occupations, 34(3): 318-44.

Ram, M. Edwards, P. Jones, T. Kiselinchev, A. and Muchenje, L. (2015), Getting Your Hands Dirty. Work, Employment and Society, 29 (3): 462-478.

Ram, M. Smallbone, D. Deakins, D. and Jones, T. (2003), Banking on 'break-out': Finance and the Development of Ethnic Minority Businesses. Journal of Ethnic and Migration Studies, 29(4):663-681.

Ram, M. Woldesenbet, K. and Jones, T. (2011), Raising the table stakes? Ethnic minority businesses and supply chain relationships. Work, Employment and Society 25(2): 309-26.

Ram, M. and Jones, T. (2008), Ethnic Minority Business: Review of Research and Policy. Government and Policy Environment and Planning 'C', 26: 352-374.

Ram, M. and Trehan, K. (2010), Critical Action Learning, Policy Learning and Small Firms: An Inquiry. Management Learning, 41(4): 415-428.

Ram, M. Theodorakopoulos, N. and Worthington, I. (2007), Policy transfer in practice: implementing supplier diversity in the UK, Public Administration, 85 (3): 779–803.

Ram, M. Trehan, K. Rouse, J. Woldesenbet. K. Jones, T. (2012), Ethnic Minority Business Support
in the West Midlands: Challenges and Developments. Government and Policy (Environment
and Planning 'C'), 30, 5: 493-512.

Ram, M., Edwards, P., Meardi, G., Jones, T, and Doldor, S. Forthcoming 'Non-Compliant Small
Firms and the National Living Wage: The Roots of Informal Responses to Regulatory Change',
British Journal of Management

Roberts, R. Ram, M. and Jones, T. (2018), It Took A Riot … Reflections on UK Government
Policymaking for Ethnic Minority Entrepreneurship over the last 50 years, 41st ISBE National
Small Firms Conference, Newcastle, UK, November, 14-15.

Shah, M. and Ram, M. (2006), Supplier Diversity and Minority Business Enterprise Development:
Case Study Experience of Three US Multinationals. Supply Chain Management: An International Journal, 11(1): 85-91.

Solano, G. Wolffhardt, A. and Xhani, A. (2019), Policies to support migrant entrepreneurship.
Report for the EU-funded project 'Migrant Entrepreneurship Growth Agenda, (MEGA).

Smallbone, D. (2005), Entrepreneurship by Ethnic Minorities: Institutions. Background paper.
OECD.

Thompson, P. and Smith, C. (2009), Labour power and labour process: Contesting the marginality
of the sociology of work. Sociology, 43(5): 913-30.

Romero, M. and Valdez, Z. (2016), Introduction to the special issue: intersectionality and entrepreneurship. Ethnic and Racial Studies, 39(9):1553-1565.

Valdez, Z. (2011), The new entrepreneurs: How race, class, and gender shape American enterprise.
California: Stanford University Press.

Valdez, Z. (2016), Intersectionality, the household economy, and ethnic entrepreneurship. Ethnic
and Racial Studies, 39(9): 1618-1636

Van de Ven, A. (2007), Engaged Scholarship, Oxford: Oxford University Press.

Villares-Varela, M. (2016), Not helping out': classed strategies of the (non) contribution of children in immigrant family businesses. Ethnic and Racial Studies, 40(10): 1758-1775.

Villares-Varela, M. Ram, M. and Jones, T. (2017), Female Immigrant Global Entrepreneurship:
From Invisibility to Empowerment? In Lewis, K. (ed) Routledge Companion to Global Female
Entrepreneurship, London: Routledge

Vertovec, S. (2007), Super-diversity and its implications. Ethnic and Racial Studies, 30(6): 1024-
1054.

Wensley, R. (2007), Beyond Rigour and Relevance: The Underlying Nature of Both Business
Schools and Management Research. AIM Research Working Paper Series, 051, January, 2007.

Whitehurst, F. and Richter, P. (2018), Engaged scholarship in small firm and entrepreneurship
research: Grappling with Van de Ven's diamond model in retrospect to inform future practice.
International Small Business Journal, 36(4): 380– 399.

Wickert, C. and Schaefer, S.M. (2015), Towards a Progressive Understanding of Performativity
in Critical Management Studies. Human Relations, 68: 107-30.

Migratory Pathways for Start-up Founders and Innovative Entrepreneurs to Austria and Estonia

Ave Lauren, Alexander Spiegelfeld[1]

Abstract

This article introduces the migration pathways available for third-country nationals intending to obtain a residence permit in Austria and Estonia to launch a start-up. It investigates both countries' strategies to attract and retain innovative third-country nationals as well as good practices and challenges associated with these policies. Since 2017, both countries have migration schemes available to start-up founders, however, in Estonia the scheme has proven to be significantly more successful. In Austria, bureaucratic obstacles and the lengthy process appear to be major challenges for third-country start-up founders wishing to obtain a residence permit. In Estonia, challenges arise from the lack of qualified labour and high labour taxes. In both countries the information on the application process is made available online, however, only in Estonia provides for the possibility to apply for the start-up assessment online.

Introduction

Due to their unique qualities, start-ups and innovative entrepreneurship contribute to creating new employment opportunities, implementing innovative technologies and securing international investments. Entrepreneurs are typically highly motivated to bring innovative products and services to market and are willing to take on certain risks. The European Union (EU) has recognised the need to improve the conditions for attracting and retaining third-country start-up founders and innovative entrepreneurs, especially in the face of demographic change and labour market needs (European Commission, 2016).

Against this backdrop, the European Migration Network (EMN)[2] has conducted a study (EMN 2019[3]) to examine the migratory pathways open to third-country start-

---

[1] The opinions, comments and analyses expressed in this report are those of the author and do not necessarily represent the views of any of the organizations with which the author is affiliated.

[2] For more information about the EMN, see https://ec.europa.eu/home-affairs/content/about-emn-0_en.

[3] For further information on the EMN study see also https://ec.europa.eu/home-affairs/sites/homeaffairs/files/00_eu_start-ups_common_template_2019_final_en.pdf.

up founders and innovative entrepreneurs who wish to establish themselves in the EU. The following two case studies from Austria (Spiegelfeld, 2019[4]) and Estonia (EMN Estonia, 2019[5]) introduce the migratory pathways for third-country start-up founders to be admitted to those countries. They also present measures to attract and retain start-up businesses and their founders. Furthermore, the case studies address challenges and good practices.

Both Austria and Estonia have adapted their immigration regulations in 2017 to attract third-country nationals intending to launch a start-up. In Estonia, the new policy has proven to be rather successful with 931 people who have already relocated to Estonia or who have been granted the right to do so under this scheme. In Austria, on the other hand, the situation appears to be drastically different with only three residence permits issued for start-up founders since 2017.

Migratory pathways for start-ups and innovative entrepreneurs to Austria

In 2011, Austria introduced the Red-White-Red Card (RWR Card), redefining the conditions under which foreign workers may immigrate to and settle in Austria (Bittmann, 2013).[6] The goal was to attract (highly) skilled workers from third countries (Faßmann, 2013: 2-4). The RWR Card was adapted in 2017, with a separate admission track introduced for start-up founders. A RWR Card for start-up founders became necessary after recognizing that previous provisions of admission of young entrepreneurs intending to start a business in Austria were overly restrictive (Federal Parliament of the Austrian Republic, 2017: 10). Introducing the RWR Card for start-up founders was also in line with the "start-up country strategy" (Gründerlandstrategie), which among other things calls for establishing a culture of welcoming start-up founders and entrepreneurs from other countries. The new migratory pathway was intended to make Austria a "start-up magnet" (Austrian Press Agency-OTS, 2017a). It should be noted, however, that the RWR Card for start-up founders has only been issued on three occasions since it was introduced in late 2017 (Federal Ministry of the Interior, 2019: 19).

Austria offers no special visas or residence permits for third-country national employees of start-ups. Such individuals can, therefore, enter Austria or immigrate only under the general visa provisions of the Aliens Police Act 2005 or based on the general legal provisions set out in the Settlement and Residence Act. Yet, such individuals could conceivably have special skills or training making them eligible

---

[4] The national report of Austria will be published soon and will then be available on the EMN website: https://www.emn.at/en/publications/studies/.

[5] The national report of Estonia will be published soon and will then be available on the EMN website: https://www.emn.ee/en/publications/.

[6] For further information on the RWR Card see also migration.gv.at, page "Dauerhafte Zuwanderung". Available at www.migration.gv.at/de/formen-der-zuwanderung/dauerhafte-zuwanderung/.

to immigrate under other categories of the RWR Card, for instance as 'other key workers'.

The admission of third-country start-ups and innovative entrepreneurs to Austria

Introducing the RWR Card for start-up founders resulted in a criteria-based migratory pathway open to start-up founders and innovative entrepreneurs. The following section provides insights into the requirements and criteria that third-country nationals need to meet in order to obtain a RWR Card for start-up founders.

In general, applicants for a residence permit must meet the general requirements set out in Part 1 of the Settlement and Residence Act.[7] To obtain a RWR Card for start-up founders, applicants must additionally meet the special requirements specified in the Settlement and Residence Act in conjunction with the Act Governing the Employment of Foreign Nationals (see information box 1). On the other hand, this entails the admission criteria based on the points system set out in the Act Governing the Employment of Foreign Nationals. The criteria include, among other things, specific skills, professional experience and language competences. On the other hand, there are special admission requirements which need to be met by start-ups, which are set out in the Act Governing the Employment of Foreign Nationals.

Applicants must apply for the residence permit for start-up founders in person at competent authority representing Austria in another country. The application, along with any documents submitted, is then forwarded to the competent settlement and residence authority in Austria. Subsequently, the settlement and residence authority requests an assessment from the provincial office of the Austrian Public Employment Service. The Public Employment Service is then responsible for deciding whether the start-up meets the requirements specified in the Act Governing the Employment of Foreign Nationals.

In the event that a positive decision on a residence permit is reached, a visa permitting entry to Austria may be issued if required (Federal Ministry of the Interior, 2019: 10). After being issued a valid visa, the applicant can travel to Austria and personally collect the residence permit from the competent settlement and resi-

---

[7] A residence permit may only be granted to a foreigner if (a) the foreigner's stay does not conflict with public interest; (b) the foreigner provides evidence of legal entitlement to accommodations meeting local standards for a family of comparable size; (c) the foreigner has health insurance that covers all risks and is valid in Austria as well; (d) the foreigner's residence would not result in a financial burden for a regional authority; (e) the granting of a residence permit does not significantly impair relations of the Republic of Austria with another State or subject of international law; (f) when applying for renewal under Art. 24, the foreigner has fulfilled module 1 of the Integration Agreement as referred to in Art. 9 of the Integration Act (FLG I No. 68/2017) within the specified period; and (g) in cases falling under Art. 58 and 58a, more than four months have passed since the departure to a third country, in accordance with Art. 58 para 5 (Art. 11 para 2 Settlement and Residence Act).

Foreign nationals are admitted as start-up founders when they:

- Achieve the minimum number of points awarded for the criteria listed in Annex D;
- Develop and bring to market innovative products, services, processes or technologies within the framework of a newly established undertaking;
- Submit a plausible business plan for founding and operating the undertaking;
- Personally have a major influence on the actual management of the planned undertaking;[8]
- Provide evidence of at least EUR 50,000 in capital for starting the company, with at least half the amount held as owner's equity.

Information box 1 Admission requirements pursuant to Art. 24 para 2 Act Governing the Employment of Foreign Nationals

Source: Act Governing the Employment of Foreign Nationals.

dence authority (AT EMN NCP, 2015: 33–34). The RWR Card for start-up founders is usually granted for two years (Spiegelfeld, 2019: 8).

Measures to attract and retain start-ups and innovative entrepreneurs from third countries

Measures to advertise Austria as a start-up location and to attract start-up founders and innovative entrepreneurs have been somewhat successful. Austria has, in fact, recorded an increased number of start-ups from other countries. This is shown by the Austrian Business Agency (ABA) annual report and other sources.[9] Particularly, the City of Vienna enjoys a good international image due to its proven high standards of living, availability of talents, and regional expertise in Central and Eastern Europe (Spiegelfeld, 2019: 53).

Introducing the RWR Card for start-up founders in 2017 represented a major step towards attracting start-ups and innovative entrepreneurs from third countries. However, there is only one additional measure implemented by the Austria Federal Government exclusively targeting third-country start-up founders or innovative entrepreneurs. In 2017, the Global Incubator Network (GIN) along with the goAustria programme was launched. The purpose of the goAustria programme is to serve as a central clearing point for international start-ups, incubators and investors wishing to take up business in Austria.[10] There are nonetheless activities aimed at helping to

---

[8] According to a decision by the Provincial Administrative Court of Vienna dated 21 January 2016, *"in addition to the applicant meeting the conditions enumerated in Art. 24 of the Act Governing the Employment of Foreign Nationals, an assessment must take place to determine whether the applicant does in fact play a key role in their company that involves making business decisions as well as business strategy decisions, thereby providing substantial input for managing that company and taking the relevant business decisions"* (Provincial Administrative Court of Vienna, 21 January 2016, VGW-151/023/5491/2015).

[9] ABA – About us. Available at https://investinaustria.at/en/about-aba/.

[10] Global Incubator Network, GO AUSTRIA. Available at www.gin-austria.com/goAustria.html.

internationalise Austria's start-up ecosystem in general. The Vienna Start-Up Package, to quote an example, targets international start-ups from all over the world while mainly seeking to nurture exchanges with stakeholders at national level (Spiegelfeld, 2019: 53).

There are no special measures aimed at retaining start-up founders and innovative entrepreneurs from third countries. However, there are measures aimed at third-country nationals already residing in the country who wish to launch a start-up. An example is the TOGETHER:AUSTRIA Start-Ups pilot project launched in 2017 by the Austrian Integration Fund as part of the Together: Austria project. The programme provides support to migrants in the process of implementing an innovative business idea. Start-up founders receive guidance from mentors over a two-year period and can participate in various events.[11]

Challenges and good practices

Bureaucratic obstacles and the lengthy process appear to be major challenges for applicants wishing to obtain a RWR Card. These challenges have nonetheless been recognised both by policymakers and administrators as well as by private businesses, research institutions and bodies representing stakeholders' interests (Austrian Press Agency-OTS, 2017b, 2017c). According to Biffl (2016: 63) the requirement to apply to the local authority representing Austria in another country is an initial challenge. Opening a bank account in Austria is another bureaucratic obstacle (Spiegelfeld, 2019: 42). A bank account is necessary, however, in order to deposit the capital required as a condition for obtaining a RWR Card for start-up founders

In an interview, a third-country national who had applied for a RWR Card for start-up founders described problems related to the admission requirements (see information box 1): during the application process, the start-up's business theoretically comes to a halt, while it is not permitted to use the EUR 50,000 in capital. This can reportedly be a major obstacle in the fast-paced start-up scene, making the difference between the success or failure of an idea. Another challenge arises from the points system for the RWR Card. The Vienna Business Agency, for instance, expressed concern at the type of inflexible points system applicable to the RWR Card, which could potentially result in losing innovative ideas where applicants did not meet all the requirements placed by the RWR Card for start-up founders (Spiegelfeld, 2019: 42-43).

On the positive side, the start-up ecosystem has matured considerably in recent years owing, among other things, to an intensified State support, according to the ABA (Ermisch, 2019). The Organisation for Economic Co-operation and Development (OECD) has attested to Austria's closely knit network of incubators and accelerators (OECD, 2018: 13–14). Austria's start-up ecosystem also stands out by virtue of its excellent services and an exceptionally well-developed culture of co-operation among businesses (Spiegelfeld, 2019: 65). In the way of good practices

---

[11]   Austrian Integration Fund, ZUSAMMEN:ÖSTERREICH Gründer/innen. Available at www.zusammen-oesterreich.at/wer-ist-zoe/akademie-gruenderinnen/.

relating to admission under the RWR Card for start-up founders, information made available online at www.migration.gv.at to prospective applicants for the RWR Card for start-up founders is reported to be adequate and transparent, allowing applicants to realistically assess their chances for obtaining the RWR Card.

Conclusion

The RWR Card for start-up founders has been issued on only three occasion since it was introduced in late 2017 (Federal Ministry of the Interior, 2019: 19). Nevertheless, introducing the RWR Card for start-up founders in 2017 can be seen as indicating an interest on the part of policymakers to have third-country start-up founders and innovative entrepreneurs immigrate to and settle in Austria. However, there seems to be a discrepancy between policymakers' avowed intention to attract start-ups and actual policies, which often appear as too restrictive (Spiegelfeld, 2019: 31, 55).

Particularly constraining are the bureaucratic procedures involved in making an application (Biffl, 2016: 63). Another major challenge arises from the points system serving as a basis for issuing the residence permit as well as the requirement to provide evidence of minimum capital of EUR 50,000, which can make the difference between the success or failure of a start-up idea (Spiegelfeld, 2019: 64). These challenges, among others, may explain why only three RWR Cards for start-up founders has been issued since its introduction in late 2017.

To increase the number of applications, high priority should be given to reducing bureaucratic obstacles involved in applying for the card. Another step would be to broaden the group of eligible applicants to include third-country nationals employed by start-ups.[12] Until now there has been no special admission track for that group of individuals.

Overview of the Start-up Regulation in Estonia

Estonia is a small, but innovative country that has made major strides towards becoming regarded as one of the most advanced digital societies in the world. The adoption of the Start-up special regulation (so-called *Startup Visa*) in 2017 should be seen as a continuation of this broader trend of innovation and building e-Estonia. In recent decades, for instance, Estonia has developed a wide range of e-services, which make doing business in Estonia convenient and fast. Moreover, Estonia is unique in the world for having the programme of e-Residency[13], a government-issued digital identity and status that provides entrepreneurs with access to Estonia's

---

[12] See the Austrian Startups website, page "Ecosystem". Available at www.austrianstartups.com/ecosystem/.
[13] Read more here: https://e-resident.gov.ee/

Major e-Estonia milestones:
   1997 - e-Governance (public e-services);
   - **e-Tax** (electronic tax filing system);
   - **x-Road** (centrally managed data exchange layer for registries);
   - **digital ID** (mandatory national ID card);
   - **i-voting** (online voting in national elections);
   - **e-Health** (common online health records);
   - **e-Residency** (digital ID for non-nationals).

Information box 2 Major e-Estonia milestones prior Startup Visa

Source: e-Estonia.com

digital business environment (see Information box 2). In parallel to these broader societal developments, fostering innovation and start-ups has also become a national priority in Estonia and tied to the broader 'e-Estonia' brand. The Estonian Entrepreneurship Growth Strategy 2014-2020, a guiding strategy in this field, envisions Estonia as a start-up hotspot in Northeastern Europe by 2020 and a range of policy areas are expected to support achieving this goal, including immigration policy[14].

Simultaneously, however, the creation of a start-up visa signifies a major departure from the more traditional approaches to immigration in Estonia. Previously existing economic, cultural, historical or family ties were seen as the main basis for entry and legal stay in Estonia, but with this policy the potential to contribute to both economy and society becomes sufficient grounds to grant an entry to the country.

The admission of third-country start-ups and innovative entrepreneurs to Estonia

In order to attract start-ups from third countries and to address the need to modernize the business environment, the start-up sector in cooperation with the state came up with the new start-up visa/residence permit scheme (Startup Visa; EMN Estonia, 2019). The regulation established a definition for a start-up: A start-up company ... is a business entity belonging to a company registered in Estonia, which is starting activity with the purpose to develop and launch such a business model with high global growth potential, innovative and replicable that shall significantly contribute to the development of the Estonian business environment. (Article 62⁴(2) of the Aliens Act 2009). The scheme came into force in January 2017 and foresees the possibility to issue a visa or a residence permit to start-up founder as well as to the start-up employees under more flexible conditions (see Information box 3).

According to the Aliens Act, the long stay visa may be issued to a start-up founder for up to one year and maybe extended for up to 548 days within 730 con-

---

[14] Estonian Entrepreneurship Growth Strategy 2014-2020. Available at https://kasvustrategia.mkm.ee/index_eng.html.

- Exemption from the immigration quota
- Exemption from investment requirements
- Exemption from salary requirements
- Exemption from the Unemployment Insurance Fund's permission
- Eligible for family reunification and family members have access to labour market

Information box 3 Flexible conditions for start-up founders and employees compared to other entrepreneurs and workers

Source: Aliens Act

secutive days and there is an exemption from the general rule regarding the rate of funds, which are sufficient to cover the expenses while being in Estonia. If a third-country national (TCN) has established a start-up enterprise in Estonia, he or she may apply for a temporary residence permit for enterprise with the duration for up to 5 years without being subject to the immigration quota and the general obligation to invest does not apply.

Estonia is one of the few countries in Europe, where the Start-up Visa Scheme applies also to employees. Hence, if a start-up which is established in Estonia wishes to employ a TCN for short term, it is possible to apply for a long-term visa with the duration up to 548 days within 730 consecutive days and register the short-term employment under more flexible conditions. As an exception from the general rule, the general salary criteria for short-term employment does not apply and as a deviation from the general rule, the short-term employment for TCNs working in a start-up is allowed for the whole duration of the legal stay. It is also possible to issue a residence permit for start-up employees with the duration of up to 5 years, if a start-up which is established in Estonia wishes to employ a TCN. This residence permit is not subject to the immigration quota and the requirement to receive a permission from the Estonian Unemployment Insurance Fund and the salary requirement does not apply.

In addition to more favourable regulations on start-up visa and residence permit TCNs have the right to be accompanied by their family members, who also have access to the labour market.

The new scheme foresees a two-level application system. At first the third-country national has to submit an online application to the start-up expert Committee for assessment whether the start-up qualifies as one. The Committee comprises of representative organisations of the start-up scene, who work on a voluntary basis. The Committee assesses whether the business has growth potential, whether the business model is innovative and repeatable, and is the added value for the Estonian business environment. After the approval from the Committee, it is possible to apply for a start-up visa or a residence permit at a foreign representation or Police and Border Guard Board or if the start-up has already been evaluated, there is no need for an extra assessment from the Committee.

Attracting and retaining start-ups and innovative entrepreneurs

Estonia has a busy, supportive and open start-up ecosystem eager to support ambitious individuals and start-ups. At the end of 2018, 103 organizations made up the local 'start-up ecosystem', providing a wide range of support services to start-ups. There are various incubator and accelerator programmes, possibilities for funding, mentoring, co-working spaces, trainings and events. [15] Except for the facilitation of admission, these measures are not meant specifically for start-up founders and employees from third countries, but for start-ups in general. The private and public sector have good cooperation in attracting start-ups. One of the main actors in attracting start-up founders and employees from third countries is Startup Estonia, a programme which was established by the Ministry of Economic Affairs and Communications. As for promotional activities Startup Estonia is carrying out roadshows in various countries together with the e-residence programme. Work in Estonia on the other hand does targeting campaigns to recruit TCN workers to work in Estonian companies including start-ups[16].

As for retention measures, it is possible to renew the residence permit for up to 10 years if the conditions are met. Start-up founders and employees are entitled to bring along their family members who are offered special services for spouses, e.g. international spouse career counselling (EMN Estonia, 2019). Given that many start-ups fail but Estonia is interested in retaining talent it is possible for individuals whose start-up did not take off but have been in the country for three years to apply for a residence permit on other grounds, e.g. settling permanently in Estonia.

Challenges and good practices

As for the main challenges from the start-up founder´s perspective there is a lack of qualified labour, the labour taxes are high and it is difficult to open a bank account in Estonia (EMN Estonia, 2019). As for good practices the start-up scheme is efficient and as it is a two-level process, no misuses have been detected so far. There were other good practices identified – e.g. the possibility to apply for the start-up assessment online and to profit from the e-residency programme that facilitates doing business in Estonia as there is no need to personally be present in the country to establish a business. Additionally, the alternative money transferring services (e.g. Transferwise) have helped in solving the difficulties with opening bank accounts.

Conclusion

Although the start-up scheme has been in place for a relatively short period of time, it can be said that it has had a positive start. With exactly two years since the launch of the scheme, 1,108 applications from companies were submitted for the start-up status, of which 385 received a positive decision, and 931 people altogether relocated already to Estonia or have been granted the right to do so (EMN Estonia,

---

[15]   Startup Estonia – Startup Ecosystem. Available at https://startupestonia.ee/startup-ecosystem.
[16]   Startup Estonia – About Startup Estonia. Available at https://www.startupestonia.ee/about.

2019). In 2018, the main countries for founders who have received a visa or a residence permit under the start-up scheme have been Russia, Turkey, India and Ukraine (ibid.). As for the sectors, temporary residence permits for working in the start-ups have mostly been issued in 2018 in the information and communication sector followed by financial and insurance activities.

Overall conclusion

After the European Union has acknowledged the need to improve the conditions for attracting and retaining third-country start-up founders, the European Migration Network has carried out a study to examine in detail the migratory pathways open to this population. The Austrian and Estonian cases stood out as particularly interesting, not least because both countries recently amended their immigration policies to better accommodate the specific situation of third-country nationals intending to launch a start-up.

On the one hand, Austria opened a new immigration track under the RWR Card as part of a national "start-up country strategy" (Gründerlandstrategie) in an attempt to facilitate the immigration of innovative third-country nationals. The effort was met with relative success, as only three individuals received the RWR Card for start-up founders since 2017. This may be due, among other things, to bureaucratic constraints or to the need to show evidence of EUR 50,000 available for capital investment.

On the other hand, Estonia's Start-up special regulation adopted in 2017 led to 1,108 applications for start-ups being lodged in a two-year timespan, of which 385 were successful. As the scheme also applies to start-up employees and their family members, a total of 931 people was granted the right to stay in Estonia in the same time period. These efforts to attract entrepreneurial third-country nationals certainly constitutes a breakaway from traditional, cultural-oriented, immigration policies in Estonia but is perfectly in synch with the country's reputation as one of the world's most advanced digital societies.

References

Aliens Act 2009, RT I 2010. Available at https://www.riigiteataja.ee/en/eli/ee/523052019002/consolide/current Accessed 26 November 2019.

Aliens Police Act 2005, FLG I No. 100/2005, in the version of FLG I NO. 56/2018.

Biffl, G. 2016 Migration and Labour Integration in Austria. Danube University Krems, Krems. Available at www.gudrun-biffl.at/publications/download/Biffl-Sopemi-2011.pdf. Accessed 21 October 2019.

Bittmann, T. 2013 Highly qualified and qualified immigration of third country nationals: Legislation, measures and statistics in Austria. IOM, Vienna. Available at www.emn.at/wp-content/uploads/2017/01/AT-EMN-NCP_Highly-qualified-and-qualified_final.pdf. Accessed 21 October 2019.

Ermisch, S. 2019 Studie: Start-up Ökosystem in Österreich reift, Wirtschaftswoche, 20 March 2019. Available at https://gruender.wiwo.de/studie-start-up-oekosystem-in-oesterreich-reift/. Accessed 21 October 2019.

Estonian Ministry of Economic Affairs and Communications 2013 Estonian Entrepreneurship Growth Strategy 2014-2020. Available at: https://kasvustrateegia.mkm.ee/pdf/Estonian%20Entrepreneurship%20Growth%20Strategy%202014-2020.pdf. Accessed 21 October 2019.

European Commission (EC) 2016 Communication from the Commission to the European Parliament and the Council – towards a reform of the Common European Asylum System and enhancing legal avenues to Europe, COM(2016) 197 final. Available at https://ec.europa.eu/home-affairs/sites/homeaffairs/files/what-we-do/policies/european-agenda-migration/proposal-implementation-package/docs/20160406/towards_a_reform_of_the_common_european_asylum_system_and_enhancing_legal_avenues_to_europe_-_20160406_en.pdf. Accessed 21 October 2019.

EMN 2019 Migratory pathways for start-ups and innovative entrepreneurs in the EU and Norway. Common Template for EMN Study 2019. Available at https://ec.europa.eu/home-affairs/sites/homeaffairs/files/00_eu_start-ups_common_template_2019_final_en.pdf. Accessed 21 November 2019.

Faßmann, H. 2013 Die Rot-Weiß-Rot-Karte in Österreich: Inhalt, Implementierung, Wirksamkeit. Bertelsmann Stiftung, Gütersloh. Available at https://www.bertelsmann-stiftung.de/fileadmin/files/BSt/Presse/imported/downloads/xcms_bst_dms_39058_39199_2.pdf. Accessed 21 October 2019.

Federal Act amending the Act Governing the Employment of Foreign Nationals and the General Social Insurance Act, FLG I No. 66/2017.

Parliament of the Austrian Republic(2017 Government Proposal - Federal Act amending the Governing the Employment of Foreign Nationals and the General Social Insurance Act, Government Proposal – Explanatory Notes. Available at www.parlament.gv.at/PAKT/VHG/XXV/I/I_01516/fname_618784.pdf. Accessed 21 October 2019.

Provincial Administrative Court of Vienna, 21 January 2016, VGW-151/023/5491/2015.

Federal Act amending the Governing the Employment of Foreign Nationals Act, FGL I No. 25/2019

Federal Ministry of the Interior, 2019 Niederlassungs- und Aufenthaltsstatistik August 2019. Available at https://www.bmi.gv.at/302/Statistik/files/2019/Niederlassungs_und_Aufenthaltsstatistik_August_2019.pdf. Accessed 21 October 2019.

National Contact Point Austria in the European Migration Network (AT EMN NCP) 2015 The organization of asylum and migration policies in Austria. IOM, Vienna. Available at www.emn.at/wp-content/uploads/2017/01/organisation-study_AT-EMN-NCP_2016.pdf. Accessed 21 October 2019.

National Contact Point Estonia in the European Migration Network (EMN Estonia) 2019 Migratory Pathways for Start-ups and Innovative Entrepreneurs to Estonia. EMN Estonia, Tallinn.

Organisation for Economic Co-operation and Development (OECD) 2018 OECD Reviews of Innovation Policy: Austria 2018 – Overall Assessment and Recommendations. OECD Publishing, Paris. Available at www.bmbwf.gv.at/fileadmin/user_upload/Pressemeldungen/OAR_2018_12_06.pdf. Accessed 21 October 2019.

Spiegelfeld, A. 2019 Migratory Pathways for Start-ups and Innovative Entrepreneurs to Austria. International Organization for Migration (IOM), Vienna.

EMN 2019 Migratory pathways for start-ups and innovative entrepreneurs in the EU and Norway. Common Template for EMN Study 2019. Available at https://ec.europa.eu/home-affairs/sites/homeaffairs/files/00_eu_start-ups_common_template_2019_final_en.pdf. Accessed 21 November 2019.

APA 2017a Mitterlehner/Mahrer: Rot-Weiß-Rot-Karte wird attraktiver – Neues Start-Up-Visum kommt. Press Release, 28 February 2017, Austrian Press Agency (APA). Available at https://www.ots.at/presseaussendung/OTS_20170228_OTS0062/mitterlehnermahrer-rot-weiss-rot-karte-wird-attraktiver-neues-start-up-visum-kommt. Accessed 21 October 2019.

APA 2017b Amon: Regierung setzt wichtige ÖVP-Maßnahmen rasch um. Press Release, 28 February 2017, Austrian Press Agency (APA). Available at www.ots.at/presseaussendung/ OTS_20170228_OTS0143/amon-regierungsetzt-wichtige-oevp-massnahmen-rasch-um. Accessed 21 October 2019.

APA 2017c Industrie: Weiterentwicklung der Rot-Weiß-Rot-Karte wichtiger Schritt. Press Release, 28 February 2017, Austrian Press Agency (APA). Available at www.ots.at/presse aussendung/OTS_20170228_OTS0123/industrieweiterentwicklung-der-rot-weiss-rot-karte-wichtiger-schritt. Accessed 21 October 2019.

Internet sources

EMN Austria: Publikationen. Available at https://www.emn.at/en/publications/studies/. Accessed 21 November 2019.

EMN Estonia: Publications. Available at https://www.emn.ee/en/publications/. Accessed 21 November 2019.

Austrian Business Agency: ABA – About us. Available at https://investinaustria.at/en/aboutaba/. Accessed 21 October 2019.

Austrian Integration Fund: ZUSAMMEN:ÖSTERREICH Gründer/innen. Available at www.zusammen-oesterreich.at/wer-ist-zoe/akademie-gruenderinnen/. Accessed 21 October 2019.

Austrian Startups: Ecosystem, available at www.austrianstartups.com/ecosystem/. Accessed 21 October 2019.

Global Incubator Network: Go Austria, available at www.gin-austria.com/goAustria.html. Accessed 21 October 2019.

European Commission (EC): About the EMN – European Migration Network at the national level. Available at https://ec.europa.eu/home-affairs/content/about-emn-0_en. Accessed 21 October 2019.

Migration Platform of the Federal Republic of Austria. Available at www.migration.gv.at, page Dauerhafte Zuwandeung, available at www.migration.gv.at/de/formen-der-zuwanderung/dau erhafte-zuwanderung/. Accessed 21 October 2019.

Startup Estonia. Available at https://startupestonia.ee/startup-ecosystem. Accessed 21 October 2019.

Rückkehrmigration im Spannungsfeld zwischen (Un)Freiwilligkeit und (Re)Integration

Conceptualising return and circular migration in the context of temporariness. Research and policy implications

Amparo González-Ferrer, Inmaculada Serrano, Adrien Vandenbunder

Abstract

This article summarizes the main issues in the conceptual discussion on return and circular migration, as well as its research and policy implications. After presenting the existing definitions and debating their pros and cons for statistical measurement and policy evaluation, the definition adopted in the TEMPER Surveys[1], conducted in 2017/18 among returned migrants and non-migrants in Argentina, Romania, Senegal and Ukraine, are explained and justified. A brief presentation of some preliminary results from the surveys illustrates the impact of applying different definitions of return migration on the estimated size of the returned populations in different migration contexts, as well as on the socio-economic and migratory profile of the returnees.

Introduction

The renewed interest in measuring and understanding return mainly derives from the increasing policy attention at the EU level to circular migration as a potential new way of managing international migration, which might serve the best interest of the migrants, their countries of origin and their countries of destination.

Past experiences in recruiting and managing temporary work suffer from a 'bad reputation', not only because they generally entailed a diminished protection of migrant workers' rights, but also for their unwanted consequences, including the settlement of large immigrant populations in the recruiting countries (Martin 1997). Being aware of the previous failures and potential risks entailed by the 'classical' temporary work programs, the European Commission (2007, 8) proposed to promote circular migration, loosely defined as *"a form of migration that is managed in a way allowing some degree of legal mobility back and forth between two countries".*

Unfortunately, EU policy documents have never provided a clear definition of circular migration that permits measuring in a precise manner its incidence and

---

[1] TEMPER is the acronym for the EU-funded Project ʹTemporary versus Permanent Migrationʹ, under grant agreement no 613468. For more info, check the website: temperproject.eu or email us to: info@temperproject.eu

characteristics, which is partially related to the multiple meanings given to the terms of return, temporary and permanent migration by different social and political actors. Obviously, lacking of clear and measurable definitions hinders (comparative) research on return and circulation, making it difficult to draw clear and meaningful policy implications.

The major challenge in agreeing on a common definition consists in combining the need to provide a concept that is statistically measurable with the sources available and, at the same time, policy relevant. Often, legal and political migration concepts lack of a clear statistical correlate, which severely hampers large-scale evidence-based evaluations and assessments of legal and political actions in the field. In addition, any definition of return and circular migration should be as inclusive as possible, in order to be meaningful in different contexts; but also strict enough to make return and circular migration easily distinguishable from other types of migration already defined, such as temporary or repeated migration.

This article summarizes the main issues in the conceptual discussion on return, temporary and circular migration based on previous research and statistical analyses. In the light of such discussion and having identified the main limitations, overlaps and contradictions of the existing definitions, we present and justify the definitions adopted in the TEMPER Surveys in different origin countries of migratory flows to the EU. Next, we present preliminary results from the TEMPER Project and discuss the statistical and policy implications of utilizing different concepts of return and circulation.

Existing definitions and conceptual discussion on return and circular migration

We start by revising existing definitions of return, and then move on to the discussion of the circular migration definitions, their main components, advantages and limitations for the study and assessment of different mobility patterns.

Return definitions. Main components, advantages and limitations

The first (statistical) definition of return migration was proposed by the United Nations Statistics Division (UNSD) in 1998. According to UNSD (1998, 26), returning migrants are *"persons returning to their country of citizenship after having been international migrants (whether short-term or long-term) in another country and who are intending to stay in their own country for at least a year."*

This definition suffers from some drawbacks with potentially important empirical implications. First, the country to which the migrant must return includes only his/her 'country of citizenship' rather than, more generally, his/her country of origin. This requirement implies, for instance, that people deprived from their previous citizenship for whatever reason (including naturalization in their country of residence when double nationality agreements are not available) but return to their country of their previous citizenship, which in most cases coincides with country of birth, will be not counted as return migrants. Secondly, even if it includes as potential returnees both short-term and long-term international migrants, it changes length criteria when it refers to return: only (intended) long-term returnees are considered as relevant ones to be included in the definition. The focus on intended duration rather than actual duration represents a major obstacle to apply the definition to available (official) sources. Intended durations are not reported by censuses or population registers, for instance, but only in surveys. In addition, intended durations change over time and the UNSD definition is not clear about when the measurement of those intentions should be made, in order to determine who should be considered or not as a return migrant. Finally, and very importantly, intentions and realized behavior often differ, especially when talking about migration.

These factors partially explain the little applicability of this definition for statistical purposes and the persistent lack of comparable and reliable statistics on return migration experienced for decades. Moreover, the UNSD definition has not been revised since its adoption in 1998, but multiple factors have changed in migration dynamics in the meantime and, therefore, also concerning the statistical needs to measure and describe them.

In 2008, the EU approved the Directive 2008/115/EC, known as the Return Directive, which contributed very little to clarify the debate around return migration by adopting a new concept that exclusively focused on non-spontaneous return. The article 3(3) of the Directive refers to return as *"the process of a third-country national going back - whether in voluntary compliance with an obligation to return, or enforced – to his or her country of origin, or a country of transit in accordance with Community or bilateral readmission agreements or other arrangements, or another third country, to which the third-country national concerned voluntarily decides to return and in which he or she will be accepted."* In other words, the Return Directive refers exclusively to returns that are the result of an administrative procedure and regardless of whether the migrant accepted it voluntarily or not. In addition, it refers only to a portion of the migrant population, the one made of third-country nationals, that is, non-EU individuals.

The two aforementioned elements render the definition of return in the Directive very restrictive, and make clear that it responds to a political motivation rather than a demographic and statistical one. However, it is important to emphasize that good statistical definitions tend to be as inclusive as possible to guarantee, precisely, the possibility to measure and evaluate different types and (political) dimensions of demographic phenomena, either directly by collecting complementary information on those aspects or dimensions, or indirectly, by combining different sources of data that utilize complementary definitions of the same phenomenon.

In fact, during the 2000s, different international agencies working in the field of migration such as International Organization for Migration (IOM) or European Migration Network (EMN) started to introduce terms like 'assisted' and 'voluntary' accompanying figures and programs on return migration, but their definitions of return remained largely inclusive. According to the IOM (2011), for instance, return migration refers to 'the movement of a person returning to his or her country of origin or habitual residence usually after spending at least one year in another country. This return may or may not be voluntary. Return migration includes voluntary repatriation.' The European Migration Network (2011) defined return in its glossary as 'the movement of a person going from a host country back to a country of origin, country of nationality or habitual residence usually after spending a significant period of time in the host country whether voluntary or forced, assisted or spontaneous'.

As can be easily observed, the definitions provided by EMN and IOM opted for a more inclusive idea of country of origin, not restricted to the one of citizenship as in the UNSD definition. In fact, in this regard, the Directive definition is the most inclusive one since any country, even if the migrant was never related to it in any way (residence, birth, citizenship), is accepted as part of the definition. This is clearly not the case in the other definitions, which assume some previous relation between the migrant and the country they return to. The EMN and IOM definitions are also more inclusive than the UNSD by suppressing the requirement of at least one year intended duration of the stay in the country of origin after the return. Neither the IOM nor the EMN imposes any requirement of length of return, intended or actual. This decision might also be criticized as too inclusive, since it makes it difficult to draw a line that separates, for instance, simple visits from returns. In contrast, both definitions decided to privilege long-term international migrants as the relevant returnees by referring to usual stay of one year (IOM) or a significant period of time[2] (EMN) in the country of destination, and potentially excluding short-term migrants from their concept of return without a clear rationale for this. In fact, in the new version of its Glossary just released in late June this year, IOM decided to suppress the reference to length of stay in country of destination when talking about return migration, which is now defined as *"the movement of persons returning to their country of origin after having moved away from their place of habitual residence and crossed an international border"* (IOM 2019, 184).

In sum, the coexistence of multiple definitions, the absence of statistical aspirations in some of them, and the lack of a proper updating of the UNSD definition in line with the new reality and demands of international migration and statistical systems, have contributed to the increasing confusion in the debate about return migration. Moreover, this situation has also reinforced the obstacles and barriers to promote evidence-based policies and adequate assessments of recent proposals and initiatives. This is particularly visible in relation to the policy debate around the idea of circular migration as a new way of managing migration by EU Member States, theoretically encouraged by the Commission since 2007, as we discuss in the following section.

---

[2]   Note that what is a 'significant period' remains an open question and offers multiple interpretations, making the definition not very helpful for statistical purposes.

Definitions of circular migration.
Main components, advantages and limitations

The term circular migration has appeared in the Commission policy documents almost exclusively referring to migration from third countries to the EU. The text of the Communication on Circular Migration and Mobility Partnerships, COM (2007) 248 final, stated that the two main forms of circular migration that could be most relevant in the EU context are:

1 *Circular migration of persons residing in a third country.*
   Circular migration could create an opportunity for persons residing in a third country to come to the EU temporarily for work, study, training or a combination of these, on the condition that, at the end of the period for which they were granted entry, they must re-establish their main residence and their main activity in their country of origin. Circularity can be enhanced by giving migrants the possibility, once they have returned, to retain some form of privileged mobility to and from the Member States where they were formerly residing, for example in the form of simplified admission/re-entry procedures.
2 *Circular migration of third-country nationals settled in the EU.*
   This category of circular migration gives people the opportunity to engage in an activity (business, professional, voluntary or other) in their country of origin while retaining their main residence in one of the Member States.

The previous references to different forms of circular migration made by the EU Commission in 2007 clearly illustrate two things. First, there was not a clear definition of circular migration but rather a wish of finding a common label that allows to refer to a certain pattern of mobility (actual or potential) between the EU and the migrant's countries of origin. Secondly, the EU Commission intended to promote this type of mobility, as far as it is linked to work or study reasons and fits into one of the different existing forms of legal migration, regardless of whether the main residence of the person is in the EU or in their country of origin.

Unfortunately, definitions of circular migration provided by other organisations also lacked the desirable precision. The European Migration Network (2012, 111) defined circular migration as *"the repetition of legal migration by the same person between two or more countries"*. IOM (2011, 19) referred to circular migration as *"the fluid movement of people between countries, including temporary or long-term movement which may be beneficial to all involved, if occurring voluntarily and linked to the labour needs of countries of origin and destination"*. In contrast to what we described for return, in the case of circular migration the definition provided by IOM (2011) results clearly less adequate for statistical and demographic purposes than the one by EMN (2012).[3]

---

[3] Note, in particular, that the definition opposes temporary and long-term movements, even if the opposite of long-term is short-term, not temporary migration, and no clear and internationally accepted definition of temporary migration (especially a statistical one) exists.

Despite the lack of precision in all the aforementioned definitions, two basic elements underlay the idea of circular migration in all of them: a) repetition and, b) two or more countries involved. Circulation automatically refers to the idea of repetition. However, if circular migration is something different from repeated migration or re-migration, it is important to specify how they both differ from each other. Re-migration refers, according to IOM (2011, 79), to *"the movement of a person who, after having returned to his or her country of origin, again emigrates"*[4], regardless of whether the country of destination is the same one as in previous migration or not. Thus, one way of distinguishing repeated migration from circular migration would be to add the condition of same destination as in previous emigration. This would be, anyhow, a strict definition of circulation departing from the more open idea contained in the EMN and IOM definitions reported above.

Beyond the a) repetition and b) number and type of countries involved, another dimension omitted in the previous definitions but crucial to achieve an inclusive but clearly delimited and measurable definition of circular migration is the c) frequency of the successive moves. Indirectly, the frequency of the moves will be defined by setting the (minimum and maximum) length of stays (both at destination and at origin) after each move and the total period of time over which successive moves need to occur to be considered as part of circular migration (within one year, three, five, ten or thirty).

Recognizing all these limitations in existing definitions of circular migration, in February 2013 the Bureau of the Conference of European Statisticians (CES) created a Task Force on Measuring Circular Migration with the objective of preparing a proposal for a common international statistical definition of circular migration, as well as further clarifying the concepts needed for measuring circular migration. The TEMPER team closely followed the work of the Task Force, and contributed to their activities in the framework of the International Workshop on Methodological Challenges for the Study of Return and Circular Migration, organized in Madrid in January of 2015. At the end of 2016, UNECE Task Force closed their activities with the publication of a report in which two proposals for a statistical definition of circular migration were presented, one general and one extended.

1 *General statistical definition for circular migration (UNECE 2016)*
   A circular migrant is a person who has crossed the national borders of the reporting country at least 3 times over a 10-year period, each time with duration of stay (abroad or in the country) of at least 12 months.

---

[4] Note that here IOM explicitly refers to return to the country of origin as a pre-condition for re-migration to occur. In contrast, this requirement was excluded from its definition of circular migration. Does it imply that circulation excludes return and, therefore, long-term migrants will never circulate in IOM terms?

2 *Extended statistical definition for circular migration (UNECE 2016)*
A circular migrant is a person who has crossed the national borders of the reporting country at least 3 times over a 10-year period, each time with duration of stay (abroad or in the country) of at least 90 days.

These definitions have minimum statistical requirements, as they only require linking migratory events to the persons. In addition, both definitions include precise details on three dimensions a) the identification of origin and destination countries, b) the minimum duration of the stays in both origin and destination and, c) the total period of time over which the incidence of return and/or circular migration has to be measured.

First of all, as UNECE (2016) noted, these statistical definitions of circular migration identify all persons with migration patterns of the form 'immigration-emigration-immigration' (when the reporting country is a destination country) and 'emigration-immigration- emigration' (when the reporting country is an origin country). However, it seems important to note that the definitions do not limit the circularity to closed sets of countries, considering only the repetition of stays in the reporting country: a trajectory A→B→A→C is as circular as the trajectory A→B→A→B, when seen from the perspective of the reporting country A. In other words, circularity is meant to be a repeated stay in the same place (the reporting country), regardless of which is/are the other place(s) where the migrant lived in between. This decision helps making the definition more inclusive but it entails some drawbacks, as commented below.

Secondly, with regard to the period of time over which repeated migrations will be considered part of the same cycle of circular migration, the choice is difficult to assess since there are no previous references or legal frameworks that can serve as helpful benchmarks. In any case, ten years seem a reasonably long period that allows, as far as the dates of the first and the last move are also known, to calculate rates of circulation over periods of shorter length to explore whether and how the incidence and profile of circular migrants changes accordingly, or not.

Finally, the length of stay at destination and at origin constitutes the only basis to distinguish between general and extended circular migration. The extended definition that lowers the minimum length of stay in any of the countries between which the circulation occurs to be at least 3 months (i.e. the typical duration of short-term visas and visa-free periods), represents a major advancement. This is especially true in the current statistical context where sources like population registers only register stays of one year or longer and short-term migrations remain largely neglected. In fact, if migrations of short duration were considered not long enough to be part of the definition – as it happens with the UNSD definition of return, for instance-, the reported incidence of circular migration risks to be seriously underestimated, and the profile of circular migrants will be potentially biased (see more in next sections).

The general definition, in contrast to the extended one, is tied to the international definition of long-term migration (UNSD 1998), and thus allows assessing the share of circular migrants in the total number of long-term international migrants. However, it avoids referring to either origin or destination country and restricts to just 'the reporting country'. By doing so, UNECE definition disconnects the concept of circulation from the concept of return, even if many migrants still qualify for both.[5] This conceptual and empirical overlap between return and circular migration needs to be technical and statistically acknowledged, but also theoretically developed and politically evaluated. In the next sections, we provide some initial hints in this regard.

Towards a better-informed discussion. The TEMPER experience

The TEMPER Surveys. Designing flexible tools for the study of return and circulation

Some available studies based on the analysis of Population Register data in different European countries have concluded that the incidence of circular migration of EU citizens among neighbor countries over periods of almost 40 years seem to be very low, when circular migration is defined from the point of view of the destination country as having emigrated more than once after periods of stay of at least one year. These results raise serious questions on the quality of official population statistics currently available to adequately measure what seems to be understood as 'circular migration' in the EU policy documents.[6] One of the most likely reasons for these results relate to the well-known issue of under-registration of exits (especially of foreigners) in most current statistical systems. In addition to this, the fact that only stays of one year of (intended) duration are registered in these statistical sources remains an additional factor that make population registers unsuitable sources for the study of return and circulation. Population censuses in the latest round at least have collected information on individuals' previous countries of residence one, five or ten years ago, which might be helpful in calculating partial return estimates. Unfortunately, not all countries included the question referred to the three points in time, and not all countries detailed the specific country of residence for each point (sometimes, like in the Argentinean example, only a general reference to 'living abroad' is available). Moreover, censuses usually also apply the same threshold of one (intended) year of stay to consider residential spells relevant to be reported.

---

[5] Migrants who after having spent at least 12 months in their last destination go back to their country of citizenship for a second time, with the intention to stay for at least one year and who actually end up staying in their country of citizenship at least 90 days or more.

[6] A review of the most recent empirical analyses of repeated, onward and circular migration using population registers can be found in the TEMPER Event Review no. 1 at: https://www.temperproject.eu/portfolio_page/international-workshop-methodological-challenges-for-the-study-of-return-and-circular-migration/

Large-scale surveys are more flexible tools than population registers and census data, since all the components of the survey (from questionnaire design to data collection technologies and sampling methodology) can be adjusted to the survey's specific goals without the strict limitations and requirements that are a necessary part of official statistics. The TEMPER Surveys were designed with the goal (among others) to capture and identify return and its characteristics, as well as migration trajectories involving multiple types of circularity, and to compare how their reintegration experiences compared to the life history and outcomes in different domains to those of non-migrants.

The surveys were conducted in four different countries - Argentina, Romania, Senegal and Ukraine - that represent different migration contexts not only because of their socio-economic, cultural and political specificities, but also based on their long-term migration history relative to our EU destinations; their geographical position and distance to those destinations; and most importantly, in terms of the limitations for travel and migration into the EU. One of our four countries is Romania, a recent member of the EU whose citizens fully enjoy freedom of circulation (since 2007). Circular migration, for instance, is likely to be higher precisely among citizens of the EU who face no legal restriction to move between the EU Member States and whose countries of origin and destination are relatively close to each other. The other three TEMPER countries occupy different positions in the range from most to least demanding entry requirements for foreigners. Argentinian citizens enjoy visa-free travel to the EU countries; Ukrainian citizens started enjoying visa-free travel to the EU only in June 2017, but until then required a visa to enter the EU; and Senegalese citizens require a visa to enter the EU. All these factors are likely to result in different levels, types and implications of temporary/permanent, and return/circular migration.

Once someone was accepted as an eligible returned migrant, the survey registered the respondent's full history of international migrations broken into 3-months periods since age 15. Next, multiple questions were made in order to explore the characteristics of interviewees' past mobility patterns and to classify their moves as temporary or not, as voluntary or not, as assisted or not, as circular or not.

To identify our target population a working definition of return was required and, in accordance to it, some basic eligibility criteria were established to allow the interviewers to decide whether someone had to be included or not in the survey. First, since fieldwork was conducted only in the so-called countries of return, we needed to decide what type of link between the interviewees and those countries was the relevant one. Aware of the limitations entailed by citizenship as non-permanent tie between individuals and countries, birth was preferred as the relevant link in this case. In this way, anyone who was born in the countries of survey was potentially eligible to be considered a returnee in his/her country of origin.

Secondly, since temporary migration was one of the foci of the project, our definition of return had to be flexible enough to allow exploring variations in the length of migrations and how they relate or not to different return patterns and outcomes. In other words, short-term migrations could not be excluded as relevant moves in the mobility history of the individuals, and the minimum length to consider someone had migrated or returned was set to 3 months, in line with the UNSD definition of short-term international migration. In addition, note that only actual durations of stay were relevant when defining return, in contrast to the combination of both actual (in destination) and intended (in origin) in the UNSD definition. However, different questions along the questionnaire asked the interviewees about their intended duration of stays to be able to measure how realized behavior differs, or not, from original intentions.

Finally, only some specific destinations within the EU were selected as relevant destinations, depending on the country of origin: Spain for Argentineans, Spain and Germany for Romanians, France and Spain for Senegalese, and Italy and Poland for Ukrainians. In addition, the return had to be a direct move from one of these selected destinations to the country of origin, without intermediate stays in other countries lasting more than three months. By imposing this condition, we ensured that both the interviewer and interviewees easily identified the concept of 'last destination country', to which multiple questions were referred.

In sum, TEMPER returnees are individuals born in one of the selected origin countries and after spending at least three months in one selected destination country go back to their country of birth and stay there for at least three months. Note that no specific effort is made in terms of eligibility to capture circular migrants apart from lowering the length of stays in both destination and origin countries to consider moves as relevant ones.[7] The interviewers, after reconstructing the entire international mobility history of the interviewees with registration of any stay that lasted 3 months or more, made different sets of questions adapted to the characteristics of the mobility trajectory of the individual in order to adequately describe each move in terms of reasons, voluntariness, assistance, legal status, etc.

Mobility trajectories can get extremely complex and messy, especially when they are studied over a long period and both long and short-term moves intend to be covered, as it was the case in TEMPER surveys. The design of a CAPI questionnaire that allowed ex-ante to identify circularity patterns was crucial in guarantee appropriate measurement and characterization of circular migration as different from return or repeated one.

---

[7]   In the case of Ukraine, the threshold was set to 2 months instead, because multiple experts on Ukrainian migration insisted that migration to Poland frequently lasted less than 3 months and we would obtain a very partial view of Ukrainian-Poland migration otherwise. However, in order to keep maximum comparability across the different flows studied in TEMPER, the Ukrainian survey included one additional eligibility requirement: only stays for study and work reasons were considered eligible, so family visits lasting between 2 and 3 months were excluded.

Return migrants:

persons who moved from one of our EU destinations (after staying for at least 3 months) back to his/her country of birth (and stayed there at least 3 months) regardless of the reasons for migration and return.

Repeated (return) migrants:

persons who moved from one of our EU destinations (after staying for at least 3 months) back to his/her country of birth (and stayed there at least 3 months) more than once, regardless of the reasons for migration and return.

Circular migrants:

a. *Strict definition*: returnees who had at least 4 consecutive stays lasting between 3 months and 1 year, alternating country of origin and one specific EU country

b. *Wide definition*: returnees who had at least 3 returns to country of origin following stays of 3 months or more in the EU (any country) over the last 10 years since last return.

Temporary migrants:

a. *Length-based definition*: returnees with stays of 3 to 12 months in their last EU migration

b. *Intentions-based definition*: returnees who intended to stay between 3 and 12 months in their last EU migration

c. *Entry status-based definition*: returnees whose documents to enter their EU selected destination did not allow them a route to permanency.

Box 1 Summary of definitions utilised in TEMPER Origin Surveys

The final samples of interviewed returnees obtained in each country were 253 in Argentina (all from Spain), 599 in Romania (285 from Germany and 314 from Spain), 600 in Senegal (299 from Spain and 301 from France) and 736 in Ukraine (369 from Italy and 367 from Poland). In the following section, we describe the main characteristics of returnees in each of the seven TEMPER flows focusing on the main dimensions considered by the definitions of return previously discussed (temporariness, voluntariness, assistance, etc.) . In addition, we also describe and discuss the impact that utilizing each definition of return has on data collection in terms of sample sizes, as well as on the profile of returnees showed by the data.

Some preliminary results

As we have previously highlighted, in TEMPER design it was crucial to define return in a way that allowed to capture and include in our samples short-term migrants, because the project was particularly aimed at describing in detail different forms of temporary migration including circular migration, which is likely to be more common among short-term migrants.

In fact, one of the first and more surprising results obtained in TEMPER Surveys consists precisely in the very high proportion of short-term migrants among returnees. Overall, approximately half of the total sample of returnees (49% of the 2,188 surveyed returnees) had been between 3 and 12 months in their country of destination in the EU during their last stay there. Obviously, there were important variations across the seven studied flows, from the lowest incidence of short-term migra-tion among returnees in Argentina (24%) to the highest among Ukrainian returnees (84%). Moreover, the proportion of returnees from EU countries previously or cur-rently engaged in circular migration multiplied by two, from approximately 7-8 per-cent to 15-16 percent of total returnees, in the case of migration flows between Sen-egal and Spain/France, depending on whether a strict or extended definition of cir-cular migration was applied. The main difference between these two definitions re-lates to the inclusion or not of short-term migrations, which highlights the limita-tions of the current statistical system to properly measure circular migration since population registers mostly are restricted to measuring changes of residence that implies stays of one year or more at destination.

The implications of this very simple result are many, both scientifically and po-litically speaking. First, by imposing a minimum length of stay at destination of one year or more, as most existing definitions have traditionally required, our statistics and estimates systematically neglect a huge part of contemporary international mo-bility. Such an omission indirectly reinforces some pre-established views on how the standard immigrant is and behaves, and it also tends to distort our ideas about how much and in which ways migrants are able to contribute to their countries of origin. Note that just by setting the minimum duration threshold (at destination) in 3 or 12 months would have implied that between 24 and 84 percent of the individ-uals interviewed by TEMPER would have been not eligible and, therefore, the ob-tained sample would have been a completely different one – not to mention the implications for a fieldwork already very difficult because of the inexistence of re-liable sampling frames for such a rare population.

Moreover, our data also suggest, as discussed above, that intended durations and actual ones often diverge. If individuals for whom intended and actual stays' dura-tion are different from the rest of migrants also in other dimensions, the type of return migrant we capture when using a definition based on intended durations will be a biased sample of total returnees. In Romania, for instance, 20% of returnees who at the time of the survey had stayed in Romania for at least 12 months declared that, at the time of returning, they intended to stay in Romania for less than a year. Thus, these individuals would have been excluded from a survey that sticks to the UNSD (1998) definition of return. In the other countries, the corresponding per-centages were 11% in Argentina, 16% in Senegal, and also 16% in Ukraine.

In addition to this, TEMPER data also illustrate how frequently other dimensions that appear in different definitions of return such as the existence of some sort of official and organized assistance, or the voluntary nature of the decision to return, actually appear among returnees. With regard to the participation of returnees in programs assisting people on their return, none of the 600 returnees interviewed in Romania had participated in such a program, in Ukraine only three individuals re-ported to have done so; in contrast, in Senegal and Argentina their numbers were higher, affecting to 6.5 and 9 percent of our samples, respectively. If we pay atten-tion to the voluntary nature of the decision, 15% of the returnees interviewed in

Senegal reported to have been expelled or deported from their last country of destination in the EU, and 21% declared their return had been 'completely non-voluntary', with an obvious large overlap between the two groups. The proportion of returnees who were expelled or deported in the other three countries was much lower (1 and 1,5% in Romania and Ukraine, and none in Argentina), although the proportion that considered their return completely non-voluntary was always a bit higher: approximately 4% in Argentina and Romania, and 5% in Ukraine.

In sum, adopting one or other definition of return strongly affects the size of the (sub)population of returnees sampled in our surveys and, most likely, their profile. In fact, our results show interesting results in this regard. Overall, sex and age composition of the samples resulting from applying different definitions of return in the data collection do not vary much for any of the migration flows studied in TEMPER. In contrast, characteristics more directly related to migration such as the period of first migration, the reasons for return or the extent to which return was prepared in advance or not, and the remittance behaviour of migrants while being abroad, vary a lot. Finally, there are some flow-specific results dimensions that appear very affected by the application of one or other definition of return such as the reunification of the partner at destination by Senegalese male returnees, or the legal status that returnees enjoyed at the time of their arrival at destination in the case of the Romanian flow.

Similarly, as expected, the proportion of circular migrants found among returnees reveals to be strongly dependent on the definition of return applied during the fieldwork. By applying the TEMPER definition that allows short-term migration and short-term returns, the proportion of repeated and circular migrants reached up to 33 and 10 percent of the Senegalese and Ukrainian flows, whereas the application of a definition that required stays at both destination and return countries of at least one year long made these percentages drop down to 10 and 0.5 percent, respectively. To the extent that circular migrants are different from one-shot migrants, the utilisation of return definitions that are very demanding in terms of stays' duration, contribute to keep them hidden from the debate, especially in their more spontaneous profile. As a consequence, the political debate about the possibilities of encouraging circulation as an effective way of managing part of current migration flows, and how to do it, becomes distorted and biased, and the myth of permanent settlement at destination indirectly reinforced.

Conclusions

The lack of a common and measurable definition has seriously hampered the collection of empirical evidence that permits to quantify the incidence of return and circular migration nowadays. In addition, it has damaged the possibility to identify possibilities for the potential encouragement of these two forms of mobility among current and prospective migrants, as well as the existing barriers and obstacles for such encouragement.

Definitions need to be made based on what needs to be known; however, it is equally important to consider what can be feasibly measured with the existing data sources. Given the multiple limitations of censuses and population registers, in their current design, to identify and properly measure return and circular migration, large-scale surveys may represent an alternative to temporarily obtain some preliminary estimates of the incidence of these relevant phenomena and their characteristics.

The current article has provided preliminary evidence, based on the TEMPER surveys, on the strong impact that using different definitions of return (and circulation) have. By comparing measurements derived from the application of different definitions of return, the results confirmed the crucial importance of including short-term migrations, if the reality of contemporary international migration (including circulation) wants to be properly captured and understood in order to design and implement effective migration and development policies. Official statistics need to start including a 3-month threshold because short-term migrations seem to represent an important and increasing share of international migration nowadays. And also because without it we are losing important phenomena such as circular migration, which has received an upsurge of policy interest from the EU, among others. In addition, the uncertainty associated with intentions in the field of migration clearly advise against using intended durations in the definition of return migration. Durations should always be directly and precisely measured.

Finally, the numerical and compositional impact of utilizing different definitions of return when we collect data on returnees reveals to be strongly context-sensitive, which obviously affects the interpretation of cross-country comparative analyses, even if the same concept of return is utilized. For instance, non-spontaneous returns can mean very different things according to the context: the 'non-spontaneous' returns in Senegal were mostly individuals who had been expelled/deported although they originally planned to stay at destination for a long time/permanently, and include almost no circular migrant. In contrast, in Ukraine it was just people coming back for administrative reasons and planning to move again, with a high share of circular migrants among them.

In terms of the returnees' profile, not all characteristics seem equally affected by changing the return definition. While socio-demographic characteristics of the interviewed returnees remain relatively stable regardless of the definition of return applied (age, sex or educational level), the impact of changing definitions is much larger when looking at other more directly migration dimensions such as incidence of repeated migration or remittances behavior.

Looking at the concrete definitions of return that we have revised in this article, it is evident that the most restrictive one is the one contained in the Return Directive, which excludes spontaneous returns as part of its concept. Although this is obviously reasonable because the Directive is just interested in this type of return, the terminology used, along with the lack of good and systematic data on spontaneous return, has strongly contributed to a very distorted and misleading political debate. Similarly, the option for return definitions that impose demanding requirements in terms of stays' duration both at origin and, especially, at destination, contributes to keep out of the public debate spontaneous forms of both short-term and circular migration to the EU, which might be especially common in some specific flows such as the Senegalese or the Ukrainian ones. It is obviously very difficult to foster a fruitful debate on the feasibility and political convenience of promoting temporary and circular migration as an alternative to long-term and settlement oriented migration, if the only types of temporariness and circularity that we are able to measure and identify are the non-spontaneous ones.

Data measure some realities, and contribute to hide others. What data are able to measure and make visible largely depends on the definition of the phenomenon adopted to start with. For this reason, when talking about return, making the definition as inclusive as possible and collecting complementary data that allow to identify different types and dimensions of return seems to be the most reasonable solution to properly capture a complex, changing and context-sensitive phenomenon as this.

References

Communication from the Commission to the European Parliament, the Council, the European Economic and Social Committee and the Committee of the Regions 'On circular migration and mobility partnerships between the European Union and third countries' COM (2007) 248 final

Directive 2008/115/EC of the European Parliament and of the Council of 16 December 2008 on common standards and procedures in Member States for returning illegally staying third-country nationals. Available at https://eur-lex.europa.eu/legal-content/EN/TXT/?uri=CELEX % 25%203A32008L0115

European Migration Network (2011) Temporary and Circular Migration: empirical evidence, current policy practice and future options in EU Member States. Available at https://ec.europa.eu/home-affairs/sites/homeaffairs/files/what-we-do/networks/european_migration_network/reports/docs/emn-studies/circular-migration/26a._sweden_national_report_circular_migration_final_version_9dec2010_en.pdf

International Organisation for Migration (2011) Glossary on Migration. International Migration Law no. 25. Available at https://publications.iom.int/system/files/pdf/iml25_1.pdf

International Organisation for Migration (2019) Glossary on Migration. International Migration Law no. 34. Available at https://publications.iom.int/system/files/pdf/iml_34_glossary.pdf

Martin, Philip (1997) Guest worker policies for the twenty-first century. New Community. Vol 23. No 4. October. 483-494

TEMPER Team (2015) International Workshop on Methodological Challenges for the Study of Return and Circular Migration. Event Review no. 1, Available at https://www.temperproject.eu/wp-content/uploads/2015/06/Event-Review-1-2015.pdf

United Nations (1998) Recommendations on Statistics on International Migration, Revision 1. Department of Economic and Social Affairs Statistics Division. Statistical Papers, no. 58, Rev.1 Available at https://unstats.un.org/unsd/publication/seriesm/seriesm_58rev1e.pdf

United Nations Economic Commission for Europe (2016) Defining and Measuring Circular Migration. Final report of the Task Force on Measuring Circular Migration. Available at https://www.unece.org/fileadmin/DAM/stats/publications/2016/ECECESSTAT20165_E.pdf

Return, Reintegration and the Role of State

Özge Bilgili, Sonja Fransen

Abstract

The main objective of this paper is to discuss the role of receiving state in the reception and reintegration of returning migrants. For a comprehensive discussion we argue that it is important first and foremost to have a good understanding of what the return and reintegration entail and how these processes are defined. Therefore, this paper firstly reflects on current definitions of return and reintegration. In particular, we highlight that there is no single type of returnee and the diverse experiences of returnees deem different approaches of support both in the process of reception and reintegration. Moreover, we acknowledge the multi-dimensional character of reintegration processes and call for a holistic approach. On the basis of these discussions, we provide examples from across the world and draw attention to what more states can do to promote reintegration. In conclusion, we emphasize the relevance of addressing reintegration through a social cohesion and socioeconomic inequality lens to address the various dimensions of reintegration and to incorporate the perspective of non-returnees.

Introduction

Return migration has been increasingly integrated into international and national development agendas over the past years. A great emphasis is put on the potential of return migrants to contribute to the economic development of their origin country through knowledge transfers, skills transfers, investments, and their transnational networks that could enable new international business collaborations (Debnath 2016). Migrants often accumulate human capital while residing abroad and apply their skills and knowledge upon return. This may improve their own livelihoods but their economic engagement may also contribute to the socioeconomic development of their communities. Because of these potential spill overs, many migrant-sending countries are increasingly interested in return migrants as a potential 'brain gain' (Olesen 2002) and create strategies to enhance their potentially positive impact on the national economy. Migrant host countries have also been quick to adopt positive views on return migration-development linkages and to integrate these into their migration and asylum policies (Van Houte & Davids 2008), e.g. through the implementation of national voluntary return programmes.

Return migration is a common social phenomenon and is often seen as a natural part of the 'migration cycle'. Migration scholarship has shown that temporary and circular migration are livelihood strategies for many individuals and households (Massey, 1998). Moreover, a permanent settlement abroad may not be possible or even desired by migrants. So, many migrants consequently return to their country of origin – either permanently or temporarily. Azose & Raftery (2019) estimated that approximately 25 percent of all global migrations between 2010 and 2015 were individuals returning to their birth country. The largest return migration flows took place within well-established migration corridors: between the United States and Mexico (1.3 million), from the United Arab Emirates to India (380,000) and from the Ukraine to Russia 358,000). Similarly, the OECD (2017) estimated that OECD countries with the largest outflows of foreign-born populations in 2017 were Germany (886,000), Korea (349,000) and Spain (280,000).

Although return migration is often seen as a natural part of the migration cycle, it is not always a natural process (Cassarino, 2004; 2014). Individuals may be forced to return, either because of a 'failed' migration attempt or because destination countries forcedly remove migrants or refugees through expulsion policies. Returnees consequently differ in their willingness to return and preparedness for their return and reintegration (Cassarino 2014). After return, the process of reintegration may consequently be difficult as well. A successful reintegration is, firstly, dependent on structural characteristics of the origin country, such as the availability of employment (Fransen 2015). Secondly, some returnees re-integrate more easily than others. Various factors related to the migration cycle, such as conditions during migration and return conditions, significantly impact the reintegration process (Fransen & Bilgili 2018).

These challenges that often accompany return and reintegration processes, call for an active involvement of the migrant-sending state to support and facilitate the return and reintegration of their citizens. To comprehend the role of the state in return and reintegration processes, we first need to have an understanding of what these processes entail and how they are defined. Therefore in this paper we will 1) reflect on current definitions of return and reintegration, the implications of applying these definitions and their potential limitations; 2) document the challenges that may occur after return and how these could be addressed by policies of the origin state; and 3) argue that reintegration should be treated through a social cohesion 'lens', to address various dimensions of reintegration and to incorporate the perspective of non-returnees.

Return migration & receiving returnees

Return migration has been defined in various ways. One of the earliest definitions of return migration was proposed by Gmelch (1980). He defined return as: *"the movement of emigrants back to their homelands to resettle"* (Gmelch, 1980: 136). Implicitly, this definition suggests that returnees go back to their country of origin to settle, which implies that return migration is a more or less permanent move. A currently commonly used definition is the one proposed by the United Nations Statistics Division (1998: 94), which defines return migrants as *"persons returning to their country of citizenship after having been international migrants (whether short-term or long-term) in another country and who are intending to stay in their country for at least a year."* Cassarino (2008) builds on the UNSD definition and defines a return migrant as:

> *"... any person returning to his/her country of origin, in the course of the last ten years, after having been an international migrant (whether short-term or long-term) in another country. Return may be permanent or temporary. It may be independently decided by the migrant or forced by unexpected/adverse circumstances."* (Cassarino 2008: 3).

These definitions clearly suggest that there is no single type of returnee. On the contrary, return populations are often very heterogeneous and consist of individuals who vary in their background characteristics, their migration experiences, their return and reintegration aspirations and their intentions for re- or onwards migration (See Figure 1). The experiences of return migrants and the conditions of return will clearly define the needs of returnees in terms of social, economic or legal support for reintegration into their origin society (Cerase, 1974). Weighing the impact of all these conditions in identifying the social, economic and legal needs of returnees is of great importance to provide the necessary support in the short to long term.

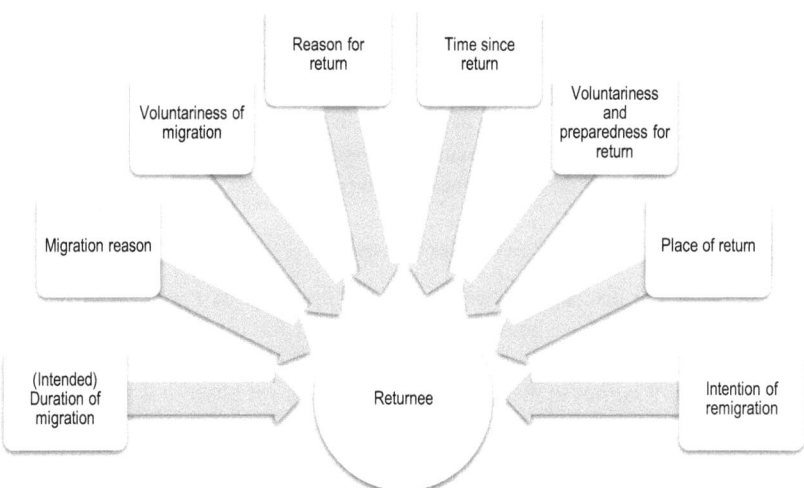

Figure 1. Returnees and their migration-related experiences

The Global Forum for Migration and Development's database collects practices across the world regarding what states have been doing to support the return process. The database provides more than 70 recent examples (see www.gfmd.org for more information). Here we highlight two existing approaches. First of all, considering the various experiences and conditions of migrants, states need to *ensure that return takes place in an orderly and safe manner*, especially for those in more vulnerable situations and those who lack resources – for example, unaccompanied minors or victims of human trafficking. The initial reception at government centres can entail short-term efforts including immediate medical needs, identity documents, legal orientation and counselling and emergency shelter when needed (Soto, Domingues-Villegas, Argueta and Capps, 2019). One way to establish orderly return includes developing One Stop Centers where returnees can receive information on economic, health and training services (Kuschminder and Ricard-Guay, 2017). Sri Lanka, with the aim of increasing reintegration services to returning workers, implements this strategy with support from International Labour Organisation.

Secondly, another strategy comprises assisting return by *supporting the preparedness of migrants for return while they are abroad*. Considering that those with more positive social and economic experiences abroad have better reintegration outcomes upon their return, this is a relevant approach that can be considered by emigration states (Fransen & Bilgili, 2018). The Philippines, a country that is known to support their labour migrants extensively through a variety of projects, has two unique programs that do just that. For example the Sa Pinas, Ikaw and Maam Sir program (see Battistella and Center, 2018), trains domestic workers in destination countries to receive their teaching qualifications. The goal is that these individuals are able to take up a teacher position in their home community upon return and get out of domestic work. Such a certification program is offered in a variety of countries including Hong Kong, Israel and Thailand (Kuschminder and Ricard-Guay, 2017). Another program provides an onsite assessment at Philippines Overseas Labor offices in destination countries to assess the competencies of migrants to see if they can take up a preferred line of work upon their return. When a worker passes the competency assessment, they can get a national certificate that is valid for five years to help them to find employment upon return.

Recommendations for receiving returnees

In relation to the discussion above, without aiming to be comprehensive, in this short section we propose some recommendations for improving the reception of returnees.

First, when it comes to receiving returnees, what we observe is that many countries lack the institutional and administrative mechanisms to effectively register return migrants. Not having a database or at least an estimation of the flow and stock of return migrants makes it more difficult for countries to assess the scope of return and reach out to returnees for support. To be able to provide effective support and enhance the potential benefit of returnees in the local development, it is important to have an estimate of who returns, with what skills, when and where. In this regard, such mechanisms of tracking are necessary both for the initial phase of return and settlement but also for the long term in terms of promoting reintegration.

Second, considering the involvement of multiple organizations in the implementation of reception strategies, it is of great importance to enhance interagency collaboration and to ensure that the activities undertaken by governmental organizations as well as civil society organizations are complementary. As suggested by the One Stop Center example in Sri Lanka, establishment of such mechanisms may help the returnees in the most effective way, but also help coordinate the processes in a more efficient way.

Third, it is crucial to take into account the fact that return conditions are very diverse for different types of returnees and their dependents. Depending on the conditions of return process, returnees may have unforeseen needs. For instance, repatriated returnees may need to obtain official identification documentation without which they may have struggles accessing services. Not to oversee, victims of human trafficking may be in need of specific support programs that may refer them to rehabilitation shelters or address their mental and physical health needs. Moreover, often returnees are not alone and may have dependents who travel with them. The services provided to returnees should not therefore only address the adult returnees themselves but also their children and their needs for example in relation to access to education and health services. While these efforts exist in multiple country contexts, they need to be incorporated in a more systematic way within a global framework on receiving returnees.

In relation to this, previous research has shown that despite information campaigns, not all returnees are aware of the programs they may benefit from. In the case of self-supported returnees, if they are not captured by government systems at reception centres, they may miss out on the opportunities that could potentially boost their reintegration.

Reintegration & supporting returnees

There is little consensus among policy makers and academics on how reintegration is defined or operationalized. Reintegration is often mentioned simultaneously with the concept of sustainable return, particularly in policy circles. Joanna Macrae for example argues that, by and large, reintegration *"is equated with the achievement of a sustainable return"* (Macrae, 1999: 36). Similarly, a UNHCR report from 1997 indicated that sustainable return is the equivalent of *"effective reintegration"* (UNHCR, 1997: 2). Implicitly the assumption is made that successful reintegration will lead to a sustainable return.

The narrow definition regards return as sustainable when return is permanent, meaning that former migrants do not emigrate again (Black and Gent, 2006). This definition is highly contested because migration can be an economically viable strategy for households. Sending a household member abroad does not necessarily occur only in the absence of successful reintegration. For financial insurance or as a safety net, families may continue to send one of the members of their family abroad (Massey, 1998). The wider definition of sustainability focuses on whether return migrants are doing well compared to non-returnees – which overlaps with the UNHCR definition of reintegration. This definition focuses primarily on legal rights and duties of returnees but in the past years researchers acknowledge more and more the fact that reintegration is a multi-dimensional concept (Bilgili, Kuschminder and Siegel, 2016; Fransen and Bilgili, 2018)). Reintegration is therefore a concept that can be operationalized and measured in relation to different dimensions of life.

Cassarino (2004), made a distinction between economic, social, legal, and cultural reintegration. In his view, economic reintegration refers to successful participation in the labour market, access to employment, and the ability to create a sustainable livelihood. Social reintegration encompasses participation in organizations, engaging in social interactions with other society members, and acceptance among family and friends. Legal reintegration denotes the establishment of citizenship and rights in the country of return, including the ability to participate in local elections and judicial processes. Finally, cultural reintegration refers to participation in local cultural events and acceptance of norms and values of the society. Cassarino's dimensions refer more to actual behaviour or acts of participation and are therefore easier to use for research purposes.

Even though the different dimensions of reintegration are acknowledged in the academic literature; when looking at policies and practices, one can easily see the major focus on economic reintegration. This emphasis most likely is driven by the expectation of states to enhance the potential economic impact of returnees on the national economy. And especially in the case of labour migration, returnees are seen as 'ordinary citizens' whose social integration is assumed to take place naturally. While we will be challenging this assumption in our discussion, this section focuses primarily on measures related to economic reintegration.

Regarding economic reintegration, in the literature we find series of interventions including: skills profiling upon return and information on training opportunities to improve employability in the country of return; providing information on business opportunities and jobs opportunity in the country of return; information on regulations concerning decent employment (salaried employment or self-employment); facilitating the portability of social security benefits; providing technical and financial support especially for entrepreneurs.

In their analysis of reintegration policies in Ethiopia, Kuschminder and Ricard-Guay (2017) illustrate that in the case of Ethiopia the governmental efforts for returnees primarily focus on economic reintegration. The authors highlight that the support for the reintegration of migrants is a relatively new area of concern for the country. While the initial support services put in place for returnees were primarily driven by emergency and humanitarian needs of the more than 160,000 labour migrants deported from Saudi Arabia in 2013, pretty quickly a shift was also made to support the economic reintegration of the returnees. Since in Ethiopia there is no national policy or strategy to tackle return and reintegration, a response to reintegration was developed through the combined efforts of international organizations, NGOs, and the Government. In the development of this response, a major emphasis was put on the economic reintegration of returnees beyond responding to humanitarian needs. The government in collaboration with International Labour Organisation and involvement of local and regional governments developed an economic reintegration strategy.

The authors summarize the approach in six aspects: 1) identification , selection and referral of returnees; 2) vocational or entrepreneurship and motivational training; 3) development of an economic reintegration or business plan during which job opportunities are mapped out or a business plan is developed; 4) allocation of land/work and acquisition of necessary licenses; 5) access to financial services and 6) monitoring of progress steps (see Kuschminder and Ricard-Guay 2017 for more detailed information).

Also in Mexico and other countries in the region including Honduras, Guatemala and El Salvador, most measures for returnees relate to economic reintegration and include components such as vocational training, microloans for small businesses and entrepreneurial projects (See Soto et al. (2019) for more detailed information). In Mexico, one additional approach is to promote sustainable employment projects that require pooled funds and collaboration among multiple returnees. While bureaucratic and implementation challenges continue to exist, it is important to note that in all these countries at least the three principles of supporting reintegration have been established. As indicated by Soto et al. (2019: 13), since 2015 the comment elements include:

- Differentiated services for migrants according to their needs and characteristics
- A whole-of-government approach in which multiple agencies coordinate efforts
- Municipal-level reintegration services with the aim of expanding the geographic coverage of such services

Recommendations for reintegration policies and practices

As mentioned earlier, receiving states acknowledge the importance of integrating returnees to the labour market. This however should not go at the expense of supporting other needs of returnees. The social, cultural and psychological dimensions of reintegration are addressed marginally, if at all in many countries, especially in the case of voluntary return. The underlying assumption of this can be that returnees are seen as 'ordinary citizens' who will naturally integrate back to their communities. They are assumed to have the same set of cultural values and norms as the local populations, have access to social networks through family and friends and go back to their origin community. This suggests that they have the necessary support available in hand to find housing and employment and to feel home again. However, this is not always the case.

The assumptions related to social dimensions of reintegration ignore the fact that migrants are self-selected and are not a random group of individuals. Returnees may originate from economically shrinking local areas or they belong to a marginalized ethnic group for whom migration is a viable short-term solution. Upon return, they may have disrupted social networks or may not necessarily go back to their origin community and therefore may need to adapt to new communities. Moreover, while they may have required new sets of skills, know-how and experiences, they may also have new sets of values and norms that may clash with their origin culture. As often mentioned in the integration literature, they may have at least temporarily a culture shock. So their return may not necessarily mean an immediate social and cultural adaptation.

All that is to say that social integration of returnees in their communities of return needs to be supported. In some countries, there is some evidence suggesting that there is prejudice and negative stereotypes towards returnees (Soto et al., 2019). These issues at the societal level are as important as structural dimensions of reintegration. In this regard, a more holistic approach to reintegration can be valuable both for returnees and their larger community. As more and more discussed in the literature, taking into consideration the subjective evaluations of returnees regarding their reintegration process can also be of great value to better understand their situation and needs (Fransen & Bilgili, 2018; Bilgili, Kuschminder & Siegel, 2017). The subjective component of reintegration may be an important element to properly understand reintegration outcomes. From an objective viewpoint, returnees may have reintegrated because they have jobs, access to healthcare and other necessities. At the same time however, feelings of reintegration may be low because of social reintegration challenges (see also McGavin, 2017). Particularly in conflict-affected context in which social ties are damaged, reintegration support should not overlook the subjective element of reintegration (see, e.g. Haider, 2009). Vice versa, returnees may feel happy to return to their origin country or community even when they are not reintegrated from an economic point of view. Moreover, reintegration and particularly social reintegration is a two-way process in which both returnees and their community or society members have to adapt. The perspectives of non-returnees are therefore crucial to fully understand the reintegration process, particularly when reintegration is perceived as a broader process

Conclusion

The main objective of this paper was to discuss the role of receiving state in the reception and reintegration of returning migrants. For a comprehensive discussion we argued that it is important first and foremost to have a good understanding of what the processes of return and reintegration entail and how they are defined. Therefore, we firstly reflected on current definitions of return and reintegration. In particular, we highlighted that there is no single type of returnee and the diverse experiences of returnees deem different approaches of support both in the process of reception and reintegration. Moreover, we acknowledged the multi-dimensional character of reintegration processes and called for a holistic approach that takes into account structural and sociocultural dimensions of reintegration. On the basis of several examples from across the world we drew attention to what states have been doing, but more importantly we brought attention some additional issues that states can consider when developing policies and programs to improve reception and re-integration of returnees. We particularly emphasized the relevance of addressing reintegration through a social cohesion lens to address various dimensions of rein-tegration and to incorporate the perspective of non-returnees.

In conclusion, we would like to address how reintegration could be approached from a social inequality perspective. The underlying assumption in this conven-tional perspective is that reintegration is achieved when all society members alike are able to exercise their rights as citizens and when returnees are fully absorbed into the local population, meaning that they do not differ significantly from other society members. This definition is most often used for research purposes as it rel-atively easy to operationalize. It is also a valuable way for states to monitor and measure reintegration in different dimensions of life in short, medium and long term. However, reintegration is an all-encompassing process that affects an entire community, including those who did not move (internationally). In cases of large-scale return, for example, resources frequently have to be shared with more people, which leads to lower living standards for all households in areas of return. Even though from an objective viewpoint returnees and locals might have equal assets and opportunities; the overall pie may have become smaller, leading to poverty (Fransen, 2015; Hammond, 1999). Therefore, an important way to tackle reintegra-tion would be to integrate reintegration issues within the larger migration govern-ance and treat them in accordance with the broader development policies of the country in a coherent manner.

We conclude by bringing attention to the fact that this paper primarily focused on economic migrants. Repatriation of internally displaced people and refugees however remain as one of the major components of return migration. Besides eco-nomic reintegration which is a big challenge, social and cultural reintegration may be particularly difficult for returnees who fled ethnic tensions and return to war-torn societies in which social ties may be damaged, or for migrants who spent long pe-riods abroad. The role of states in these contexts which is often combined with hu-manitarian actors' efforts is therefore a relevant topic of further inquiry. Rogge (1994) specifically draws attention to the ways in which reintegration support is provided by humanitarian actors in these contexts. He states that humanitarian sup-port is often present for a few years only until all refugees are returned and therefore focuses mainly on short-term reintegration goals (See Fransen, 2015 for a case study of Burundi). However, ignoring the issues related to long-term reintegration which may take 10-15 years, if not generations is extremely important to consider. Future discussions on reintegration may particularly highlight what states can do in collab-oration with other relevant stakeholders (international organisations, NGOs and CSOs) with short to long-term vision.

References

Azose, J. J., & Raftery, A. E., 2019. Estimation of emigration, return migration, and transit migration between all pairs of countries. *Proceedings of the National Academy of Sciences, 116*(1), 116-122.

Bilgili, Ö. Kuschminder, K. & Siegel, M., 2017. Return Migrants' Perceptions of Living Conditions in Ethiopia: A Gendered Analysis. *Migration Studies*. Published online: 10 August 2017.

Battistella, G. and Center, S.M., 2018. Return Migration: A Conceptual and Policy Framework. 2018 International Migration Policy Report Perspectives on the Content and Implementation of the Global Compact for Safe, Orderly, and Regular Migration.

Black, R., & Gent, S., 2006. Sustainable return in post-conflict contexts. *International Migration*, 44(3), 15–38.

Cassarino, J. P., 2004. Theorising Return Migration: The Conceptual Approach to Return Migrants Revisited. International Journal on Multicultural Societies, UNESCO, 2004, 6 (2), pp. 253-279.

Cassarino, J. P., 2014. A case for return preparedness. In Global and Asian perspectives on international migration (pp. 153-165). Springer, Cham.

Cassarino, J. P. (ed.). 2008. Return Migrants to the Maghreb Countries: Reintegration and Development Challenges. Return Migration and Development Platform (RDP). MIREM, RSCAS, EUI, Florence.

Cerase, F.P., 1974. Expectations and reality: a case study of return migration from the United States to Southern Italy. *International Migration Review*, 8(2), pp. 245-262.

Debnath, P., 2016. Leveraging Return Migration for Development: The Role of Countries of Origin- A Literature Review. KNOMAD Working Paper 17, November 2016. Washington D.C.: World Bank.

Fransen, S., 2015. The socio-economic sustainability of refugee return: Insights from Burundi. *Population, Space and Place*. Early view available online. DOI: 10.1002/psp.1976.

Fransen, S., & Bilgili, Ö., 2018. Who reintegrates? The constituents of reintegration of displaced populations. *Population, Space and Place*. 24 (6), 1-13.

Global Forum for Migration and Development, 2019. Policies and Practices Database. Accesible at: https://www.gfmd.org/pfp/ppd

Gmelch, G., 1980. Return migration. Annual review of anthropology, 9(1), 135-159.

Haider, H., 2009. (Re) Imagining coexistence: Striving for sustainable return, reintegration and reconciliation in Bosnia and Herzegovina. *International Journal of Transitional Justice*, 3(1), pp.91-113.

Hammond, L., 1999. Examining the discourse of repatriation: towards a more proactive theory of return migration. *The end of the refugee cycle*, pp. 227-244.

Kuschminder, K. and Ricard-Guay, A., 2018. Reintegration background report. International Labour Organizational. Accesible at https://www.ilo.org/addisababa/information-resources/publications/WCMS_647745/lang--en/index.htm

Macrae, J., 1999. Aiding peace... and war: UNHCR, returnee reintegration, and the relief-development debate. United Nations High Commissioner for Refugees, Centre for Documentation and Research

Massey, D. et al. 1998. Chapter 2 Contemporary theories of international migration. In "Worlds in motion" (pp. 17-59). Oxford: Clarendon Press.

McGavin, K. 2017. (Be)Longings: Diasporic pacific islanders and the meaning of home. In Taylor, J. and H. Lee (Eds) (2017). Mobilities of Return. Pacific Perspectives (pp. 123–146). Canberra: ANU Press.

OECD, 2017. OECD International Migration Database and Labour Market Outcomes of Immigrants. Paris: OECD.

Olesen, H., 2002. Migration, return, and development: An institutional perspective. *International migration*, 40(5), 125-150.

Soto, A.G.R., Dominguez-Villegas, R., Argueta, L. and Capps, R., 2019. Sustainable Reintegration: Strategies to Support Migrants Returning to Mexico and Central America. Migration Policy Institute. Washington.

United Nations High Commissioner for Refugees, 1996. Handbook Voluntary Repatriation: International Protection. Geneva: UNHCR.

United Nations Statistics Division, 1998. Recommendations on Statistics of International Migration, Revision 1. New York: United Nations.

Van Houte, M., & Davids, T., 2008. Development and return migration: from policy panacea to migrant perspective sustainability. *Third World Quarterly*, 29(7), 1411-1429.

Back to Afghanistan: Expectations and Challenges between Development and Reintegration

Marieke van Houte

Abstract

Repatriation programmes of refugees and asylum seekers, initiated by receiving countries, are based on the implicit or explicit assumption that going back 'home' is the most natural and desirable thing to do. Particularly after international military intervention, repatriating refugees is intended to demonstrate that stability was created and that the mission was successful. Yet poor reintegration and re-emigration and altogether low return rates show the often-limited success of these repatriation programmes. Based on fieldwork from 2012 among 35 Afghan return migrants, this chapter addresses the need for a better and more in-depth understanding of the lived experiences of (return) migrants, in order to better respond to their needs. The chapter shows that rather than their repatriation signifying the end of their journey, mobility continues to be an essential desire in the lives of Afghan return migrants. This chapter questions the notion of sustainable reintegration and highlights the importance of post-return mobility as an indicator for the wellbeing of returnees.

Introduction

Return and sustainable reintegration of refugees and asylum seekers after conflict is high on the humanitarian and political agenda of receiving states. Increasingly since the 1990s, return and sustainable reintegration has become the preferred durable solution for refugees and rejected asylum seekers that is even expected to contribute to development[1]. Despite the increasing interest however, repatriation programmes both fail to meet the needs of returnees and consistently fail to achieve policy goals.

Research shows that return assistance does not have a positive effect and is even negatively correlated with reintegration (Ruben, Van Houte, and Davids 2009, Fransen and Bilgili 2018, Flahaux 2017), and many returnees re-emigrate or aspire to do so (Schuster and Majidi 2015). In terms of policy efficacy, after an initial increase of return rates of refugees in the 1990s, these return rates significantly decreased from 2004 onwards and are now globally at less than 3 per cent of the refugee population (UNHCR 2016). Zooming in on rejected asylum seekers from Europe, research on 12 European countries for six main asylum-seeking nationalities

---

[1] See Van Houte 2016 for a more elaborate discussion of this trend.

shows that the majority of rejected asylum seekers do not return, with estimated return rates between 4 and 44 per cent (Van Houte and Leerkes 2019). Research consistently shows that rejected asylum seekers often do everything that is in their power, and will prefer very marginal living circumstances in the 'host' country over returning (Leerkes, Galloway, and Kromhout 2010). A better understanding of the experience of return, including successes but also challenges and concerns after return and the factors that affect the post-return experience, will therefore not only help to do more justice to the situation of returnees, but can also contribute to more effective policy making that responds to the needs of returnees.

In this chapter I specifically discuss the case of Afghan returnees from Europe to the capital Kabul, where I did fieldwork among 35 returnees in 2012. Based on insights from a study from 2007-2008, in which it appeared that the motivation to return was a key factor, I purposefully sampled the widest possible scope of return motivations and conditions: from deportees to Afghan-European citizens returning as expats. The methodology entailed an autobiographical narrative approach with participatory elements such as timeline drawing and photo voice with returnees, complemented with group discussions and expert interviews.

Afghanistan has experienced recurrent conflicts over the past 40 years, with subsequent refugee flows. It has been estimated that ten million Afghans – one third of the population – have been refugees at least once during this period (Koser 2014); and that more than half of the Afghan population has migrated at some point since the conflict started (Oeppen 2009). Repatriation movements occurred after each episode of conflict. The overthrow of the Taliban in 2002 in particular sparked Afghan return movements from Europe. In addition to forced and assisted return of rejected asylum seekers and undocumented migrants, the improved ability to travel to Afghanistan also prompted small-scale voluntary return movements of Afghans who were not legally obliged to return (Blitz, Sales, and Marzano 2005, Van Houte, Siegel, and Davids 2016). Some took advantage of job opportunities in areas of reconstruction, interpreting and consultancy sectors or sold or rented family properties (Oeppen 2012). Others returned to take up positions within ministries, government institutions and the private sector (Fischer and van Houte 2019).

The case of Afghanistan continues to be relevant, and even increasingly so: Since 2014, increased Afghan outmigration as well as intensified repatriation and deportation programmes are co-occuring (Ruttig 2015, Majidi 2018, Dimitriadi 2018), as well as re-emigration of deported migrants (Schuster and Majidi 2015). The Afghan case shows the changing nature of repatriation and deportation: the spaces and grounds to find protection are shrinking, and repatriation and deportation increasingly extends to vulnerable groups (Majidi 2018).

In previous publications, I have discussed in detail how involuntary returnees had less room to manoeuvre than voluntary returnees to negotiate a sense of belonging in both economic, social, institutional and cultural terms (Van Houte 2016). This may be a rather intuitive finding that is also confirmed by other studies (Ruben, Van Houte, and Davids 2009, Fransen and Bilgili 2018, Flahaux 2017). Nevertheless, a study on Mexican return shows no significant differences between deported and non-deported returnees (Hagan, Wassink, and Castro 2019). I argue in this chapter that a closer analysis on the mechanisms behind the perceived differences between voluntary and involuntary return reveals structural patterns of inequality as well as resilient responses underneath the voluntary – involuntary divide.

In what follows, I will first briefly discuss the policy rationales and academic and empirical discussion on the assumptions and shortcomings of the concept of reintegration, and introduce an alternative concept of 'belonging'. Next, I will discuss different post-return strategies of belonging and determinants of these strategies, before discussing the concept of mobility as the key driver of these strategies. I conclude that return and 'reintegration' is only 'sustainable if return occurs under the condition of continued transnational mobility and strengthened human capacity and its implications for policy.

Policy rationales and empirical realities of return and 'sustainable reintegration'

The problem of our lack of understanding of return really starts with the concepts with which we study it: Sustainable reintegration is a policy term that most of the times remains implicit or is assumed to be self-explanatory. Yet the term emerges from three different policy frames, leading to three different implicit or explicit assumptions on what sustainable reintegration is. Below, I will discuss each of them and will discuss how they differ from the empirical reality.

Finding a durable solution for refugees

Second, when the need to return first came up in the 1990s, it was accompanied with a humanitarian frame, which was about supporting the right of return of refugees after conflict as the preferred 'durable solution' for refugees. In this understanding, return is seen as a means of undoing the negative consequences of conflict that were embodied in refugee flows (Black 2001, Eastmond 2006). Going back 'home' where one 'belongs' is considered to be in the best interest of the migrant in question (Allsopp and Chase 2019). Moreover, return is seen as a way to restore the social order in the country of origin that was disrupted by conflict (Chimni 2000, Hammond 1999). Within this frame, return is sustainable when *"any observable distinctions which set returnees apart from their compatriots, particularly in terms of their socio-economic and legal status"*, disappear (UNHCR 1997, 9).

However, research shows that return after conflict is not always the most logical or natural option for refugees and asylum seekers (Monsutti 2008, Omata 2013b). Their initial decision to move is often part of dynamic and collective livelihood strategies that include security, but also political, economic, social and cultural aspects. The financial, physical and emotional investment required for migration implies that migrants have a lot to lose if they go back, even if the conflict has ended and the country is considered safe (Zimmermann 2012). Uncertainty about political and economic developments in the future, a lack of opportunities for education, family pressure to stay and cultural issues can lead to reluctance to return (Dolan 1999, Blitz, Sales, and Marzano 2005, Braakman and Schlenkhoff 2007, Black et al. 2004). Moreover, return and reintegration programmes cannot ensure justice, political stability or personal security for those returning (Webber 2011). Last, opportunities or gains achieved in exile can be a factor that affects migrants' decisions to return (Zimmermann 2012).

In addition to the socio-political and economic challenges of return, research on the experience of return also highlights the tension between return, identity, home and belonging (Pedersen 2003). The post-war economic, social, cultural and political situation in the society of origin is often very different from what it was when people left it (Ghanem 2003). Moreover, the notion of the homeland as a taken for granted familiarity and intimacy (Werbner 2013), no longer fits the experience of migrants; their identifications become more complicated with each migration movement (Werbner 2013, Hammond 1999, Long and Oxfeld 2004, Zevulun et al. 2018). In addition, protracted refugee situations produce second-generation migrants who were born outside of the country of 'origin', which further complicates the notions of 'home' (Zevulun et al. 2018, King and Christou 2010, Lee 2016). By consequence, while some migrants may feel a strong affinity to their country of origin, others may experience multiple belongings, or feel that they belong in the host country, or have no sense of belonging at all (Allsopp and Chase 2019). These dynamic and multilocal notions of home and belonging challenge the conceptual understanding of return as a natural option.

Across the different lines of empirical evidence that challenges the 'naturalness' of return and reintegration, it is clear that the return experience varies according to personal characteristics such as age, marital status, education level, as well as years spent abroad (Paasche and Skilbrei 2017, Arowolo 2000, Fransen and Bilgili 2018, Mohammadi, Abbasi-Shavazi, and Sadeghi 2018). A relatively understudied topic is the differences in motivation for return. While I found in my own work that involuntary returnees had a more difficult time to find a sense of belonging than voluntary returnees (Van Houte 2016). Flahaux also sees an important difference between those who were able to choose the time and conditions of return to Senegal and DR Congo and those who could not (Flahaux 2017), as do Mohammadi et al. for the case of Afghan return from Iran (Mohammadi, Abbasi-Shavazi, and Sadeghi 2018). By contrast, Hagan et al., looking at the case of Mexican returnees from the United States, conclude that in the long run, economic perspectives for deported migrants were not worse than voluntary returnees (Hagan, Wassink, and Castro 2019).

Development and stability in origin countries

On top of the previous two, a third policy frame concerns promoting development and stability in origin countries and regions and, by extension, regional and global peace and stability. Return then has a function of serving geo-political interests and legitimising post-conflict states and enhance donor confidence (Fransen and Bilgili 2018), particularly after international military intervention (Blitz, Sales, and Marzano 2005). Following this rationale, return is sustainable when it does not do harm to fragile or (post) conflict countries or people, and, or when returnees even contribute to post-conflict reconstruction and reconciliation.

While there are reasons to believe that returnees might contribute to development upon return, there is also evidence that instead of contribution to a return to normalcy, return migration may increase tensions in this precarious process, for different reasons. First, large-scale return movements can stretch the absorption capacity of local economies and labour markets (Özerdem and Sofizada 2006, Arowolo 2000). Second, returnees may be associated with former ethnic and political structures or face challenges in restoring their livelihoods, property, documents and rights (Blitz, Sales, and Marzano 2005, Özerdem and Sofizada 2006). Third, distrust and resentment around questions of loyalty between returnees and those who stayed in the country can form a new source of conflict (Zunzer 2004, Chan and Tran 2011, Arowolo 2000). In turn, any destabilizing effects of return migration may initiate new conflict and migration movements.

Effective migration law enforcement for host states

A third policy rationale of return and reintegration that comes from yet another different angle is that of effective migration law enforcement by the host state, with the goal of managing, controlling and regulating the movements of migrants who are economically and politically superfluous to and relieving the burden from host countries by returning them to the country of origin (Peutz 2006, Walters 2002). Following this rationale, return is sustainable if people leave the host country and find a livelihood in the country of origin or elsewhere, without the intention to leave again (Ghosh 2000, Carr 2014, Flahaux 2017).

Here, research on migration enforcement regimes often considers both the legitimacy and efficacy of such policies. Many contributions discuss the tensions of legitimacy and legality of deportation in liberal democratic states (Fekete 2005, Ellermann 2010, Henderson 2014, Schoultz 2014, Lenard 2015, Chetail 2016), which also shows an empirical bias on The European Union and the United States. In addition to this legitimacy deficit, studies on the efficacy gap (Czaika and De Haas 2013) or deportation gap (Gibney 2008) between those ordered to leave and those actually leaving the 'host' state, show the limited capacity and, or willingness to enforce deportation or repatriation policies (Van Houte and Leerkes 2019).

Beyond assumptions of reintegration:
Belonging as a way forward in research on return

The discussion of the literature above suggests that the concept of reintegration is problematic and confusing, as there are multiple meanings emerging from competing policy frames, which are also incompatible: return can never be sustainable in all three senses of the word at the same time. In my studies on the experience of return migration, I have therefore applied the concept of embeddedness rather than reintegration. While avoiding to artificially trying to 'measure' something that cannot easily be measured, the concept helps to understand peoples' decision-making processes in their migration and return, how they were doing after return, and the diversity in such migration patterns and dynamics (Tsuda 1999, Wissink, Düvell, and van Eerdewijk 2013). Over the past few years, I have tried to conceptualize the term with more clarity (Van Houte 2016). Embeddedness links to the term 'emplacement' which, Hammond describes as a continuous and ongoing process to construct a physical, social and emotional 'home' in a new setting (Hammond 2004, Sturridge, Bakewell, and Hammond 2018). However, while the essence of the concept is clear, I have found that the term also raises some confusion. Therefore, I now want to rebrand the same concept as 'belonging' (Hammond 2004), which is a more intuitive term. Below, I will explain the essence of this concept.

Belonging (or embeddedness), is defined here as the process of an individual's identification with and participation in one or multiple spaces of belonging, which includes institutional, economic, social and cultural dimensions (See Van Houte 2016). To be sure, 'belonging' here does not merely entail the 'soft' aspects of life such as emotions, psychology and identity, but is meant to include the more 'tangible' aspects as well, such as where one has property and makes money[2]. Such a holistic and multidimensional understanding of belonging provides a lens to look at return migration in a more encompassing and non-normative way, by analysing a person's identification with and participation in society, beyond the ideas of 'reintegration' or 'going home'. I will highlight some of its benefits with regard to the discussion above.

First, the encompassing and multilocal approach of belonging or embeddedness helps in studying the possibility of 'simultaneous' (Levitt and Schiller 2004) or 'double' (Mazzucato 2008) engagements of migrants, and the reality that this sometimes leads to rich, transnational lifestyles, and sometimes leaves people in-between and in limbo (Lietaert, Broekaert, and Derluyn 2017, Majidi 2018, Allsopp and Chase 2019). In addition, since finding a sense of belonging is not exclusively about migration, the concept can be used to compare migrants and non-migrants.

Second, the relational aspect of belonging or embeddedness stresses that human behaviour, including migration, is not an isolated process, but is the result of the interaction between individuals and their social environment (Kloosterman, Van Der Leun, and Rath 1999, Van Liempt 2011). Human beings are proactive, intentional agents who influence and are influenced by the social worlds in which they are located. This relational aspect of belonging shows that it is a complex process in which notions of self, other, home, and place are fluid, and affect and are affected by migration (Pedersen 2003, Erdal 2012).

---

[2]   Other conceptualizations of reintegration make the distinction between 'objective' socio-economic measures and 'subjective' measures of return, of which the latter includes a sense of belonging (Fransen and Bilgi 2018).

Third, the multidimensional aspect of embeddedness highlights the interplay between social, cultural, economic and institutional aspects, and the notion that migrants may selectively engage in or retreat from these different dimensions. In any particular space of belonging, migrants may be embedded strongly in one dimension and less strongly in the other (Jones 2011, Oeppen 2009, Levitt, Lucken, and Barnett 2011), leading to a splitting of 'home' as an everyday experience (Ahmed 1999).

The concept of belonging provides a lens to look at how people are doing after return, rather than measuring how they are doing according to certain standards. To some, this may sound too unspecific to be useful for policy-making. Still, as I will show by discussing my case study of Afghan returnees, this lens can provide useful in-depth insights that are concrete and valuable for policy as well.

Strategies of belonging of Afghan returnees

Rather than a mark on a singular scale of reintegration, three main strategies to negotiate belonging and feel 'at home' after return to Kabul came forward from my studies among Afghan returnees. A first strategy was making differences disappear. This meant identifying and complying with the existing structures, claiming belonging to 'Afghan' practices and values. In practice, this meant living with and blending in with their relatives, and doing what was expected of them in terms of work and family life. Agreeing with a traditional, arranged marriage was mentioned by many informants as a significant example of this strategy of belonging.

Conversely, the opposite strategy was to seek continuation of a 'European' lifestyle. This meant in practice leading an 'expat' life in Afghanistan, living and working in the international community, which also included living on compounds, working for international organizations or companies, going to 'international' restaurants and attending occasional parties. A life, in short, that was dedicated towards contributing to rebuilding Afghanistan, while not necessarily adapting to all aspects of Afghan lifestyle.

A third strategy involved bridging gaps between 'European' and 'Afghan' spaces of belonging. This led to a transnational or in-between lifestyle, in which the boundaries of both had to be pushed. This strategy was about forming hybrid identities, and applying creative responses to new situations in their personal lives (Sewell 1992, Emirbayer and Mische 1998, Bakewell 2008, Mai and King 2009). It included, with varying degrees of success, working in Afghan companies or administration while trying to change something of the culture of corruption, discussing new or controversial things such as liberal habits or human rights with family and friends, or trying to negotiate a level of choice in an arranged marriage.

Next, I tried to determine which kind or returnees chose what kind of strategy of belonging after return. With the strategy of their choice, returnees tried to match what they wanted to do with what they were able to do. Involuntary returnees felt less room to manoeuvre to negotiate a sense of belonging than voluntary returnees, which often lead to choosing 'Afghan' strategies of belonging. This is perhaps not surprising considering the what Lietaert et al. describe as restricted access to the transnational field, with fewer resources and limited mobility (Lietaert, Broekaert, and Derluyn 2017). Still, some involuntary returnees tried to maintain some form of hybrid lifestyle, which also mirrors Lietaert et al.'s findings. By contrast, voluntary returnees had more room to choose between either European, hybrid or Afghan strategies of belonging. While many chose European or hybrid lifestyles, others still chose mainly Afghan strategies of belonging. The deviances in the pattern shows that there is more to explore. Below, I will briefly discuss and illustrate three structural patterns of inequality underneath the voluntary – involuntary divide[3], before discussing mobility as the factor that connects the dots between them.

Winning or losing:
Socio-economic background, timing of migration, and legal status

The first set of factors that affects post-return strategies of belonging is the interplay between socio-economic background, timing of migration, and legal status. In the case of Afghanistan, socio-economic differences that existed prior to migration strongly affected the timing of migration, and were in turn also reinforced by the migration experience. Members of the Afghan élite often benefitted from their migration experience. They were able to leave early in the conflict and combined with their high profile this led to refugee status. Moreover, an overall more welcoming environment towards refugees in Europe, enabled their full participation in the host country, resulting in strong and multilocal belonging and continued transnational mobility after return, where they also could rely on stronger networks. This is portrayed by the narrative of Nadir[4], a voluntary returnee from the Netherlands:

> "During my internship, September 11 happened. Then I was in demand. I was able to help a lot then. In 2002 I went to Afghanistan. Just to see how it was, just looking, for two weeks, and to see the family. I accidentally ran into someone of an American organization. Media. I helped them with some interviews. They are an organization that brought the Afghan media back on their feet. I accidentally got in contact with them and we had a conversation. I worked first two weeks and after that two months for them."

Nadir (m, interview, original in Dutch)

By contrast, Afghan migrants who were of more modest descent lost rather than won from their migration experiences. They took longer to travel, or spent time in neighbouring countries first. Their late arrival meant that they faced the disadvantages of increasingly restrictive asylum policies, leading to insecure legal status. This stood in the way of participating in the host country and resulted in involuntary return, where they were often supported by their families, despite stretching already strained household budgets.

---

[3] These patterns are discussed in more detail in, amongst others, Van Houte 2016.
[4] All names of informants are pseudonyms.

"(A)ll the Afghanistan people, they just split up and they went to different places. I went to the UK and ... Afghanistan just broke out like a tree. ... One branch falls down, the other branch goes another way, one branch just burns and the other branch just gets dry and then at the end the actual tree has nothing. It's only a dry tree. This is what happened to me and at this time."
Omar (m, interview, original in Dari, via translator)

The stratifying effects of migration and return on previously existing inequalities has been confirmed by studies showing that economic wellbeing after return was related to *„ cumulative human capital skills learned on and off the job at all stages of the migratory circuit"* (Wassink and Hagan 2018, see also Fransen and Bilgili 2018). It also shows the importance of (family) networks to get life after return back on track (Omata 2013a).

Comparing these two quotes, what stands out is the difference in emotion and tone in the voices of these migrants. While Nadir felt that his opportunities were reinforced by the migration experience, Omar highlighted the destructive force of conflict and displacement. This confirms the feelings of exclusion and loss of power reported by Majidi among deportees to Afghanistan (Majidi 2018), and the suggestion by Von Lersner et al. (2008), that pressured return led to an increase of psychiatric disorders, mostly Post Traumatic Stress Disorder and depression.

The sentiment of having 'won' or having 'lost' from the migration experience is the first underlying pattern that informs strategies of belonging: A feeling of loss and failure seemed to inspire a strategy to 'blend in' and become invisible, thus take up an Afghan strategy of belonging. Conversely, a feeling of having won made people feel confident to stand out from the crowd, be different, by either choosing 'European' or hybrid strategies of belonging.

Light or heavy return: Agency in return decisions

The aspects discussed in the section above affects the degree of agency over the return decision, which forms a factor that affects strategies of belonging. There are no clear-cut boundaries between voluntary and involuntary return (see also Monsutti 2008). Almost no return decision was entirely free, as there were legal constraints, family pressure, economic needs or sociocultural difficulties at the basis of every decision. Almost no return decision was entirely forced, either, as most people had an alternative, however extreme, to being deported: from living a precarious life as an undocumented migrant to, as one deportee mentioned, committing suicide as a last resort.

Rather than a dichotomy of voluntary and forced return, there is a gradual scale, depending on social, economic, institutional and cultural capacities and desires within structural opportunities, which lead to different levels of agency over the decision to return. Nevertheless, legal status strongly plays into the amount of external pressure applied to the decision-making to return (Flahaux 2017), and the meaning of return, as these two quotes illustrate:

„After I finished my studies and all this time I worked, and I was quite bored about everything. And didn't know why ... I'm not happy because I had every-thing. ... And then what was still something missing and I was looking for it what can it be, should I change my job, should I change my style, should I change my life, and what's the problem. ... And then I found out, maybe it's a good thing to go back to my roots and start again as a human being ... can you live in Afghan-istan, it is something for you, do you still identify yourself as an Afghan?"
Eshan (m, interview, original in English)

"How long do you want to stay in the Netherlands? You will never get a perma-nent status. Here, every time I call here, my mother says you have to go back, my father says come back. And I heard my father died. Only then I say OK, I go back to Afghanistan."
Areef (m, interview, original in Dutch)

The lack of a legal basis to remain in the host country strongly restricted all other dimensions of life in the host country, as well as their mobility options upon return. Conversely, people with permanent residence status and often citizenship of the host country felt stayed as long as the opportunities were there, while they felt that they could always undo this decision.

The experienced sense of agency and the kind of choice is a second underlying pattern informing strategies of belonging: for people for whom return was a last resort, either because of legal restrictions, or, as also happened, problems in the private sphere, their return felt quite 'heavy' or irreversible, leading to a stronger inclination to focus on Afghanistan. This does not mean that these returnees are completely immobile, as many deportees decide to re-emigrate again (Majidi 2018), yet the financial and psychological burden of this mobility becomes increasingly heavy. Conversely, returnees who had made an initially 'light' and open-ended de-cision to return, such as Eshan, understandably were more ambiguous about their belonging, keeping their options open.

Experiences of present and future security / stability

A third factor affecting strategies of belonging was the experience of the present and future security situation. Life in Kabul was unstable in 2012, and all my re-spondents acknowledged that. People who were in a strong and privileged position felt that they could protect themselves from generalized violence and at the same time keep their dependants safe in the European country of residence. At the same time, their strong affiliation with the West and their sometimes-high profiles as suc-cessful returnees created a risk for them. Younger voluntary returnees found a sense of belonging in the Afghan society by taking that risk. Conversely, those who were in an overall more vulnerable situation also felt exposed to generalized violence, as they did not have the means to protect themselves and their dependants, although their lower profile made them less of a target.

However, returnees were actually surprisingly calm about the day-to-day risks of getting caught in a suicide attack, a kidnapping, or other forms of extreme violence. The main security concerns for these returnees related to the future. All returnees expected the planned gradual withdrawal of the international military and civil presence after 2014 to lead to either a return of the Taliban or a return to civil conflict.

Migration has always been a means for Afghans to deal with problems such as conflict, violence and economic crisis (Monsutti 2008), and the barrier to leave seems to be even lower for people who have used this coping strategy before. So when asked for their outlook for the next five years, returnees whose continued transnational mobility was an important prerequisite for their return in the first place, felt comfortable enough in the unstable Afghan environment, knowing that they could constantly re-evaluate their decision to stay, return or move elsewhere. By contrast, some returnees who felt restricted in their mobility presented a very dark perspective for their own lives and the future of Afghanistan, which withheld them from making any plans. The following quotes reflect the different positions:

„After two years it starts to be unsafe for me here. ... people know that when they put a gun against my head, that daddy will pay a hundred thousand. And he will. "
Amir (m, interview, original in Dutch)

"I'm not really worried about getting killed or dying or whatever, one day you're born and the other day you just die. I'm not really worried about that. But the only thing I'm worried about is my kids. And my wife. So. if I get killed what will happen to them?"
Ajmal (m, interview, original in Dari, via translator)

The experienced present and expected security is a third underlying pattern affecting strategies of belonging. In the context of resurgence of conflict, people who feel insecure and anxious about their present and future safety can be expected to resort to familiar and close-knit structures such as family networks, which requires adherence to the habits, values and traditions of that network. Conversely, people who felt confident that they would be able to keep themselves safe independent of support networks, also felt freer to depart from tradition and try out different things.

Connecting the dots: Mobility

The sense of winning or losing from migration; the sense of agency over migration decisions and the experience of present and future security all come together in one main issue: mobility. Returnees who felt they lost from their migration experience, had limited say over their return decision and felt vulnerable in the face of recurring conflict, experienced involuntary immobility (Carling 2002). This immobility caused a lot of unrest and discontent, and a feeling of being 'stuck' in a potentially explosive environment.

By contrast, returnees who felt they had won from their migration experience, had had a degree of choice over their return and felt they could protect themselves against violence, did so because they felt transnationally mobile, which gave these returnees a crucial sense of security and comfort, and allowed them to take advantage of geographical differences (ibid.). Their mobility is therefore their strongest asset that may facilitate their most valuable contributions.

Mobility continues to be an essential desire in the lives of return migrants. I therefore propose to centralize mobility in the analysis of return. While involuntary immobility had a paralysing effect on returnees in the light of the expected post-2014 changes, transnationally mobile returnees chose to return to Afghanistan despite these expected changes. Although they were likely to re-emigrate in the face of '2014', this very mobility also allowed them to take the risk of being different from the dominant society. Rather than a weakness, their mobility is therefore their strongest asset that may facilitate their most valuable contributions. Two quotes illustrate the differences between these two groups:

> *"These people have the advantage that they can always leave again. So therefore they can easily come back. That is a great advantage. ... Because I like to come and work here, not because it's that safe here, but because you can mean a lot. And that gives a lot of satisfaction for your work. And when it goes bad then I'm out again."*
> Salim (m, interview, original in Dutch)

> *"(T)he thing is that in Afghanistan once you're in a circle, if the circle gets tighter and tighter you have to live with it. And you have to deal with it. ... You cannot just get yourself out of the circle."*
> Omar (m, interview, original in Dari, via translator)

Conclusion

In the beginning of this chapter I have highlighted a number of issues with the topic of return and sustainable reintegration. I have found that in essence, the main issue is that many repatriated and deported migrants are less worried about being back in their country of origin as they are about not being able to leave anymore. Even in a highly insecure environment like Afghanistan where deported migrants struggled to set up a livelihood, many deported migrants did highlight the advantage of being back in a country where they were citizens again rather than unwanted visitors. Many of them were highly resilient and doing everything they could to get their life back on track. What frightened them, however, was the prospect of not being able to leave when their situation would deteriorate, due to lack of funds, and decreased opportunities of shelter both in the neighbouring countries and further afield. For people who have lived with harsh circumstances such as insecurity, drought and scarcity through strategies of mobility, the immobilising effect of deportation was what concerned them the most. These findings suggest that we can only prevent that return inflicts harm on vulnerable people and places if return occurs under the condition of continued transnational mobility.

Policy implications

These conclusions have an important implication for policy. The majority of migrants who are obliged to leave, know that they will be more or less stuck once they have returned, and hence do everything in their power to resist return, leading to extremely inefficient and ineffective return policies (Van Houte and Leerkes 2019).

Innovative solutions for the lack of return and reintegration of rejected asylum seekers and former refugees could be to offer more flexible rights to post-return transnational mobility in the event of recurring instability or conflict. Alternatives could be that return comes with a guarantee that re-emigration is possible if the person in question becomes a de facto refugee at some point in the future, or in the ten subsequent years, which may increase the willingness of people to leave.

It may sound naïve to claim that in order to succeed in removal, mobility needs to be guaranteed. It may also seem like a stretch to propose a policy switch from return and reintegration to mobility. Yet considering the overall failure of migration enforcement policies, it is necessary to consider completely new approaches to return.

References

Ahmed, Sara. 1999. "Home and Away." *International Journal of Cultural Studies* 2 (3):329-347. doi: 10.1177/136787799900200303.

Allsopp, Jennifer, and Elaine Chase. 2019. "Best interests, durable solutions and belonging: policy discourses shaping the futures of unaccompanied migrant and refugee minors coming of age in Europe." *Journal of Ethnic and Migration Studies* 45 (2):293-311. doi: 10.1080/1369183X.2017.1404265.

Arowolo, Oladele O. 2000. "Return Migration and the Problem of Reintegration." *International Migration* 38 (5):59-82. doi: 10.1111/1468-2435.00128.

Bakewell, Oliver. 2008. "'Keeping Them in Their Place': The Ambivalent Relationship Between Development and Migration in Africa." *Third World Quarterly* 29 (7):1341-1358. doi: 10.1080/01436590802386492.

Black, Richard. 2001. "Return and Reconstruction in Bosnia-Herzegovina: Missing Link, or Mistaken Priority?" *SAIS Review* XXI (2):177-199.

Black, Richard, Khalid Koser, Karen Munk, Gaby Atfield, Lisa D'Onofrio, and Richmond Tiemoko. 2004. Understanding Voluntary Return. In *Home Office Report* London: Home Office.

Blitz, Brad K., Rosemary Sales, and Lisa Marzano. 2005. "Non-Voluntary Return? The Politics of Return to Afghanistan." *Political Studies* 53 (1):182-200. doi: 10.1111/j.1467-9248.2005.00523.x.

Braakman, Marije, and Angela Schlenkhoff. 2007. "Between Two Worlds: Feelings of Belonging While in Exile and the Question of Return." *Asien* 104 (3):9-22.

Carling, Jørgen. 2002. "Migration in the Age of Involuntary Immobility: Theoretical Reflections and Cape Verdean Experiences." *Journal of Ethnic and Migration Studies* 28 (1):5-42. doi: 10.1080/13691830120103912.

Carr, H. 2014. "Returning 'Home': Experiences of Reintegration for Asylum Seekers and Refugees." *British Journal of Social Work* 44:140-156. doi: 10.1093/bjsw/bcu046.

Chan, Yuk Wah, and Thi Le Thu Tran. 2011. "Recycling Migration and Changing Nationalisms: The Vietnamese Return Diaspora and Reconstruction of Vietnamese Nationhood." *Journal of Ethnic and Migration Studies* 37 (7):1101-1117. doi: 10.1080/1369183x.2011.572486.

Chetail, Vincent. 2016. "Is There any Blood on my Hands? Deportation as a Crime of International Law." *Leiden Journal of International Law* 29 (3):917-943. doi: 10.1017/s092215 6516000376.

Chimni, Bhupinder S. 2000. "Globalization, Humanitarianism and the Erosion of Refugee Protection." *Journal of Refugee Studies* 13 (3):243-263. doi: 10.1093/jrs/13.3.243.

Czaika, Mathias, and Hein De Haas. 2013. "The Effectiveness of Immigration Policies." *Population and Development Review* 39 (3):487-508. doi: doi:10.1111/j.1728-4457.2013.00613.x.

Dimitriadi, Angeliki. 2018. Irregular Afghan Migration to Europe: At the Margins, Looking In. London: Palgrave Macmillan.

Dolan, Chris. 1999. "Repatriation from South Africa to Mozambique–Undermining Durable Solutions?'." In *The End of the Refugee Cycle? Refugee Repatriation and Reconstruction*, edited by Richard Black and Khalid Koser, 85-108. New York / Oxford: Berghahn.

Eastmond, Marita. 2006. "Transnational returns and reconstruction in post-war Bosnia and Herzegovina." *International Migration* 44 (3):141-166. doi: 10.1111/j.1468-2435.2006.00375.x.

Ellermann, Antje. 2010. "Undocumented Migrants and Resistance in the Liberal State." *Politics & Society* 38 (3):408-429. doi: 10.1177/0032329210373072.

Emirbayer, Mustafa, and Ann Mische. 1998. "What Is Agency?" *American Journal of Sociology* 103 (4):962-1023. doi: 10.1086/231294.

Erdal, Marta Bivand. 2012. "'A Place to Stay in Pakistan': Why Migrants Build Houses in their Country of Origin." *Population, Space and Place* 18 (5):629-641. doi: 10.1002/psp.1694.

Fekete, L. 2005. "The deportation machine: Europe, asylum and human rights." *Race & Class* 47 (1):64-78. doi: 10.1177/0306396805055083.

Fischer, Carolin, and Marieke van Houte. 2019. "Dimensions of Agency in Transnational Relations of Afghan Migrants and Return Migrants." *Migration Studies*. doi: 10.1093/migration/ mnz012.

Flahaux, M. L. 2017. "Home, sweet home? The effect of return migration support mechanisms on reintegration." *Espaces-Populations-Societes* (1):17. doi: 10.4000/eps.7118.

Fransen, S., and O. Bilgili. 2018. "Who reintegrates? The constituents of reintegration of displaced populations." *Population Space and Place* 24 (6):13. doi: 10.1002/psp.2140.

Ghanem, Tania. 2003. When Forced Migrants Return 'Home': The Psychological Difficulties Returnees Encounter in the Reintegration Process. In *RSC Working Paper*. Oxford: University of Oxford.

Ghosh, Bimal. 2000. "Return migration: reshaping policy approaches." *Return migration: Journey of hope or despair*:181-226.

Gibney, Matthew J. 2008. "Asylum and the expansion of deportation in the United Kingdom." *Government and Opposition* 43 (2):146-167. doi: 10.1111/j.1477-7053.2007.00249.x.

Hagan, J., J. Wassink, and B. Castro. 2019. "A longitudinal analysis of resource mobilisation among forced and voluntary return migrants in Mexico." *Journal of Ethnic and Migration Studies* 45 (1):170-189. doi: 10.1080/1369183x.2018.1454305.

Hammond, Laura. 1999. "Examining the Discourse of Repatriation: Towards a More Proactive Theory of Return Migration." In *The End of the Refugee Cycle? Refugee Repatriation and Reconstruction*, edited by Richard Black and Khalid Koser, 227-244. New York / Oxford: Berghahn.

Hammond, Laura. 2004. *This Place Will Become Home: Refugee Repatriation to Ethiopia*: Cornell University Press.

Henderson, Claire. 2014. "Australia's Treatment of Asylum Seekers From Human Rights Violations to Crimes Against Humanity." *Journal of International Criminal Justice* 12 (5):1161-1181. doi: 10.1093/jicj/mqu062.

Jones, Richard C. 2011. "The Local Economic Imprint of Return Migrants in Bolivia." *Population, Space and Place* 17 (5):435-453. doi: 10.1002/psp.626.

King, Russell, and Anastasia Christou. 2010. "Cultural Geographies of Counter-Diasporic Migration: Perspectives from the Study of Second-Generation 'Returnees' to Greece." *Population, Space and Place* 16 (2):103-119. doi: 10.1002/psp.543.

Kloosterman, Robert C, Joanne Van Der Leun, and Jan Rath. 1999. "Mixed Embeddedness: (In) Formal Economic Activities and Immigrant Businesses in the Netherlands." *International Journal of Urban and Regional Research* 23 (2):252-266.

Koser, Khalid. 2014. Transition, Crisis and Mobility in Afghanistan: Rhetoric and Reality. Geneva: IOM.

Lee, H. 2016. ""I was forced here': perceptions of agency in second generation "return' migration to Tonga." *Journal of Ethnic and Migration Studies* 42 (15):2564-2579. doi: 10.1080/1369183x.2016.1176524.

Leerkes, A., M. Galloway, and M. Kromhout. 2010. Kiezen tussen twee kwaden : Determinanten van blijf- en terugkeerintenties onder (bijna) uitgeprocedeerde asielmigranten. In *Cahiers*. Den Haag: WODC.

Lenard, Patti Tamara. 2015. "The ethics of deportation in liberal democratic states." *European Journal of Political Theory* 14 (4):464-480. doi: 10.1177/1474885115584834.

Levitt, Peggy, Kristen Lucken, and Melissa Barnett. 2011. "Beyond Home and Return: Negotiating Religious Identity across Time and Space through the Prism of the American Experience." *Mobilities* 6 (4):467-482. doi: 10.1080/17450101.2011.603942.

Levitt, Peggy, and Nina Glick Schiller. 2004. "Conceptualizing Simultaneity: A Transnational Social Field Perspective on Society." *International Migration Review* 38 (3):1002-1039. doi: 10.1111/j.1747-7379.2004.tb00227.x.

Lietaert, Ine, Eric Broekaert, and Ilse Derluyn. 2017. "The boundaries of transnationalism: the case of assisted voluntary return migrants." *Global Networks-a Journal of Transnational Affairs* 17 (3):366-381. doi: 10.1111/glob.12141.

Long, Lynellyn D., and Ellen Oxfeld, eds. 2004. *Coming Home? Refugees, Migrants, and Those Who Stayed Behind*. Philadelphia: University of Pennsylvania.

Mai, Nicola, and Russell King. 2009. "Love, Sexuality and Migration: Mapping the Issue(s)." *Mobilities* 4 (3):295-307. doi: 10.1080/17450100903195318.

Majidi, Nassim. 2018. "Deportees lost at "home": Post-deportation outcomes in Afghanistan." In *After Deportation*, 127-148. Springer.

Mazzucato, Valentina. 2008. "The Double Engagement: Transnationalism and Integration. Ghanaian Migrants' Lives Between Ghana and The Netherlands." *Journal of Ethnic and Migration Studies* 34 (2):199-216. doi: 10.1080/13691830701823871.

Mohammadi, Abdullah, Mohammad Jalal Abbasi-Shavazi, and Rasoul Sadeghi. 2018. "Return to Home: Reintegration and Sustainability of Return to Post-conflict Contexts." In *Demography of Refugee and Forced Migration*, 251-270. Springer.

Monsutti, Alessandro. 2008. "Afghan Migratory Strategies and the Three Solutions to the Refugee Problem." *Refugee Survey Quarterly* 27 (1):58-73. doi: 10.1093/rsq/hdn007.

Oeppen, Ceri. 2009. "A Stranger at Home: Integration, Transnationalism and the Afghan Elite." PhD Thesis, University of Sussex.

Oeppen, Ceri. 2012. "A Stranger at 'Home': 'Interactions Between Transnational Return Visits and Integration for Afghan-American Professionals." *Global Networks* 13 (2):261-278. doi: 10.1111/glob.12008.

Omata, N. 2013a. "Repatriation and Integration of Liberian Refugees from Ghana: the Importance of Personal Networks in the Country of Origin." *Journal of Refugee Studies* 26 (2):265-282. doi: 10.1093/jrs/fes023.

Omata, Naohiko. 2013b. "The Complexity of Refugees' Return Decision-Making in a Protracted Exile: Beyond the Home-Coming Model and Durable Solutions." *Journal of Ethnic and Migration Studies* 39 (8):1281-1297. doi: 10.1080/1369183X.2013.778149.

Özerdem, Alpaslan, and Abdul Hai Sofizada. 2006. "Sustainable Reintegration to Returning Refugees in Post-Taliban Afghanistan: Land-Related Challenges." *Conflict, Security & Development* 6 (1):75-100. doi: 10.1080/14678800600590678.

Paasche, E., and M. L. Skilbrei. 2017. "Gendered Vulnerability and Return Migration." *Temida* 20 (2):149-166. doi: 10.2298/tem1702149p.

Pedersen, Marianne Holm. 2003. Between Homes: Post-war Return, Emplacement and the Negotiation of Belonging in Lebanon. In *New Issues in Refugee Research*. Geneva: UNHCR.

Peutz, N. 2006. "Embarking on an anthropology of removal." *Current Anthropology* 47 (2):217-241. doi: 10.1086/498949.

Ruben, Ruerd, Marieke Van Houte, and Tine Davids. 2009. "What Determines the Embeddedness of Forced-Return Migrants? Rethinking the Role of Pre- and Post-Return Assistance." *International Migration Review* 43 (4):908-937.

Ruttig, Thomas. 2015. "An "Afghan Exodus" (1): Facts, figures, trends." Afghanistan Analysts Network, Last Modified 14 November 2015. https://www.afghanistan-analysts.org/an-afghan-exodus-facts-figures-trends/.

Schoultz, Isabel. 2014. "Seeking Asylum and Residence Permits in Sweden: Denial, Acknowledgement, and Bureaucratic Legitimacy." *Critical Criminology* 22 (2):219-235. doi: 10.1007/s10612-013-9206-3.

Schuster, Liza, and Nassim Majidi. 2015. "Deportation Stigma and Re-migration." *Journal of Ethnic and Migration Studies* 41 (4):635-652. doi: 10.1080/1369183X.2014.957174.

Sewell, William H., Jr. 1992. "A Theory of Structure: Duality, Agency, and Transformation." *American Journal of Sociology* 98 (1):1-29. doi: 10.2307/2781191.

Sturridge, Caitlin , Oliver Bakewell, and Laura Hammond. 2018. Return and (Re) Integration after Displacement: Belonging, Labelling and Livelihoods in Three Somali Cities. Research and Evidence Facility: EU Trust Fund for Africa (Horn of Africa Window).

Tsuda, Takeyuki. 1999. "Transnational Migration and the Nationalization of Ethnic Identity among Japanese Brazilian Return Migrants." *Ethos* 27 (2):145-179. doi: 10.1525/eth.1999.27.2.145.

UNHCR. 1997. *The State of The World's Refugees 1997: A Humanitarian Agenda*. Geneva: UNHCR.

UNHCR. 2016. *Global Trends. Forced Displacement in 2015* .Geneva: United Nations High Commissioner for Refugees.

Van Houte, Marieke. 2016. *Return Migration to Afghanistan: Moving Back Or Moving Forward?*, *Migration, Diasporas and Citizenship*. London: Palgrave Macmillan.

Van Houte, Marieke, and Arjen Leerkes. 2019. Dealing with (non-) Deportability. A comparative policy analysis of the post-entry migration enforcement regimes of Western European countries. A Report commissioned by the 'Van Zwol committtee'. Maastricht: UNU-Merit.

Van Houte, Marieke, Melissa Siegel, and Tine Davids. 2016. "Deconstructing the Meanings of and Motivations for Return: An Afghan Case Study." *Comparative Migration Studies* 4 (1):21. doi: DOI: 10.1186/s40878-016-0042-y.

Van Liempt, Ilse. 2011. "Young Dutch Somalis in the UK: Citizenship, Identities and Belonging in a Transnational Triangle." *Mobilities* 6 (4):569-583. doi: 10.1080/17450101.2011.603948.

von Lersner, Ulrike, Thomas Elbert, and Frank Neuner. 2008. "Mental health of refugees following state-sponsored repatriation from Germany." *Bmc Psychiatry* 8. doi: 10.1186/1471-244x-8-88.

Walters, William. 2002. "Deportation, Expulsion, and the International Police of Aliens." *Citizenship Studies* 6 (3):265-292. doi: 10.1080/1362102022000011612.

Wassink, J. T., and J. M. Hagan. 2018. "A Dynamic Model of Self-Employment and Socioeconomic Mobility Among Return Migrants: The Case of Urban Mexico." *Social Forces* 96
(3):1069-1096. doi: 10.1093/sf/sox095.

Webber, Frances. 2011. "How voluntary are voluntary returns?" *Race & Class* 52 (4):98-107. doi:
10.1177/0306396810396606.

Werbner, P. 2013. "Mothers and Daughters in Historical Perspective: Home, Identity and Double
Consciousness in British Pakistanis' Migration and Return." *Journal of Historical Sociology*
26 (1):41-61. doi: 10.1111/johs.12011.

Wissink, Marieke, Franck Düvell, and Anouka van Eerdewijk. 2013. "Dynamic Migration Intentions and the Impact of Socio-Institutional Environments: A Transit Migration Hub in Turkey."
Journal   of   Ethnic   and   Migration   Studies   39   (7):1087-1105.   doi:
10.1080/1369183x.2013.778026.

Zevulun, D., W. J. Post, A. E. Zijlstra, M. E. Kalverboer, and E. J. Knorth. 2018. "Migrant and
asylum-seeker children returned to Kosovo and Albania: predictive factors for social-emotional
wellbeing after return." *Journal of Ethnic and Migration Studies* 44 (11):1774-1796. doi:
10.1080/1369183x.2017.1391076.

Zimmermann, Susan. 2012. "Understanding Repatriation: Refugee Perspectives on the Importance
of Safety, Reintegration, and Hope." *Population, Space and Place* 18 (1):45-57. doi:
10.1002/psp.647.

Zunzer, Wolfram. 2004. Diaspora Communities and Civil Conflict Transformation. In *Berghof
Occasional Paper*. Berlin: Berghof Research Centre for Constructive Conflict Management.

From Austria (back) to Afghanistan: Assisted Voluntary Return and Reintegration

Andrea Götzelmann-Rosado

Summary

When migrants decide to return to countries in conflict, like Afghanistan, a lot of questions arise. The article provides background information to the project RE-START II, which is implemented by the International Organization for Migration (IOM) and provides assistance for the voluntary return and reintegration of Afghans returning from Austria, and analyses the demographic data of the project beneficiaries and their feedback collected during 2,5 years of project implementation. It sheds light on the return motivations of project beneficiaries as well as on the realities they encounter upon return – both in terms of assistance they can receive, as well as the many considerable challenges they encounter.

Introduction

Return migration is, like migration in general, a complex phenomenon. However, it is by no means exceptional: When people leave their countries of origin, it is very often under the expectation that they will return at some point. This is the case for persons who migrate for promising purposes such as education or work, but even more so in cases of forced migration, where return is usually conditional to an improvement of the situation that has led to the decision to leave (King 2000; OHCHR 2001).

While for some migrants, the return intention never materializes (for instance because the situation in the country of origin does not improve for many years, life becomes centred in the new country, contacts to the country of origin become scarce, or because the economic opportunities in the host country are considered more favourable), return becomes a reality for many migrants under a variety of different circumstances.

When migrants return to countries in conflict, like Afghanistan, a lot of questions arise. Their choices are often questioned, and in contexts where choices are limited, implications need to be debated.

The International Organization for Migration (IOM) helps migrants who decide to go back to their countries of origin in their voluntary return and reintegration in the framework of specific projects. One such project is also open to voluntary returnees from Austria to Afghanistan.

The project RESTART II (Reintegration Assistance for Voluntary Returnees to Afghanistan and Iran) is implemented from 1 January 2017 until 31 December 2019 and co-funded by the Asylum, Migration and Integration Fund of the European Union and the Austrian Federal Ministry of the Interior. Implemented by IOM in Austria, Afghanistan and Iran, it aims to assist third country nationals in their voluntary return to as well as in their sustainable reintegration in Afghanistan and Iran.

As of 30 June 2019, 320 Afghans have already returned to Afghanistan in the framework of the project. Information with regards to their profiles, preliminary results and experiences may provide insights and inputs for further informed discussion on that topic.

This article aims to provide background information on IOM's work in the area of assisted voluntary return and reintegration (AVRR), and the project RESTART II in particular. With a specific focus on Afghan beneficiaries, it will present some of the main data collected as part of the project and provide a brief analysis of possible implications and limitations thereof. While the data has been gathered mainly for case management and monitoring purposes and thus cannot compete with data gathered in dedicated research projects, the article hopes to contribute to an evidence-based understanding of AVRR from Austria to Afghanistan.

The decision to return

A migrant's return decision is often complex and influenced by diverse, sometimes overlapping, considerations (Black, Koser and Munk 2004). These can include conditions in the country/region of origin, such as an improved political, economic, and/or social situation, improved security conditions and stability, as well as family reasons and the social environment. In ideal scenarios, migrants return according to their plan, for instance after having completed their education or work contract. Conditions in the host country/region may also lead to the decision to return, such as lack of (perspectives of gaining) residence permit, or lack of economic opportunities, including for those who have a secure residence status (for instance, due to a lacking recognition of qualifications gained abroad, language difficulties, or absence of networks). Other integration obstacles can also prompt a decision to return, such as limited social connections, discrimination, or unfamiliar cultural environments. Often, familial duties (care of sick or elderly relatives, protection of vulnerable family members) are reasons for returning. Many studies have indicated that non-economic factors tend to be more relevant than economic factors and pull factors in the country of origin are more relevant than push factors in the host country (see for instance Black, Koser and Munk 2004); however, some researchers have found conditions in the country of origin to be relatively unimportant in the decision-making process (Koser and Kuschminder 2015).

A migrant's decision to return voluntarily does not necessarily imply that return is the migrant's unambiguous wish. It is possible that alternative options are limited, for instance if a migrant has no legal entitlement to remain on a State's territory, or if economic opportunities are scarce. In cases where a migrant has the legal obligation to leave the country and chooses to return at his/her own volition, voluntary return is sometimes referenced as obliged, mandatory, compulsory or accepted return (see, for instance, ECRE 2018; Newland 2018). In the context of assisted voluntary return and reintegration, IOM holds that voluntariness is assumed to exist if two conditions apply: (a) freedom of choice, which is defined as the absence of physical or psychological pressure to enrol in an AVRR programme; and (b) an informed decision, which requires the availability of timely, unbiased and reliable information upon which to base the decision (IOM 2018).

Assisted Voluntary Return and Reintegration (AVRR)

IOM defines "assisted voluntary return and reintegration" as the administrative, logistical or financial support, including reintegration assistance, to migrants who are unable or unwilling to remain in the host country or country of transit and who decide to return to their country of origin (IOM 2019a). As a core activity of IOM, AVRR activities aim to facilitate voluntary return of migrants in safety and in dignity and to support their sustainable reintegration, in full respect for human rights, regardless of their status. Since the start of its first AVRR programmes in 1979, IOM has assisted more than 1.3 million returning migrants and increasingly expanded its services to more countries. In 2018, IOM assisted more than 63,000 migrants to voluntarily return and reintegrate in ca. 170 countries of origin. 53 per cent returned from the European Economic Area (IOM 2019b).

According to IOM, the legal foundations of AVRR are anchored in international law and rest on two main pillars: the protection of the rights of migrants during the return and reintegration process and State sovereignty. In its *Framework for Assisted Voluntary Return and Reintegration*, IOM has formulated seven principles which form a common basis for engagement in AVRR-related activities: voluntariness, a migrant-centred response, safety, sustainable reintegration after return, confidentiality, dialogue and partnerships, and evidence-based programming (IOM 2018).

IOM advocates for the adoption of an integrated approach to return, including post-return reintegration assistance. According to IOM, reintegration is a process which enables individuals to re-establish the economic, social and psychosocial relationships needed to maintain life, livelihood and dignity and inclusion in civic life (IOM 2019a). IOM considers reintegration to be sustainable when returnees have reached levels of economic self-sufficiency, social stability within their communities, and psychosocial well-being that allow them to cope with (re)migration drivers. Having achieved sustainable reintegration, returnees are able to make further migration decisions a matter of choice, rather than necessity. Considering the complexity of reintegration, achieving sustainability requires an approach that addresses the needs of individual returnees as well as the communities in a mutually beneficial way while responding to the structural factors at play (IOM 2017).

In Austria, IOM offers logistical assistance for the voluntary return of migrants who are unable or unwilling to stay in Austria but lack the means to return to their countries of origin in the framework of its General Return Programme. In contrast to various other IOM offices worldwide, IOM Austria does not offer return counselling, but cooperates with partners. Return counselling in Austria is offered by NGOs commissioned by the Austrian Ministry of the Interior (Caritas, Verein Menschenrechte Österreich); as well as by the Provincial Government in Carinthia. Once a migrant has taken the decision to return and coverage of costs has been confirmed (e.g. by the Ministry of the Interior), the return counsellors refer the cases to IOM Austria who organizes the return journey according to IOM standards and provides assistance at the airport. While IOM is not involved in return counselling, the organization meets every migrant upon departure at the airport and thus verifies to the extent possible that return is truly voluntary in accordance with the above definition. Migrants can withdraw their decision any time prior to departure.

In 2018, IOM Austria assisted 3,469 voluntary returns to 77 different countries; the majority of cases were funded by the Austrian Ministry of the Interior. In addition, IOM Austria has been implementing a number of projects offering reintegration measures in the returnees' countries of origin. In this context, IOM Austria has been managing projects offering reintegration assistance in Afghanistan since 2012.

Afghanistan: The Context

As of 01 January 2019, 44,420 Afghan nationals were registered in Austria (Statistics Austria 2019). In 2018, Afghan asylum seekers filed 2,120 new asylum applications, constituting the second biggest group of persons seeking international protection in Austria. Out of all asylum decisions regarding claims from Afghan nationals that were issued in 2018, positive decisions were taken in 4,979 cases (50%), 3,986 decisions were negative (40%), and 914 cases (10%) were decided otherwise (Federal Ministry of the Interior 2019).

Social and economic reintegration in Afghanistan, however, remains challenging. Afghanistan ranked number 168 (out of 189 countries) in the UNDP Human Development Index (HDI) for 2017 (UNDP 2018).

Decades of conflict have led to a pervasive protection crisis. The UN strategic review of 2017 reclassified Afghanistan from a post-conflict country to one in active conflict (UN OCHA 2017). UN OCHA reports systematic violations of international humanitarian law and international human rights law and warns that ongoing hostilities across large parts of the country are causing extreme levels of physical and psychological harm; almost two-thirds of the Afghan population live in areas directly affected by conflict (UN OCHA 2018).

Population movement is a permanent feature of the crisis, impacting both displaced and host communities and limiting access to essential services. Each year, many thousands of Afghans return from the neighbouring Islamic Republics of Iran

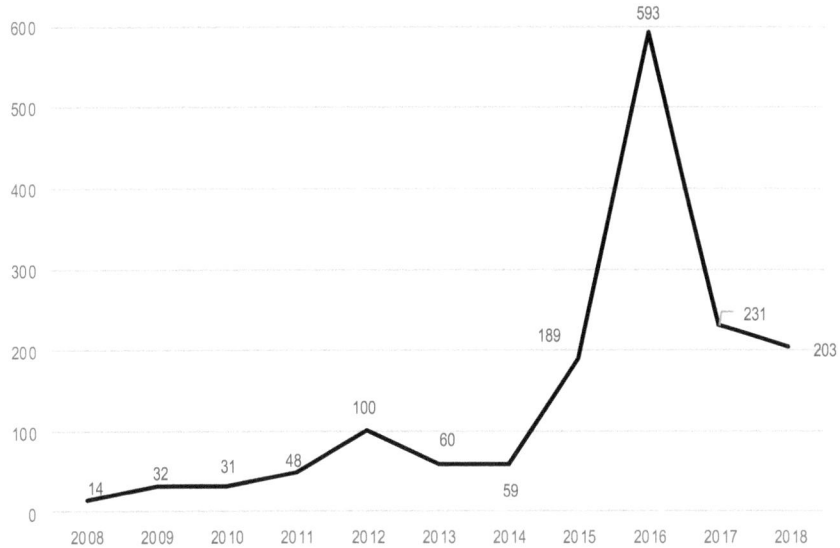

Graph 1 Voluntary returns to Afghanistan assisted by IOM Austria 2008-2018

Source: IOM Austria.

and Pakistan and other countries, burdening the already over-stretched absorption capacity of local host communities; over 820,000 Afghans returned from these two countries in 2018 (IOM and UNHCR 2019). In addition, in 2018 one of the worst droughts in living memory struck Afghanistan and impacted the lives of more than two-thirds of Afghans, devastating the agricultural sector and leaving some 4 million people across the country in need of life-saving assistance, including 3.9 million in need of food and livelihoods support (UN OCHA 2018).

UN OCHA counts 6.3 million people in need of some form of humanitarian or protection assistance including 3.7 million in severe and major need. Active conflict, large-scale population movements, and limited livelihood options continue to disrupt and deprive people of access to essential services, particularly health and education. While limited access to essential services affects all members of the population, internally displaced people (IDPs) and returnees are particularly disenfranchised due to either their loss or lack of appropriate civil documentation (ibid).

In light of this situation, a comparatively small number of Afghans return to Afghanistan from Austria.

While many Afghans have received asylum in Austria, Austria is also amongst those countries that deport Afghans found not to be in need of international protection (Wilkes 2017, Parliament, BM.I 2018). From 01 January 2017 to 30 November 2018, 283 persons were deported to Afghanistan; in the same timeframe, the Austrian Ministry of the Interior recorded 450 voluntary departures to Afghanistan (Parliament, BM.I 2019).

Between 2008 and 2018, IOM Austria assisted 1,560 beneficiaries in their voluntary return to Afghanistan. 2016 saw a peak in returns from Austria to Afghanistan, when IOM provided assistance to 593 voluntary returnees to Afghanistan. In 2018, the number of voluntary returns assisted by IOM amounted to 203 cases (compared to 231 cases in 2017).[1]

Reintegration Assistance for Voluntary Returnees to Afghanistan: RESTART II

In order to assist migrants in their voluntary return to Afghanistan and Iran as well as in their sustainable reintegration in their respective country of origin, IOM Austria and IOM Afghanistan, together with IOM Iran, are implementing the project RESTART II (Reintegration Assistance for Voluntary Returnees to Afghanistan and Iran). The project is implemented from 1 January 2017 until 31 December 2019 and foresees the participation of 490 project beneficiaries, thereof 345 voluntary returnees to Afghanistan (and 145 to Iran). Only one person per household is eligible to participate as main beneficiary.

The project benefits voluntary returnees to Afghanistan (and Iran) who belong to one of the following target groups specified by the EU's Asylum Migration and Integration Fund for return-related activities:

- third-country nationals who have not yet received a final negative decision in relation to their request to stay, their legal residence and/or international protection in Austria and who may opt for voluntary return;
- third-country nationals enjoying the right to stay, legal residence and/or international protection within the meaning of EU Directive 2011/95/EU, or temporary protection within the meaning of EU Directive 2001/55/EG in Austria and who have opted for voluntary return;
- third-country nationals who are present in Austria and do not or no longer fulfil the conditions for entry and/or stay in a Member State, including those third-country nationals whose removal has been postponed in accordance with article 9 and article 14 paragraph 1 of the EU Directive 2008/115/EG.

This target group description includes all Afghan nationals who decide to return voluntarily to Afghanistan; it excludes persons who do not want to return voluntarily. In addition, the participation in the project is subject to approval of the Federal Office for Immigration and Asylum, which excludes for instance migrants who have sufficient means of their own, who have criminal procedures pending, or in case of doubts that the person is interested in a voluntary return. In cases where a deportation is already under preparation, the Federal Office may decline participation.

---

[1] In 2018, IOM assisted 2,232 Afghans in their voluntary return from all over the world (IOM 2019b).

Afghan nationals can apply for voluntary return support as well as for participation in the project RESTART II by submitting an application to the Federal Office for Immigration and Asylum. This is usually done with the help of the return counsellors, who send the application to the Federal Office and IOM and subsequently inform the migrant of the Federal Office's decision.

The assistance offered in the framework of RESTART II encompasses various elements: The migrant's decision making process regarding whether or not to return is supported through project-specific information material, pre-departure information sessions for migrants, family assessments in the country of origin (in particular for unaccompanied or separated children), as well as gathering of relevant country of origin information, including on available health care. The return travel is organized by IOM in line with IOM standards, including the provision of specific support for migrants in vulnerable situations (e.g. check of travel requirements, fitness to travel, organization of escorts, etc.). The migrant receives assistance at the Vienna International Airport in check-in and border control, transit assistance at relevant transit airports, as well as reception assistance (if requested), at the airport of arrival in Kabul. Upon request, IOM can organize temporary accommodation in a hotel in Kabul for two weeks immediately after arrival in Afghanistan and organize the onward travel to the returnee's final destination.

After arrival, project beneficiaries meet with IOM Afghanistan project staff in one of the IOM offices in Kabul, Badakhshan, Balkh, Bamyan, Herat, Kandahar, Nangarhar, Nimroz and Paktia[2]. Beneficiaries receive financial support in the form of cash worth the equivalent of € 500 to address their immediate needs after return. In addition, they receive in-kind assistance worth € 2,800 to invest in individual reintegration projects, such as education measures or income-generating activities. Available funds can be invested in services or goods that allow starting or joining a small business or agricultural activities, e.g. by purchasing wares for a shop or livestock. A small part of the in-kind assistance (max. € 300) can be invested in child support and accommodation (e.g. rent, renovation of housing). In addition, the project can also fund measures to address health-related needs, e.g. reimburse costs for medical treatments. In-kind assistance is not provided in cash directly to the beneficiaries but provided through direct payments to the service providers/suppliers of their choice, after review and check-up of supporting documents through IOM staff in Afghanistan and Austria.

---

[2]   It should be noted that due to the overall unstable security situation in Afghanistan, all nine offices in the country have to follow tight security measures as mandated by the United Nations Department of Safety and Security (UNDSS) in order to safeguard its staff members, the beneficiaries and the infrastructure of the offices.

Data Collection and analysis

For case management and monitoring purposes, data of RESTART II beneficiaries are collected systematically throughout the project cycle in accordance with IOM data protection principles and based on the beneficiaries' consent.

Initial data on the migrants' profiles are collected via the project applications submitted prior to departure from Austria. Additional data on the legal status – an indication of the three target groups specified above – are provided by the Federal Office for Immigration and Asylum. Data captured in the application forms are biographic data (name, date and location of birth, etc.), contact details, basic qualifications, intended location of return, reasons for return and preliminary reintegration plans.

After return, further information is collected through standardized questionnaires during an *initial assessment* carried out by the IOM case workers very soon after return. Data captured in the initial assessments include current living and income situation, reintegration plans as well as challenges encountered so far. It provides the basis for the reintegration support activities that are implemented in the framework of the project.

In Afghanistan, in-kind reintegration assistance is provided in two instalments; the second instalment is released after monitoring through IOM. Monitoring is done two to four months after the first instalment was released, based on a standardized monitoring questionnaire developed by IOM Austria and IOM Afghanistan staff. The questionnaire aims to capture the project beneficiaries' experiences with regards to the overall situation after return, the economic reintegration, and the project implementation. Beneficiaries have the right to decline monitoring for justified reasons and if they can provide other proof that their individual project is sustained. As monitoring is conducted by IOM, project beneficiaries may be subject to response bias, i.e. they may not be open about possible dissatisfaction due to reasons of politeness vis-à-vis IOM staff working to support them; or for fear of not receiving the second instalments in case of critical feedback (despite IOM's efforts to gain returnees' trust and assurance that critical feedback will not lead to negative consequences).

Profile of voluntary returnees to Afghanistan

From 01 January 2017 to 30 June 2019 (30 months), 320 project beneficiaries returned to Afghanistan within the framework of the project RESTART II. The following information represents data collected from their project application forms (n=320) and additional data provided by the Federal Office for Immigration and Asylum.

Out of the 320 beneficiaries, 315 are male, and five female. The overwhelming majority returned on their own, only nine project participants returned with family members (17 family members in total).

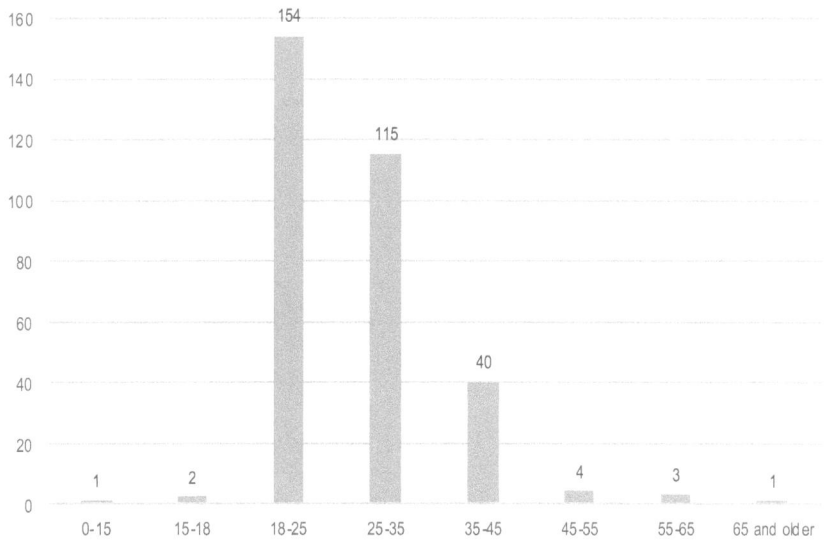

Graph 2 Age groups of RESTART II beneficiaries

Source: IOM Austria

Almost 85 per cent of the project beneficiaries are under the age of 35, the biggest group of beneficiaries (154 persons) was between 18 and 25 years old. Three of the beneficiaries were minors.

90.9 per cent of the beneficiaries indicated that they were born in Afghanistan. 19 persons (5.9%) indicated that they were born in Iran, two in Pakistan, and eight persons did not indicate any location of birth.

In Afghanistan, Kabul and Ghazni were the provinces that were indicated most frequently as locations of birth.

73.1 per cent of beneficiaries indicated Dari as their first language, 8.4 per cent indicated Farsi, 16.3 per cent indicated Pashto, and 2.2 per cent indicated Uzbek as their first language. 24.7 per cent of the returnees indicated that they had no education at all. 34.4 per cent indicated that they had completed primary education, 28.1 per cent had completed secondary education, 4.1 per cent vocational trainings, and 7.8 per cent had completed higher education.

The majority of beneficiaries (66.3%) were in Austria between two and five years before returning to Afghanistan. 6.2 per cent were in Austria less than a year, 18.1 per cent were in Austria for more than one but less than two years. 8.1 per cent were in Austria between five and ten years, while 1.3 per cent (four persons) were in Austria between ten and 20 years.

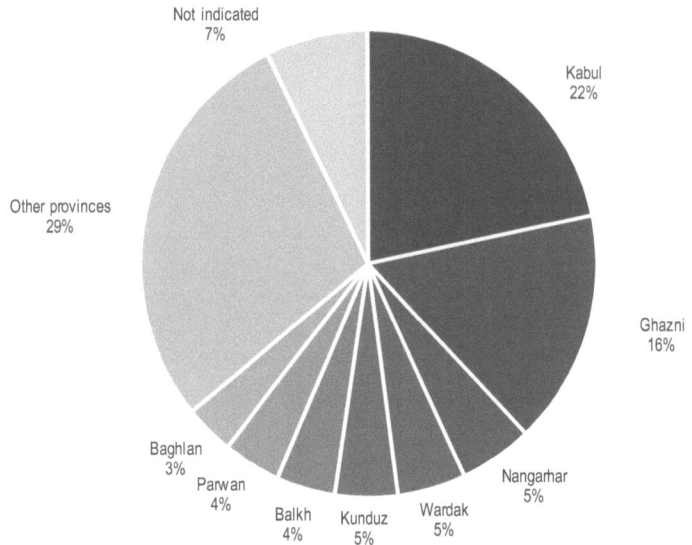

Graph 3 Location of birth of RESTART II beneficiaries born in Afghanistan (shares of provinces from total)

Source: IOM Austria

51.9 per cent of beneficiaries had not yet received a final decision with regards to their request to stay, their legal residence and/or international protection; 7.5 per cent had received a positive decision, and 40.6 per cent had received a negative decision. However, the percentage of the three different groups changed over the years: While 16 per cent of returnees in 2017 had received a negative decision, 45 per cent of returnees in 2018 had a negative decision, and 60 per cent of those who returned in the first six months of 2019. 12.8 per cent of all project registrations were submitted from administrative detention.

RESTART II – The decision to return to Afghanistan

RESTART II beneficiaries indicated various reasons for returning; many of them quoted multiple reasons at once. The reasons were provided in the returnees' own formulation in response to an open-ended question, as recorded in the project application forms. Here are some examples: "*My asylum procedure takes too long, I want to go back to my family*" (returnee, male, 30); "*My mother is very sick and needs my help*" (returnee, male, 30); "*I received a negative decision and I have no more strength*" (returnee, male, 29).

In some cases, the exact reason remained vague due to the chosen formulation, and in several cases different formulations may actually hint at the same motivation. For instance, while many people indicated that they had decided to return due to a negative asylum decision, others indicated that the *lack of perspectives in Austria* was their motivation for return; while in fact the lack of perspectives may be linked to a negative asylum decision not explicitly mentioned by the applicant. At the same time, *a negative asylum decision* did not necessarily imply that the person was already under an obligation to leave the country, since this formulation was used by those who had received a negative decision on their asylum claim in the first instance (i.e., with a possibility to appeal against it), as well as by those who had received a negative decision in the second instance (with little possibilities for further appeals). 35 persons did not provide any reason for their return.

Drawing on categorizations used in studies with similar focus (Black, Koser and Munk 2004; Koser and Kuschminder 2015)[3], the returnees responses were clustered in three different categories: (1) Conditions and perspectives in Afghanistan, (2) conditions and (lack of) perspectives in Austria, and (3) Personal reasons. Interestingly, policy interventions such as incentives for the voluntary return were not quoted by returnees as reasons for their return.

Reasons for Return - Categories	Total
Conditions & Perspectives in Afghanistan	6
Personal situation in Afghanistan has improved	2
„My country needs me"	1
Wants to start a new life	1
Continuation of studies	1
Wants to be in own country and earn money	1
Conditions & (Lack of) Perspectives in Austria	202
Negative asylum decision	108
Lack of perspectives in Austria	62
Long asylum procedures	19
Unemployment	5
Withdrawal of legal status	3
Dublin transfer pending	2
Homeless in Austria	2
Lack of legal documents	1
Personal Reasons	145
Family Reasons	128
Mental health affected in Austria	5
Homesick	5
Doesn't want to live in Austria	4
Perceived integration challenges	2
Improved personal health situation	1
Reasons not indicated	35

Table 1 Reasons for return in categories

Source: IOM Austria

The majority of returnees (63.1%) indicated the conditions and (the lack of) perspectives in Austria as a factor in their return decision. Not surprisingly, beneficiaries who did not or no longer fulfil the legal conditions for staying in Austria referred

---

[3] Note that this article does not use exactly the same categorization that the mentioned authors have used, because they differ in consistency and in data collection.

to the conditions and (lack of) perspectives in Austria as reason for the return decision more often (85.4%) than others (47.9%).

Another very important category of motivation were personal reasons (indicated by 45.3 per cent of all returnees), especially reasons linked to the family (e.g. the beneficiary wanted to join the family he/she had left behind in Afghanistan; a family member was in danger or ill and he/she wanted to take care of them or provide support, etc.). 33 per cent of all reasons provided were related to the family.

Persons who had not yet received a final decision in relation to their request to stay, their legal residence and/or international protection, and those who had received a positive decision, quoted personal reasons (59%), before conditions and lack of perspectives in Austria (48%) and conditions and perspectives in Afghanistan (2.6%) as their main reasons for deciding to return. By contrast, persons who had received a negative decision on their asylum or alien law claim quoted conditions and lack of perspectives in Austria (85.4%) before personal reasons (25.4%) as their main reasons for deciding to return. This shows that there is a very clear connection in the motivation to return linked to the legal status in Austria.

RESTART II – Assistance received

As of 30 June 2019, 265 out of the 320 returnees received reception assistance at the airport in Afghanistan, 312 returnees received cash assistance (€ 500); 53 persons received temporary accommodation after return, and 104 persons received support for their onward journey to their final destination.

Interestingly, persons who had filed a project application while in administrative detention in Austria (n=41) were more likely to request temporary accommodation after return (provided in 41.5 per cent of cases) than others (16.6 per cent of all beneficiaries had received temporary accommodation).

By 30 June 2019, IOM staff in Afghanistan had conducted 252 initial assessments with returnees soon after their return. At the time of the initial assessments, 62.7 per cent of the returnees were living in Kabul Province, 9.5 per cent were living in Herat Province, 9.1 per cent in Balkh Province, and the other 18.7 per cent lived in 15 other provinces.[4] When asked about the main challenges they had encountered so far, beneficiaries could provide multiple choices of pre-defined categories as well as indicate any other challenge. They indicated no/low income (91.3%), unemployment (82.8); security issues (76.6%), lack of adequate housing (19.4%), family related problems (1.6%), health related problems (2%), and lack of child-care (1.2%) as major challenges.

Until 30 June 2019, 247 beneficiaries had already submitted plans for the investment of the in-kind assistance. All of them focused on building or joining a small

---

[4]   It is very important to note that the choice of places of return is often shaped by various factors and does not imply that they are necessarily safe.

business in the areas of retail (84.6%; 66.1% of which were grocery stores), agriculture (6.1%, mostly animal husbandry), handicraft (7.3%, 44.4% of which were bakeries) or service (2%).

In 206 cases, one or both parts of the in-kind assistance for individual reintegration plans had already been provided.[5]

RESTART II – Situation a few months after return

As of 30.06.2019, 153 monitoring interviews with project beneficiaries had been undertaken by IOM staff in Afghanistan (six over the telephone, the rest in person). Monitoring had usually taken place between two and six months after the beneficiaries had received the first part of the reintegration assistance. In average, monitoring had taken place about four months after the first tranche of the reintegration assistance had been paid, and around seven months after they had returned.

More than 60 per cent of the interviewees (n=153) were living and interviewed in Kabul Province, followed by Herat Province (11.8%) and Balkh Province (9.2 %).

Out of 132 persons who had indicated a location of birth in Afghanistan, only 48.5 per cent were living in their province of birth. 57 per cent of those who were living in Kabul Province at the time of the monitoring (n=93) had indicated to have been born elsewhere, either in another province (51.6%), or in Iran or Pakistan (5.4%).

When asked to compare the current situation in the areas economy, health, infrastructure, cultural life and public safety and security to the situation before they had left, project beneficiaries responded as follows:

Responses	Economy	Health	Infrastructure	Cultural Life	Public Safety/ Security
don't know		2	5		2
improved	137	97	124	24	25
the same	14	53	23	128	89
worsened	1		1		37
no response	1	1		1	

Table 2 Comparison of situation before having left to now

Source: IOM Austria

Interestingly, among those who had been away from Afghanistan between two and five years (n=98), 27 per cent indicated that they felt that public safety and security had worsened (51 per cent felt it had remained the same), while among

---

[5]   Out of 89 RESTART II project beneficiaries who had returned in 2017, 15.7 per cent had not received a first tranche of in-kind reintegration support until 30 June 2019, either because they had not submitted the required documentation, or because they had not picked up the assistance afterwards. While they can still do so and may receive support until the end of 2019, it is fairly safe to assume that they have dropped out from the project. Similar figures for 2018 and 2019 would not allow such a conclusion, as beneficiaries are more likely to be still in the process of preparing the relevant steps.

those who had been away between one and two years from Afghanistan (n=36), eight per cent indicated that the security situation had worsened (83 per cent felt it had remained the same). Those who had an obligation to leave Austria were more likely to indicate that the security situation had worsened (36%) than the others (18.5%).

Reports about a perception of improved security situation came only from four out of 13 provinces, and with one exception (Herat), the responses that indicated a worsened security situation in these provinces equalled or outnumbered those that indicated an improvement.

94.1 per cent of the 153 returnees reported that they had not encountered any difficulties in re-accustoming to everyday life in Afghanistan. 94.8 per cent reported that their family and friends had reacted positively to their return.

95.4 per cent indicated that their only source of income resulted from the business they had set up or joined with the help of the RESTART II project. Most claimed that they were rather satisfied with their business and income situation: on a scale from 0 (not at all satisfied) to 10 (extremely satisfied), no one indicated 0-5. 96.7 per cent of respondents still had the business they had started with the project support, only five persons had changed their business. 9.2 per cent of the respondents indicated that their business had created jobs for either family members or other persons.

When asked how satisfied they were with the IOM assistance in general on a scale from 0 (not at all satisfied) to 10 (extremely satisfied), all respondents answered with marks 6 or higher. 66.6 per cent gave 10 points, 16.3 per cent gave nine points, 9.2 per cent gave eight points, 7.2 per cent gave seven points, and 0.7 per cent gave six points. 98 per cent of respondents indicated that the project met their needs fully, three persons indicated it met their needs partially.

Project beneficiaries were also asked whether they had gained any experiences, skills and/or qualifications abroad that were helpful for their life in Afghanistan. Only 11.1 per cent of them answered in the affirmative, quoting mostly work experience as something they could now make use of. Out of the 136 others, 51.5 per cent stated that they had gained some language skills, which however they didn't feel were helpful in the context of Afghanistan. The following quote sums up what many of the respondents indicated:

> *"I have taken a language course for nine months but that is not helpful as I cannot get any advantage from it here in Afghanistan. I couldn't gain any other experience or qualifications as I was in the migrants camp all the time and I was not allowed to work."* (Returnee, male, 22)

Conclusions

The profile of Afghan returnees who have participated in IOM's project RESTART II is not surprising for anyone working with Afghan migrants in Europe: Almost 85 per cent are between the age of 18 and 35 years old, male, and returned without family members.

Another well-known phenomenon is reflected in the fact that 21 persons "returned" to Afghanistan, despite having been born and likely grown up in another country (mostly Iran), and that many others indicated *Farsi* rather than *Dari* as their first language (and many indicated to speak both languages). IOM can only assist in the voluntary return to a country in which the returnee can stay legally; this means that Afghans cannot be assisted in the return to Pakistan and Iran if they have no legal residence status in these countries, even if they have grown up and have family there. It is known among return counsellors that some Afghan returnees intend to move on to Iran or Pakistan after their return to Afghanistan; in such cases, return counsellors usually do not present the project RESTART II as an option, since its aim is to facilitate reintegration in Afghanistan (reintegration assistance in Iran is only offered to Iranian returnees). However, it is possible that some RESTART II beneficiaries decided to move on to Iran after their return.

A fact less well known to most people who do not work with returnees in Austria is that contrary to popular belief, returnees do not only return because they have no legal right to remain on Austria's territory. In fact, almost 60 per cent of the beneficiaries had no legal obligation to leave the country. For them, personal reasons, especially reasons linked to the family, are more important than conditions or (lack of) perspectives in Austria. However, there is a changing trend that can be perceived over the years, as the percentage of those who do not or no longer have the right to stay increases. Furthermore, the number of those who still have an asylum case pending but who indicate a first negative decision, long asylum procedures, and other lack of perspectives as reasons for return is considerable.

One sad implication of the lack of perspectives is the low figure of people who report that they have gained skills or qualifications while abroad. It is sometimes argued that such skills or qualifications could be an advantage upon return to Afghanistan; however, the data gathered in RESTART II cannot confirm this.

In addition, the proportions of those who return compared to those who come to Austria (and are entitled to stay) must also be highlighted. While the number of Afghan asylum seekers in Austria has decreased in the past years, more than 40,000 applications for asylum were filed by Afghan nationals between 2015 and 2018. In the same timeframe, only about 1,200 Afghans have received voluntary return assistance from IOM Austria.

This contrast is also reflected in the enormous challenges that returnees face upon return. 76.6 per cent report that security is a major challenge for them. This could also explain why many people did not return to the provinces where they had been born. While the project aims to address the two other major challenges named by returnees (unemployment and no/low income), the security situation is something the project cannot address, and which remains highly volatile.

Addressing the economic situation is, however, a priority both for returnees as well as for IOM. While the high level of the beneficiaries' satisfaction with the project should be regarded with caution, since monitoring is usually conducted by

IOM staff and not by independent external parties, the high satisfaction rate with the businesses they had chosen, together with the low rate of changes in business, can be indicative of the good effect of the reintegration support. It must be taken into account, however, that the project monitoring usually takes place fairly soon after the reintegration assistance has been provided. Longer term effects cannot be deducted from these monitoring results.

For this reason, the project RESTART II intends to roll out an additional monitoring in the second half of 2019, to revisit at least ten per cent of the caseload and gather information about mid-term and long-term reintegration success. Using IOM's reintegration sustainability survey and its related scoring system (see Majidi and Nozarian 2019), the additional monitoring will evaluate sustainable reintegration of project beneficiaries across the economic, social and psychosocial dimensions.

This information will be important to better understand the reintegration process of individuals returning to Afghanistan and can inform future information activities that allow migrants in Austria and elsewhere to take informed decisions about their voluntary return.

References

Black, Richard, Khalid Koser, Karen Munk et al. (2004) Understanding Voluntary Return, Home Office Online Report (UK Home Office, London);

European Council on Refugees and Exiles (ECRE) (2018) Voluntary Departure and Return: Between a Rock and a Hard Place. ECRE's Analysis of European Practices in the Area of Return Including "Voluntary Departures" and Assisted Return, with its Recommendations to the EU. Policy Note (ECRE).

International Organization for Migration (IOM) (2019a) International Migration Law No. 34: Glossary on Migration (IOM, Geneva).

International Organization for Migration (IOM) (2019b) 2018 Return and Reintegration Key Highlights (IOM, Geneva).

International Organization for Migration (IOM) (2018) A Framework for Assisted Voluntary Return and Reintegration (IOM, Geneva).

International Organization for Migration (IOM) (2017) Towards an Integrated Approach to Reintegration in the Context of Return (IOM, Geneva).

International Organization for Migration (IOM) and Office of the United Nations High Commissioner for Refugees (UNHCR) (2019) Returns to Afghanistan 2018. Joint IOM-UNHCR Summary Report (IOM/UNHCR, Kabul).

King, Russell (2000) Generalizations from the history of return migration. In: Gosh, Bimal (ed.) Return Migration. Journey of Hope or Despair (IOM, Geneva) 7-56.

Koser, Khalid, and Katie Kuschminder (2015) Comparative Research on the Assisted Voluntary Return and Reintegration of Migrants (IOM, Geneva).

Majidi, Nassim., and Nazanine Nozarian (2019) Measuring sustainable reintegration. In: Migration Policy Practice 2019(IX, 1) 30-39.

Federal Ministry of the Interior, Republic of Austria (2019) Asylstatistik 2018 (*Asylum Statistics 2018*) (Federal Ministry of the Interior, Vienna). Available at https://www.bmi.gv.at/301/Statistiken/files/Jahresstatistiken/Asyl-Jahresstatistik_2018.pdf (accessed on 28.05.2019).

Newland, Kathleen (2017) Migrant Return and Reintegration Policy: A Key Component of Migration Governance. In: McAuliffe, Marie, and Michele Klein Solomon (conveners) Ideas to Inform International Cooperation on Safe, Orderly and Regular Migration (IOM, Geneva).

Office of the United Nations High Commissioner for Human Rights (OHCHR) (2001) Training Manual on Human Rights Monitoring; Chapter XI, Monitoring and Protecting the Human Rights of Returnees and Internally Displaced Persons (OHCHR, Geneva).

Parliament, BM.I (2018) Kosten und Sicherheitsrisiken von Abschiebungen nach Afghanistan. Response of the Federal Minister of the Interior Herbert Kickl (1792/AB) to a parliamentarian written re-quest for information (1770/J), Ref. BMI-LR2220/0557-II/2/b/2018, 26.11.2018; available at https://www.parlament.gv.at/PAKT/VHG/XXVI/AB/AB_01792/index.shtml

Parliament, BM.I (2019) Daten zur Abschiebung. Response of the Federal Minister of the Interior Herbert Kickl (2483/AB) to a parliamentarian written re-quest for information (2498/J), Ref. BMI-LR2220/0007-V/8/2019BMI-LR2220/0007-V/8/2019, 20.02.2019, Vienna; available at https://www.parlament.gv.at/PAKT/VHG/XXVI/AB/AB_02483/index.shtml

Statistics Austria (2019) Bevölkerung zu Jahresbeginn 2002-2019 nach detaillierter Staatsangehörigkeit (*Population at beginning of the year 2002-2019 according to detailed nationality*) (Statistics Austria, Vienna). Available at http://www.statistik.at/wcm/idc/idcplg?IdcService= GET_PDF_FILE&RevisionSelectionMethod=LatestReleased&dDocName=071715 (accessed on 15.10.2019).

United Nations Development Programme (UNDP) (2018) Human Development Indices and Indicators: 2018 Statistical Update Afghanistan (UNDP, Kabul).

United Nations Office for the Coordination of Humanitarian Affairs (UN OCHA) (2017) 2018 Humanitarian Needs Overview. Afghanistan (UN OCHA, Kabul).

United Nations Office for the Coordination of Humanitarian Affairs (UN OCHA) (2018) 2019 Humanitarian Needs Overview. Afghanistan (UN OCHA, Kabul).

Wilkes, Tommy (2017) Afghans deported from Europe arrive home, to war and unemployment, in: Reuters World News, March 31, 2017, available at: https://www.reuters.com/article/us-afghanistan-refugees/afghans-deported-from-europe-arrive-home-to-war-and-unemployment-idUSKBN1721VJ

NACH DER MIGRATION IST VOR DER MIGRATION: POSTMIGRANTISCHER WANDEL ZU EINWANDERUNGSGESELLSCHAFTEN

Staatsbürgerschaft und Wahlrecht: Österreich im internationalen Vergleich

Rainer Bauböck

Zusammenfassung

Ein globaler Vergleich von 175 Staatsbürgerschaftsgesetzen zeigt die regionale Dominanz des Abstammungsprinzips in Europa und Asien und des Territorialprinzips in Nord- und Südamerika. Dabei ist jedoch zu berücksichtigen, dass das Geburtsrecht auf Staatsbürgerschaft dort ineffektiv ist, wo Staaten nicht fähig oder willens sind, alle Geburten in ihrem Staatsgebiet zu registrieren. Bei Einbürgerung, Verzicht auf und unfreiwilligem Verlust von Staatsbürgerschaft zeigen sich deutliche Unterschiede zwischen liberalen und autoritären Regimen. Auffallend ist jedoch, dass die Toleranz von Doppelstaatsbürgerschaft sowohl für Einwanderer als auch für Auswanderer heute weltweit zur Norm geworden ist. Im Vergleich mit anderen europäischen Einwanderungsländern ist das österreichische Staatsbürgerschaftsrecht sowohl bei den Bedingungen für die Einbürgerung als auch bei der Zulassung mehrfacher Staatsbürgerschaften besonders restriktiv.

Ein starker globaler Trend ist die Entkoppelung des Wahlrechts in nationalen Wahlen vom Aufenthalt, d.h. die Einführung von Wahlrechten für die „Diaspora" der Auslandsbürger. In Europa und Südamerika gibt es aber auch eine starke Gruppe von Staaten, die das Wahlrecht auf kommunaler Ebene von der Staatsbürgerschaft entkoppeln und alleine auf den Aufenthalt in der Gemeinde abstellen. Österreich hat sich dem ersten Trend angeschlossen, dem zweiten jedoch verweigert.

I. Ein globaler Vergleich der Staatsbürgerschaftsgesetze[1]

Die Allgemeine Erklärung der Menschenrechte aus dem Jahr 1948 proklamiert: *„Jeder Mensch hat ein Recht auf Staatsbürgerschaft."*[2] Andererseits gilt der völkerrechtliche Grundsatz: *„Jeder Staat bestimmt nach seinem eigenen Recht, wer seine Staatsangehörigen sind."*[3] Der Konflikt zwischen diesen beiden Grundsätzen zeigt

---

[1] Abschnitt I ist eine Übertragung ins Deutsche eines DELMI-GLOBALCIT Policy Briefs: Rainer Bauböck, Iseult Honohan and Maarten Vink: How Citizenship Laws Differ: A Global Comparison, Delmi Policy Brief 2018:9, verfügbar auf www.delmi.se und www.globalcit.eu. Dabei wurden einzelne Daten korrigiert.

[2] AEMR Art. 15 (1)

[3] Haager Abkommen zu einigen Fragen der Staatsangehörigkeit (1930), Art. 1 und Europäisches Übereinkommen über Staatsangehörigkeit (1997), Art. 3.

sich darin, wie unterschiedlich der Zugang zur Staatsbürgerschaft und deren Wechsel in nationalen Gesetzen geregelt wird. Im Folgenden werden wir die Ergebnisse eines aktuellen globalen Vergleichs referieren und insbesondere auf die Situation in Österreich eingehen.

Vergleichende Studien über Staatsbürgerschaftsgesetze waren bisher meist auf westliche Demokratien beschränkt und untersuchten lediglich den Zugang von Einwanderern[4] zur Staatsbürgerschaft. Dabei wurde oft angenommen, dass diese Gesetze durch einen Kontrast zwischen ethnischen und republikanischen Konzeptionen geprägt sind, wobei die erstere das Abstammungsprinzip (ius sanguinis) in den Vordergrund rückt und letztere das territoriale Geburtslandprinzip (ius soli). Ein weltweiter und umfassender Vergleich nationalen Staatsangehörigkeitsrechts in 175 Ländern zeigt ein komplexeres Bild. Wir haben dazu 12 Indikatoren kalkuliert, welche messen, wie inklusiv einzelne Bestimmungen von Staatsangehörigkeitsgesetzen für die jeweilige Zielgruppe sind, wieviel Freiheit sie dem einzelnen beim Wechsel der Staatsbürgerschaft einräumen und ob sie grundlegende Standards der Nichtdiskriminierung und Rechtsstaatlichkeit erfüllen. Diese Indikatoren erfassen die gebräuchlichsten Regeln für die Zuerkennung der Staatsbürgerschaft bei Geburt, für gewöhnliche (d.h. auf dem Aufenthalt im Inland beruhende) Einbürgerung, für bevorzugte Einbürgerung von EhepartnerInnen und kulturell verwandter Gruppen, für die freiwillige Rücklegung der Staatsbürgerschaft, sowie für den Entzug aufgrund eines längeren Auslandsaufenthalts oder im Fall des freiwilligen Erwerbs einer anderen Staatsangehörigkeit. Zusätzlich verwenden wir UNICEF Daten über die Registrierung von Geburten um zu bewerten, ob Personen mit Rechtsanspruch auf Staatsbürgerschaft per Abstammung oder Inlandsgeburt diese auch tatsächlich erhalten können.

Staatsbürgerschaft per Geburt: Starke Regionale Divergenz

Alle Staaten verleihen ihre Staatsangehörigkeit per Geburt. Die beiden Grundregeln des ius soli und ius sanguinis haben ihren modernen Ursprung jeweils im englischen Common Law und dem französischen Code Napoléon, der Anfang des 19. Jahrhunderts das Modell für allgemein bürgerliche Gesetzbücher in Kontinentaleuropa war. Das ius soli wurde von den ehemaligen britischen Siedlerkolonien in Nordamerika, Australien und Neuseeland übernommen, es dominiert aber auch in Lateinamerika, wo seine Ursprünge auf die liberale spanische Verfassung von Cádiz aus dem Jahr 1812 zurückgehen. Im Rest der Welt wird Staatsbürgerschaft hauptsächlich per Abstammung übertragen; das gilt auch in vielen ehemaligen britischen Kolonien, die ihre Gesetze kurz nach der Unabhängigkeit in diesem Sinn änderten.

Die meisten Staaten mischen allerdings Elemente beider Regeln. Alle Staaten, in denen im Inland das ius soli vorherrscht, verleihen zumindest der ersten Generation von Kindern ihrer Auswanderer die Staatsbürgerschaft per Abstammung. Und 51%

---

[4] Aus Gründen der besseren Lesbarkeit wird auf geschlechtsneutrale Formulierungen verzichtet. Die männliche Form bezieht sich daher in der Regel sowohl auf Frauen als auch auf Männer.

	Welt	Afrika	Amerika	Asien/ Ozeanien	Europa
Ius Sanguinis (im Inland)					
- unbeschränkt	59%	72%	17%	64%	71%
- bedingt	14%	17%	3%	13%	21%
- stark beschränkt	10%	8%	-	22%	7%
- keine Anwendung	17%	4%	80%	-	-
Ius Sanguinis (im Ausland)					
- unbeschränkt	41%	62%	29%	22%	43%
- bedingt	38%	25%	43%	42%	48%
- keine oder stark beschränkte Anwendung	21%	13%	29%	36%	10%
Ius Soli					
- unbeschränkt	18%	4%	83%	2%	-
- bedingt	21%	23%	14%	16%	29%
- stark beschränkt	6%	8%	-	13%	2%
- keine Anwendung	55%	66%	3%	69%	69%
Ius Soli (für Staatenlose)					
- besondere Anwendung	51%	32%	23%	60%	88%
- keine besondere Anwendung	49%	68%	77%	40%	12%
Zahl der Staaten	**175**	**53**	**35**	**45**	**42**

Tabelle 1: Geburtsrecht auf Staatsbürgerschaft

Quelle: http://globalcit.eu/wp-content/uploads/2018/11/Policy_Brief_Delmi_GLOBALCIT.pdf

der untersuchten Gesetze enthalten spezielle ius soli Bestimmungen für Kinder, die in ihrem Territorium ohne andere Staatsangehörigkeit geboren werden. In Europa gilt dies für 88% aller Staaten, in Asien für 60%, in Afrika allerdings nur für 32%. Da in diesen drei Kontinenten das Abstammungsprinzip vorherrscht, ist das Fehlen von ius soli Bestimmungen eine wesentliche Ursache für Staatenlosigkeit.

Es ist wichtig zu betonen, dass das ius soli zwar die im Zielland geborenen Kinder von Einwanderern automatisch in Staatsbürger verwandelt, aber meist jene Kinder, die im Ausland geboren wurden und als Minderjährige mit oder nach ihren Eltern einreisen (die sogenannte „Generation Eineinhalb") in der rechtlichen Unsicherheit des Ausländerstatus belässt, bis sie die Volljährigkeit erreicht haben und die Einbürgerung beantragen können. Dagegen werden auch die Kinder von Einwanderern in ius sanguinis Staaten zu Staatsbürgern per Geburt oder bald nach dieser, wenn es für ihre Eltern leicht war, sich einbürgern zu lassen oder wenn minderjährige Kinder einen Rechtsanspruch auf Staatsangehörigkeit nach wenigen Jahren Aufenthalt haben – wie es etwa in Schweden der Fall ist, wo die Eltern nach fünf Jahren lediglich eine Erklärung abgeben müssen. Der Kontrast zwischen inklusivem ius soli und ausschließendem ius sanguinis ist also selbst für den Einwanderungskontext weniger eindeutig als oft angenommen wird.

Sowohl ius sanguinis als auch ius soli können entweder unbedingt oder bedingt verliehen werden. Nur in Nord- und Südamerika werden in den meisten Staaten (83%) alle im Inland geborenen Menschen unabhängig von Aufenthaltsdauer oder -status automatisch Staatsbürger, wogegen Großbritannien, Irland, Australien und

Neuseeland unterschiedliche Bedingungen eingeführt haben, wie etwa eine bestimmte Aufenthaltsdauer eines Elternteils. Europäische Staaten, die das ius soli neu als Antwort auf Einwanderung eingeführt haben, wie etwas Deutschland oder Griechenland, haben sich immer für eine bedingte Variante entschieden. Ius sanguinis ist dann unbedingt, wenn es ohne Beschränkung über Generationen hinweg auf im Ausland geborene Nachkommen übertragen werden kann. Dadurch entstehen potenziell sehr umfangreiche Diaspora-Populationen, die im Herkunftsland ihrer Vorfahren Niederlassung und Staatsbürgerrechte beanspruchen können. In Afrika gibt es in 62% der Staaten keine Begrenzung für die extraterritoriale Anwendung des ius sanguinis, in Europa trifft dies für 43% zu, während in Asien, Ozeanien und Amerika der Anteil bei unter 30% liegt.

Ineffektives Geburtsrecht bei unvollständigem Geburtenregister

Das Geburtsrecht auf Staatsbürgerschaft sollte eigentlich allen Individuen den lebenslangen staatlichen Schutz ihrer Rechte sichern. Wo jedoch Staaten Geburten in ihrem Territorium und die Elternschaft ihrer Staatsbürger nicht zuverlässig registrieren, wird Kindern dieser Schutz entzogen. Oft werden sie de facto staatenlos. Die Kinderhilfsorganisation der Vereinten Nationen UNICEF benennt 60 Staaten, in denen der Anteil der registrierten Geburten an allen Inlandsgeburten geringer als 90% ist. In Afrika sind dies mehr als drei Viertel aller Staaten (77%, wobei für weitere 8%, die wahrscheinlich zur selben Gruppe gehören, Daten fehlen). Unvollständige Geburtenregister sind auch ein gravierendes Problem in lateinamerikanischen und asiatischen Staaten. Die Hauptursache sind mangelnde Kapazitäten der öffentlichen Verwaltung, aber Bronwen Manby findet in ihrer Analyse afrikanischer Staaten auch Fälle, wo vor allem die Registrierung von Geburten in ethnischen, „rassischen" oder religiösen Minderheiten vernachlässigt wird.[5]

Einbürgerung: ein Recht oder ein Privileg?

Eine Staatsangehörigkeit, die bei Geburt erworben wurde, kann im späteren Leben durch Einbürgerung gewechselt oder durch eine zusätzliche ergänzt werden. Anders als beim Geburtsrecht gibt es eine viel größere Vielfalt von Gründen, warum Staaten Anträge auf Einbürgerung annehmen und von Bedingungen, die sie auferlegen. Wir haben einige wenige signifikante Einbürgerungsgründe und –bedingungen ausgewählt, indem wir die gewöhnliche Einbürgerung aufgrund längeren Aufenthalts von bevorzugter Naturalisierung unterscheiden, bei der meist die geforderte Aufenthaltsdauer verkürzt oder gänzlich erlassen wird.

In fast der Hälfte aller Staaten (48%) genügen 5 Jahre regulären Aufenthalts oder mit Daueraufenthaltsbewilligung um sich für Einbürgerung zu qualifizieren. In Nord- und Südamerika trifft das auf 2/3 aller Staaten zu. Am anderen Ende des Spektrums liegen jene 34% aller Staaten, die eine Aufenthaltsdauer von 10 oder mehr Jahren verlangen, explizit diskriminierende Kriterien anwenden oder die Ent-

---

[5]   Manby, B. Citizenship in Africa: The Law of Belonging, Hart Publishing, 2018.

	Welt	Afrika	Amerika	Asien/ Ozeanien	Europa
Aufenthaltsbedingung					
- 5 Jahre oder weniger	48%	36%	66%	51%	45%
- 6 bis 9 Jahre	18%	13%	29%	2%	33%
- 10 bis 12 Jahre	22%	38%	3%	18%	21%
- 15 Jahre oder mehr / Keine oder diskriminierende Regeln	12%	13%	3%	29%	0%
Doppelstaatsbürgerschaft für Einwanderer	63%	72%	71%	56%	52%
Wirtschaftliche Bedingungen	53%	43%	37%	67%	64%
Erstreckung auf EhegattInnen					
- Ja	60%	57%	69%	31%	88%
- keine besonderen Regeln	13%	0%	17%	27%	12%
- Geschlechtsdiskriminierung	27%	43%	14%	42%	0%
Erleichterung für "kulturell Verwandte"	23%	13%	14%	18%	48%
Zahl der Staaten	**175**	**53**	**35**	**45**	**42**

Tabelle 2: Gewöhnliche und beschleunigte Einbürgerung

Quelle: http://globalcit.eu/wp-content/uploads/2018/11/Policy_Brief_Delmi_GLOBALCIT.pdf

scheidung über Einbürgerungsanträge zur Gänze dem Ermessen der Behörden überlassen. Unter den zahlreichen anderen Bedingungen, die Staaten für gewöhnliche Naturalisierung verlangen greifen wir jene heraus, die wahrscheinlich die höchsten Hürden bilden. Toleranz von Doppelstaatsbürgerschaft bei Einbürgerung gibt es häufiger in Afrika (72%) und Amerika (71%) als in Asien/Ozeanien (56%) und Europa (52%). Wirtschaftliche Kriterien, wie ein bestimmtes Einkommensniveau, stabile Beschäftigung oder die Nichtinanspruchnahme von Sozialhilfebezügen werden relativ häufig in Europa (64%) und Asien/Ozeanien (67%) angewendet, aber viel seltener in Amerika (37%).

60% aller untersuchten Staaten und 88% der europäischen erleichtern die Einbürgerung für jene, die mit Staatsangehörigen verheiratet sind. Bis in die 1970er Jahre diskriminierten die meisten Staaten zwischen Männer und Frauen, indem Ehegattinnen gezwungen wurden, die Staatsbürgerschaft ihrer Ehemänner anzunehmen. Obwohl solche Gesetze heute gegen bindendes Völkerrecht verstoßen, haben 47 Staaten (in Afrika und Asien sind das mehr als 40%) noch immer solche Geschlechterdiskriminierung in ihren Staatsbürgerschaftsgesetzen. Der privilegierte Zugang zur Staatsbürgerschaft für jene, die eine offizielle Staatssprache sprechen oder einer ethnischen und kulturellen Mehrheitsbevölkerung zugerechnet werden, ist dagegen in Europa mit 48% viel häufiger anzutreffen als im Rest der Welt (15%).

Verlust der Staatsbürgerschaft –
durch freiwillige Entscheidung oder unfreiwilligen Entzug

Staatsbürgerschaft kann freiwillig durch Verzicht verloren werden oder durch unfreiwilligen Entzug seitens des Staats. Der zweite Absatz des eingangs zitierten Artikel 15 der Allgemeinen Erklärung der Menschenrechte lautet: *„Niemandem darf*

	Welt	Afrika	Amerika	Asien/ Ozea- nien	Europa
Freiwillige Rücklegung möglich					
- Ja	84%	85%	69%	80%	100%
- nur beschränkt	3%	0%	17%	0%	0%
- nein	13%	15%	14%	20%	0%
Entzug nach langem Auslandsaufenthalt	30%	26%	23%	40%	31%
Doppelstaatsbürgerschaft für Auswanderer	66%	64%	89%	44%	74%
Zahl der Staaten	175	53	35	45	42

Tabelle 3: Freiwilliger und unfreiwilliger Verlust der Staatsbürgerschaft

Quelle: http://globalcit.eu/wp-content/uploads/2018/11/Policy_Brief_Delmi_GLOBALCIT.pdf

		Bei Erwerb einer fremden Staatsbürgerschaft		
		Nein	Ja	Gesamt
	Nein	32 (18%)	33 (19%)	65 (37%)
Bei Einbürgerung	Ja	27 (15%)	83 (47%)	110 (63%)
	Gesamt	59 (34%)	116 (66%)	175 (100%)

Tabelle 4: Toleranz der Doppelstaatsbürgerschaft

Quelle: Maarten Vink, Berechnungen auf Basis von GLOBALCIT Daten

die eigene Staatsangehörigkeit willkürlich entzogen noch das Recht versagt werden, die Staatsangehörigkeit zu wechseln. " Respektieren alle Staaten diesen Grundsatz?

13% hindern ihre Bürger daran, ihre Staatsangehörigkeit zu wechseln aufgrund einer Doktrin der „immerwährenden Treuepflicht". Weitere 3% erlauben die Rücklegung der Staatsbürgerschaft nur unter sehr eingeschränkten Bedingungen. Interessant ist, dass solche illiberalen Regeln nicht nur in nicht-demokratischen Staaten (besonders in Asien und Nordafrika) weitverbreitet sind, sondern auch in den lateinamerikanischen ius soli Staaten (11 dieser Staaten kennen keine oder nur stark eingeschränkte Verzichtsoptionen). Häufiger – und durchaus im Einklang mit menschenrechtlichen Normen – wird der freiwillige Verzicht dann nicht erlaubt, wenn Staatenlosigkeit die Folge wäre, oder wenn die Person ihren Hauptwohnsitz im Inland hat.

Etwas weniger als ein Drittel der Staaten (bei geringer Varianz zwischen den Weltregionen) nimmt an, dass langjähriger Auslandsaufenthalt einen Verlust genuiner Bindung an den Staat bewirkt, der den Entzug der Staatsbürgerschaft dann rechtfertigt, wenn bereits eine andere erworben wurde. Für genau ein Drittel (33%) ist es hingegen der freiwillige Erwerb einer anderen Staatsangehörigkeit selbst, der die Ausbürgerung rechtfertigt. Diese Haltung ist allerdings seit den 1960er Jahren deutlich seltener geworden, weil immer mehr Staaten daran interessiert sind, die Bindungen zu ihrer „Diaspora" zu stärken und deshalb Doppelstaatsbürgerschaften bei Auswanderern tolerieren.[6] Das trifft auf 74% der europäischen Staaten und 66%

---

[6]   Siehe https://macimide.maastrichtuniversity.nl/dual-cit-database/

aller Staaten weltweit zu. Nur in Asien gibt es noch mehrheitlichen Widerstand gegen diesen globalen Trend.

Kombiniert man die Doppelstaatsbürgerschaft bei Einbürgerung und beim freiwilligen Erwerb einer fremden Staatsangehörigkeit, so zeigt sich, dass eine starke relative Mehrheit von 47% aller Staaten Doppelstaatsbürgerschaft sowohl für Einwanderer als auch für Auswanderer akzeptiert und nur 18% die österreichische Haltung einer symmetrischen Ablehnung teilen. Die Gruppen jener Staaten, die Doppelstaatsbürgerschaft nur für Einwanderer akzeptieren ist mit 15% kleiner als jene, die sie nur für Auswanderer tolerieren (19%). Dabei ist jedoch zu berücksich tigen, dass selbst generell ablehnende Staaten wie Österreich Doppelstaatsbürgerschaften meist dann anerkennen, wenn diese bei Geburt entstehen und nicht durch den späteren Erwerb einer zusätzlichen Staatsbürgerschaft.

Politikempfehlungen

(1) Unsere Studie zeigt: Um das 1948 proklamierte Menschenrecht auf Staatsangehörigkeit zu verwirklichen, müssten globale Mindeststandards für Gesetze und Politiken eingeführt werden. Diese sollten die Ziele verfolgen, Staatenlosigkeit zu verringern, offene Diskriminierung zu bekämpfen, und Rechtsstaatlichkeit zu stärken. Das Schwergewicht sollte auf die folgenden Reformen gelegt werden:

- Staatsbürgerschaft aufgrund der Geburt im Inland für Kinder, die sonst staatenlos würden, muss in allen Staaten eingeführt werden, in denen es kein ius soli gibt (insbesondere in Afrika).
- Diskriminierung von Frauen, ethnischen, religiösen und "rassischen" Minderheiten in ius soli Bestimmungen, bei der Einbürgerung, beim Erwerb der Staatsbürgerschaft durch Abstammung oder Eheschließung muss beseitigt werden (vor allem in Asien und Afrika).
- Die Länge des geforderten Aufenthalts für gewöhnliche Einbürgerung sollte begrenzt werden und die entsprechenden Gesetze sollten alle Anforderungen klar und vollständig enthalten, um Behördenwillkür bei Ermessensentscheidungen zu vermeiden (besonders in Asien und Afrika).
- Das Recht, die Staatsbürgerschaft durch Verzicht zu wechseln, muss gesichert werden (besonders in Asien, Afrika und Lateinamerika).

(2) Inklusive Regeln für das Geburtsrecht auf Staatsbürgerschaft bleiben ineffektiv, wo Staaten die Verwaltungskapazität fehlt, Geburten zu registrieren, oder wo Kinder, die zu ethnischen, religiösen und „rassischen" Minderheiten gehören, bewusst nicht registriert werden. Internationale Organisationen sollten die Erstellung vollständiger Geburtenregister fordern und fördern, insbesondere in den afrikanischen Staaten.

(3) Völkerrechtliche Normen können auf regionaler Ebene leichter entwickelt und durchgesetzt werden. Organisationen wie die Afrikanische Union, UNASUR

und ASEAN sollten zwischenstaatliche Prozesse initiieren, aus denen regionale Abkommen über Staatsangehörigkeit hervorgehen. Das Abkommen des Europarats über Staatsangehörigkeit aus dem Jahr 1997 kann dafür als Vorbild dienen.

(4) Demokratische Staaten müssen danach streben, höhere Standards als die menschenrechtlichen Mindestnormen zu erfüllen. Viele europäische Staaten haben ihre Staatsbürgerschaft für große und wachsende Bevölkerungen mit Migrationshintergrund nicht geöffnet. Diese europäischen Einwanderungsländer, darunter auch Österreich, sollten zumindest bedingte Formen des ius soli einführen oder die Kinder der Immigranten durch starke Rechtsansprüche auf Einbürgerung inkludieren. Sie sollten auch die Einbürgerung der ersten Generation fördern, indem sie Hindernisse wie wirtschaftliche Kriterien, schwierige Sprach- und Wissenstests und die Notwendigkeit der Rücklegung einer bisherigen Staatsbürgerschaft beseitigen.

II. Erwerb und Verlust der österreichischen Staatsbürgerschaft

Europa unterscheidet sich von anderen Weltregionen durch ein relativ einheitliches Staatsangehörigkeitsrecht. Das kann einerseits damit erklärt werden, dass in Europa die meisten Staaten gefestigte Demokratien sind und andererseits damit, dass sowohl der Europarat als auch die Europäische Union Mindeststandards für Grundrechte und Rechtsstaatlichkeit festlegen. Das bereits erwähnte Abkommen des Europarats über Staatangehörigkeit enthält weltweit die stärksten Normen, von denen viele in anderen Weltregionen systematisch verletzt werden. Dazu zählt etwa das Verbot von Diskriminierung, einschließlich jener zwischen Staatsbürgern per Geburt und per Einbürgerung (Art. 5), die Festlegung einer maximalen Aufenthaltsfrist von 10 Jahren für Einbürgerung (Art. 6(3)), die Aufzählung einer abschließenden Liste zulässiger Gründe für den Entzug der Staatsbürgerschaft (Art. 7) und das Recht, auf die Staatsbürgerschaft zu verzichten, wenn man eine andere besitzt und seinen gewöhnlichen Aufenthalt im Ausland hat (Art. 8).

Die Entwicklung des österreichischen Staatsbürgerschaftsrechts seit der Zeit der Gastarbeiterrekrutierung in den 1960er und frühen 1970er Jahren lässt sich mit den folgenden Schlagworten beschreiben: zunehmende Politisierung, Komplexitätssteigerung und Erhöhung der Einbürgerungshürden. Bis in die späten 1990er Jahre gab es nur wenige Novellen des Staatsbürgerschaftsgesetzes und kaum politische Debatten über Einbürgerung. Das lag daran, dass die Republik sich nach wie vor nicht als Einwanderungsland verstand, trotz des demographischen Wandels durch Familiennachzugs zu den „Gastarbeitern" und die große Zuwanderung von Flüchtenden aus dem Westbalkan zu Beginn der 1990er Jahre. Schon vor der Jahrtausendwende änderte sich dies. Die konservative ÖVP entwickelte – auch als Antwort auf die Mobilisierung des Themas durch die Freiheitliche Partei – einen neuen Diskurs, dass die Staatsbürgerschaft ein „hohes Gut" sei, dessen Wert durch allzu leichten Zugang vermindert würde. Seither gilt in Österreich (wie in einigen anderen westeuropäischen Staaten) die Devise, dass Einbürgerung kein Mittel für die Integration von Einwanderern sei, sondern deren krönender Abschluss, der als Auszeichnung für besondere Integrationsleistungen zu verleihen ist. Diese Bekräftigung des symbolischen Werts der Staatsbürgerschaft erforderte immer neue Novellen, in denen die Bedingungen für die Einbürgerung verschärft wurden.[7] Heute zählt das österreichische Staatsbürgerschaftsgesetz ohne Zweifel zu den komplexesten und gleichzeitig restriktivsten innerhalb der Europäischen Union und insbesondere unter den Staaten mit hohen und langansässigen Bevölkerungsanteilen mit Migrationshintergrund. Der Migrant Integration Policy Index von 2015 reiht Österreich an fünftletzte Stelle unter 38 Staaten, nach der Schweiz und vor der Slowakei, Bulgarien, Estland und Lettland.[8]

Angelehnt an die für den globalen Vergleich ausgewählten Indikatoren sollen im Folgenden die wesentlichen Merkmale des österreichischen Staatsbürgerschaftsgesetzes beschrieben werden.

Geburtsrecht

Das österreichische Recht beruht fast ausschließlich auf dem Abstammungsprinzip (ius sanguinis). Die einzigen Elemente des ius soli betreffen den Erwerb der Staatsbürgerschaft durch Findlinge solange ihre Staatsangehörigkeit nicht geklärt werden kann. Das österreichische ius sanguinis ist nicht begrenzt, d.h. die Staatsbürgerschaft wird an Kinder, die im Ausland geboren werden, ohne Beschränkung in der Generationenfolge weitergegeben, wenn ein Elternteil die österreichische Staatsbürgerschaft hat. Eine Begrenzung der Zahl der Auslandsösterreicher ohne genuine Verbindung zur Republik ergibt sich nur indirekt über den Verlust der Staatsbürgerschaft im Fall der Einbürgerung im Gastland. Im Inland geborene Kinder mit zwei ausländischen Eltern bleiben Ausländer, wenn sie sich nicht einbürgern lassen. Allerdings gibt es für im Inland geborene Kinder eine Verkürzung der Aufenthaltsfrist von 10 auf 6 Jahre, wobei jedoch alle anderen Voraussetzungen für die gewöhnliche Einbürgerung gelten – einschließlich der Rücklegung einer anderen Staatsbürgerschaft. Doppelstaatsbürgerschaften werden in Österreich (mit Ausnahmen, etwa bei Einbürgerung im besonderen Interesse der Republik) nur dann toleriert, wenn sie per Geburt entstehen, weil nur ein Elternteil die österreichische Staatsbürgerschaft besitzt oder wenn ein im Ausland geborenes Kind österreichischer Eltern eine fremde Staatsbürgerschaft aufgrund des ius soli erwirbt.

Gewöhnliche Einbürgerung

Mit einer geforderten Aufenthaltsdauer von mindestens zehn Jahren für gewöhnliche Einbürgerung schöpft Österreich das Maximum aus, das vom Europäischen Abkommen vorgesehen ist. Dazu kommt besonders erschwerend, dass dieser Aufenthalt nicht nur rechtmäßig sondern auch ununterbrochen sein muss. Einwanderer, die für längere Zeit in ihr Herkunftsland zurückkehren müssen, etwa um sich um enge

---

[7]   Siehe Joachim Stern und Gerd Valchars (2013) Country Report: Austria. GLOBALCIT, Florenz
[8]   Siehe http://www.mipex.eu/access-nationality.

Familienangehörige zu kümmern, werden damit von der Staatsbürgerschaft auf lange Zeit ausgeschlossen. Auch bei den anderen Einbürgerungsvoraussetzungen gehört Österreich fast durchwegs zu den restriktivsten Staaten in Europa. Das betrifft insbesondere die Pflicht zur Rücklegung der bisherigen Staatsbürgerschaft, die schwer zu erfüllenden wirtschaftlichen Kriterien und extrem hohen Einbürgerungsgebühren, sowie die besonders strenge Auslegung der Bedingung der Unbescholtenheit. Bei der Einführung von Sprach- und Wissenstests folgt Österreich dagegen einem breiteren europäischen Trend. Ob solche Tests tatsächlich als Integrationsnachweis gelten können und einen Anreiz für das Lernen der deutschen Sprache bilden oder vielmehr den Zugang zur Staatsbürgerschaft für bildungsferne Einwanderer blockieren, ist empirisch bisher nicht abschließend geklärt.

Erleichterte Einbürgerung

Neben der gewöhnlichen Einbürgerung nach 10 Jahren Aufenthalt gibt es in Österreich mehrere Möglichkeiten, die Staatsbürgerschaft bereits früher und teilweise auch unter großzügigeren Bedingungen zu erhalten. Für die meisten Gruppen verkürzt sich dadurch die Wartefrist auf 6 Jahre. Dazu gehört die Einbürgerung von Ehepartnern und minderjährigen Kindern österreichischer Staatsbürger bzw. die Erstreckung der gewöhnlichen Einbürgerung einer Ankerperson auf solche engen Familienangehörige. Auch Personen, die „nachhaltige persönliche Integration" nachweisen können (etwa durch dreijähriges ehrenamtliches Engagement in einer gemeinnützigen Organisation) können schon vier Jahre früher als andere eingebürgert werden. Österreich gehört zu den wenigen EU-Staaten, in denen auch die Bürger anderer Mitgliedsländer vorzeitig eingebürgert werden können, wobei der Zwang zur Aufgabe der bisherigen Staatsbürgerschaft und die Tatsache, dass Unionsbürger auch ohne inländische Staatsbürgerschaft rechtlich weitgehend gleichgestellt sind, wenig Anreize für die Einbürgerung bieten. Bemerkenswert ist, dass unter der Regierung Kurz-Strache die vorzeitige Einbürgerung von anerkannten Konventionsflüchtlingen aus dem Gesetz gestrichen wurde.

Einige öffentliche Diskussion hat auch die Bestimmung ausgelöst, wonach keine bestimmte Aufenthaltsdauer und keine Rücklegung der bisherigen Staatsbürgerschaft notwendig ist, wenn *„die Verleihung der Staatsbürgerschaft wegen der vom Fremden bereits erbrachten und von ihm noch zu erwartenden außerordentlichen Leistungen im besonderen Interesse der Republik liegt"* (StBG, Art. 10(6)).

Verlust der österreichischen Staatsbürgerschaft

Auf die österreichische Staatsbürgerschaft kann freiwillig verzichten, wer eine andere Staatsangehörigkeit besitzt, und – falls er ein Mann ist – den Militär- oder Zivildienst abgeleistet hat und gegen den kein Strafverfahren anhängig ist. Hauptwohnsitz im Ausland ist keine Voraussetzung, allerdings entfallen nach 5 Jahren Auslandsaufenthalt die zuletzt genannten Bedingungen.

Unfreiwillige Ausbürgerung erfolgt in Österreich vor allem im Fall des freiwilligen Erwerbs einer fremden Staatsbürgerschaft. Doppelstaatsbürgerschaft wird daher – im Gegensatz zu den meisten anderen Staaten in Europa und weltweit weder für die meisten Einwanderer noch für Auswanderer toleriert. Allerdings können letztere einen Antrag auf Beibehaltung der österreichischen Staatsbürgerschaft aufgrund besonderer persönlicher und familiärer Gründe stellen – solche Gründe werden nicht in gleicher Weise bei der Rücklegungspflicht für Einwanderer anerkannt.

III. Wahlrechte für Staatsbürger im Ausland und Nichtstaatsangehörige: Österreich im internationalen Vergleich

Das Wahlrecht auf nationaler Ebene bleibt international überwiegend an die Staatsbürgerschaft gekoppelt, aber es wurde in den letzten Jahrzehnten zunehmend vom Wohnsitz entkoppelt. Laut International IDEA (International Institute for Democracy and Electoral Assistance) können Staatsbürger im Ausland in 58% aller Staaten weltweit sich an legislativen Wahlen auf nationaler Ebene beteiligen, in 41% an Präsidentschaftswahlen und in 34% an nationalen Referenden.[9] In Wahlen auf substaatlicher Ebene (etwa zu Landtagen oder Gemeinderäten) bleibt das Wahlrecht dagegen überwiegend an den Wohnsitz in der jeweiligen Gebietskörperschaft gebunden und kann nur im Inland ausgeübt werden.

Auch Auslandsösterreicher sind seit einem Urteil des Verfassungsgerichtshofs aus dem Jahr 1990 grundsätzlich bei Nationalratswahlen, Präsidentschaftswahlen und nationalen Volksabstimmungen wahlberechtigt, wobei die Modalitäten der Ausübung dieses Wahlrechts sukzessive erleichtert wurden. Ungewöhnlich im internationalen Vergleich ist, dass sich Auslandsösterreicher mit früherem Wohnsitz in Niederösterreich, Tirol und Vorarlberg auch an Landtagswahlen in diesen Bundesländern beteiligen können.

Lediglich in 5 Staaten (Chile, Ecuador, Malawi, Neuseeland und Uruguay) hängt die Wahlberechtigung in nationalen Wahlen nicht von der Staatsbürgerschaft ab. Auch in diesen Staaten können aber nur Staatsbürger als Abgeordnete oder in andere hohe öffentliche Ämter gewählt werden. Daneben gibt es noch einige Staaten, die nationale Wahlrechte auf der Basis von Wechselseitigkeit oder historischer Verbindungen den Angehörigen bestimmter anderer Staaten zuerkennen. Dazu gehören Großbritannien und Irland sowie Portugal und Brasilien.

Viel weiter verbreitet sind Ausländerwahlrechte jedoch auf der kommunalen Ebene. In der EU können EU Bürger sich in anderen Mitgliedsstaaten an kommunalen Wahlen beteiligen, sie sind jedoch nicht überall bei Wahlen zum Amt des Bürgermeisters zugelassen und wählbar. 12 der EU Mitgliedstaaten, ebenso wie Island und Norwegen und eine Reihe von Schweizer Kantonen haben das aktive Wahlrecht auf der kommunalen Ebene völlig von der Staatsbürgerschaft entkoppelt.

---

[9] Siehe https://www.idea.int/data-tools/data/voting-abroad.

Eine solche Konzeption der lokalen „Wohnbürgerschaft" gibt es auch in 8 südamerikanischen Staaten und in Südkorea.[10]

In Österreich sind Reformbestrebungen in dieser Richtung im Jahr 2004 an der Auslegung der Bundesverfassung durch den Verfassungsgerichtshof gescheitert, der – ähnlich wie schon im Jahr 1990 das deutsche Bundesverfassungsgericht – die Zugehörigkeit zum österreichischen Volk an die Staatsangehörigkeit knüpft und für den der Grundsatz des Artikels 1 der Bundesverfassung, dass das Recht der Republik vom Volk ausgeht, impliziert, dass in allen politischen Wahlen nur Staatsbürger das Wahlrecht genießen können. Die Ausnahme sind lediglich EU Bürger, die aufgrund des EU-Vertrags Wahlrechte in Gemeinderats- und Europäischen Parlamentswahlen genießen. In Wien, das zugleich Gemeinde und Bundesland ist, sind EU Bürger jedoch nur auf der Ebene von Bezirksvertretungen wahlberechtigt.

Starke Zuwanderung nach Österreich, strenge Einbürgerungskriterien und entsprechend niedrigen Einbürgerungsraten von etwa 0,7%[11] in den letzten Jahren, sowie fehlende Ausländerwahlrechte bewirken zusammen genommen den Ausschluß von 1,2 Millionen Menschen, das sind 15% der Wohnbevölkerung von demokratischer Beteiligung und parlamentarischer Repräsentation. In der Bundeshauptstadt Wien beträgt der Anteil der nichtwahlberechtigten Bevölkerung fast 30%. Daraus entsteht ein demokratisches Legitimationsdefizit, das – da Einwanderung nicht mit rechtsstaatlichen Mittel rückgängig gemacht werden kann – nur durch Reform der Staatsbürgerschaft oder des Wahlrechts reduziert werden kann.

---

[10] Für eine Analyse der Wahlrechte von Auslandsbürgern und Ausländern in Europa und Lateinamerika siehe: Jean-Thomas Arrighi und Rainer Bauböck: „A multilevel puzzle: Migrants' voting rights in national and local elections", European Journal of Political Research, 2017, vol. 56 (3): 619–639.

[11] Das bedeutet, dass von 1.000 in Österreich lebenden Ausländern nur 7 pro Jahr eingebürgert werden.

Für eine andere Globalisierung. Der Zorn über die Hyperglobalisierung und die Politik mit der Angst

Ernst Fürlinger

Zusammenfassung

Skeptische und kritische Stimmen gegenüber der neoliberal orientierten ökonomischen Globalisierung verstärkten sich ab den 1990er Jahren, als die sozialen Folgen der Globalisierungsprozesse deutlicher wurden. Der Aufstieg rechtspopulistischer Parteien, die Wahl von Trump und der Brexit können als spezifische rückwärtsgewandte Reaktion auf den epochalen Umbruch von der Industrie- in die globale Moderne verstanden werden, die auf den Rückzug in das Nationale, nationale Abschottung setzt. Dagegen geht es progressiven Konzepten nicht um einen Rückzug aus der globalisierten Welt, sondern um eine andere Form der ökonomischen Globalisierung. Es gilt, die "Hyperglobalisierung" (Dani Rodrik) institutionell zu bändigen, um zu einer intelligenten, fairen und nachhaltigen Form der Globalisierung zu gelangen. Entscheidend wird sein, inwiefern die „Agenda 2030" der UNO mit ihren 17 Zielen für eine globale nachhaltige Entwicklung (SDGs) zu dieser nötigen tiefgreifenden Revision des dominierenden WTO-Modells der Globalisierung führen kann.

Historische Phasen der Globalisierungsdiskussion

Der Begriff der „Globalisierung" kam in den 1960er Jahren auf, fand in den 1980er Jahren allgemeine Verbreitung und wurde ab Mitte der 1990er Jahren mit großer Geschwindigkeit außerordentlich populär, sowohl in der Wissenschaft als auch in den Medien (vgl. Osterhammel 2017: 15). Jürgen Osterhammel unterscheidet mehrere historische Phasen des Globalisierungsdenkens. In der ersten Phase wurde das neue „globale Zeitalter" von einigen prominenten Autoren/innen euphorisch gefeiert: Manche betonten die Chancen grenzenloser Mobilität, die Chancen der Verbreitung des Internets ab Ende der 1980er Jahre; neoliberale Ansätze feierten die grenzenlose Marktfreiheit und waren überzeugt von Globalisierung als Wachstumsmotor. Für die Proponenten der Globalisierung und den Mainstream der Ökonomen bedeutete Globalisierung – im Sinn des Abbaus von Handelsschranken und der Integration der nationalen Ökonomien – schlicht Fortschritt. Alle würden von der Globalisierung profitieren. Es dominierten in den

1990er Jahren, nach dem Ende der Systemkonkurrenz und dem Fall der Mauer 1989 der Optimismus und die Globalisierungseuphorie.[1]

Gleichzeitig gab es Warnungen und skeptische Stimmen, die die Hemmfaktoren der Globalisierung betonten, auf die Widerständigkeit nationaler Institutionen und lokaler Traditionen gegen die Globalisierung hinwiesen, und ebenso die problematischen Aspekte der Globalisierung herausstrichen. Selbst ein Befürworter der Globalisierung wie Thomas Friedmann definierte die ökonomische Globalisierung als *„lose Kombination aus Freihandels-Vereinbarungen, dem Internet und der Integration der Finanzmärkte, die Grenzen auslöscht und die Welt in einen einzigen, lukrativen aber brutal wettbewerbsorientierten Marktplatz vereinigt"* (Friedmann 1996).

2002 erschien beispielsweise das Buch „Globalization and Its Discontent" des Wirtschaftsnobelpreisträgers Joseph Stieglitz. Als Chefökonom der Weltbank 1997 bis 2000 hatte er die Wirkung der Finanzkrise 1997-98 erlebt, die in Ostasien begann und sich dann global verbreitete. Das Buch basiert auf seinen Erfahrungen aus erster Hand über die Folgen einer Politik auf Basis der Ideologie des freien Marktes, so wie er im Vorwort sagt: *„die verheerende Wirkung, die die Globalisierung auf die Entwicklungsländer haben kann, speziell auf die Armen innerhalb dieser Länder"* (Stieglitz 2002: ix). Stieglitz anerkannte die Tatsache, dass die ökonomische Globalisierung für hunderte Millionen von Menschen, vor allem in Asien, speziell China und Indien, aber auch in einigen Ländern Afrikas, eine Verbesserung ihrer Lebensbedingungen mit sich brachte – gleichzeitig waren aber auch Armut, soziale Ungleichheit und die Krisenanfälligkeit des globalen Wirtschafts- und Finanzsystems verstärkt worden.

Der Ökonom Dani Rodrik, damals an der Princeton University, stellte 1997 in einem Buch die Frage, ob die Globalisierung zu weit gegangen sei (Rodrik 1997). Die internationale Integration der Märkte für Waren, Dienstleistungen und Kapital stelle Gesellschaften unter Druck und breche als disruptive Kraft gesellschaftliche Traditionen auf, z.B. die Tradition stabiler, lebenslanger Beschäftigungsverhältnisse in Japan. Zu beobachten sei eine wachsende Kluft zwischen Gruppen, die die Fähigkeit und die Mobilität haben, sich in globalen Märkten zu bewegen, und denen, die diese Möglichkeiten nicht nutzen können und die *„Ausdehnung unregulierter Märkte als feindlich gegenüber sozialer Stabilität und tief verankerten Normen wahrnehmen"* (Rodrik 1997: 2). Rodrik wies beispielsweise darauf hin, dass die Löhne von schlecht ausgebildeten Arbeitern/innen in Europa und den USA seit den 1970er Jahren um 20% niedriger geworden waren, aufgrund der Konkurrenz zwischen Arbeitern/innen in Industrieländern und in Entwicklungsländern. Die Möglichkeit, die Produktion in Billiglohnländern auszulagern, erzeugte Druck auf die Belegschaften, niedrigere Löhne zu akzeptieren. Insgesamt gab die stark gewachsene Verhandlungsmacht den Unternehmen die Möglichkeit,

---

[1]   Zur Geschichte des Freihandels und der neoliberalen Globalisierung siehe jüngst Slobodian 2019a.

Löhne und Arbeitsbedingungen zu drücken. Rodrik sah voraus, dass der Preis der stärkeren ökonomischen Integration eine größere soziale Desintegration sein würde. Rodriks 2011 erschienenes Buch „The Globalization Paradox", drei Jahre nach der großen Finanzkrise, vertiefte die Analyse der Globalisierung im Sinn der wirtschaftlichen Liberalisierung und tiefgreifenden weltwirtschaftlichen Integration in den 1980er und 90er Jahren – ein Prozess, der zu weit gegangen sei und den er als „Hyperglobalisierung" bezeichnet. Der Übergang von der Globalisierung zu Hyperglobalisierung ist für ihn wesentlich mit zwei Vorgängen verbunden:

- die Wende von der staatlichen Kontrolle von Kapitalflüssen hin zu einer Liberalisierung – in Form der Entscheidung der OECD 1989, alle Beschränkungen für grenzüberschreitende finanzielle Ströme zu beseitigen;
- die Etablierung der World Trade Organization (WTO) im Jahr 1995, die es für Länder nicht nur schwieriger machte, sich gegen den globalen Wettbewerb zu schützen, sondern auch tief in nationale Politikbereiche eingriff, wie Landwirtschaft, Industriepolitik, intellektuelles Eigentum usw. (vgl. Rodrik 2011: 78f).

Hyperglobalisierung bedeutet die Priorität der *„Bedürfnisse der multinationalen Unternehmen, der großen Banken und Investmentgesellschaften vor anderen sozialen und wirtschaftlichen Zielen"* (Rodrik 2011: 206). Dabei ist die Balance zwischen der Kontroll- und Regulierungsmöglichkeit der nationalen Regierungen und den globalen Märkten verloren gegangen. Es kam zu einer maximalen Globalisierung, die Rodrik u.a. von einer intelligenten und inklusiven Form der Globalisierung unterscheiden. Lori Wallach, Direktorin der 1995 von ihr gegründeten NGO „Public Citizen's Global Trade Watch" (Washington, D.C.) charakterisiert *„Hyperglobalisierung"* als *„weltweite Aufzwingung von Regeln nach dem Muster ‚eine Größe passt allen', die von den globalen Finanzmärkten befürwortet wird und die Fähigkeit demokratischer Regierungen beschränkt, auf die Bedürfnisse ihrer Gesellschaften einzugehen."* (Wallach 2019)

Sieht man sich die Eckdaten an, was eine „hyperglobalisierte Welt" konkret bedeutet, dann sticht vor allem das Hyper-Wachstum des globalen Finanzbereichs seit 1980 heraus und der enorme Machtzuwachs, der damit einhergeht. Laut Daten des „Financial Stability Board" von 2017 sind die Finanzvermögen von 12 Billionen Dollar im Jahr 1980 auf rund 300 Billionen Dollar im Jahr 2016 gewachsen (vgl. Gallagher/ Kozul-Wright 2019, 5, Table 1). Diese Machtkonzentration der globalen Eliten erklärt auch, warum selbst die globale Finanzkrise von 2008 nicht dazu führte, der Hyperglobalisierung als dominierendes Konzept der ökonomischen Globalisierung die Legitimität zu entziehen und eine grundlegende Reform der Struktur der globalen Wirtschaft einzuleiten. Ein anderer Aspekt der hyperglobalisierten Welt ist beispielsweise die extreme Unregelmäßigkeit der globalen Finanzflüsse in die sich entwickelnden Ökonomien in den letzten 30 Jahren (vgl. Gallagher/ Kozul-Wright 2019, 10, Figure 3): Eine Grafik, die den Kapitalzufluss in wirtschaftlich guten Zeiten und den plötzlichen Stopp und Kapitalabzug in schwierigen Zeiten darstellt, wirkt wie eine extreme Fieberkurve und illustriert anschaulich die anarchische Instabilität der ungeregelten finanziellen Globalisierung mit ihren massiven Auswirkungen auf ganze Gesellschaften. Insgesamt hat das v.a. von der WTO getragene Hyperglobalisierungsregime zu wachsender Ungleichheit bei den Einkommen und Vermögen und der damit verbundenen Polarisierung auch in den Industrieländern geführt, wie der von Thomas Piketty, Emmanuel Saez u.a. koordinierte „World Inequality Report" belegt, der sich auf Daten von mehr als 100 Wissenschaftler/innen aus allen Kontinenten stützt (World Inequality Report 2018). Beispielsweise hat sich die Einkommensungleichheit in den USA seit 1980 – in deutlichem Unterschied zu Europa – verdoppelt: 1980 betrug der Anteil des obersten Prozents der Einkommensbezieher am nationalen Gesamteinkommen in den USA knapp 10%, 2016 bereits 20%. Gleichzeitig sank der Anteil der unteren 50% am Gesamteinkommen zwischen 1980 und 2016 von gut 20% auf 13% (vgl. Bericht zur weltweiten Ungleichheit 2018, 6).

„Ungleichheit" und globale Ungerechtigkeit sind auch Zentralbegriffe, wenn es um die Klimakrise geht. Die ärmsten 50% der Weltbevölkerung (3,5 Milliarden Menschen) sind nur für rund 10% der CO_2-Emissionen, die die Erderwärmung verursachen, durch individuellen Konsum verantwortlich,[2] aber am meisten von den Folgen des Klimawandels (v.a. Extremwetterereignisse, Anstieg des Meeresspiegels etc.) betroffen und haben die geringsten finanziellen Mittel, um sich daran anzupassen. Die reichsten 10% der Weltbevölkerung produzieren dagegen rund 50% der globalen Emissionen (vgl. Gore 2015; siehe auch Chancel/ Piketty 2015). „Was klar ist: Klimawandel und ökonomische Ungleichheit sind untrennbar miteinander verbunden. Es ist eine Krise angetrieben durch die ‚Habenden', die die ‚Nicht-Habenden' am meisten trifft." (Gore 2015, 6).

Aufstand gegen die neoliberale Globalisierung

Bereits 1996 sprachen Befürworter/innen der ökonomischen Globalisierung sorgenvoll von einem „Backlash" gegenüber der Globalisierung als globalem Trend. Am Tag vor der Eröffnung des Weltwirtschaftsforums Davos im Februar 1996 veröffentlichte beispielsweise der Gründer des Forums Klaus Schwab zusammen mit dem Manager des Forums einen Artikel, in dem sie u.a. ausführten:

> „Die ökonomische Globalisierung hat eine kritische Phase erreicht. Ein wachsender Rückschlag gegen ihre Wirkungen, vor allem in den industrialisierten Ökonomien, bedroht eine sehr disruptive Wirkung auf die wirtschaftliche Aktivität und die soziale Stabilität in vielen Ländern. Die Stimmung in diesen Demokratien ist eine von Hilflosigkeit und Angst, die hilft, den Aufstieg einer neu-

---

[2]   Individueller Konsum oder „Lebensstil-Emissionen" sind insgesamt für 64% der globalen CO_2-Emissionen verantwortlich, die restlichen 36% sind dem Konsum durch Regierungen, Investitionen (u.a. in Infrastruktur) und internationalen Transport zugeordnet (vgl. Gore 2015, 3).

en Art populistischer Politiker zu erklären. Dies kann sich leicht in einen Aufstand wenden. " (Schwab/ Smadja 1996; vgl. Friedman 1996).

Diesen Aufstand erleben wir heute, im Aufstieg rechtspopulistischer Parteien in Europa,[3] in Form des Brexit und vor allem in der Wahl von Donald Trump in den USA. Die zentrale These des Buches „Die Gesellschaft des Zorns" der Soziologin Cornelia Koppetsch lautet, *„dass der Aufstieg der Rechtsparteien eine aus unterschiedlichen Quellen gespeiste Konterrevolution gegen die Folgen der (...) Globalisierungs- und Transnationalisierungsprozesse darstellt"* (Koppetsch 2019: 23).

Eine strukturelle Folge u.a. ist die Spaltung in ein transnationales Oben und Unten, die Herausbildung von transnationalen Klassenlagen von Globalisierungsgewinnern und –verlierern, während die mittlere und untere Mittelschicht zunehmend unter Druck gerät (Koppetsch 2019: 18ff). Für Koppetsch resultiert der Aufstieg des Rechtspopulismus *aus einem kollektiven emotionalen Reflex*, der sich auf den epochalen Umbruch von der Industriemoderne in die globale Moderne und eine neoliberal orientierte ökonomische Globalisierung richtet. Dieser Reflex kann in gewisser Hinsicht als Teil einer umfassenden Tendenz zur Rückwärtsgewandtheit, der Nostalgie des Regionalen, Kleinräumlichen, lokaler Traditionen betrachtet werden. Zygmunt Bauman hat diese Tendenz in seinem letzten Buch als Aufschwung der *„Retrotopie"* charakterisiert, als *„Zurück ans Stammesfeuer"*, zur eigenen Horde, in einem *„Zeitalter der Nostalgie"*: ein Aufschwung von Utopien, die auf die Vergangenheit vor diesem Epochenbruch gerichtet sind (Bauman 2017). Diese Tendenz besitzt ein reaktionäres Gesicht in Form eines ausgrenzenden Nationalismus, von Abschließungsprozessen der nationalen Mehrheit, Isolation. Sie kann aber meiner Ansicht nach auch ein progressives Gesicht besitzen, in Form des selbstbestimmten, offenen Zusammenlebens, der Solidarität und der Partizipation auf lokaler Ebene,[4] in Form des Aufrechterhaltens von Vielfalt, der Pflege des regionalen Eigensinns gegen den homogenisierenden Druck der global agierenden Konzerne, der Förderung von regionalen kulturellen Traditionen und Besonderheiten – bei gleichzeitiger kosmopolitischer Offenheit für ganz andere lokale Felder, Traditionen und Weltbilder.

Eine Reihe von Studien bestätigt den Zusammenhang zwischen den Folgen der ökonomischen Globalisierung und der Unterstützung rechtspopulistischer Parteien (vgl. Rodrik 2018a). Sie liefern u.a. den empirischen Nachweis, dass der gestiegene Wettbewerb mit Importen aus Niedriglohnländern in den letzten 20 Jahren (v.a. aus China) und die wachsende Ungleichheit in den Industrieländern für einen

---

[3]   Seit den 1960er Jahren hat sich der durchschnittliche Stimmenanteil der rechtspopulistischen Parteien in Europa bei Wahlen mehr als verdoppelt (von 5,1% auf 13,2%) und die Anzahl der Parlamentssitze verdreifacht (von 3,8% auf 12,8%) (vgl. Inglehart/ Norris 2016: 2). Kalkuliert von Holger Döring and Philip Manow: Parliaments and governments database (ParlGov), 'Elections' dataset (http://www.parlgov.org/).

[4]   Ein Beispiel dafür ist die Transition Town-Bewegung, die 2006 vom britischen Umweltaktivisten Rob Hopkins initiiert wurde (s. Hopkins 2014) und auch in Österreich verbreitet ist, z.B. in Friesach (Kärnten). Weblink: https://transition.at/

wesentlichen Teil des Anstiegs des Rechtspopulismus bei Wahlen verantwortlich ist (vgl. Fadinger 2019). So hat beispielsweise ein internationales Forschungsteam empirisch nachgewiesen, dass eine starke Korrelation zwischen Stimmen für Trump bei der Präsidentschaftswahl 2016 und den Auswirkungen von ökonomischen Schocks in bestimmten Gebieten in den USA besteht: Je größer die Jobverluste aufgrund der Importe aus China waren, die ab 2001 – dem Beitritt Chinas zur WTO – stark und abrupt anstiegen, desto höher war die Unterstützung für Trump (vgl. Autor et al. 2017). Eine ähnliche Untersuchung hat nachgewiesen, dass die Unterstützung für den Brexit beim Referendum im Juni 2016 signifikant höher war in Regionen, die von der ökonomischen Globalisierung, vor allem dem „Chinesischen Import-Schock", in den letzten 30 Jahren härter betroffen waren, in Form des Niedergangs lokaler Industrien, höherer Arbeitslosigkeit und Armut. Umgekehrt fanden die Forscher keine Evidenz dafür, dass stärkere Einwanderung mit einer höheren Unterstützung des Brexit verbunden war – auch wenn bei der Brexit-Kampagne das Thema Migration stark im Zentrum stand (vgl. Colantone/ Stanig 2017). Auch für andere Länder hat man den Zusammenhang zwischen Handelsschocks und Wahlverhalten untersucht.[5] Man wird also die Motive für die Unterstützung des Brexit nicht adäquat verstehen, wenn man sich dabei vor allem auf den öffentlichen, populistisch geführten Diskurs konzentriert, aber die harte ökonomische Dimension und die verheerenden Folgen des Thatcherismus in Großbritannien vor allem für die „kleinen Leute", die Arbeiterschicht, zu wenig berücksichtigt.

Eine alternative Erklärung für den Aufstieg des Rechtspopulismus betrachtet kulturelle Faktoren, die kulturelle Spaltung der Gesellschaften, als prioritär. Pippa Norris und Ronald Inglehart vertreten auf Basis ihrer empirischen Forschung, u.a. einer Auswertung der Daten des European Social Survey (2002-2014) die These, dass nicht ökonomische Unsicherheit, sondern vielmehr ein „Cultural Backlash" entscheidend ist: Der autoritäre Populismus sei eine Gegenreaktion auf den progressiven Wertewandel, der sich ab den 1970er Jahren vollzog. Die Spaltung verlaufe zwischen Gruppen mit kosmopolitischen und postmaterialistischen Werten wie Säkularismus, persönliche Autonomie und Diversität und kulturkonservativen „Traditionalisten", denen Religion, traditionelle Familienstrukturen und Konformität wichtig seien und die Migranten/innen ablehnen (vgl. Inglehart/ Norris 2016; Norris/ Inglehart 2019). Im Rechtspopulismus komme der Protest jener Bevölkerungsgruppen zum Ausdruck, die sich in ihrem Wertesystem von der Öffnung der Gesellschaft bedroht fühlen.

Ökonomische und kulturelle Ursachen müssen sich nicht widersprechen, sondern ergänzen einander. In diesem Sinn spricht Koppetsch von einer „zusammengesetzten Konfliktlinie", wie u.a. auch Analysen der deutschen Bundestagswahl 2017 bestätigen würden. Die Teilung der Gesellschaft verlaufe sowohl entlang der

---

[5] Für Deutschland: Dippel/ Gold/ Heblich (2015); für Frankreich: Malgouyres (2017). Für den Literaturhinweis danke ich Prof. Harald Fadinger (Universität Mannheim).

sozioökonomischen Dimension, zwischen der sozial gehobenen Schicht mit höherer Bildung und den Milieus der unteren Mittel- und Unterschicht, *als auch* in der Wertedimension entlang der Grundorientierungen *„Tradition"* versus *„Modernisierung"* (Koppetsch 2019: 104; unter Bezug auf Vehrkamp/ Wegschaider 2017).

Ökonomische und kulturelle Faktoren überlagern sich auch in der Ablehnung von Migranten/innen durch die Wähler/innen rechtspopulistischer Parteien: „Sie" – die Migranten/innen - würden „uns" Jobs wegnehmen und den Sozialstaat belasten; gleichzeitig würden sie die Einheit der nationalen Kultur und ihrer Werte unterminieren und bedrohen. Anhand der Moscheebaukonflikte in Österreich in den letzten Jahren habe ich das Moment der kulturellen Abwehr gegenüber den muslimischen Fremden als ein zentrales Element rechtspopulistischer Politik herausgearbeitet. Dabei überlagern sich soziale, ökonomische und kulturelle Dimensionen in einer komplexen Weise. Kulturelle und sozialökonomische Faktoren bei der Analyse gegeneinander auszuspielen, würde eine Vereinfachung der Komplexität der sozialen Welt bedeuten (vgl. Fürlinger 2013: 437).

Soziale, ökonomische und kulturelle Ängste verstärken sich gegenseitig, und eine *„Politik der Angst"* (vgl. Wodak 2016; Nussbaum 2019) bewirtschaftet diese Ängste. In letzter Zeit treten auch immer mehr ökologische Ängste dazu - Ängste vor den Folgen der modernen Industriezivilisation und des entfesselten Spätkapitalismus für die Lebensgrundlagen, wie er z.B. paradigmatisch in Form der Preisgabe des Amazonas-Regenwalds für kurzfristige Wirtschaftsinteressen durch den neuen brasilianischen Präsidenten Jair Bolsonaro Gestalt annimmt, berechtigte Ängste vor den Folgen des Überschreitens planetarer Grenzen, vor allem vor dem Klimawandel und dem Artensterben. Für die Strategie rechtspopulistischer Parteien bietet es sich an, Unbehagen, Unmut und Ängste im Zusammenhang mit der entfesselten Globalisierung primär auf die Migranten/innen und Flüchtlinge zu lenken, weil in ihnen der schwer fassbare und verstehbare strukturelle Wandel hin zur globalen Moderne konkret greifbar wird: *„Die Sozialfigur des Migranten vereinigt in sich, wie keine andere Figur, grenzüberschreitende Mobilität, kulturelle Fremdheit, identitäre Hybridität und transnationale Verflechtungen"* (Koppetsch 2019: 41).

Reform der Globalisierung

Wie mit dem *„Cultural Backlash"* (vgl. Inglehart/ Norris 2016; Norris/ Inglehart 2019) umgegangen wird, ist eine Frage der gesellschaftlichen Auseinandersetzung über grundlegende Werte und Orientierungen, nicht zuletzt eine Auseinandersetzung zwischen den Generationen. Wichtig ist dabei der methodische Hinweis von Koppetsch, dass das wissenschaftliche Milieu seine Standortgebundenheit reflektieren müsse, wenn es um die Auseinandersetzung mit Globalisierung und Rechtsparteien geht: Wissenschaftler/innen sind Teil der globalisierten Kultur- und Wissensökonomien, profitieren von der Globalisierung, sind überwiegend kosmopolitisch orientiert und stehen den Rechtsparteien meist kritisch gegenüber (vgl. Koppetsch 2019: 31f).

Wenn ökonomische Faktoren – ökonomische Unsicherheit, soziale Ungleichheit und Deklassierung im Zuge der Hyperglobalisierung – eine zentrale Rolle für den Aufstieg des Rechtspopulismus spielen, dann müsste genau dort angesetzt werden, bei strukturellen ökonomischen Reformen und einer inklusiveren Politik. Aus der Sicht von Dan Rodrik ist die Rückkehr zum Protektionismus keine zukunftsfähige Alternative. Zwischen der Scylla der Hyperglobalisierung und der Charybdis der Abschottung von Märkten, die zum Zusammenbruch des Welthandels führen würden, gehe es um eine *„neue, gesündere Globalisierung"* (Rodrik 2018b), um eine breitere Unterstützung für eine Weltwirtschaft zu gewinnen, *„die in wesentlichen Teilen offen ist, auch wenn sie das hyperglobalistische Ideal nicht erfüllt"* (Rodrik 2019a). Er plädiert für neue internationale Normen, die den Spielraum nationaler Wirtschaftspolitik gegenüber den globalen Märkten vergrößern sollen.[6] Seiner Meinung nach wäre die adäquate Kur gegen den autoritären Populismus ein *„Populismus anderer Art"*, der gegen ökonomische Ungerechtigkeit und auf Inklusion gerichtet ist (vgl. Rodrik 2019b).

Der kanadische Historiker Quinn Slobodian hat anlässlich des Jahrestags der Massenproteste gegen die Ministerkonferenz der WTO in Seattle am 30. November 1999, die zur Verhinderung der Konferenz führten, darauf hingewiesen, dass es den Akteur/innen der Proteste nicht um einen Ausstieg aus der Globalisierung in Richtung nationaler Isolation ging, vielmehr um ein anderes Konzept der ökonomischen Globalisierung, in der das Gemeinwohl und nicht die Profitinteressen von Unternehmen und Finanzwirtschaft im Zentrum stehen. Zu den zentralen Forderungen gehörte die Einführung von Arbeits- und Umweltrichtlinien in die Handelsabkommen, gegen die sich die WTO wehrt, weil diese den Handel blockieren würden (vgl. Slobodian 2019b).[7]

Gegenwärtig existieren unterschiedliche, vielfältige Ansätze für eine Reform der ökonomischen Globalisierung, die das Regime der Hyperglobalisierung beendet und eine Transformation der Globalisierung hervorbringt, die mit den ethischen Prinzipien Gemeinwohl. Gerechtigkeit und Nachhaltigkeit vereinbar ist. Ein Beispiel sind die „Geneva Principles for a Global Green New Deal", die in einem breiten Diskussionsprozess vom Global Development Policy Center der Boston University in Kooperation mit UNCTAD formuliert und Anfang 2019 veröffentlicht wurden (Gallagher/ Kozul-Wright 2019). Diese Prinzipien wollen ein dringendes Forschungsprogramm und eine politische Agenda fördern „für einen neuen Multilateralismus, der die Regeln der globalen Wirtschaft wiederherstellt zugunsten der Ziele koordinierter Stabilität, geteilten Wohlstands und ökologischer

---

[6] Siehe dazu die Vorschläge des im Februar 2019 gegründeten Netzwerks „Economics for Inclusive Prosperity" für unterschiedliche Bereiche (Handel, Finanzsystem, Arbeitsmarktpolitik usw.): https://econfip.org
[7] Siehe den Dokumentarfilm zu den Seattle-Protesten „This Is What Democracy Looks Like" (2000) von Jill Friedberg und Rick Rowley.

Nachhaltigkeit, während gleichzeitig der Raum für die Souveränität nationaler Politik respektiert wird." (Gallagher/ Kozul-Wright 2019, 1) Im Grunde geht es um eine Orientierung an den grundsätzlichen Prinzipien der Internationalen Handelsorganisation (ITO) in Richtung einer auf Werten und Regeln basierenden globalen Verwaltung der Weltwirtschaft. Die ITO wurde 1948, nach der Katastrophe des Zweiten Weltkriegs, ins Leben gerufen, scheiterte aber 1950 am US-Kongress, der die Beteiligung der USA verhinderte. Lori Wallach erinnert an die Orientierung der ursprünglichen Welthandelsorganisation: Die ITO stellte Vollbeschäftigung und fairen Wettbewerb ins Zentrum ihrer Tätigkeit und setzte sich für Arbeitsstandards und Vorkehrungen gegen Monopole ein, sodass möglichst viele Menschen von den Vorteilen des Handels profitieren können. So gesehen stelle das Modell der ITO eine bereits bereitliegende „Grundlage dar, um bessere globale Handelsregeln zu schaffen" (Wallach 2019, 10).

Die UN-„Agenda 2030" und die Revision der Hyperglobalisierung

Für eine Überwindung der gegenwärtig dominierenden Hyperglobalisierung wird wichtig sein, ob die „Agenda 2030" der UNO und der damit verbundene Prozess tatsächlich zu einem konkreten politischen Reformprojekt für eine andere, faire und nachhaltige ökonomische Globalisierung führt - ob das bestehende asymmetrische, unfaire Handelssystem durch eine selektive Lektüre der „Agenda 2030" und der SDGs seitens der Industrieländer des Nordens noch verschärft wird (vgl. Sengupta 2016, 137).

Das zentrale Anliegen der „Agenda 2030" ist die Integration der sozialen Gerechtigkeitsdimension und der ökologischen Dimension für die Lösung der globalen Probleme. Sie wurde von der Vollversammlung der UNO im September 2015 unter dem Titel „Transformation unserer Welt" beschlossen und in Form von 17 neuen globalen Zielen und 169 dazugehörigen Zielvorgaben für die Umsetzungsmittel für nachhaltige Entwicklung (SDGs) konkretisiert, die auf den Milleniums-Entwicklungszielen basieren und die am 1. Jänner 2016 in Kraft traten. Die Erklärung der UN-Generalversammlung betont dabei die Unteilbarkeit dieser wirtschaftlichen, sozialen und ökologischen Ziele (Nr. 55) und bringt diesen integralen Ansatz u.a. in folgender Weise zum Ausdruck:

> *„Nachhaltige Entwicklung beruht auf der Erkenntnis, dass die Beseitigung der Armut in allen ihren Formen und Dimensionen, die Bekämpfung der Ungleichheit in und zwischen Ländern, die Erhaltung unseres Planeten, die Herbeiführung eines dauerhaften, inklusiven und nachhaltigen Wirtschaftswachstums und die Förderung der sozialen Inklusion miteinander verbunden und wechselseitig voneinander abhängig sind."* (UN GA 2015: S. 4 (Erklärung Nr.13))

Diese grundsätzliche Verzahnung der Gerechtigkeits- und Ökologie-Dimension steht ebenso im Zentrum der Enzyklika *„Laudato Si' über die Sorge für das ge-*

meinsame Haus" von Papst Franziskus, die im gleichen Jahr – im Vorfeld der historisch bedeutenden Pariser Weltklimakonferenz im Dezember 2015, bei der der Weltklimavertrag beschlossen wurde – veröffentlicht wurde (Papst Franziskus 2015). Der Schlüsselsatz der Enzyklika dazu lautet: *„Wir kommen jedoch heute nicht umhin anzuerkennen, dass ein wirklicher ökologischer Ansatz sich immer in einen sozialen Ansatz verwandelt, der die Gerechtigkeit in die Umweltdiskussion aufnehmen muss, um die Klage der Armen ebenso zu hören wie die Klage der Erde."* (Papst Franziskus 2015: LS Nr. 49) Damit gehen zentrale globale Akteure – der eine im säkularen, der andere im religiösen Bereich – grundsätzlich in die gleiche Richtung, wenn es um die nötige umfassende, tiefgreifende strukturelle Transformation unserer Wirtschafts- und Lebensweise auf planetarer Ebene geht. Bei der Agenda 2030 zeigt sich die UNO entschlossen,

> *„die für die Umsetzung dieser Agenda benötigten Mittel durch eine mit neuem Leben erfüllte Globale Partnerschaft für nachhaltige Entwicklung zu mobilisieren, die auf einem Geist verstärkter globaler Solidarität gründet, insbesondere auf die Bedürfnisse der Ärmsten und Schwächsten ausgerichtet ist und an der sich alle Länder, alle Interessenträger und alle Menschen beteiligen."* (UN GA 2015: S. 1 (Präambel); vgl. S. 11 (Erklärung Nr. 39))

Für die notwendige Reform der wirtschaftlichen Globalisierung in Richtung Nachhaltigkeit, Gemeinwohl und sozialer Gerechtigkeit und den Rückbau der Hyperglobalisierung ist vor allem SDG 17 relevant: *„Umsetzungsmittel stärken und die Globale Partnerschaft für nachhaltige Entwicklung mit neuem Leben erfüllen"* (UN GA 2015: S. 15 und 28ff. (Ziel 17)). Das Ziel wird in Form von 19 Zielvorgaben zu SDG 17 sowie 43 weiteren Zielen, die die Umsetzungsmittel („Means of Implementation", MOI) betreffen und auf die 16 anderen SDGs verteilt sind, konkretisiert.

Kritische Entwicklungsexperten aus dem Globalen Norden und Süden holen die hochfahrende UN-Rhetorik der „Agenda 2030" gewissermaßen auf den harten Boden der Realität des gegenwärtigen Weltwirtschaftssystems herunter, in dem nicht die ethischen Normen für eine „Transformation der Welt" zählen, sondern die rechtlich verbindlichen Handelsvereinbarungen und -verträge. Sie buchstabieren im Detail durch, was es bedeutet, dass die Governance der Weltwirtschaft von der WTO, dem IMF, der Weltbank und anderen Organisationen – der *„global club governance"* (vgl. Bissio 2019) - bestimmt wird, nicht von der UNO. Ranja Sengupta vom „Third World Network" beispielsweise kommt zu einem sehr skeptischen Schluss, was die Ausführungen zum internationalen Handel in der „Agenda 2030" wie auch ihre praktische Umsetzung betreffen. So weist er darauf hin, dass Versuche z.B. im Rahmen des Asia Forums on Sustainable Development oder im ersten „Financing for Development Forum" im April 2016 zu mehr Kooperation, Klarheit und Verbindlichkeit zu gelangen, was Mechanismen zur Gewährleistung der Umsetzungsmittel (MOI) betrifft, gescheitert sind. Der Widerstand seitens der Industrieländer dagegen sei *„stark und proaktiv"* (Sengupta 2016, 130). Sengupta analysiert etwa die Problematik der drei Zielvorgaben zum internationalen Handel bei SDG 17, nämlich die Ziele 17.10., 17.11. und 17.12. Das Ziel 17.10 beispielsweise verankert ein universales, offenes, regel-basiertes multilaterales Handelssystem nur unter dem Dach der WTO. Aber: *„WTO-Verfahren machen es für Entwicklungsländer und am wenigsten entwickelte Länder (LDCs) schwierig, jederzeit ‚offen' zu sein, insofern es für sie nötig sein kann, ihre Märkte zu schützen, abhängig von ihrer Stufe der Entwicklung".* (Sengupta 2016, 131).

Ein anderes Beispiel: SDG 2b spezifiziert die Korrektur und Verhinderung von Handelsbeschränkungen auf den globalen Agrarmärkten – gleichzeitig bleibe der „Elefant im Raum", nämlich die hohen nationalen Agrarsubventionen seitens der OECD-Länder, vor allem USA und EU, unberührt (vgl. Sengupta 2016, 131). Sengupta zieht das Fazit: *„Die gegenwärtigen Handelsvereinbarungen stehen in einem inhärenten Konflikt mit dem gesamten Rahmen der Agenda 2030 und ihren SDGs."* (ibid.)

Abgesehen von der *„Agenda 2030"*, mit ihrer transformativen Vision, aber auch ihren inneren Widersprüchen und Inkonsistenzen und den Schwierigkeiten bei ihrer Umsetzung[8] existieren andere Ansätze für eine Überwindung der hyperglobalisierten Welt, in der wir heute leben. Um die Verlierer der ökonomischen Globalisierung einzubeziehen und Ungleichheit zu bekämpfen, wird z.B. die steuerliche Entlastung von Beziehern niedriger Einkommen vorgeschlagen, die Einführung einer globalen Vermögenssteuer, wie sie Thomas Piketty konzipiert hat (vgl. Pickety 2014) oder die Einführung einer sogenannten *„Robin-Hood-Steuer"*, einer Steuer auf Transaktionen am Finanzmarkt, um Finanzspekulationen unattraktiver zu machen und Investitionen in die Realwirtschaft zu stimulieren (vgl. Schäfer 2015).

Schlussfolgerungen für politische Strategien

Politik und Zivilgesellschaft sollten nicht hinnehmen, dass rechtspopulistische Parteien den öffentlichen Diskurs auf jenes Spielfeld verschieben, auf dem sie besonders erfolgreich punkten - nämlich Migration, Zuwanderung, Ausländer/innen - sondern aktiv andere diskursive Schwerpunkte setzen, die bei den zugrundeliegenden ökonomischen und sozialen Problemen ansetzen. Häufig passiert aber das Gegenteil: Kritiker/innen des Rechtspopulismus agieren oft zu sehr mit dem rechtspopulistischen Diskurs mit, der Migration, Flüchtlinge, nationale Abschottung und Errichtung von neuen Mauern ins Zentrum der politischen Kommunikation stellt, während gleichzeitig Themen der ökonomischen Ungleichheit und der wachsenden sozialen Spaltung vernachlässigt werden. Der Einsatz für kulturelle Vielfalt und Multikulturalismus und gegen Diskriminierung durch Proponenten des Konzepts der *„postmigrantischen Gesellschaft"* greift zu kurz,

---

[8] Siehe dazu u.a. die jährlichen Berichte „Spotlight on Sustainable Development", koordiniert vom Global Policy Forum. Internetquelle: socialwatch.org.

wenn die ökonomischen Bedingungen für den Aufstieg der Feinde der offenen, kosmopolitischen, globalisierten Gesellschaft ausgeblendet bleiben und die neoliberale Gestalt der Globalisierung wie eine Naturerscheinung aufgefasst wird. Nötig wäre es, die jeweiligen „Blasen" des konservativen Milieus und des Modernisierungs-Milieus zu verlassen und einen echten Dialog zwischen den verschiedenen sozialen Schichten zu führen, um die bestehenden Polarisierungen zu überwinden und die jeweiligen, unterschiedlichen Ängste, Sichtweisen und Lebenssituationen besser verstehen zu können. Das gilt nicht zuletzt für das akademische Milieu. Vorschläge und erste praktische Versuche z.B. in Frankreich und UK, die wachsende gesellschaftliche Polarisierung rund um die Klimakrise und die Transformation in Richtung Nachhaltigkeit und Regeneration der Erde mit Hilfe von lokalen Bürgerversammlungen zum Thema Klimawandel und gesellschaftliche Transition („Mini-Öffentlichkeiten") abzubauen und aufzufangen, gehen in diese Richtung (vgl. Lenzi 2019).

Es ist eine wichtige Frage der politischen Strategie, wie die Grundorientierungen *„Anerkennung"* und *„Umverteilung"*, wenn es um den Kern von Gerechtigkeit geht, gewichtet werden (vgl. Honneth/ Fraser 2003). Will man eine politische Antwort auf den Aufstieg des Rechtspopulismus formulieren und den Rechtspopulisten den Wind aus den Segeln nehmen, dann müssen die großen ökonomischen Fragen, die Fragen der sozialen Gerechtigkeit und sozialen Sicherheit wieder stärker in den Mittelpunkt der politischen Auseinandersetzung gestellt werden. Der Fokus auf Identitätspolitik muss ergänzt werden durch die Auseinandersetzung mit den harten ökonomischen Fakten, mit konkreten Arbeitsbedingungen, dem Kampf gegen soziale Ungleichheit und mit einem Reformkonzept für eine neue, inklusive Form der Globalisierung (vgl. Raza 2018). Der deutsche Soziologe Andreas Reckwitz hat für dieses neue Paradigma, das aus seiner Sicht das ab 1980 dominierende Dynamisierungsparadigma (auf ökonomischer Ebene: Öffnung zugunsten der Märkte; auf kultureller Ebene: Öffnung der individuellen und kollektiven Identitäten) nun abzulösen beginnt, den Begriff *„einbettender Liberalismus"* verwendet, im Sinn einer Regulierung der Märkte, etwa in den Bereichen Infrastruktur, Wohnen, Grundsicherung. Es gehe dabei um ein *„neues Regulierungsparadigma, das aber die Dynamisierung nicht abwürgt, aber eben ‚einbettet'."* (Reckwitz 2019a; vgl. 2019b)

Abschließend: Die *„Alter-Globalisierung von rechts"* (Slobodian 2019b), der weltweite Aufstieg des Rechtspopulismus, die rechtspopulistische Politik mit der Angst und die zunehmende Polarisierung der Gesellschaften wird nur gestoppt werden können, wenn es gelingt, die ökonomischen Gründe für Angst und Unsicherheit zu eliminieren, die Hyperglobalisierung zu überwinden und eine andere Globalisierung durchzusetzen. Wie etwa das Global Policy Forum in seinem jüngsten Bericht betont, liegt der Schlüssel in einer neuen Gestalt globaler Governance: Es bedarf einer grundlegenden Reform der „Hardware", der Strukturen und Institutionen auf globaler Ebene, um das transformative Potential der „Agenda

2030" tatsächlich umzusetzen (siehe Global Policy Forum 2019).[9] Die existenzielle Bedrohung, in die wir durch das zunehmende Überschreiten von „planetaren Grenzen" (Rockström et al. 2009; Steffen et al. 2015) geraten, u.a. den anthropogenen Klimawandel, birgt jedenfalls eine Chance, weil sie zu einer grundlegenden Wende zwingt, wenn wir das Projekt Menschheit fortsetzen wollen.

Literatur

Autor, David/ Dorn, David/ Hanson, Gordon/ Majlehsi, Kaveh (2017): Importing Political Polarization? The Electoral Consequence of Rising Trade Exposure (National Bureau of Economic Research Working Paper Nr. 22637). Cambridge, Mass.: NBER. Revised version.

Bauman, Zygmunt (2017): Retrotopia. Aus dem Englischen von Frank Jakubzik. Berlin: Suhrkamp.

Bericht zur weltweiten Ungleichheit (2018): Kurzfassung, deutsche Fassung. Internetquelle: https://wir2018.wid.world/files/download/wir2018-summary-german.pdf (Abruf 3.12.2019).

Bissio, Roberto (2019): "Club governance: Can the world still be run by gentlemen's agreements?": Spotlight on Sustainable Development 2018. Koordination: Global Policy Forum. Internetquelle: https://www.2030spotlight.org/sites/default/files/spot2019/Spotlight_Innenteil_2019_web_ge samt.pdf (Abruf: 4.12.2019).

Bosselmann, Klaus (2015): Earth Governance: Trusteeship of the Global Commons. Cheltenham, UK: Edward Elgar.

Bosselmann, Klaus (2017): "The Next Step: Earth Trusteeship". Seventh Interactive Dialogue of the United Nations General Assembly on Harmony with Nature, New York, 21.4.2017. Internetquelle: http://files.harmonywithnatureun.org/uploads/upload96.pdf (Abruf: 10.12.2019).

Colantone, Italo/ Stanig, Piero (2017): „Global Competition and Brexit": American Political Science Review 112 (2), 201-218.

Dippel, C. R./ Gold, R./ Heblich, S. (2015): „Globalization and its (Dis) Content: Trade Shocks and Voting Behaviour": National Bureau for   Economic Research Working Paper No. 21812.

Fadinger, Harald (2019): „Das Gesicht der Verlierer. Wie Freihandel und Globalisierung den Aufstieg der Rechtspopulisten fördern": Die Zeit, 10.April 2019.

Friedman, Thomas (1996): „Revolt of the Wannabes": Foreign Affairs, 7. Februar 1996.

Fürlinger, Ernst (2013): Moscheebaukonflikte in Österreich. Nationale Politik des religiösen Raums im globalen Zeitalter. Göttingen/ Wien: v & r unipress/ Vienna University Press.

Gallagher, Kevin P./ Richard Kozul-Wright (2019): A New Multilateralism for Shared Prosperity. Geneva Principles for a Global Green New Deal. Boston University. Internetquelle: https://www.bu.edu/gdp/files/2019/04/A-New-Multilateralism-GDPC_UNCTAD.pdf (Abruf: 3.12.2019).

Global Policy Forum (2019): Spotlight on Sustainable Development 2019. Internetquelle: https://www.2030spotlight.org/en/book/1883/chapter/reshaping-governance-sustainability

Gore, Timothy (2015): Extreme Carbon Inequality. Oxfam Media Briefing, 2.12.2015. Internetquelle: https://www.oxfam.org/en/research/extreme-carbon-inequality (Abruf: 3.12.2019).

---

[9] Eine Initiative dafür ist beispielsweise auf die Einrichtung einer Institution für die Treuhandschaft der globalen Gemeingüter (u.a. der Atmosphäre) gerichtet, die von mehreren globalen Netzwerken getragen wird, u.a. vom „Planetary Integrity Project" und der „Earth Trusteeship Initiative" (Bosselmann 2015; 2017).

Honneth, Axel/ Fraser, Nancy (2003): Umverteilung oder Anerkennung? Eine politisch-philosophische Kontroverse. Berlin: Suhrkamp.

Hopkins, Rob (2014): Einfach. Jetzt. Machen! Wie wir unsere Zukunft selbst in die Hand nehmen. München: oekom.

Inglehart, Ronald F./ Norris, Pippa (2016): Trump, Brexit, and the Rise of Populismus. Economic Have-Nots and Cultural Backlash (Harvard Kennedy School, Faculty Research Working Paper Series 16-026, August 2016).

Koppetsch, Cornelia (2019): Die Gesellschaft des Zorns. Rechtspopulismus im globalen Zeitalter. Bielefeld: transcript.

Lenzi, Dominic (2019): „Deliberating about Climate Change: The Case for ‚Thinking and Nudging‘“: Moral Philosophy and Politics, ISSN (Online) 2194-5624.

Osterhammel, Jürgen (2017): Die Flughöhe der Adler. Historische Essays zur globalen Gegenwart. München: Beck.

Malgouyres, Clément (2017): „Trade Shocks and Far-Right Voting: Evidence from French Presidential Elections“. European University Institute, Robert Schuman Centre for Advanced Studies, Working Paper 2017/21, März 2017. Norris, Pippa/ Inglehart, Ronald F. (2019): Cultural Backlash: Trump, Brexit, and Authoritarian Populism. Cambridge: Cambridge University Press.

Nussbaum, Martha (2019): Königreich der Angst. Gedanken zur aktuellen politischen Krise. Aus dem Englischen von Manfred Weltecke. Darmstadt: Wissenschaftliche Buchgesellschaft.

Papst Franziskus (2015): Laudato si. Die Umwelt-Enzyklika des Papstes. Freiburg i.Br.: Herder.

Piketty, Thomas (2014a): Das Kapital im 21. Jahrhundert. München: Beck.

Piketty, Thomas (2014b): „A global progressive tax on individual net worth would offer the best solution to the world's spiralling levels of inequality“. London School of Economics and Political Science, British Politics and Policy Blog, 17. April 2014.

Raza, Werner (2018): „For the many, not the few! Anmerkungen zur Zukunft der Globalisierung“, A&W Blog, 10.9.2018.

Reckwitz, Andreas (2019a): "Krise der Selbstentfaltung" (Interview mit Jens Bisky): Süddeutsche Zeitung, 11. November 2019, 15.

Reckwitz, Andreas (2019b): Das Ende der Illusionen. Politik, Ökonomie und Kultur in der Spätmoderne. Berlin: edition Suhrkamp.

Rockström, Johan/ Steffen, Will/ Noone, Kevin,, et al. (2009): "Planetary Boundaries: Exploring the Safe Operating Space for Humanity": Ecology and Society 14 (2). Internetquelle: https://www.ecologyandsociety.org/vol14/iss2/art32/

Rodrik, Dani (1997): Has Globalization Gone Too Far? New York: Columbia University Press.

Rodrik, Dani (2018a): „Populism and the economics of globalization“: Journal of International Business Policy. Internetquelle: https://drodrik.scholar.harvard.edu/files/dani-rodrik/files/pop ulism_and_the_economics_of_globalization.pdf (Abruf: 12.10.2019).

Rodrik, Dan (2018b): Straight Talk on Trade: Ideas for a Sane World Economy. Princeton, N.J.: Princeton University Press.

Rodrik, Dan (2019a): „Globalization's Wrong Turn and How It Hurt America“: Foreign Affairs, 19. Juni 2019. Internetquelle: https://www.foreignaffairs.com/articles/united-states/2019-06-11/globalizations-wrong-turn (Abruf: 13.10.2019).

Rodrik, Dan (2019b): „What's Driving Populism?“ Project Syndicate, 9. Juli 2019. Internetquelle: http://www.project-syndicate.org/ (Abruf: 12.10.2019).

Schwab Klaus/ Smadja, Tanja (1996): „Start Taking the Backlash Against Globalization Seriously“: The International Herald Tribune, 1. Februar 1996.

Schäfer, Dorothea (2015): Fiskalische und ökonomische Auswirkungen einer eingeschränkten Finanztransaktionssteuer. Gutachten im Auftrag der SPD-Bundestagsfraktion. Berlin: Deutsches Institut für Wirtschaftsforschung.

Sengupta, Ranja (2016): „International Trade and the 2030 Agenda for Sustainable Development“, in: Spotlight on Sustainable Development 2016. Report by the Reflection Group on the 2030 Agenda for Sustainable Development, Koordination: Global Policy Forum. Beirut/

Bonn/ Montevideo et al., 130-140. Internetquelle: https://neu.globalpolicy.org/sites/default/fi les/contentpix/spotlight/pdfs/Agenda2030_engl_160708_WEB.pdf

Slobodian, Quinn (2019a): Globalisten: Das Ende der Imperien und die Geburt des Neolibera- lismus. Aus dem Englischen von Stephan Gebauer. Berlin: Suhrkamp.

Slobodian, Quinn (2019b): „Sie wollten bloß eine andere Globalisierung": Süddeutsche Zeitung, 2.12.2019, 9.

Steffen, Will/ Richardson, Katherine/ Rockström, Johan, et al. (2015): "Planetary boundaries: Guiding human development on a changing planet": Science 347 (6223). Internetquelle: https://science.sciencemag.org/content/347/6223/1259855

Stieglitz, Joseph (2002): Globalization and Its Discontent. London: Penguin Books.

UN GA (2015) Transformation unserer Welt: die Agenda 2030 für nachhaltige Entwicklung. Resolution 70/1 der Generalversammlung, verabschiedet am 25. September 2015. United Na- tions General Assembly (UN GA). https://www.un.org/Depts/german/gv-70/band1/ar70001 .pdf (Abruf: 2.12.2019).

Vehrkamp, Robert/ Wegschaider, Klaudia (2017): Populäre Wahlen. Mobilisierung und Gegen- mobilisierung der sozialen Milieus bei der Bundestagswahl 2017. Gütersloh: Bertelsmann- Stiftung.

Wallach, Lori (2019: „The WTO is dying, but we can fix it": The New York Times, international edition, 30.11./1.12.2019, 1 und 10.

Wodak, Ruth (2016): Politik mit der Angst. Zur Wirkung rechtspopulistischer Diskurse. Wien/ Hamburg: Edition Konturen.

World Inequality Report (2018). Internetquelle: https://wir2018.wid.world

FORSCHUNGSVORHABEN

Long Way to go:
Re-integration Processes into post-conflict Bosnia

Friedrich Altenburg

Abstract

This article examines the question in which way return after conflict induced flight migration can contribute to an inclusive society and restoration of peace and stability, taking up the case of Bosnia and Herzegovina. Indeed the Dayton Peace Agreement as guiding policy document declared return as one of the objectives and means for peace at the same time. As we will see this objective was hardly met, as return was only partial in numbers, reinforced ethnic divisions and relocation of persons. Contributing factors to that end were the lack of focus on re-integration, the dominance of host countries' perspective on return and too little attention on returnees' own agenda.

Introduction

"Going home" suggests a positive feeling, and politicians play this tune when enticing refugees to return home, as was the case with the "Rückkehr-Tausender" (a cheque of 1,000 EURO) offered by the then Minister for Interior in Austria, Sobotka in March 2017 for voluntary return. Return is presented as a "solution in the best interest of the refugee", but at the same time as a message to the home audience as an instrument to reduce migrant stocks in times of large influx numbers and growing concern about migration across Europe.

The UNHCR concept of three permanent solutions (UNHCR 1995) might have two flaws: One is the idea of permanence in the first place, and the second is to forget that integration is not only needed in countries of exile, but also a factor in resettlement and last but not least in return.

Return is presented as a remedy for post-conflict situations, as a restoration to the status quo ante for both the returnees, the societies in the countries of origin and the recipient societies. But do these expectations hold true? Will return be the restoration to normality in Syria, South Sudan, Afghanistan or Myanmar? With the Bosnian case Europe has a prototype on its doorstep, which can provide lessons from the long-term perspective. The size of refugee movement (2.2 million persons), the complexity of the conflict (ethnic, religious and diaspora components) and the international implications and involvement make it a special case indeed.

The Bosnian Case

The conflicts between the three main groups, the Bosniacs, Croats and Serbs, engulfing other groups such as the Roma and the small Jewish community, resulted in a massive displacement of persons: 1 million persons were displaced within the country, and 1.2 million sought refuge across international borders: Almost half of those (519,000) in former member states of the Republic of Yugoslavia, an equally large number (465,000) in three Western European countries Germany, Austria and Sweden, the remainder across other European countries and overseas (Harild et al. 2015; Valenta/Ramet 2016b).

Rape and torture, *"domicide"* (the intentional destruction of private property and cultural capital) and the massive expulsion later known infamously as "ethnic cleansing", were part of the strategic portfolio of all warring parties and first moves in what a street art poster in Sarajevo labelled as *Refuchess* (Jansen 2011), where refugees and returnees became pawns in a political game of the (former) warring parties.

Return to Bosnia

The Dayton Peace Agreement (DPA) formerly ended the hostilities on December 14, 1995 and created a state consisting of two entities, the Federation of Bosnia and Hercegovina and the Republica Srpska. In its Annex VII[1] the DPA declares that *"all refugees and displaced persons have the right freely to return to their homes of origin"*, postulating that the *"early return of refugees and displaced persons is an important objective of the settlement of the conflict in Bosnia and Herzegovina."*(DPA 1995: Annex VII, Art.1) Return objective was to restore the status quo ante and thus to reverse ethnic cleansing, favour minority return and to foster return to the "original home".

In the first year after the DPA some 250,000 returned and it took until 2004 for UNHCR to be able to declare a return rate somehow close to 50%: 440,000 international refugees and 560,000 IDPs were recorded as having retuned (for figures we rely on Harild et al. 2015; Valenta/Ramet 2016a; Valenta/Strabac 2013). So on one hand return was slower the rates smaller than projected by UNHC (Walsh et al. 1999).

Return was not the favoured option, certainly not for the international refugees. Their average return rate was 40%, and only Germany, from where 77% returned, is standing out among the others. It appears that the various repatriation packages offered by different European states had less effect. Whereas other countries sooner or later offered integration and naturalisation such as Sweden or Austria (after an initial reluctance) Germany ended the temporary protection regime after 1997 (Hageboutros 2017). It seems that structure or external frameworks rather than individual agency of the refugees were the driving momentum.

---

[1]   https://www.refworld.org/docid/3de497992.html

The result of return movements in Bosnia can be described as equally uneven and far away from the objectives proclaimed by Annex VII of the DPA. Main issues were housing (including property rights and reconstruction), safety (especially because of land mines) and security in view of the continuous tensions as well as livelihood in genera. There is a broad consensus that return was not sustainable, at least measured against the terms of the DPA (Dahlman/Ó Tuathail 2005; Hageboutros 2017; Jansen 2011; Kleck 2007; Valenta/Strabac 2013).

Return happened mainly to majority areas, not necessarily to the original home area, thus cementing the ethnic division and undermining the intentions of the DPA. At the same time the return to other places than the original home increased the case load of IDPs. An additional issue is the contribution to urbanisation, as minority return would have meant return to rural areas. Actually Bosniacs mainly returned into Federation towns.

According to UNDP returnees (together with continuous IDPs) tended to be marginalised with high unemployment rates and need for social assistance (UNDP 2002). Bosnian Diaspora is still double the size than the refugee caseload from 1992-1995 and the wish to emigrate in Bosnia is equally large (up to 80% among young people), given the shaky political situation and continuous division of the country as well as the weak economy.

This assessment prompts the question for the reasons for this unsatisfactory outcome of return migration, measured against the publicly proclaimed expectations and the text of the DPA. What might be the lessons to be learned for present and future refugee movements and return operations? And may we generalise Bosnian experiences to other contexts such as Syria, Sudan or Venezuela? We can deduct three main issued which contributed to these outcomes:

The conception of return as such

The notion that return would mean a movement back to an ideal, even mythical home and thus solve the problem of the refugee as well as his or her society, implies not only that home was an ideal place to be indeed, and negates the fact that home must have changed in the first place, otherwise people would not have left.(Houte 2017: 6–8) If Bosnia was a divided society prior to the war, along ethnic lines of segregation, it was even more so after the war. We can distinguish four groups (Basic 2013):

- Remainees, who had never left
- Returnees, who came back from displacement within the country or abroad
- Refugees (people settling as displaced from else-where in the Bosnian context)
- Diaspora (people having left Bosnia as refugee, but returning home for vacation)

Members of the diaspora as expelled refugees could be interpreted as victims, but become perpetrators through the apparent gains: also returnees were viewed negatively by remainees, mainly on economic grounds. Refugees from other parts of Bosnia (or Croatia) were to be considered as victims because of their displacement, but became a threat to remainees and hindrance to return of diaspora.

So in fact the war created four distinctive groups, each of these in either an in- or out position, and all competing for resources, notably housing and employment, but also attention of the political representation, which again was organised along ethnic lines of separation.

International Community and its Operations

The presence and intervention of the international community was characterised by two aspects, which were new and to a certain extent specific for Bosnia at the time: The establishment of the Office of the High Representative on one hand and the large number of international NGOs operational on the ground. Both may have been the result of the proximity in the midst of Europe, the heavy media coverage of the conflict and the massive displacement of refugees into Europe.

The Office of the High Representative (OHR) was established in 1995 by Resolution 1031 of the UN Security Council and strengthened significantly in 1997 by the Bonn Powers. Whereas some describe this form of international bureaucracy as "benevolent despots" comparable to British Colonial administration in India in the 19th century or postcolonial protectorate (Džihić 2006; Knaus/Martin 2003), others recognise it as decisive player once it was established to promote minority return (Dahlman/Ó Tuathail 2005). Its establishment with the Reconstruction and Return Task Force and the Property Law Implementation Plan are credited as innovative instruments in the return process.

But these innovations were in place only in 1999, i.e. 7 years after displacement took place, whereas the actors of ethnic cleansing were still in power and used all bureaucratic means and social pressure to prevent minority return.

Another shortcoming of the reconstruction process (Dahlman/Ó Tuathail 2005; Jansen 2011; Kleck 2007) can be accredited to the sheer number of relief agencies on the ground. This led to what some observers described as "flag mentality" of NGOs, distributing the country among themselves. Reconstruction was perceived as chaotic, too often concentrating on single houses based on a case-to-case approach and not on spatial and social planning, including schools and infrastructure etc.

Case lists were developed by village leaders, often based on bribes. Thus deprived families were disadvantaged. On top of that allegations were made that aid was used to reconstruct houses of people living abroad without intention to return and indirectly used for holiday residencies.

The start of reconstruction by and with aid agencies without common standards created new divisions and problems: Some NGOs supplied just building materials, whereas other followed a "finished house approach". In the first case roof and door constituted the house as habitable, even if there was no bathroom, kitchen or plastering. This "habitable" status resulted in pressure to vacate temporary accommodation either in Bosnia or abroad (Kleck 2007). The subsequent obligation to pay tradesmen in order to finish the job led into debt. Women, elderly persons and single households were disadvantaged, as they got less priority on the lists and were not involved in the design process, which was a male domain.

Returnees' strategies

Given these shortcomings and challenges refugees and IDPs alike developed their own coping strategies, including intergenerational, gender, spatial, and timing aspects (Jansen 2011). Partial return became a method of risk distribution:

Elderly persons returned in order to claim property and reconstruction assistance, while younger ones remained in the place of displacement. Another form of intergenerational strategy would be the return of (particularly male) adults, leaving the children (and women) with relatives or friends in save places. Staying over weekends or commuting across internal demarcation lines were strategies particularly of IDPs, but also valid for refugees in neighbouring countries.

Based on these observations Jansen (2011) compared these return practices to a hedging bet, trying to assure property rights and future options on one hand and safety and livelihood on the other. If return to the original home was to be considered as the objective and an indicator for sustainability, then the evaluation of return to Bosnia is certainly ambiguous. Not only did the majority of displaced persons (1.2 out of 2.2 millions) opt to stay in their place of displacement or travel onwards, turning spatial and timing strategies into transnational ways of living. Many of those actually returning to Bosnia ended up in different places and contributed to the entrenchment of an already ethnically divided country and through urbanisation to further social segregation (See also Harild et al. 2015; Kleck 2007).

Lessons to be learned for
future post-conflict return programmes

Now which lessons may we draw from the Bosnian case? Bosnia may have been unique as refugee source country in the midst of Europe, but many other features are shared by hot spots of the presence: The division along ethnic, religious or other social lines of segregation, the elements of ethnic cleansing and domicide, the massive displacement and the political instability as well as the involvement of the international community.

A first lesson would be to change the perception of return as such, away from a seemingly automatic "end of the refugee cycle" (Black/Koser 1999) to an understanding of a migratory move in its own right. Therefore return to normality needs to be replaced by an integration process, involving all parties involved as integration not only the migrant's affair but requires efforts from the recipient society, even more so if it is divided in a post–conflict scenario as was the case in Bosnia.

The Bosnian experience was guided by a case to case approach, emphasising the divisions rather than integrative interventions: Affiliation to an ethnic group, return from a particular country of exile, age and gender started to play a role. It was the European host country perspective, driven by the endeavour to reduce migrant stocks that became the guiding principle.

So the answer would be a holistic and integrative approach based on the common understanding to be developed on the ground. Basic needs like schooling, health services as well as technical infrastructure need to be taken into account as part of such a holistic approach. Such an approach requires appropriate coordination structures and the willingness of all actors to submit to such mechanisms and a certain loss of autonomy in planning and programming.

All of that would be futile without a framework for safety and livelihood. These are of paramount importance for successful and sustainable return and re-integration. The model of the OHR pointed the way into the right direction; without its establishment and the presence of SFOR peace keeping troops the partial successes would have been impossible.

A last lesson to be learned would be to respect and work with the fluidity in the strategies of refugees and not to work against it. Any programming approach requiring firm decisions on the side of an individual refugee or displaced household might prompt a decision against sustainable return to the original home, such as staying in exile, moving to urban spaces or leaving at the earliest convenience.

"[L]ook ..., you cannot stand it there, you are feeling bad, but here, my friend, it is all FOR NOTHING".[2] In other words: If no chances for re-integration and accommodation of livelihood aspects into returnees' development perspectives are offered, sustainability of return programmes remains questionable.

References

Basic, Goran (2013): Stories after the Bosnian War: Competition for Victimhood. In: Cheng, L-L (Hrsg.), Proceedings of the 1st Annual International Conference on Forensic Sciences & Criminalistics Research (FSCR 2013). 68–77.

Black, Richard/Koser, Khalid (1999): The End of the Refugee Cylcle?: In: Black, Richard/Koser, Khalid (Hrsg.), The End of the Refugee Cylcle?: Refugee Repatriation and Reconstruction. New York: Berghahn Books, 2–17.

Dahlman, Carl/Ó Tuathail, Gearóid (2005): Broken Bosnia: The Localized Geopolitics of Displacement and Return in Two Bosnian Places. In: *Annals of the Association of American Geographers*, 95, 3.

DPA (1995): General Framework Agreement for Peace in Bosnia and Hercegovina. Text abrufbar unter: https://peacemaker.un.org/sites/peacemaker.un.org/files/BA_951121_DaytonAgreement.pdf (Zugriff am 2.12.2019).

Džihić, Vedran (2006): Bosnien-Herzegowina. Europa als bosnischer Mythos vs. Bosnischer Balkan als europäisches politisches Trauma. In: Džihić, Vedran/Ndjivan, Silvia/Paic, Hrvoje/ Stachowitsch, Saskia (Hrsg.), Europa - verflucht begehrt: Europavorstellungen in Bosnien-

---

[2] From the rap song *„Za Mirzu"* by Edo Majke (2006), translation Vedran Dzihic/Friedrich Altenburg

Herzegowina, Kroatien und Serbien. Wien, Braumüller, 13–94. Text abrufbar unter: http://deposit.ddb.de/cgi-bin/dokserv?id=2825367&prov=M&dok_var=1&dok_ext=htm (Zugriff am 3.4.2019).

Hageboutros, Joelle (2017): The Bosnian Refugee Crisis: A Comparative Study of German and Austrian Reactions and Responses. In: *Swarthmore International Relations Journal*, 1 (1), 50–60.

Harild, Niels/Christensen, Asger/Zetter, Roger/Weltbankgruppe (2015): Sustainable refugee return [Elektronische Ressource]: triggers, constraints and lessons on addressing the development challenges of forced displacement. World Bank.

Houte, Marieke van (2017): Return Migration to Afghanistan: Moving Back or Moving Forward? Migration, Diasporas and Citizenship: Cham: Palgrave Macmillan.

Jansen, Stef (2011): Refuchess: Locating Bosniac Repatriates after the War in Bosnia–Herzegovina. In: *Population, Space and Place*, 17 (2), 140–152.

Kleck, Monika (2007): Refugee Return - Success Story or Bad Dream. A Review from Eastern Bosnia. In: Fischer, Martina (Hrsg.), Peacebuilding and civil society in Bosnia-Herzegovina: ten years after Dayton. 2. ed. Berlin: LIT, 107–122.

Knaus, Gernot/Martin, Felix (2003): Travails of the European Raj. Lessons from Bosnia and Herzegovina. Text abrufbar unter: https://www.esiweb.org/index.php?lang=en&id=156&document_ID=59 (Zugriff am 8.1.2019).

UNDP (2002): UNDP Human Development Report Bosnia and Herzegovina (2002). Text abrufbar unter: http://hdr.undp.org/sites/default/files/bosnia_and_herzegovina_2002_en.pdf (Zugriff am 9.10.2019).

UNHCR (1995): The State of The World's Refugees 1995: In Search of Solutions. UNHCR. Text abrufbar unter: http://www.unhcr.org/publications/sowr/4a4c70859/state-worlds-refugees-1995-search-solutions.html (Zugriff am 1.2.2018).

Valenta, Marko/Ramet, Sabrina (2016a): Bosnian Migrants. An Introduction. In: Valenta, Marko/Ramet, Sabrina (Hrsg.), The Bosnian Diaspora. Integration in Transnational Communities. Routledge, 1–24.

Valenta, Marko/Ramet, Sabrina (Hrsg.) (2016b): The Bosnian Diaspora. Integration in Transnational Communities. Routledge.

Valenta, Marko/Strabac, Zan (2013): The Dynamics of Bosnian Refugee Migrations in the 1990s, Current Migration Trends and Future Prospects. In: *Refugee Survey Quarterly*, 32 (3), 1–22.

Walsh, Martha/Black, Richard/Koser, Khalid (1999): Repatriation from the European Union to Bosnia-Herzegovina: The Role of Information. In: Black, Richard/Koser, Khalid (Hrsg.), The End of the Refugee Cylcle?: Refugee Repatriation and Reconstruction. New York: Berghahn Books, 110–125.

Turkish Policy Developments towards Highly Skilled Immigration and the position of Austria[1]

Hakan Kilic, Gudrun Biffl

Abstract

Highly skilled migrants are much sought after in an international quest for talent. Not only highly developed countries are devising policies to attract them but also traditional source countries of migrants. Their focus is on return migration of former emigrants and their offspring. By attracting highly skilled Turkish origin migrants, Turkey is hoping to diversify its workforce and upgrade the skills in areas of high economic growth potential. The paper identifies the role of policies in the decision to return. The focus is on Turkey's National Development Plans which aim at the return of highly qualified Turkish (origin) migrants and the change of the migration policy strategy.

Introduction

Before addressing the research approach, we draw attention to three factors which are decisive for the methodology chosen and the outcome of the study:

- The statistical as well as research data on return migration of highly skilled Turkish origin migrants from Austria is scarce and does not provide conclusive quantitative evidence about the stocks and flows involved by gender, age, profession and educational attainment level.
- Turkish migration to Austria is the result of a temporary worker recruitment agreement between Austria and Turkey of 1964 – never had Austria nor Turkey the intention to thereby pave the way for permanent immigration to Austria. Given the supposedly temporary nature of worker migration from Turkey, the Austrian labour migration policy did not implement social integration measures. As it turned out, settlement and family migration occurred nonetheless from the mid-1980s onwards while a comprehensive integration policy was only implemented in 2009, following the request of the European Union to develop a National Action Plan for Integration.

---

[1] This Policy Brief is based on the PhD research project "Back to the Roots. Return Migration of Highly Skilled Turkish Origin Migrants from Austria to Turkey", which is one of the PhD-projects under the title "PhD Migration & Sozialer Friede – Interdisziplinäre Umweltforschung im Rahmen des PhD Programms Migration Studies" funded by the EU-Asylum, Migration and Integration Fund and the Austrian Federal Ministry of the Interior.

- With political stabilization, economic reforms and increasing integration into the global economy from 1999 onwards, Turkey was in need of skilled labour to sustain its successful economic development. This was the driving force for the promotion of return migration of highly skilled migrants of Turkish origin in 2010.

Turkey and its migration policy

On 15 May 1964, the Republic of Austria and the Republic of Turkey concluded an Agreement on the Recruitment of Turkish 'guest-workers'.[2] After more than 50 years of the signing of the agreement, one may judge the outcomes by juxtaposing them with the intentions of the policy. According to the First Turkish Five-Year Development Plan 1963-1967, it was the objective of Turkey to promote emigration of its workers, just as Austria was keen on employing Turkish workers, albeit only on a temporary basis. Thus, large-scale Turkish emigration started as a government policy (Abadan-Unat 2011), even though the migration decision itself remains an individual/family choice. The following paragraph in the development plan dealing with "manpower, employment, education and research" points out the political objectives but also the potential risks for Turkey:

> *"Another aspect of employment policy is the export of surplus labour to those countries of Western Europe, which suffer from a dearth of labour. However, Turkey, while having a surplus of unskilled labour, it has insufficient numbers of skilled labour. Therefore, it is essential that measures be taken to ensure that Turkey's deficiency in skilled labour not be exacerbated by Turkey's labour export policy"* (State Planning Organization 1962; 456).

From Turkey's point of view, labour migration was a national development strategy that was primarily intended to promote socio-economic development, in particular via remittances (Martin 1991). In addition, as stated above, Turkey was keen on reducing its surplus of unskilled labour, thereby reducing the need for social expenditure on poverty alleviation. After World War II, Turkey did not only struggle for political but also for economic stability, experiencing slow economic growth and high unemployment (Biffl 2013). Thus, Turkey was in a similar situation as many Southern European countries, in particular Italy, Spain, Greece and former Yugoslavia. Austria, on the other hand, experienced a scarcity of labour, as many Austrians had emigrated to overseas countries after WWII, reducing labour supply to the extent that the economic growth potential was at stake. Therefore, Austria

---

[2]   Refer to: Abkommen zwischen der Republik Österreich und der Türkischen Republik über die Anwerbung türkischer Arbeitskräfte und deren Beschäftigung in Österreich. http://www.ris. bka.gv.at/GeltendeFassung.wxe?Abfrage=Bundesnormen&Gesetzesnummer=10008198. 21.10.2019.

considered recruiting migrant labour and adopting the German guestworker recruitment model. Germany had signed the recruitment agreement with Turkey in 1961.

A new step in in the promotion of labour migration as well as economic development was taken with the signing of the Turkish agreement with the European Economic Community (EEC), the so-called Ankara Agreement (1963). This was an association agreement of the EEC with Turkey, followed by an additional Protocol to the Agreement in 1970. The Agreement initiated a three-step process towards a customs union, beginning with the integration of economic and trade policy; envisaged was Turkey's full membership in the EEC at a later stage. An Association Council, set up by the Agreement, controlled its development and gave the Agreement a detailed road map of actions to be taken. In this vein, the Association Council Decision No 1/80, spells out in Article 6(1) that regular Turkish migrant workers may obtain, after a certain period of legal work, the right to renew their work permits and to extend their residence in accordance with their entitlement to work (Rieser-Angulo Garcia 2012).

As it was, large numbers of originally temporary Turkish labour migrants settled in one or the other EU-Member State. Then, the gist of Turkish policy towards migration was to ensure Turkish workers' rights in the EU rather than promoting their return to Turkey. Some countries, e.g. Germany, terminated the recruitment of labour migrants from Turkey in 1973, reduced family benefits to children in Turkey and promoted return migration to Turkey (Meier-Braun 1996; Hönekopp 1987).

The Turkey - EU relationship features several milestones: the association agreement and the beginning of an accession process in 1987, the signing of a Customs Union agreement with the EU in 1995 and the official recognition of Turkey as a candidate for full membership on 12 December 1999. In addition, migration policy of Turkey evolved in the wake of bilateral treaties and experienced a turnaround from promoting emigration of workers to inviting them back, once they had obtained high educational attainment levels and skills.

As far as migration flows go, the nature of return migration to Turkey differs markedly between the 1970s and 80s and the return flows of the 2000s (Icduygu 2009). In the 1970s and 1980s, migration flows were largely mono-directional, as they resulted mainly from labour shedding in Austria (as well as Germany and Switzerland) in the wake of the economic recession 1973/74 and the rise in domestic labour supply (Biffl 1985). In the years since 2000, on the other hand, the flows were largely circular, partly based on family re-union, partly resulting from economic opportunities in a transnational context. In that context it is becoming increasingly evident that the second and third generations tend to "return to their roots" for various reasons, one being their expectations of obtaining a higher socio-economic status than their parents, the other hoping for better employment opportunities flowing from their higher foreign education. Family ties, cultural factors and an increasingly hostile (Austro-German) host society relative to Turkish migrants may be additional factors (Merey 2018). In addition, the rapid increase in the number of private universities in Turkey has also promoted the return of Turkish scientists to Turkey (Bilgili & Siegel 2014).

This more recent development raises the question to what extent this new trend of highly skilled return migration of Turkish (origin) migrants may be interpreted as a result of a change in Turkish migration policy. Is Turkey adopting a selective (return) migration policy in line with immigration countries? Recent surveys show that in the 2000s the majority of OECD countries, as well as a growing number of non-OECD countries, employ selective immigration policies specifically aiming at highly qualified labour (Czaika 2017). Turkey is one of those countries which implemented programs and policies to attract highly skilled migrants. The aim is to encourage young university graduates and other highly skilled Turkish (origin) migrants abroad to 'return' to Turkey. These initiatives may be taken as an indication for a rudimentary selective migration policy without the adoption of a comprehensive system of immigration typical for traditional immigration countries.

Among the policy instruments in place is the International Postdoctoral Research Scholarship Program, initiated by the Scientific and Technological Research Council of Turkey (TUBITAK); it encourages young scientists who have successfully completed their doctoral studies abroad in natural sciences, medicine, social sciences and the humanities, as well as engineering and technical sciences to return to Turkey for research (Bilgili & Siegel; p. 224). Through this project, 562 scientists have returned to Turkey in the years 2007-2015 (Hürriyet 2019). This new policy focus is also surfacing in the most recent National Development Plan, aiming at highly qualified labour via migration.

"The importance of a skilled workforce is increasing on a global scale. The educational attainment level and competences of the labour force will continue to have an impact on the economic development of countries and individuals. It is expected that the quality of the labour force will be a determining factor for labour productivity together with their educational attainment level. Demand for skilled labour is expected to increase in all countries. The twenty-first century will be the century of countries that, in addition to creating their own skilled workforce, will be able to attract these people on a global scale (...)" (State Planning Organization 2013).

A further political step in that direction was the adoption of Law No. 41129 in 1995, according to which additional rights are granted to foreign citizens of Turkish origin, aiming at maintaining or expanding their contact with Turkey. Thereafter, in 2004 and 2009, several legislative changes were undertaken, again to facilitate labour market access of highly skilled foreign citizens of Turkish origin. The most recent changes along the roadmap of promoting highly skilled Turkish origin return migration has taken place in May 2012, allowing persons who had previously given up Turkish citizenship to apply for the (Turkish) 'Blue Card'; the latter grants Turkish origin foreign citizens living abroad unrestricted residence and free access to the labour market in Turkey. Accordingly, 'Turkish Blue Card' holders have similar rights as Turkish citizens, with only few restrictions such as the right to vote in elections or to hold public office; they are also exempt from military service. All these are examples of an increasingly explicit diaspora engagement policy of Turkey (Bilgili & Siegel; p. 225).

Conclusion

As the political concern of Turkey switched from the 1960s to the 1990s from ensuring labour and social rights of their diaspora in the host countries to the promotion of the return of skilled Turkish origin migrants in the years of 2000, so changed their policy tool kit. To ensure equal or even preferential treatment of Turkish migrants in other European countries, Turkey had signed bilateral agreements either with individual countries or the EEC/EU. In contrast, the more recent strategy to welcome back Turkish (origin) skilled migrants is a unilateral approach, offering preferential treatment to the highly skilled Turkish(origin) diaspora in terms of access to employment and social participation in Turkey. To what extent the policy change has resulted in increasing return flows to Turkey is difficult to establish, given the dearth of specific data in Turkey and Austria respectively. What we can see, however, is a continuous decline in inflows of Turkish citizens to Austria between 2008 and 2017 from some 5,000 individuals annually in 2008 to 3,300 in 2017. Over the same period the outflow of Turkish citizens from Austria has been surprisingly stable at some 3,000 persons, implying a steady decline of net inflows of Turkish citizens, reaching a low of 300 in 2017. At the same time the inflow of Austrian citizens, possibly of Turkish origin, from Turkey is declining steadily (to 557 in 2017) while the outflow of Austrians, possibly of Turkish origin, to Turkey is rising (to 1,017 in 2017), reaching a net outflow of 500 in 2017. While these may still be small numbers, they may be indicative of the effectiveness of the Turkish policy lure. A more comprehensive picture as to the factors responsible for the (return) migration decision can only be derived from interviews of Turkish (origin) migrants.

What we can learn from the analysis of Turkish policy papers and from the effective outflow of skilled Turkish (origin) migrants from Austria to Turkey is the changing character of migration between the two countries. An adequate policy response on the part of Austrian policy could be to specifically address these migrants as "bridge-builders". Their skills are augmented by transnational attributes and hybrid cultural characteristics, which enable them to move freely between the two countries and to interact effectively with either society. They may therefore not only contribute to the innovative capacity of Turkey but also of Austria, if adequately addressed. In so doing the economic and social networks and ties between the two countries may be strengthened and economic growth promoted in both countries.

References

Abadan-Unat, Nermin (2011). Turks in Europe: From Guestworkers to Transnational Citizen, Berghahn Books, New York.

Bilgili, Özge/Siegel, Melissa (2014). Policy perspectives of Turkey towards return migration: From permissive indifference to selective difference. In: Migration Letters, Volume: 11, No: 2, pp. 218-228.

Czaika, Mathias (2017). "Global Competition for Talent": Eine migrationspolitische Herausforderung. In: Altenburg, F.; Faustmann, A.; Pfeffer, T.; Skrivanek, I. (Ed.). Migration und Globalisierung in Zeiten des Umbruchs, edition Donau-Universität Krems, Krems.

Biffl, Gudrun (2013). The Role of Migration in Economic Relations between Europe and Turkey. European Review, Vol. 21, No. 3, 372–381.

Biffl, Gudrun (1985). „Die Entwicklung der Ausländerbeschäftigung in den wichtigsten europäischen Industriestaaten." WIFO-MB 8/1985. https://www.wifo.ac.at/jart/prj3/wifo/resources/person_dokument/person_dokument.jart?publikationsid=838&mime_type=application/pdf.

Hönekopp, Elmar (1987). Rückkehrförderung und Rückkehr ausländischer Arbeitnehmer und ihrer Familien. In: Hönekopp, Elmar (Ed.). Aspekte der Ausländerbeschäftigung in der Bundesrepublik Deutschland, Nürnberg, pp. 287-343.

Hürriyet (2015). 562 bilim insanı ülkeye geri döndü (562 scientists returned to the county). http://www.hurriyet.com.tr/egitim/562-bilim-insani-ulkeye-geri-dondu-28990197.

Icduygu, Ahmet (2009). International Migration and Human Development in Turkey. MPRA Paper No. 19235. 2009. https://mpra.ub.uni-muenchen.de/19235/1/MPRA_paper_19235.pdf.

Martin, Philipp L (1991). The unfinished story: Turkish labour migration to Western Europe: with special reference to the Federal Republic of Germany, International Labour Organization, Geneva.

Meier-Braun, Karl-Heinz (1996). 40 Jahre „Gastarbeiter" in Deutschland. In Meier-Braun, Karl-Heinz/ Martin A. Kilgus (Ed.): 40 Jahre „Gastarbeiter" in Deutschland und Ausländerpolitik in Deutschland – Tagungsbericht zum 4. Radioforum Ausländer bei Uns, 20. bis 22. März 1995 in Stuttgart. Nomos, Baden-Baden.

Merey, Can (2018). „Der ewige Gast – Wie mein türkischer Vater versuchte, Deutscher zu werden", Verlag Blessing.

Rieser-Angulo García, Yvonne (2012). Assoziationsabkommen der Europäischen Union. Überblick über die Auswirkungen auf das Fremdenrecht der Mitgliedstaaten anhand des EWG-Türkei-Abkommens. In: SIAK-Journal – Zeitschrift für Polizeiwissenschaft und polizeiliche Praxis (2), pp.4-16. https://www.bmi.gv.at/104/Wissenschaft_und_Forschung/SIAK-Journal/SIAK-Journal-Ausgaben/Jahrgang_2012/files/Rieser_2_2012.pdf.

State Planning Organization (1962). Turkish Five-Year Development Plan, Ankara.

State Planning Organization (2013). Tenth Development Plan 2014-2018, Ankara.

Afghan refugees return ‚home' to migrate again

Ali Ahmad Safi

Abstract

In the second half of 2016, Pakistan forcibly expelled more than half a million Afghan refugees, the greatest number of returnees from Pakistan since U.S. forces ousted the Taliban in 2001. This massive influx exacerbated Afghanistan's already critical socioeconomic situation. Tens of thousands of returnees settled in and around Kabul and other major cities in eastern Afghanistan, hoping to access services and integrate in the labour market. Many, however, have inadequate skills to adapt to life in urban economic settings. This paper provides information on how much the life of returnees have changed since their return from Pakistan. It also presents some highlights of poor (re)integration programs in two informal settlements in eastern Afghanistan and one formal near the capital, Kabul. The returnees experienced social exclusion, unemployment and lack of reintegration programs by the Afghan government.

Introduction

In the second half of 2016, Pakistan forcefully repatriated 618,156 refugees (370,102 documented and 248,054 undocumented) to Afghanistan (Ministry of Refugees and Repatriation, 2018), the highest number of returnees from Pakistan in the post-Taliban era. Human Rights Watch described this expulsion as *„the world's largest unlawful mass forced return of refugees in recent times (HRW, 2016)."* The Afghan government and international organizations lacked the sufficient resources to provide social services to large influx of returnees. The UN refugee agency described the situation as *"humanitarian emergency".* Among various factors for forceful return, Pakistan threatened not to renew the residence cards of Afghan refugees. The host resorted to daily extortion, arbitrary detention and unlawful use of force (HRW, 2016). Another factor that evoked the involuntary return was the political tensions between the two countries. The Afghan government and its international allies accuse Pakistan of harbouring international 'terrorists' and the Taliban insurgents who launch attacks on government and foreign targets inside Afghanistan. Although Afghans' legal status in Pakistan is increasingly precarious and their life has become more difficult, millions of Afghans still call Pakistan their 'home' (Siddiqui, 2019).

Afghanistan remains one of the largest refugee producing countries in the world over the last four decades (UNHCR and World Bank Group, 2019). Over seven million refugees returned 'home' (Ministry of Refugees and Repatriation, 2018) since the beginning of a new political era when the US forces ousted the Taliban from power in 2001. The majority of returnees came from Pakistan and Iran, the main host countries of Afghan refugees since the Soviet Union invasion of Afghanistan in 1979 (Jazayery, 2002: 215) that triggered the first massive waves of displacement. The plague of war and the large return challenged the government of Afghanistan in regards with their (re)integration program in social and economic life.

At the end of 2014, the US-led NATO forces pulled out their combat troops from Afghanistan and redefined their involvement as ‚Resolute Support Mission (RSM)'. The new mission aimed to assist, train and advise the Afghan security forces (Report to German Bundestag, 2018). The security deteriorated and the economic opportunities were restricted after the departure of international troops (Thier and Worden, 2017). Thousands of Afghans lost their jobs in the country. Political instability and uncertainty have added to the confusion over the fact in which direction the country was moving to. Fraud and irregularities in the 2014 presidential elections led to the formation of National Unity Government by two leading contenders with direct intervention by the then US Secretary of State (Their and Worden, 2017, Van Houte, 2016: 50-51).

More than half of Afghanistan's estimated 30 million population suffer from poverty, both in urban and rural areas. Access to irrigated or rain-fed land is vital to economic security in rural Afghanistan (NSIA, 2019). Recent drought has severely affected 1.4 million Afghans in the north and west of the country, creating a massive humanitarian crisis that has received minimal attention and assistance from the international community (Ben and Makoii, 2018). The former Afghan government Minister of Labour, Social Affairs, Martyrs and Disabled (MoLSAMD) said that his government designed programs to create one million jobs over the next three years (Zaki, 2017), a promise which was unlikely to fulfil and integrate the low skilled returnees due to limited resources and deteriorating security situation.

The United Nations Development Program (UNDP), International Labour Organization (ILO) and UN High Commissioner for Refugees (UNHCR) designed Support Afghanistan Livelihood and Mobility (SALAM) program with the aim to provide vocational training for returnees and assist them with finding work (UNDP, 2017). According to MoLSAMD, SALAM is unlikely to cope with the scale of migration, unemployment and poverty that Afghanistan is facing (Zaki, 2017). Eastern Nangarhar province for example and major cities have accommodated most of the returnees and internally displaced persons (IDPs) from Pakistan (Turton and Marsden, 2002). The relative better security, access to services and the labour market have been the pull factors for the returnees to settle in urban areas.

Waves of Afghan displacement and return

Migration has existed in various forms in social, economic and cultural landscape of Afghans throughout its turbulent history (Monsutti, 2008: 60, van Houte, 2016: 40). The strategic location of Afghanistan along the Silk Road has connected the trading countries in East and West and has formed transnational networks (Will-ner-Reid, 2017, Monsutti, 2008). The communist coup in 1978 and subsequent invasion of Afghanistan by the Soviets in 1979 have forced millions of Afghans out of their country and dispersed them around the world (Turton and Marsden, 2002, Monsutti, 2008: 60, van Houte, 2016:42). By the early 1980s there were some three million Afghan refugees, mainly in Pakistan and Iran (Jazayery, 2002: 215) and this number reached to its peak in 1990 of 6,22 million (Monsutti, 2008) mostly in Afghanistan's neighbouring countries. Today, Afghanistan remains the second largest refugee producing countries in the world after Syria, with 2.7 million people living outside the country's national borders (UNHCR, 2018). These statistics represents only documented refugees registered with the United Nations High Commissioner for Refugee (UNHCR).

The withdrawal of Soviet troops from Afghanistan in 1989 generated a lot of optimism that the pull-out of Russian Army would mean the end of the "refugee cycle" – both the end of violent resistance and the return of Afghan refugees (Black and Koser, 1999). On the contrary, the Soviet-backed government survived until 1992 when the resistant fighters known as Mujahiddin toppled it (Jazayery, 2002). Close to one million Afghan refugees returned home after the withdrawal and the fall of the communist regime (Marsden, 2003) but soon inter-Mujahiddin fighting fuelled a second wave of displacement both internally as IDPs or transna-tionally mainly to Pakistan and Iran (Jazayery, 2002, Monsutti, 2008). This mi-grated group constituted mainly the city elites who were associated with the com-munist People's Democratic Party of Afghanistan (PDPA) government and mostly from urban areas. Many with better resources migrated to the US or Europe who obtained refugee status and residence permits (van Houte, Siegel, Davids, 2014, Monsutti 2008).

A third wave fled to Pakistan as the Taliban took control of vast parts of the country between 1996 until 2001 (Alimia, 2014). The Taliban emerged as the outcome of the civil war who conquered Kabul in 1996 and installed a very harsh Islamic government that also restricted women's education and mobility (van Houte, 2016, Turton and Marsden, 2002). Torture, lashing, amputation and execu-tion were the routine practices by the Taliban (van Houte, 2016). In the aftermath of the 9/11 attacks, the US-led international forces toppled the Taliban for har-bouring Osama bin Laden and his Al-Qaeda in Afghanistan. Hope for peace, pros-perity and a new Afghanistan began to grow as international community poured its political and military support to the war-ravaged country. This optimism for peace was short-lived though. More than five million Afghans returned to Afghanistan in the post-Taliban era, which Alessandro Monsutti has described it as *"the larg-est repatriation campaigns in the history of the UN agency"* (Monsutti, 2008: 60).

They returned with the assistance of UNHCR or spontaneously. The pace of the return, however, slowed down since 2005 (Monsutti, 2008:61) as the security situation started to deteriorate.

Over the following decade, the Taliban began to reassert power, spreading violence across the country and triggering a new wave of migration. The political, economic and military transitions in 2014 left behind huge economic and security challenges. The US-led NATO forces pulled out their combat troops from Afghanistan and redefined their engagement as to *"assist, train and advise"* (Shanker, 2014) the Afghan security forces. The military and economic transition affected migration movements as well. The largest group of Afghans refugees are currently in Pakistan with nearly three millions (documented and undocumented) followed by around two millions in Iran (Alimia, 2014). The majority of Afghan refugees in Pakistan live in Khyber Pakhtunkhwa and Baluchistan provinces along the border with Afghanistan (Ahmad, 2018, Alimia, 2018) while another significant number live in Islamabad, Karachi and Lahore. Almost three quarters (74%) of Afghan refugees in Pakistan were born in Pakistan, with only 26% born in Afghanistan (Alimia, 2018)

Return means when refugees have the ability to make decisions to choose freely when and whether to return home country without any pressures (ECRE, 2017, Sydney, 2019). Forced return takes place against the will of the refugee and migrant (ECRE, 2017). Return is also believed to be a 'durable solution' for any type of post-war situation (Eastmond, 2006) that should lead to sustainable reintegration in the country of origin. The protracted Afghan refugees in Pakistan, however, have not enjoyed much of integration services during their decades-long stay. The return of most of the over 600,000 Afghans from Pakistan in 2016 (Muzhary, 2017) due to extortion and unlawful detention by Pakistan to force Afghan refugees out cannot be treated as 'durable solution'. Many returned after decades and for many was the first time to see the country of their parents. The large exodus of Afghan refugees from Pakistan exerted enormous pressure on social services like healthcare, education and shrinking labour market (Muzhary, 2017) with little prospect for future. For them, return meant the continuation of their displacement journey.

Research Methodology

The entire research project targeted fifty in-depth interviews with returnees, policy makers and key-informants on the topic of Afghan migration, reintegration and return that included twenty-one interviews, eight women and thirteen men, with returnees from Pakistan. The researchers visited two informal settlements in eastern Afghanistan and one formal in north of the capital, Kabul where they conducted face-to-face interviews. All interviews were recorded, translated and transcribed by the research team. The analysis of interviews was carried out using a multi-step process. This publication focuses only on the findings of the returnees' interviews in two informal settlements and one formal. This research paper attempts to provide an analysis on how the lives of Afghan refugees have changed after their return to their home country. It also provides an answer to the question of whether or not these returnees have benefited from social services and employment opportunities after return.

This paper begins with an overview of Afghanistan situation and the realities on the ground for employment and labour market. It explains the joint initiatives by the international organisations and Afghan government to improve the lives of returnees. It also presents an overview on various waves of displacements and returns and it also provides a brief summary on conceptual framework. The paper ends with a very brief summary of the field research with the returnees and conclusion.

Informal settlements in eastern Afghanistan

The following section provides an in-depth analysis of the situation of life in two informal and one formal settlements where interviews with twenty-one returnees was carried out. The study attempts to provide a quick analysis about the life of returnees after they were forcibly returned to Afghanistan. Most of the returnees interviewed for this research were low skilled persons, which made their integration even harder.

The Eastern Nangarhar province has accommodated more than 400,000 returnees/IDPs across 26 informal settlements, the first of which was established in 1990. Around two third of this population are recent returnees from Pakistan, along with a small number from Iran. The other third are IDPs who have predominantly moved in from other districts of Nangarhar due to conflict (REACH, 2017). In the capital Kabul, more than 10,000 IDP and returnee households live in 60 different informal settlements of various sizes (REACH, 2017).

Pul-e Behsud is a small informal settlement within Jalalabad, the capital of eastern Nangarhar province with around 100 returnee families who have spent the majority of their lives as refugees in Pakistan. Located in a poor rural area between Nangarhar and Laghman provinces, Gambiri is characterized by poor accommodation, lack of water, electricity, insufficient sanitation facilities and insecurity. Around six hundred families (10,500 persons) live in Gambiri who have returned from Pakistan and still live in makeshift houses and tents.

In 2016, refugees had decided to return to Afghanistan as their lives were becoming harder in Pakistan. Physical and verbal harassment, beatings, threats of arrest and extortion by Pakistani authorities was routine. Each time a security or criminal incident occurred, Pakistani police would raid homes of Afghan refugees in different parts of Pakistan, in particular in Khyber Pakhtunkhwa. The returnees said that daily harassment ultimately forced them to become ‚refugee' again in their ‚home' country. *„We could not sleep all night long. The Pakistani police entered our homes at night while we were asleep. We were so much under pres-*

sure that we decided to leave" (AYB, a teacher returnee in Gambiri)[1]. AYB complained from the systematic pressure that Pakistani government inflicted on Afghan refugees especially after a criminal or terrorism-related incident. According to research respondents, the police in Pakistan had the power to raid Afghan refugee houses, make arbitrary arrests and imprison them for weeks.

Returning to ,home' country did not change their pains as they expected. Contrary to their expectations, life worsened for Afghan refugees after the return. Harassment by Afghan provincial authorities has become a daily occurrence. Local warlords and police regularly visited in Pul-e Behsud, for example, to force them out of government-owned land, but they had no other place to go. *,, We have lived in this desert for over six months, in cold, hot and windy weather. Local commanders threaten us and call us land grabbers. We used to have a better situation in Pakistan"* (ZGL, a returnee in Gambiri).

The returnees constantly made comparisons between their life as refugees in Pakistan and at ,home'. They expected their home country would have developed socially and economically since the fall of the Taliban in 2001 due to the enormous amount of international aid that poured to Afghanistan for the reconstruction, but were shocked to see their ancestral land was poorer than the country that hosted them for decades. Lack of security, employment, roads, drinking water, shelter/housing, health and education services were critical issues in both of informal settlements. Loss of identity was obvious element as the Afghans considered them as Pakistanis while in Pakistan they were called to be Afghan refugees. „I sold my shop in Pakistan and opened a new one here but that collapsed financially. I made no profit" (ZRGA in Gambiri settlement).

In both Pul-e Behsud and Gambiri, returnee boys attend school until a certain grade then drop out to work, while girls go to primary school then stay home. Women are only able to work with permission from their male guardians, and even then only in exclusively rare female workplaces. The women in both settlements have never attended school. Male interviewees believed that it was their job to earn and provide for women and children. *,, Men feel ashamed if they see their women work outside the home"* (FRZ returnee in Pul-e Behsud).

Life for women household-heads is far more difficult, as patriarchal support is non-existent. Forty years old ZRNA lives in an informal male-dominated settlement with her three children. In Pakistan she worked as a cleaner, but since her return she has been living on charity especially Zakat.

Integration in the labour market at home country: Most of the state resources are either allocated to fight insurgency or wasted due to the rampant corruption within the Afghan government. Nearly two years after their return to Afghanistan, many interviewees had little knowledge on how to find work in the chaotic Afghan labour market. At the time the interviews were conducted, housing, water, and roads were more urgent issues than the lack of employment. Returnees also

---

[1]   All names of returnees have been changed to abbreviations to protect their identities.

felt insecure about leaving belongings and women unprotected while they searched for jobs. *„Housing first and then work"* (AZM in Gambiri).

In Pul-e Behsud, women and girls are engaged in home-based carpet weaving while men are daily labours in the nearby market. Earning from both activities is inconsistent and unstable, though. Male returnees in Gambiri had acquired skills in running grocery stores, keeping cows and carpentry in Pakistan, while the women had earned money from cleaning, embroidery and carpet weaving. According to WRM in Gambiri, the young people were weaving carpets most of the time in Pakistan, but that skill is little use in Afghanistan as there is insufficient investment in the sector.

Since their forceful return in 2016, there is intense competition with both locals and IDPs for the limited employment opportunities that is available in their rural communities. Many returnees in Gambiri have already regretted to be in their ‚home‘ country. *"My children now ask me why we returned to a country that has nothing to live on. No house, no water, no jobs,"* returnee AZM said in Gambiri.

Formal settlement of Barikab

The residents in Barikab settlement had a different narrative about their life in this formal settlement. Despite its establishment over a decade ago, residents of Barikab complained from lack of access to social and employment services. Lack of water and electricity, poor healthcare centre and lack of medical supplies were the primary complaints of interviewees. The settlement has one intermediate school catering for children up until the ninth grade. The only high school is many miles walk away, and girls in particular drop out of school after reaching high school. Security issues, distance to the high school, cost and lack of public transport were cited by all eight interviewees in Barikab as major factors hindering girls from continuing their education. The existing school in Barikab is inadequately resourced, with insufficient teachers and learning materials to meet the demands of school children.

Over one thousand residents have moved away from Barikab to seek employment in the city, despite receiving repeated promises from the Afghan government and international donors that their concerns will be addressed. Most women in Barikab don't work and rely on their husbands and/or male relative's earnings to cover expenses. *„Men still hardly find any work. We are barely surviving here. We don't have enough water, no electricity, no good roads. There is no regular work neither for men nor for women"* (SMR, Barikab).

The returnees described the situation of returning in a country they called ‚home‘ and the myth of (re)integration in receiving social and labour services. One of the female recent returnees illustrates the situation as this: *"I regret returning to Afghanistan. My life as refugee in Pakistan was much better. I expected things would get better each year but it has been the opposite. I would not hesitate to migrate again if I ever get a chance again" (SMR, Barikab).*

Conclusion

Afghanistan's last forty years is a history of protracted conflict and displacement. Millions of Afghans were forced to flee their country and seek refuge mostly in neighboring Pakistan and Iran. Today, Afghans represent the second largest refugee population around the world after Syria. Pakistan hosts nearly three millions of these Afghan refugees since the start of the war in 1978. Millions have returned after the collapse of the Taliban government in 2001 when US-led forced ousted them from power. The major forceful return, however, took place in the second half of 2016 when Pakistani authorities forcibly repatriated more than half a million in short span of time.

Return to Afghanistan after decades of life as refugee in Pakistan has added to the pain of their displacement. For all respondents, the return as a "durable solution" is a myth and they considered remigration. Most returnees from Pakistan in all three settlements were financially and socially worse off in Afghanistan than they were in Pakistan. They have resorted to unstable and random jobs that earned them low and inconsistent income. With already critically high levels of unemployment, the huge number of IDPs and returnees have little prospect of finding work in the near future. They also suffer from lack of housing, education, health care, food, and water. Insecurity, poverty and loss of identity were identical. The Afghan government and its international allies have been distracted by an expanding Taliban insurgency which has led to a lack of plans to (re)integrate the returnees into their home country. The Afghan government offered almost no social services the returnees could benefit from. The lives of returnees have gone worse than what they experienced as refugees in Pakistan.

References

Ahmad, Ali. (2018). Refugees return to poverty, unemployment and despair: Afghanistan's labor market and the status of women. Vienna, Vienna Institute for International Dialogue and Cooperation (VIDC). http://www.vidc.org/fileadmin/Bibliothek/DP/Foto_Veranst/Fanizadeh/Afghanistan_5.11.18/Afghanistan_s_labor_market_and_the_status_of_women.pdf [Accessed 16 December 2019)]

Alimia, Sanaa (2014). Violence and vulnerabilities: Afghans in Pakistan. https://www.fmreview.org/sites/fmr/files/FMRdownloads/en/afghanistan/alimia.pdf [Accessed 17 October 2019]

Alimia, Sanaa (2012). Afghans in Pakistan face a perilous future. Al Jazeera English. https://www.aljazeera.com/indepth/opinion/2012/07/20127291012146593.html [Accessed 12 July 2018]

Alimia, Sanaa (29. July 2012). Afghans in Pakistan face a perilous future. Al Jazeera English. https://www.aljazeera.com/indepth/opinion/2012/07/20127291012146593.html [Accessed 15 October 2019]

Anon, (2017). AFGHANISTAN Multidimensional Poverty Index 2016–2017 Report and Analysis. [online] Available at: https://www.nsia.gov.af:8080/wp-content/uploads/2019/04/A-MPI-2019-full-report-English-1 [Accessed 2 Dec. 2019]

Anon, (2017). EU Migration Policy and Returns: Case Study on Afghanistan. [online] Available at: https://www.ecre.org/wp-content/uploads/2017/11/Returns-Case-Study-on-Afghanistan.pdf [Accessed 9 Dec. 2019]

Black, Richard. and Koser, Khalid. (1999). The End of the Refugee Cycle?: Refugee Repatriation and Reconstruction. New York and Oxford: Berghahn Books.

Carling, Jorgen., Mortensen, Elin Berstad. and Wu, Jennifer. (2011). A Systematic Bibliography on Return Migration. [online] Prio.org. Available at: https://www.prio.org/Publications/Publication/?x=7199 [Accessed 29 Nov. 2019]

Cassarino, Jean-Pierre. (2015). Theorising Return Migration: The Conceptual Approach to Return Migrants Revisited. International Journal on Multicultural Societies (IJMS), 6(2), pp.253-279.

Die Bundesregierung (2018). Federal Government Report on the Status of and Outlook for Germany's Afghanistan Engagement. Die Bundesregierung, https://www.auswaertiges-amt.de/blob/1789270/e84f878742c319e5d93337c0b8b13c37/180315-perspektivbericht-data.pdf. [Accessed 9 Dec. 2019]

Eastmond, Marita. (2006). Transnational Returns and Reconstruction in Post-war Bosnia and Herzegovina. [online] Files.ethz.ch. Available at: https://onlinelibrary.wiley.com/doi/pdf/10.1111/j.1468-2435.2006.00375.x [Accessed 9 Dec. 2019].

Farmer, Ben and Makoii, Akhtar (2018). Afghanistan faces worst drought in decades, as UN warns 1.4 million people need help. The Telegraph https:// www.telegraph.co.uk/news/2018/07/22/afghanistan-faces-worst-drought-decades-un-warns-14 m-need-help/ [Accessed 15 October 2019]

Glaser, Barney G. and Strauss, Anselm L. (1967). The discovery of grounded theory: strategies for qualitative research. Aldine, Chicago.

Human Rights Watch. (2016). Pakistan Coercion, UN Complicity | The Mass Forced Return of Afghan Refugees. [online] Available at: https://www.hrw.org/report/2017/02/13/pakistan-coercion-un-complicity/mass-forced-return-afghan-refugees [Accessed 28 Nov. 2019].

Jazayery, Leila. (2002). The Migration-Development Nexus: Afghanistan Case Study. In: N. Van Hear and N. Sørensen, ed., The migration-development nexus. [online] Geneva, pp.231-254. Available at: https://publications.iom.int/system/files/pdf/migration_dev_nexus.pdf [Accessed 9 Dec. 2019].

Kuschminder, Katie. (2017). Taking Stock of Assisted Voluntary Return from Europe: Decision Making, Reintegration and Sustainable Return Time for a Paradigm Shift. [online] Available at: https://pdfs.semanticscholar.org/249c/de0621d6411f510269a4bf615c6254b4b3b5.pdf [Accessed 9 Dec. 2019].

Ministry of Refugees and Repatriation (2018). Return and Reintegration Response Plan - 2018. Kabul: Ministry of Refugees and Repatriation (MoRR).

Ministry of Refugees and Repatriation (2019). Statistics | MORR. [online] Available at: https://morr.gov.af/en/statistics-0 [Accessed 27 Nov. 2019].

Monsutti, Alessandro. (2006). Afghan Transnational Networks: Looking Beyond Repatriation. Synthesis Paper Series. [online] Kabul: Afghanistan Research and Evaluation Unit (AREU). Available at: https://reliefweb.int/sites/reliefweb.int/files/resources/6A583751924F6A31492571F400099A52-areu-afg-31aug.pdf [Accessed 28 Nov. 2019].

Monsutti, Alessandro. (2008). Afghan Migratory Strategies and the Three Solutions to the Refugee Problem. Oxford Journal, 27(1).

Muzhary, Fazal. (2017). Resettling Nearly Half a Million Afghans in Nangrahar: The consequences of the mass return of refugees. [online] Kabul: Afghanistan Analysts Network. Available at: https://www.afghanistan-analysts.org/resettling-nearly-half-a-million-afghans-in-nangrahar-the-consequences-of-the-mass-return-of-refugees/ [Accessed 29 Nov. 2019].

Nangarhar Informal Settlement Profiling. (2017). [online] REACH: An initiative of IMPACT Initiatives ACTED and UNOSAT. Available at: https://www.impact-repository.org/document/reach/e0b49e79/reach_afg_factsheet_nangarhar_informal_settlement_booklet_january2017_1.pdf [Accessed 30 Nov. 2019].

Publications.iom.int. (2019). [online] Available at: https://publications.iom.int/system/files/pdf/ migration_dev_nexus.pdf [Accessed 25 Nov. 2019].

REACH. (2019). Afghanistan: 80% of Informal Settlements households have limited access to food | REACH. [online] Available at: https://www.reach-initiative.org/what-we-do/news/afg hannistan-80-of-informal-settlements-households-have-limited-access-to-food-2/ [Accessed 25 Nov. 2019].

Shankar, Thom. (2014). Military Plans Reflect Afghanistan Uncertainty. [online] Nytimes.com. Available at: https://www.nytimes.com/2014/01/30/world/asia/us-and-nato-afghanistan.html [Accessed 12 Dec. 2019].

Siddiqui, Zuha., (2019). For Afghan Refugees, Pakistan Is a Nightmare—but Also Home. [online] Foreign Policy. Available at: https://foreignpolicy.com/2019/05/09/for-afghan-refugees-pakistan-is-a-nightmare-but-also-home/ [Accessed 28 Nov. 2019].

Van Hear, Nicholas, Sørensen, Ninna Nyberg. (2003). The migration-development nexus. [New York, N.Y.]: United Nations, pp.207-218.

Support Afghanistan Livelihoods and Mobility (SALAM). (2017). [ebook] UNDP. Available at: https://info.undp.org/docs/pdc/Documents/AFG/SALAM%203rd%20Quarterly%20Report% 20%202017.pdf [Accessed 25 Nov. 2019].

Sydney, Chloe. (2019). Return decision making by refugees | Forced Migration Review. [online] Fmreview.org. Available at: https://www.fmreview.org/return/sydney [Accessed 9 Dec. 2019].

Taylor-Powell, Ellen. and Renner, Marcus. (2003). Analyzing Qaulitative Data. [online] Deltas-tate.edu. Available at: https://deltastate.edu/docs/irp/Analyzing%20Qualitative%20Da ta.pdf [Accessed 30 Nov. 2019].

The Center for Migration Studies of New York (CMS). (n.d.). Return Migration: A Conceptual and Policy Framework - The Center for Migration Studies of New York (CMS). [online] Available at: https://cmsny.org/publications/2018smsc-smc-return-migration/ [Accessed 29 Nov. 2019].

Thier, Alex. and Worden, Scott. (2019). Political Stability in Afghanistan. [online]. Available at: https://www.usip.org/sites/default/files/2017-07/sr408-political-stability-in-afghanistan-a-2020-vision-and-roadmap.pdf [Accessed 25 Nov. 2019].

Turton, David. and Marsden, Peter. (2002). Taking Refugees for a Ride? The politics of refugee return to Afghanistan. [online] Kabul: Afghanistan Research and Evaluation Unit (AREU). Available at: https://www.refworld.org/pdfid/47c3f3cb1a.pdf [Accessed 28 Nov. 2019].

UNHCR (2018). Global trends: Forced displacement in 2018. [online] pp. 2-33. Available at: https://www.unhcr.org/5d08d7ee7.pdf [Accessed 26 Nov. 2019].

Van Houte, Marieke. (2016). Return Migration to Afghanistan: Moving Back or Moving For-ward?. Oxford: University of Oxford.

Van Houte, Marieke., Siegel, Melissa. and Davids, Tine. (2014). Return to Afghanistan: Migrati-on as Reinforcement of Socio-Economic Stratification. [online] Merit.unu.edu. Available at: http://www.merit.unu.edu/publications/uploads/1416828959.pdf [Accessed 9 Dec. 2019].

Willner-Reid, Matthew. (2017). Afghanistan: Displacement Challenges in a Country on the Move. [online] migrationpolicy.org. Available at: https://www.migrationpolicy.org/article/ afghanistan-displacement-challenges-country-move [Accessed 28 Nov. 2019].

Zaki, Faizullah. (2017). Afghanistan labor market and returnees.

Zimmermann, Susan. (2010). Understanding repatriation: refugee perspectives on the importance of safety, reintegration, and hope. [online] Available at: https://onlinelibrary.wiley.com/ doi/pdf/10.1002/psp.647 [Accessed 9 Dec. 2019].

Engaging the Host Community in Refugee Relocations: A Proposed Framework

Margarita Fourer

Abstract

This paper proposes a framework for taking into account host communities in situations where an external group of people is moved to a locale. For this purpose, it analyses the concept of "regional disembarkation platforms", which has been suggested by the European Council, a concept that attempts to emulate the "Australian model" by moving irregularly arriving asylum seekers and refugees to a third (non-EU) state for processing of refugee claims and potential settlement. The paper looks to the Australian model for gaps relating to the consideration of host communities. Any unaddressed real or perceived disadvantage to the host community as a result such a settlement process can not only lead to delays in the integration of the relocated persons but also, often, in violence against the newcomers by members the host community. The framework of host community safeguards proposes that in drafting and implementing disembarkation agreements, EU (as individual Member States and/or institution) supports the disembarkation partner(s) in mitigating any negative effects on the host population.

What are Disembarkation Arrangements

Following its meeting of 28-30 July 2018, the European Council reached a number of conclusions on migration. One of which directed the European Commission to explore the concept of "regional disembarkation platforms",[1] in close cooperation with relevant third countries (European Council 2018, pp. 2 and 4). This envisages the taking of people intercepted at sea to reception centres in developing countries. IOM and UNHCR are to potentially process the asylum seekers' refugee claims or assist the third countries of reception to develop their asylum systems in order to process these claims themselves (European Commission 2018, p. 2-3). The plan for disembarkation arrangements intends not only for the processing of refugee claims

---

[1] The term "disembarkation platforms" is used by the European Commission to mean "disembarkation arrangements", (ie an agreement between two states regarding processing of refugee claims and consequent settlement) and an element thereof (ie, the place of disembarkation). For clarity purposes this paper discusses disembarkation arrangements.

on the territory of a third state but also settlement of the refugees in that state, together with other durable solutions such as resettlement and voluntary return (European Commission 2018, p. 3).

The exploration of disembarkation arrangements can be argued to be the latest attempt to emulate the much criticised Australian model (called the 2001 and 2012 Pacific Solutions). This can be seen in the similarity of the European Council proposal and the Australian Pacific Solution, being the transfer, processing and settlement of irregularly arriving asylum seekers and refugees by Australia to the third state nations of Nauru and Manus Island, Papua New Guinea (PNG).

Host community violence and lessons learned from other fields

Criticism of the Australian model

Much of the criticism of the Australian model focuses on the breach of refugees' human rights, especially, with regards to rights against *refoulement*, arbitrary detention and treatment amounting to torture (UNHRC 2015, p. 7). What has, as yet, to be addressed is the interaction between the refugees and the host communities[2] into which they have been placed for both the processing of asylum claims and potential settlement. On Nauru and Manus Island, tensions arose between the host communities and refugees for a number of reasons. One of the reasons relates to misconceptions about refugees being given jobs and better benefits in a country with a high unemployment rate (Fedele 2016). Host communities also expressed frustration at not being consulted in the decision-making process as well as not benefitting directly from hosting refugees. Finally, the negative historical colonial experience with Australia (Taylor 2005) has made the local population resentful of having a group of people "dumped" onto their islands (Fedele 2016). As a result of this tension and frustration, there have been numerous cases of recorded violence against refugees on the two islands (SBS News 2017; HRW 2017; Law Students for Refugees 2016; Commonwealth of Australia Senate Legal and Constitutional Affairs Committee 2017).

Other regimes for dealing with host communities

Looking at the above experience with the Australian model, any attempt to relocate refugees into a host community in a planned manner, should not only consider the human rights of refugees but also address the concerns of the host communities by investing in and engaging with them from the outset. This paper attempts to provide the framework that addresses the needs of the host communities by looking at other

---

2   Host communities are also called "host populations" and "local communities". These are communities that receive groups of people called "displaced persons", "relocated persons", "resettled persons", "resettlers" etc.

regimes that have experience with tensions between host communities and relocated persons and have developed guidelines[3] for host community safeguards, engagement and capacity development.

The *refugee governance* field itself can provide lessons to be learnt regarding the interactions between host communities and the refugees settled amongst them.[4] The experience of tensions and violence between the host and refugee communities has been reflected in the drafting and adoption of the *New York Declaration for Refugees and Migrants* (UNGA 2016) and *Global Compact on Refugees* (GCR) (UNGA 2018). Other lessons for the framework are drawn from the field of *industry resettlement*, which often encompasses private sector- and/or government-run "natural resource projects" such as mining, and "major infrastructure projects", such as dam construction, that require the relocation of people (Reddy et al. 2015, p. 2). Finally, lessons are drawn from the field of *environmental relocations*, which includes the planned relocation of people, both internally (UNHCR et al. 2015; UNHCR et al. 2017) and across borders (Nansen Initiative 2015a and 2015b) for environmental reasons as a result of and/or in preparation for sudden (eg, floods) and slow-onset (eg, rising sea levels) climate events.

While environmental relocation is emerging as its own field at the crossroad of industry resettlement, internal displacement and refugee laws (Ferris 2014), industry resettlement, in particular, has many decades (and in the colonial context, centuries) of resettlement experience (Michel 2008; Ba and Bluen 2018). Thus, authors writing in the 1990s (Lassailly-Jacob 1996; Scudder 1997) and 2000s (Mathur 2006), clearly outlined that *"the potential for ... conflict always exits in relocation situations"* and that *"[f]ew resettlement projects have been documented where conflict has not appeared ... sooner or later conflicts between the two [host communities and resettled/relocated people] can be expected."* (Mathur 2006, p. 59).

---

3   The non-binding guidance documents relied on are UN General Assembly, New York Declaration for Refugees and Migrants: resolution / adopted by the General Assembly, 3 October 2016, A/RES/71/1; UN General Assembly, Report of the United Nations High Commissioner for Refugees, Part II, Global compact on refugees, A/73/12, New York, 2018; UN Human Rights Council, Basic Principles and Guidelines on Development-Based Evictions and Displacement, Annex 1 of UN Human Rights Council: Report of the Special Rapporteur on Adequate Housing as a Component of the Right to an Adequate Standard of Living, 5 February 2007, A/HRC/4/18, International Finance Corporation World Bank Group, IFC Performance Standards on Environmental and Social Sustainability: Performance Standard 5: Land Acquisition and Involuntary Resettlement, 2012; UNHCR and Brookings Institution, Georgetown University, Guidance on Protecting People from Disasters and Environmental Change through Planned Relocations, 2015; and UNHCR, SFS and IOM, A Toolbox: Planning Relocations to Protect People from Disasters and Environmental Change, 2017.

4   Although in the case of refugee governance, the settlement of refugees is spontaneous, as a result of displacement rather than being a planned process.

Reasons for conflicts between host communities and relocated persons

Some of the reasons for these conflicts include *"competition of a larger population over a diminished (in terms of per capita) land base, as well as over access to job opportunities, social services and political power"* (Mathur 2006, p. 59). According to Vanclay (2017, p. 11) host communities experience social impacts such as an increase in the demand for public services, which are often not adequately adjusted for an increase in population, causing delay or even shortages of key requirements, water, electricity, fuel and even food (Vanclay 2017, p. 15). There even exists a risk to the host community of follow-on economic displacement, due to local inflation resulting from greater demand for goods and services (van der Ploeg and Vanclay 2017, p. 37). A further possibility for *"resentment between the host community and the resettled households, especially if the host community perceives that the reset-tled people are being given special treatment, like modern houses, preferential access to jobs or other benefits that are not available to them."* (Vanclay 2017, p. 15). Rural resettlement is seen as particularly challenging, requiring greater mitigation measures to *"avoid compromising the social and cultural continuity of affected communities, including those host communities to which displaced populations may be resettled"* (Mathur 2006, 40).

While industry resettlement has the most experience in planned relocations of people, the experience of all the fields reflect that host communities are affected by the settlement of external groups into their locale, but are not adequately considered or consulted during the settlement process, nor do they receive commensurate benefits from the process. Consequently, any unaddressed real or perceived disadvantage to the host community as a result of the settlement process can not only lead to delays in the integration of the resettled persons but also, in extreme, but not rare, situations, in violence against the newcomers by members the host community (Vanclay 2017, p.15). It is for this reason that Mathur laments that planners do not take the above into account, relying only on the generosity and hospitality of the host community. When looking at the proposal for the disembarkation arrangements as well as the experience of the Australian Pacific Solution, it is clear that host communities are not, on the whole, being taken into account (neither their generosity nor their needs) during the planning stages. By the time the host community is addressed, the situation has already escalated and violence has occurred, leading to continued and not easily dissipated tension and mistrust between the host and relocated communities.

Specific gaps of the Australian model

The UNHCR did set out guidelines for the Australian model of transferring asylum seekers and refugees. These guidelines focused primarily on the needs and rights of the asylum seekers and refugees. However, no guidance was provided for the host communities. Thus, the *Guidance note on bilateral and/or multilateral transfer arrangements of asylum-seekers* (UNHCR 2013) makes no mention of a host community, requesting only that such agreements *"should ideally contribute to the enhancement of the overall protection space in the transferring State, the receiving State and/or the region as a whole"* (UNHCR 2013, p. 2). The 2016 Position Paper by the UNHCR Regional Office in Canberra makes a minor amendment to the 2013 Guidance Note, requiring a guarantee that there would be a *"commitment of the local community"* that they *"are able to sustain such an arrangement"* (UNHCR 2016, p. 3). This guarantee requirement is awkwardly-phrased in the paper and therefore is somewhat unclear in its meaning.

The Memorandum of Understanding (MoU) signed in 2013 by Australia with Nauru and separately with PNG, does discuss some benefits to the host communities. It must however be noted that these MoUs were an update to the ones signed in 2012 and that asylum seekers and refugees were already on the two islands for a year with little consideration given to the host communities. The 2013 MoUs promised some capacity development. For instance, if the Nauru processing centre *"requires additional development of infrastructure or services, it is envisaged that there will be a broader benefit for communities in which transferees are initially placed"* (Australia-Nauru 2013, p. 3). Similarly, the PNG *"Regional Processing Centres will be developed so that they can be utilised flexibly for the benefit of local communities for wider national purposes"* (Australia-PNG 2013b, p. 2). Additionally, the PNG MoU addressed the development of *"a package of assistance and other bilateral cooperation, which will be in addition to the current allocation of Australian development cooperation assistance to PNG"* (Australia-PNG 2013a, p. 3). It must be noted that no explicit mention was made regarding direct (rather than incidental) benefit to the host communities. Importantly, no provision is available for the engagement, at the local level, directly with the host communities of either Nauru or Manus Island, PNG (as opposed to governments at the national level).

While the Australian model can be argued to be an isolated phenomenon, the European Council proposal for disembarkation arrangements shows the need to ensure that a framework exists that provides host community safeguards, engagement and capacity development in any situation where an external group of people are relocated to a locale in a planned manner. This is particularly important, considering that no documents on disembarkation arrangements to date mention host or local communities.

Proposed framework of host community safeguards, engagement and capacity development

In drafting and implementing disembarkation agreements, it is important for the EU (as individual Member States and/or institution) to support the disembarkation partner(s) in mitigating any negative effects on the host population. This includes the safeguarding of the host communities' human rights, engaging the host communities through dissemination of information, consultation and participation, and the development of host communities' capacities. This will assist in ensuring that the experience of hosting facilitates improved engagement and living conditions of the host population, and by extension their reception and acceptance of the asylum seekers and refugees.

Safeguarding the human rights of the host communities

As citizens of the host state, host communities must have their rights respected, protected and fulfilled by that state. Thus, guidance documents for industry resettlement clearly state that host communities are to have those human rights protected (ie, prevent and/or not suffer detriment), including their progressive realization of the right to adequate housing. Nor are host communities to have their right to the continuous improvement of their living conditions infringed (UNHRC 2007, pp. 12-13). Similarly, the Environmental Relocation Guidance argues for the safeguarding of political, economic, social and cultural rights, in particular rights to self-determination, preservation of identity and culture and control of land and resources (UNHCR et al. 2015, pp. 11, and 19-20).

Host community engagement

The GCR makes clear that *"[r]esponses are most effective when they actively and meaningfully engage those they are intended to protect and assist"* (UNGA 2018, p. 7). Thus, *"consultative processes that enable refugees and host community members to assist in designing appropriate, accessible and inclusive responses"* are to be developed and supported by states and other relevant actors (UNGA 2018, pp. 6 and 15). While the GCR expands community (stakeholder) engagement into consultation and participation (UNGA 2018, pp. 4, 6, 7 and 15), for industry resettlement and environmental relocation, engagement is broken up into provision of information, consultation and participation (IFC 2012a, p. 11; UNHCR et al. 2015, p. 6, 11 and 19); UNHCR et al. 2017, pp. 20-22).

Host community engagement does not necessarily mean consent. In industry resettlement *free prior and informed consent* (FPIC) does exist. However, it only applies to formally recognized indigenous groups. Where indigenous groups with either traditional or legal ownership of the land are present, no resettlement project can go ahead without their express agreement that land can used (IFC 2012b).

What is envisaged by engagement includes the dissemination of *information* at every stage (including planning) of the process allows host communities to make informed decisions (UNHCR et al. 2015, p. 6, 11, and 19-20; UNHCR et al. 2017, p. 20; IFC 2012a, pp. 21-22).[5] *Consultation* is an important element of engagement, and together with *participation*, allows for host communities (directly as well as through traditional and non-traditional community leaders) to take ownership of the way they are affected by the settlement process (IFC 2012a, p. 11; UNHRC 2007,

---

[5] While not clearly specified to apply to host communities, dissemination of information is put forward in the Basic Principles and Guidelines on Development-Based Displacement (UNHRC 2007, pp. 9 and 12).

p. 9; UNHCR et al. 2015, pp. 6, 11, 15-17 and 19; UNHCR et al. 2017, pp. 21-2 and 26; UNGA 2018, pp. 3, 6 and 7). Importantly, *"the outcomes of Planned Relocation are likely to depend on the extent to which those that are affected by it actively engage in all aspects of the process and perceive that they have been sufficiently involved and controlled the process"* (UNHCR et al. 2015, p. 6).

Grievance mechanism is also a key element of engagement. While the GCR does incorporate the need for a grievance mechanism that includes the host community, the objective is to ensure accountability through receipt of complaints and investigation and prevention of fraud, abuse and corruption (UNGA 2018, p. 6). Although this is necessary, the type of grievance mechanisms utilized in the fields of industry resettlement and environmental relocation should also be implemented. The latter provides host communities *"access to impartial and equitable grievance, review, conflict resolution, and redress mechanisms throughout a planned relocation"*, including as early as at the *"project development phase"* (UNHCR et al. 2015, p. 14; UNHCR et al. 2017, p. 20; IFC 2012a, p. 11).

The importance of host community engagement cannot be overemphasised. It should be involved in all parts of planned relocation, including and especially as it relates to capacity development (discussed below). Another essential element where, in particular, host community participation should be utilised is refugee *integration*. Community cohesion is to be achieved by interaction of refugees and migrants with the host communities, which include direct contact as well as the establishment of *"supportive systems and networks"* (UNGA 2018, p. 2), and which *"take into account the needs of both refugees and host communities"* (UNGA 2018, p. 19). This facilitates integration by the refugee community and an informed, active and participatory welcome by the host communities (UNHCR et al. 2017; UNGA 2016, p. 3; UNGA 2018, pp. 2, 16 and 19).

Capacity development

Capacity development benefiting the host community, through the development of services, such as the building up of local authorities and NGOs capacities, infrastructure development, jobs and livelihoods (including compensation), service facilities and services such as health, education, accommodation, (clean, renewable) energy, as well as the management of resources such as food and water (UNGA 2016, p. 14; UNGA 2018, pp. 6-7, 10, 12-16 and 19). While the GCR has the most comprehensive approach to development for the host community, industry resettlement and environmental relocation experience suggests that this level of investment into development should not be attempted without consultation with and participation of the host community as to their infrastructure, livelihoods, services and compensatory needs.

Development opportunities for the host communities can only be achieved through careful *planning* (IFC 2012a, pp. 1 and 17). Amongst other considerations, planning includes collecting baseline data as part of undertaking careful *monitoring and evaluation* (UNGA 2016, p. 18). An important consideration of the baseline is the identification of vulnerable groups together with an analysis of any historic relationship between the relocated persons and the host community, as well as the *"similarities and differences in social, cultural, political and economic characteristics and structures"* (UNHCR et al. 2017, pp. 16-7).

The results of the baseline – together with the continuous monitoring and evaluation – can be used for guiding the development necessary to benefit host communities (UNGA 2016, p. 18). The GCR and NY Declaration mainly focus on appropriate disaggregated data collection in order to identify the needs of the host communities and plan appropriate solutions, including capacity development (UNGA 2016, p. 8; UNGA 2018, pp. 8-9). Guidance documents on environmental relocation are more detailed, requiring the baseline data to *"develop indicators and benchmarks against which to assess ... on-going monitoring and evaluation activities"*. The latter is to be achieved by states *"together with ... Host Populations"* (UNHCR et al. 2015, p. 22). Thus, host communities must not only be benefited by capacity development, the development must be planned through the establishment of baseline data and implemented not only with continuous monitoring and evaluation, but the results thereof must be disseminated to the host communities in a timely manner (UNHCR et al. 2015, p. 22).

Conclusion

As can be seen from the proposed framework, the safeguarding of host community human rights, their engagement and capacity development is a continuous, accumulative and interconnected process. The human right of continuous improvement of living conditions is connected to and enacted by capacity development. Capacity development cannot be successfully implemented without community engagement. Neither community engagement nor capacity development can be effective without planning the relocation process (prior to the actual relocation) through the collection of baseline data and continuous monitoring and evaluation.

The development of this framework proposal was instigated by the consideration by the European Council (together with individual European states) of disembarkation arrangements. These arrangements are based on the Australian model, which has been used in this paper to demonstrate that omitting the protections proposed in the framework leads to host community frustration, resentment and consequent tension and violence towards the newcomers. However, the fact that host community violence has been seen in different fields – refugee governance, industry resettlement and environmental relocation, – suggests the application of this framework can be more wide-ranging, including in refugee return, and intra-EU refugee relocations and placement of refugees in rural areas of countries such as Austria. Further research into these areas can contribute a fruitful test and refinement of the proposed framework.

Acknowledgement

This project is co-financed by the Asylum, Migration and Integration Fund and the Austrian Federal Ministry of the Interior (Project No 141235506).

References

Ba, Oumar / Bluen, Kelly-Jo (2018) The Chagos Islands: Colonialism on trial at the ICJ. In: Al-Jazeera, Opinion, 12 September 2018

Commonwealth of Australia / Independent State of Papua New Guinea (2012) Memorandum of Understanding between the Government of the Independent State of Papua New Guinea and the Government of Australia, Relating to the Transfer to and Assessment of Persons in Papua New Guinea, and Related Issues, 8 September 2012

Commonwealth of Australia / Independent State of Papua New Guinea (2013a) Memorandum of Understanding between the Government of the Independent State of Papua New Guinea and the Government of Australia, Relating to the Transfer to, and Assessment and Settlement in, Papua New Guinea, and Related Issues, 6 August 2013

Commonwealth of Australia / Independent State of Papua New Guinea (2013b) Regional resettlement arrangement between Australia and Papua New Guinea on Further Bilateral Cooperation to Combat People Smuggling, 19 July 2013

Commonwealth of Australia / Republic of Nauru (2012) Memorandum of Understanding between the Republic of Nauru and the Commonwealth of Australia, Relating to the Transfer to and Assessment of Persons in Nauru, and Related Issues, 29 August 2012

Commonwealth of Australia / Republic of Nauru (2013) Memorandum of Understanding between the Republic of Nauru and the Commonwealth of Australia, relating to the Transfer to and Assessment of Persons in Nauru, and Related Issues, 3 August 2013

Commonwealth of Australia Senate Legal and Constitutional Affairs Committee (2017) Serious allegations of abuse, self-harm and neglect of asylum seekers in relation to the Nauru Regional Processing Centre, and any like allegations in relation to the Manus Regional Processing Centre, 21 April 2017

European Commission (2018) Non-paper on regional disembarkation arrangements, 24 July 2018

European Council (2018) European Council meeting (28 June 2018) – Conclusions, ST 9 2018 INIT

Fedele, David (2016) Resettling refugees in Papua New Guinea: a tragic theatre of the absurd. In: The Guardian, 20 May 2016

Ferris, Elizabeth (2014) Planned Relocations, Disasters and Climate Change: Consolidating Good Practices and Preparing for the Future - Background Document, Soremo Consulatation, 12-14 March 2014 (UNHCR, Brookings Institute, Georgetown University)

Human Rights Watch (HRW) (2017) Australia/PNG: Refugees Face Unchecked Violence, 25 October 2017

International Finance Corporation World Bank Group (IFC) (2012a) IFC Performance Standards on Environmental and Social Sustainability: Performance Standard 5: Land Acquisition and Involuntary Resettlement

International Finance Corporation World Bank Group (IFC) (2012b) IFC Performance Standards on Environmental and Social Sustainability: Performance Standard 7: Indigenous Peoples

Lassailly-Jacob, Veronique (1996) Land-Based Strategies in Dam-Related resettlement Programmes in Africa. In: McDowell, Chris (Ed.) Understanding Impoverishment: The Consequences of Development-Induced Displacement (Berghahn Books, Providence/Oxford) 187-199

Law Students for Refugees (2016) Submission 10 to the Inquiry into Conditions and Treatment of Asylum Seekers and Refugees at the Regional Processing Centres in the Republic of Nauru and Papua New Guinea

Mathur, Hari Mohan (2006) Resettling People Displaced by Development Projects: Some Critical Management Issues. In: Social Change, 2006 (36(1), 36-86

Michel, Jeffrey H (2008) Status and Impacts of the German Lignite Industry. In: The Swedish NGO Secretariat on Acid Rain Air Pollution and Climate Series, Göteborg, 2008, (18)

Nansen Initiative on Disaster-Induced Cross Border Displacement (2015a) Agenda for the Protection of Cross-Border Displaced Persons in the Context of Disasters and Climate Change Volume I

Nansen Initiative on Disaster-Induced Cross Border Displacement (2015b) Agenda for the Protection of Cross-Border Displaced Persons in the Context of Disasters and Climate Change Volume II

Reddy, Gerry / Smyth, Eddie / Steyn, Michael (2015) Land Access and Resettlement: A Guide to Best Practice (Greenleaf Publishing, Sheffield)

SBS News (2017) Timeline of Manus Island detention centre. In: SBS News, 31 October 2017

Scudder, Thayer (1997) Resettlement. In Biswas, Andrea (Ed) Water Resources: Environmental Planning, Management and Development (McGraw Hill, New York)

Taylor, Savitri (2005) The Pacific Solution or a Pacific Nightmare?: The Difference between Burden Shifting and Responsibility Sharing. In: Asia-Pacific Law & Policy Journal, 2005 (6(1)), 1-43

UN General Assembly (UNGA) (2016) New York Declaration for Refugees and Migrants: resolution / adopted by the General Assembly (A/RES/71/1, including Annex 1 Comprehensive Refugee Response Framework)

UN General Assembly (UNGA) (2018), Report of the United Nations High Commissioner for Refugees, Part II, Global compact on refugees (A/73/12)

UN High Commissioner for Refugees (UNHCR) (2013) Guidance Note on bilateral and/or multilateral transfer arrangements of asylum-seekers

UN High Commissioner for Refugees (UNHCR) (2016) Bilateral and/or Multilateral Arrangements for Processing Claims for International Protection and Finding Durable Solutions for Refugees - Position paper, 20 April 2016

UN High Commissioner for Refugees (UNHCR) / Brookings Institution / Georgetown University (2015) Guidance on Protecting People from Disasters and Environmental Change through Planned Relocations

UN High Commissioner for Refugees (UNHCR) / IOM / Georgetown University (2017) A Toolbox: Planning Relocations to Protect People from Disasters and Environmental Change

UN Human Rights Council (UNHRC) (2007) Basic Principles and Guidelines on Development-Based Evictions and Displacement, Annex 1 of UN Human Rights Council: Report of the Special Rapporteur on Adequate Housing as a Component of the Right to an Adequate Standard of Living (A/HRC/4/18)

UN Human Rights Council (UNHRC) (2015) Report of the Special Rapporteur on Torture and Other Cruel, Inhuman or Degrading Treatment or Punishment, Juan E. Méndez : addendum, (A/HRC/28/68/Add.1)

van der Ploeg, Lidewij / Vanclay, Frank (2017) A human rights based approach to project-induced displacement and resettlement. In: Impact Assessment & Project Appraisal, 2017 (35(1)), 34-52

Vanclay, Frank (2017) Project induced displacement and resettlement: From impoverishment risks to an opportunity for development. In: Impact Assessment & Project Appraisal, 2017 (35(1)), 3-21

PRAXISBERICHTE

Interkulturelles Selbstmanagement von Expatriates

Christiane Schnetzer

Zusammenfassung

Expats müssen komplexe Veränderungsprozesse unter anfangs oft nur schwer ‚durchschaubaren' Rahmenbedingungen meistern und unter kulturell und soziostrukturell unterschiedlichen Voraussetzungen erfolgreich performen können. Den interkulturellen Fähigkeiten des Selbstmanagements kommt hierbei eine Schlüsselrolle zu. Vor diesem Hintergrund stellte sich die Frage nach einem praktikablen und unterstützenden Tool für das interkulturelle Selbstmanagement von Expats.

Der im Folgenden vorgestellte *„Erweiterte Selbstmanagement-Fragenkatalog"* (Schnetzer 2015: S. 73 ff.) ist ein solches Instrument. Selbstmanagementfähigkeiten, die die Herausforderungen und Rahmenbedingungen unterschiedlicher Expatgruppen – auch die von begleitenden Familienangehörigen – reflektieren, werden zielgerichtet hinterfragt, so dass die individuelle situative Selbststeuerungskompetenz abgebildet werden kann. Ressourcen können erkannt, Entwicklungsziele für ein darauf aufbauendes interkulturelles Coaching abgeleitet werden.

Es handelt sich um ein Tool, das – im Vorfeld und während eines Assignments oder für die Kompetenzentwicklung eingesetzt – die Selbststeuerung und interkulturelle Handlungsfähigkeit von Expats im Rahmen eines hochgradig mobilen Lebens unterstützen kann.

Einleitung

Expatriates sind Personen, die für einen langen Zeitraum außerhalb des Heimatlandes (ex patria) leben und ein vorrangig internationalisiertes Berufs- und Privatleben führen. Sie werden umgangssprachlich auch als Expats bezeichnet.

Viele von ihnen sind hochqualifizierte Personen und gehen direkt nach dem Studium ins Ausland, denn: *„wer ‚in der Spitzenliga' mitspielen wolle, müsse mobil sein"*, erklärt Univ. Prof. Jean-Robert Tyran, Vizerektor für Forschung und Internationales an der Universität Wien (Herzog 2018, S. 10). Etwa ein Viertel der Alumni an der Universität Wien geht direkt nach dem Studium ins Ausland.

Auch Expats aus Wirtschaft und Diplomatie führen ein internationalisiertes Berufs- und Privatleben, short time and rotational assignments gehören zum beruflichen Alltag. Das bedeutet, dass sie unter der Voraussetzung häufiger *Wechsel und Brüche* und unter soziokulturell sehr unterschiedlichen Vorzeichen Aufgaben und Leistungen erbringen müssen.

Um ein solch hochgradig mobiles Leben, auch mit Familie, führen und trotz komplexer Veränderungen beruflich erfolgreich performen zu können, sind neben fachlicher Kompetenz *individuelle skills* und entsprechende Unterstützungsmaßnahmen notwendig.

„Also was ich mir wünschen würde, dass Firmen besser vorbereitet werden ... mit der Entsendung, mit der Betreuung während des Expatlebens, aber auch mit der Wiedereingliederung, und da mangelt's heftig in Firmen, finde ich, und das ergibt dann emotional Schübe, die VIEL Energie kosten." (Expat in Schnetzer 2015, S. 36)

Vor einer Entsendung wird häufig die Bedeutung einer guten Vorbereitung und einer unterstützenden Begleitung während der Entsendung unterschätzt.

Wofür brauchen Expats interkulturelles Selbstmanagement?

„Employees are assigned abroad often as of the employer's need of their special skills in host country. It is expected that they shall be fully devoted to their job, which will not be possible if they have concerns in other areas. The employee will not be fully devoted to their job abroad if there are uncertainty connected to health coverage for themselves and their family members." (Deloitte 2013, S. 8)

Im Zusammenhang mit einer Entsendung muss der Spagat zwischen familiären, sozialen und professionellen Verantwortungen unter den Vorzeichen fremdkultureller Herausforderungen geschafft werden. Letztere ergeben sich vor allem dadurch, dass im Kontakt mit einer neuen Kultur, mit anderen kulturellen Standards, die gelernten bisherigen Standards in Frage gestellt werden. Die Wahrnehmung unterschiedlichen Denkens, Beurteilens und Handelns sowie von unterschiedlichen Beziehungs-, Arbeits-, und Konfliktstilen führt zu einer persönlichen Auseinandersetzung mit dem Eigenen und dem Fremden und kann zu Verunsicherung führen. Es handelt sich um einen *„Balanceakt zwischen eigener Stabilität und Modellierbarkeit als Grundthema interkultureller Wandlungsprozesse"* mit dem Ziel eines gelungenen Kulturkontakts (vgl. Steixner 2007, S. 170). Dies zeigt die Komplexität der Herausforderungen, denen Expats gegenüberstehen. Und es verwundert nicht, dass auch hochqualifizierte und fachlich kompetente Personen straucheln können.

Die Ergebnisse von Interviews, welche im Zuge der Masterarbeit *„Einfluss und Entwicklung des Selbstmanagements im Rahmen beruflicher Auslandseinsätze"* (Schnetzer 2015) mit entsandten und self-initiated Expats aus Wirtschaft und Diplomatie in Norwegen geführt und im Hinblick auf Selbstmanagementfähigkeiten qualitativ ausgewertet wurden, bestätigen dies.

Im Rahmen dieser Arbeit wurde – in Auseinandersetzung mit Steixners „Fähigkeitenkatalog interkultureller Kompetenz" (Steixner 2007, S. 168) – der Frage nach den interkulturellen Selbstmanagementfähigkeiten von Expats, und wie diese gegebenenfalls gefördert werden können, nachgegangen.

Hierzu wurden leitfadengeführte Experteninterviews geführt, um die Selbstmanagementfähigkeiten – als Voraussetzung für erfolgreiche Auslandsentsendung –

zu überprüfen. Die Ergebnisse der Untersuchung bildeten die Grundlage für die Ableitung der Fragen für den Erweiterten Selbstmanagement-Fragenkatalog, der als Tool im Rahmen von Assessments sowie im Rahmen von Kompetenz- und Persönlichkeitsentwicklungsmaßnamen eingesetzt werden kann.

Erweiterter Selbstmanagement-Fragenkatalog: Ein ressourcenorientiertes Tool für Assessment und Kompetenzentwicklung

Es kann davon ausgegangen werden, dass Expats grundsätzlich einem mobilen Leben gegenüber aufgeschlossen und gewillt sind, dieses erfolgreich zu gestalten. Eine konstruktive Auseinandersetzung mit Veränderung, mit den eigenen Voraussetzungen und Lernbereitschaft vorausgesetzt, trägt dies zur Kompetenz- und Persönlichkeitsentwicklung bei. Der vorliegende Erweiterte Selbstmanagement-Fragenkatalog ist hierfür ein unterstützendes Tool. Es fokussiert auf die interkulturellen Selbstmanagementfähigkeiten im Kontext komplexer Veränderungen wie Expatriation, Repatriation und Transition. So können notwendige Ressourcen für das Meistern internationaler Assignments und Unterstützungsbedarf erkannt und mögliche Entwicklungsziele definiert werden, um die Selbststeuerungskompetenz und Handlungssicherheit einer Person zu stärken und einem potentiellen Scheitern von Entsendung vorzubeugen.

Fähigkeiten interkulturellen Selbstmanagements

Reflexion und Selbstreflexion spielen eine zentrale Rolle, sind sie doch Voraussetzung jedes Lernprozesses, für den Abgleich von Lernerfolg und Lernbedarf. Dies veranschaulicht das folgende Zitat eines self initiated Wirtschaftsexpats:

> *„... man wahrscheinlich immer mehr reflektiert über: was muss man selber machen, was muss man ändern, um erfolgreich zu sein in einer neuen Kultur."* (Expat in Schnetzer 2015, S. 70)

Es zeigt sich, dass Führungskräfte, die Ergebnisse liefern und ehrgeizige Ziele verfolgen bzw. Expats mit hohen Ansprüchen im Hinblick auf Erfolg eine besondere Bereitschaft zur Selbstreflexion zu haben scheinen (Schnetzer 2015, S. 71). Die unterschiedlichen Motive bei der Verwirklichung beruflicher und persönlicher Ziele gehen häufig mit unterschiedlichen Anpassungs- und Integrationsabsichten einher.

Selbstmanagementfähigkeiten

Als Selbstmanagementfähigkeiten wird die Summe aller Fähigkeiten definiert, die für die Selbststeuerung im interkulturellen Kontext und im Zusammenhang mit komplexer Veränderung notwendig sind. Das Ergebnis der Expat-Interviews und deren qualitative Auswertung machen deutlich, dass neben fachlichem und kulturellem Wissen (hard facts) noch weitere Fähigkeiten für das Selbstmanagement und interkulturelle Handlungssicherheit entscheidend sind.

Selbstvertrauen

Selbstvertrauen beinhaltet die Fähigkeit zu relativieren. bzw. die Fähigkeit zur realistischen Selbsteinschätzung. Sie steht in Verbindung mit einer positiven Grundhaltung gegenüber Veränderungen, es fördert das Meistern von Umbrüchen und Neuanfängen.

Selbstvertrauen in Verbindung mit einer ethnorelativistischen Haltung erlaubt die Relativierung von auftauchenden Problemen und der Richtigkeit der eigenen kulturellen Werte, wie das folgende Zitat eines Expats zeigt:

> *"Well, I am in that country, if I don't like it I leave it, I mean, whether I like it or not it's my problem not theirs"* (Expat in Schnetzer 2015, S. 51)

Auf der Grundlage von Selbstvertrauen können fremdkulturelle Erfahrungen positiv verarbeitet, fremdkulturelle Denk- und Handlungskonzepte in den eigenen Referenzrahmen integriert werden. Dadurch kann Expatriation per se als Bereicherung erlebt werden.

Kulturelle Selbstbewusstheit/ Identität

Kulturelle Selbstbewusstheit für die eigene Identität beinhaltet die Fähigkeiten Zuhören, Beobachten, Beobachtungen teilen und Sensibilität (Fühlen). Selbstbewusstheit ist eine Voraussetzung für Reflexionsbereitschaft und Verständnis. Zuhören und Beobachten spielen dabei eine wichtige Rolle.

> *„... es ist schon wichtig, um die andere Seite, zum Beispiel die ... Kultur zu VERSTEHEN, um zu verstehen, wie denn das WIRKT oder ... wie auch ICH wirke - oder wie MEINE Verhaltensweisen, MEINE Reaktionen wirken auf eine andere Kultur.“* (Expat in Schnetzer 2015, S. 52)

Sie erlaubt das Nachdenken über eigen- und fremddeterminierte Anteile in einem Lernprozess, der zu Persönlichkeitsentwicklung, zu Stabilität und Wohlbefinden im fremdkulturellen Umfeld beiträgt:

> *„Also was ich nicht vermissen will, ist also lernen, über die fremden Kulturen sich SELBER besser kennen zu lernen. ... man erlebt wieder, dass man LEBT, das ist das Schöne! ... bewusster, ja man lebt viel bewusster plötzlich wieder, ja.“* (Expat in Schnetzer 2015, S. 52)

Dies setzt Stabilität voraus und trägt zur persönlichen Reife bei.

Reife und Stabilität

Stabilität und Reife sind Fähigkeiten, die vor allem durch eine positive Verarbeitung von Erfahrungen in einem kontinuierlichen Lernprozess entwickelt werden und so zu Persönlichkeitsentwicklung beitragen, wie das folgende Zitat eines sehr erfahrenen Expats verdeutlicht.

„Ich glaub schon, dass jemand der VIEL Expat ist, also Leute, die 5, 6, 7-mal gewechselt haben, dass die schon sehr also ihre Erfolge sehen, was sie in jedem Land, bei jedem Umzug, mit allen Schwierigkeiten erreicht haben." (Expat in Schnetzer 2015, S. 64)

Reife und Stabilität zählen zu den wichtigsten individuellen Akkulturationsbedingungen, da jede Situation von Expatriation mit einer Infragestellung des Selbstkonzeptes verbunden ist.

„Having a new country is always a new way of - it's a way to put into question the way you're working, am I right or not." (Expat in Schnetzer 2015, S. 52)

Expatriates mit einer reifen und stabilen Persönlichkeit können den Kulturkontakt als Reflexionsfläche nutzen, ohne verunsichert zu werden. Sie verfügen in hohem Maße die Fähigkeit zu relativieren.

Stressresistenz und Belastbarkeit

Berufliche und private Herausforderungen unter sich ändernden kulturellen Rahmenbedingungen können Instabilität und Stress verursachen. Stress und Überbelastung sind eine häufige Ursache für physische und psychische Probleme, die nicht selten zu Partnerproblemen führen. So ist die Situation der mitgereisten (wie auch zurückgelassenen) Familienmitglieder ein Stressfaktor, vor allem in unsicheren Situationen des Übergangs.

In dieser kommt es zu Reflexionen über die – sich oft unfreiwillig ändernden – Zugehörigkeiten, unbekannte fremde Kommunikation im Gastland und veränderte Verantwortungen und Aufgaben (*Rollen*). So macht sich in Übergangsprozessen oft ein Verlust des Selbstwertgefühles bemerkbar, der mit Entwurzelung einhergeht.

„Selbst wenn wir äußerlich wie Erwachsene aussehen, kommen wir uns emotional wie Kinder vor." (vgl. Pollock u.a. (2003), S. 82).

Stressresistenz und Belastbarkeit kommen daher im Kontext sich verändernder Rahmenbedingungen eine hohe Bedeutung zu.

Vertrauensfähigkeit und positive Grundeinstellung

Vertrauensfähigkeit und eine positive Grundeinstellung sind eng mit Stressresistenz verbunden.

„Be positive" (Expat in Schnetzer 2015, S. 66) ist *nicht nur ein* Zitat einer Person mit viel Expaterfahrung. Es beschreibt zugleich eine wesentliche Voraussetzung für

das positive Meistern beruflicher Auslandsentsendungen. Diese hilft andere, bisher unbekannte Wege und Möglichkeiten des Denkens und Handelns im fremdkulturellen Umfeld wahrzunehmen und Vorurteile zu reduzieren.

Sie ist neben der Vertrauensfähigkeit in Personen und in Lösungen eine Voraussetzung dafür, Schwierigkeiten überwinden zu wollen und Wege zu finden.

> *„Wenn ich da ruhig rangehe, ... dann gibt es bestimmt eine Lösung, zurückhaltend, ich versuch erst einmal positiv zu sein."* (Expat in Schnetzer 2015, S. 66)

Vertrauensfähigkeit fördert die kulturelle Kontaktaufnahme, erleichtert die interkulturelle Zusammenarbeit. und unterstützt Anpassungsprozesse.

Kontaktfreudigkeit

Kontaktfreudigkeit gehört zu jenen Fähigkeiten des Selbstmanagements eines Expatriates, welche sich mit Erfahrung entwickelt und zu Gelassenheit und Selbstvertrauen beiträgt. Im beruflichen Kontext handelt es sich vor allem um professionelle erlernbare Kontaktfreudigkeit. Hingegen ist die Kontaktfreudigkeit privater Natur Voraussetzung für den Aufbau des sozialen Umfeldes, sozialer Netzwerke und Unterstützungssysteme. Diese sind im Kontext beruflicher Auslandsentsendungen Ersatz für nicht vor Ort ansässige Freunde und Familie.

Motivation

Motivation ist stark kontext- und personenabhängig. Sie beeinflusst in hohem Maße die Bereitschaft für interkulturelles Lernen und interkulturelle Anpassungsprozesse. Motivation korreliert eng mit der Dauer einer Entsendung und dem persönlichen Interesse an Neuem.

Reflexion und Selbstreflexion

Reflexion und Selbstreflexion sind dem Selbstmanagement übergeordnete Fähigkeiten, sie sind eine Voraussetzung für das positive Meistern von Veränderung und beruflichen Erfolg.

Sie wurden von allen Interviewpartnern hoch bewertet. Dies verweist auf die Notwendigkeit des kontinuierlichen Abgleichens von Realitäten und Erfordernissen für eine persönliche Entwicklung.

Kreativität

Kreativität ist – wenn auch nicht direkt analytisch erfasst – von hohem Stellenwert für die Entwicklung neuer Denk- und Handlungsmöglichkeiten. Sie ist die Fähigkeit, bisher nicht genutztes Wissen und nicht genutzte Fähigkeiten im Kontext fremdkultureller Begegnungen wahrnehmen und nutzen sowie fremdkulturelle Standards im eigenen Referenzrahmen integrieren zu können.

„... man in so einem interkulturellen Leben lebt, dann sieht man, dass es tausende Möglichkeiten gibt sein Leben zu meistern und alles GUT sein kann ..."
(Expat in Schnetzer 201, S. 60)

Das kreative Potential wird erweitert, indem neue Möglichkeiten des Denkens und Handelns einbezogen werden. Dies stärkt wiederum das Selbstvertrauen und trägt zur Persönlichkeitsentwicklung bei.

Gegenüberstellung

Die Zugehörigkeit zu einer bestimmten Expatgruppe – entsandt für eine begrenzte Dauer oder self-initiated und langfristig – korreliert mit der Ausprägung bestimmter Fähigkeiten des Selbstmanagements.

Dass die Interviewpartner beider Gruppen Selbstvertrauen, eine positive Grundhaltung, Reife und Stabilität sowie Stressresistenz *ähnlich oder gleich wichtig beurteilen,* verweist darauf, dass es sich hierbei um unspezifische und daher essentielle Fähigkeiten für das Selbstmanagement im Rahmen von Expatriation handelt.

Die unterschiedlich bewerteten Fähigkeiten Selbstbewusstheit, Kontaktfreudigkeit und Reflexionsbereitschaft verweisen auf den Einfluss der unterschiedlichen Rahmenbedingungen von Assignments und unterschiedlicher Notwendigkeiten für Handlungssicherheit. Self initiated Expats haben eine im Allgemeinen höhere Bereitschaft, sich in eine fremdkulturelle Gesellschaft zu integrieren als routinemäßig für nur wenige Jahre entsandte Expats, wie zum Beispiel Diplomaten.

Erweiterter Selbstmanagement-Fragenkatalog

Der „Erweiterte Selbstmanagement-Fragenkatalog" (Schnetzer 2015) fokussiert auf die zuvor beschriebenen Fähigkeiten und resultiert aus empirisch gewonnenen, qualitativen Interviewergebnissen mit Expats. Er dient der Feststellung der individuellen, situativen Selbstmanagementkompetenz von Personen im Kontext von Entsendung mit zielgerichteten Fragen. Einige werden nachfolgend angeführt.

Potentiale, Ressourcen sowie Entwicklungsziele können so abgeleitet werden und bilden den Ausgangspunkt für weiterführende unterstützende Maßnahmen, zum Beispiel im Rahmen eines interkulturellen Coachings. In diesem können andere Tools mit dem vorliegenden Erweiterten Fragenkatalog kombiniert werden.

Auszug aus dem Fragenkatalog:

Selbstreflexion

- Wie wichtig ist es Ihnen, sich selbst und im Kontext eines fremdkulturellen Umfeldes bewusst zu reflektieren?
- Wie beurteilen Sie Ihre Erfahrungen mit Selbstreflexion?

Selbstvertrauen

- Sind Sie gegenüber neuen / kulturellen Herausforderungen positiv eingestellt?
- Wie wichtig ist es Ihnen, was und wie andere Menschen über Sie denken?
- Sind Sie selbstkritisch?

Fähigkeit zu relativieren

- Wie schätzen Sie Ihr Verständnis für andere Denk- und Verhaltensweisen ein?
- Vergleichen Sie eigene mit fremden/anderen Denk- und Verhaltensweisen?
- Lassen Sie sich von anderen Werten überzeugen?

Kulturelle Selbstbewusstheit / Identität

- Sind Sie sich der wichtigsten Quellen Ihrer kulturellen Prägungen bewusst?
- Können Sie sich mit der Kultur/den Kulturen, in der/denen Sie arbeiten bzw. leben, identifizieren?
- Sind Ihnen Zugehörigkeiten zu Personengruppen (Familie, Sport, Freunde, Beruf) wichtig?
- Sind Sie daran interessiert, in einem neuen kulturellen Umfeld Mitglied von Interessensgruppen/Vereinen zu sein?

Beobachten, Zuhören, Fühlen

- Sind Sie in einer fremdkulturellen Situation in erster Linie Beobachter und Zuhörer?
- Achten Sie im fremdkulturellen Alltag/ in Gesprächen/ Verhandlungen auf Zwischentöne, nonverbale Gesten/ Mimik?
- Inwieweit achten Sie auf Ihre Gefühle in einer kulturellen Begegnung?

Vertrauensfähigkeit/ positive Grundhaltung

- Würden Sie sagen, dass Sie eine positive Lebenseinstellung haben?
- Würden Sie sich in einem neuen Arbeitsumfeld Personen anvertrauen?
- Können Sie Rat und Hilfe annehmen?

Reife und Stabilität

- Wie können Sie mit anderen kulturellen Umgebungen umgehen?

- Gibt es Faktoren, die Ihre innere Balance besonders beeinflussen? Sind Sie bereit, neue Strategien auszuprobieren?

Kontaktfreudigkeit

- Fällt es Ihnen leicht, mit bisher unbekannten Personen in einer fremdkulturellen Umgebung Kontakt aufzunehmen?
- Sind Sie bereit, in der Situation eines Neuanfangs auf
  a) neue Teamkollegen
  b) unbekannte Organisationen
  c) Personen im unmittelbaren persönlichen Lebensumfeld
  zuzugehen?

Stress

- Fühlen Sie sich unter Druck, wenn Sie bemerken, dass Sie Ihren Alltag nicht in gewohnter Weise managen können?
- Wie können Sie mit beruflichem Stress umgehen?
- Können Sie Belastungsgrenzen erkennen und sind Sie in der Lage, die Stopptaste zu drücken?

Motivation

- Entwickeln Sie berufliche Ziele und Visionen für und während eines Auslandsaufenthaltes?
- Entwickeln Sie private Ziele und Visionen für und während eines Auslandsaufenthaltes?

Kreativität

- Würden Sie sagen, dass das fremdkulturelle Umfeld Sie zu neuen Ideen anregt?
- Haben Sie dadurch bisher unbekannte Fähigkeiten an sich entdeckt?

Allgemeine Ressourcen von Expats

Expats verfügen im Allgemeinen über gute interkulturelle und organisatorische Stärken, die sie aufgrund ihrer Erfahrungen entwickeln. Zu diesen Ressourcen gehören:

- eine positive Grundhaltung gegenüber Veränderung und Fremdkulturellem
- Neugierde, Interesse und Freude an fremdkulturellen Herausforderungen und kultureller Abwechslung
- Kulturelle Herausforderungen genießen können, aufgrund von Offenheit, Lernbereitschaft und Flexibilität
- Internationale, interkulturelle Erfahrungen, Mehrsprachigkeit
- Beobachten, Zuhören; Fühlen und Relativieren können, Respekt
- Wissen um eine Vielzahl gleichwertiger Denk- und Handlungsmöglichkeiten

- Kreativität
- Gelassenheit
- Altes loslassen und Neues beginnen können/ wollen

Auch wenn viele Expats über die angeführten allgemeinen Ressourcen verfügen, heißt das nicht, das jede/r hoch qualifizierte Expat für ein Leben im Kontext wechselnder kultureller, sprachlicher, beruflicher sowie sozialer Bedingungen geeignet ist. Es bedarf einer positiven Grundeinstellung gegenüber Veränderungen und Fremdem, sowie einer gezielten Vorbereitung und Unterstützung durch das Entsendemanagement. Daher ist der Erweiterte Selbstmanagement-Fragenkatalog sowohl für Expats als auch für Personalentwickler, Trainer und Coaches von Relevanz.

Resümee

Vielfältige Anwendungsmöglichkeiten

Der hier vorgestellte „Erweiterte Selbstmanagement-Fragenkatalog" beleuchtet die notwendigen Selbstmanagementfähigkeiten im interkulturellen Kontext und von Expatriation.

Er beruht auf empirisch gewonnenen Ergebnissen von Interviews mit hochqualifizierten Expats und deren qualitativen Auswertung. Er kann im Rahmen eines Assessments oder als Grundlage für ein darauf aufbauendes Coaching von Expats eingesetzt werden. Das „Messergebnis" eines solchen Assessments ist ein Indikator für die individuelle situative Selbstmanagementkompetenz einer Person.

Der ressourcenorientierte Ansatz ermöglicht es, die individuellen Voraussetzungen von Personen im Umgang mit kulturellen Differenzen und für das Arbeiten unter den Rahmenbedingungen von Expatriation zu reflektieren und das Selbstmanagement zu fördern. Potentiale können aufgezeigt, Ziele für eine verbesserte Selbststeuerung und das Arbeiten im Rahmen internationaler Assignments und interkulturellen Kontext abgeleitet, Maßnahmen im Interesse eines nachhaltigen Entsendemanagements ergriffen werden.

Dies trägt zur Stärkung des interkulturellen Selbstmanagements und Entwicklung interkultureller Kompetenz zu entsendender oder von entsandten Personen bei.

Einsatz- und Anwendungsmöglichkeiten bei internationalen Assignments

Der „Erweiterte Selbstmanagement-Fragenkatalog" kann im Rahmen internationaler Assignments für die folgende Zwecke eingesetzt werden:

1. für die Auswahl der „richtigen" Akteure und deren Vorbereitung,
2. zur Assistance und Unterstützung während Auslandsentsendung und bei Repatriation
3. für eine verbesserte Handlungssicherheit im Rahmen internationaler Projektarbeit und

4. als Tool für diversitätsorientierte/ interkulturelle Coachings und Trainings.

Grundsätzlich ist der Erweiterte Selbstmanagement-Fragenkatalog ein universelles Tool zur Feststellung und Förderung des Selbstmanagements von Personen, die sich in einer Situation kultureller Transformation und komplexer Veränderungen befinden.

Literaturangabe

Deloitte Advokatfirma AS (2013). Global Employer Services – support for employers everywhere. Werbebroschüre für Rechtsberatung in Fragen der transnationalen Mobilität von hochqualifizierten Mitarbeitern multinationaler Unternehmen. Deloitte Advokatfirma AS, Norway

Gröschke, Daniela (2007) Kulturelle Unterschiede im Selbstkonzept: ein Differenzierungsschema. interculture journal:Online-Zeitschrift für interkulturelle Studien, 6(5), 39-70. https://nbn-resolving.org/urn:nbn:de:0168-ssoar-454497

Schnetzer, Christiane (2015) „Einfluss und Entwicklung des Selbstmanagements im Rahmen beruflicher Auslandseinsätze." (Master thesis, Donau-Universität Krems)

Steixner, Margret (2009): "Fine-tuning" durch interkulturelles Coaching. interculture journal: Online-Zeitschrift für interkulturelle Studien, 8 (9), 83-110. https://nbn-resolving.org/urn:nbn:de:0168-ssoar-454799

Herzog, Siegrun (2018) Im Mobilitäts Karussell. In: univie. Alumni-Magazin der Universität Wien, Nr. 2/2018, Juni-Oktober 2018, S. 8-15. https://issuu.com/univie/docs/univie_218_screen_einzel

Integrationsmanagement für Hochqualifizierte Migrantinnen und Migranten in der Erste Group Bank AG – ein Praxisbericht

Franziska Simader-Schober

Zusammenfassung

Die Erste Group Bank AG ist bekannt für ihren Expansionskurs und den daraus resultierenden ausländischen Tochterbanken vor allem in Zentral- und Osteuropa und Niederlassungen an strategischen Finanzmärkten weltweit. Das Unternehmen hat schon früh erkannt, dass eine erfolgreiche Integrationspolitik wichtig ist, um die im Ausland rekrutierten Mitarbeiterinnen und Mitarbeiter zu entlasten und damit den Start im Unternehmen und im Gastland bzw. in der neuen Heimat zu erleichtern. Das bedeutet, dass der Rekrutierungsprozess und das Onboarding im Haus abgewickelt werden und bei Personen, die aus dem Ausland in das Unternehmen geholt werden zusätzlich das sogenannte Integrationsmanagement eingebunden wird. Das Integrationsmanagement ist neben der Erlangung des nötigen Aufenthaltstitels bzw. der nötigen Beschäftigungsbewilligung für die Gesamtbetreuung dieser Personengruppe zuständig. Im nachfolgenden Beitrag möchte ich dazu einen Einblick in die Praxis geben und auch auf Schwierigkeiten bei der Zulassung zum österreichischen Arbeitsmarkt eingehen, im Speziellen auf den Verfahrensablauf bei den zuständigen Behörden

Einleitung

Die Erste Group Bank AG versteht sich als internationales Unternehmen und spiegelt das auch in ihrer Personalpolitik. Transnationaler Mobilität innerhalb der Gruppe wird seit Jahren ein hoher Stellenwert beigemessen. Darüber hinaus wird die Rekrutierung von Fachkräften und Spezialistinnen und Spezialisten, aber auch von Praktikantinnen und Praktikanten und Trainees nicht nur innerhalb der Gruppe oder innerhalb Österreichs betrieben. Vielmehr wird weltweit nach den besten Köpfen und talentiertesten Personen gesucht. Sowohl Expertinnen und Experten mit jahrelanger praktischer Erfahrung werden gesucht, als auch Studienabsolventinnen und Studienabsolventen diversester Studienrichtungen. Diese finden sich sehr oft im Ausland oder in Form von ausländischen Studentinnen und Studenten, die ihr Studium in Wien bzw. Österreich absolvieren oder absolviert haben.

Seit dem Jahr 2007 bin ich in der Funktion des „Integration Managers" für die Ausländerbeschäftigung in der Erste Group Bank AG verantwortlich. Dieses Aufgabengebiet umfasst Unterstützung bei der Erlangung der nötigen Zulassungen zum österreichischen Arbeitsmarkt, wie z.B. der „Rot-Weiss-Rot Karte", der „Blaue Karte EU" oder anderer nötiger Beschäftigungsbewilligungen, aber auch die Beantragung der Aufenthaltstitel für die Familie sowie in weiterer Folge auch die regelmäßig notwendigen Verlängerungsanträge der jeweiligen Bewilligungen. Weitere Bedarfe, wie etwa die Wohnungssuche oder die Suche nach einem entsprechendem Kindergarten- oder Schulplatz, werden ebenfalls vom Unternehmen unterstützt. Konkrete Details, die die Integration im Allgemeinen, aber auch speziell im Unternehmen betreffen, finden Sie nachfolgend unter dem Punkt „Integration am Arbeitsplatz". Dort werde ich auch auf die Probleme bei der Erlangung von Aufenthaltstiteln und Beschäftigungsbewilligungen eingehen und gleichzeitig Lösungsvorschläge unterbreiten, die auf jahrelanger praktischer Erfahrung basieren.

Um diesen Aufgaben noch besser gerecht werden zu können, habe ich im Jahr 2015 meinen „Master of Science in Migrationswissenschaften" an der „Donau-Universität Krems am Department für Migration und Globalisierung erworben und auch meine Master Thesis dem Thema „Arbeitsmigration in der Erste Group Bank AG" gewidmet.

Politik

Wie bereits eingangs erwähnt, ist der Erste Group Bank AG die Internationalität ihrer Belegschaft ein wichtiges Anliegen. Zum einen ist der Konzern bestrebt, den Mitarbeiterinnen und Mitarbeitern der Gruppe in ihren in- und ausländischen Tochterfirmen Mobilität zu ermöglichen. Zum anderen sollen offene Stellen mit den besten Personen besetzt werden. Diese findet man oftmals nicht am österreichischen Arbeitsmarkt.

Diese Vielfalt an offenen Stellen ist auch darauf zurückzuführen, dass die Finanzdienstleistungsbranche Reglements unterworfen ist, die nur mit der Hilfe hochspezialisierten Personals erfüllt werden können. Personen, die diese Positionen einnehmen können, benötigen eine fundierte akademische Ausbildung, sollten aber oft auch über mehrjährige berufliche Erfahrung verfügen. Unser Ziel ist es daher, die besten Köpfe für das Unternehmen zu gewinnen, um die Erfolgsgeschichte der Bank weiterführen zu können. Das bedeutet aber auch, sich nicht nur auf den nationalen Arbeitsmarkt zu beschränken

Die Erste Group Bank AG beschäftigt mit Stand August 2019 insgesamt ca. 47.000 Personen, in Österreich etwa 8.000. Von diesen in Österreich Beschäftigten sind etwa 80% österreichische Staatsbürgerinnen und Staatsbürger und 20% Personen mit nicht-österreichischer Staatsbürgerschaft. Von diesen 20% wiederum sind etwa zwei Drittel EU-Bürgerinnen und EU-Bürger und ein Drittel Drittstaatenangehöriger. 6 Personen gelten als staatenlos. Das Unternehmen weist zurzeit 73 unterschiedliche Nationalitäten auf.

Die Anzahl an Personen mit nicht-österreichischer Staatsbürgerschaft, die für das Unternehmen rekrutiert werden und einen Zugang zum österreichischen Arbeitsmarkt benötigen, ist im Laufe der Jahre immer wieder gestiegen, von 2018 auf 2019 aber besonders stark. Waren es im Jahr 2018 insgesamt 23 Anträge auf „Rot-Weiß-Rot Karte" oder „Blaue Karte EU", sind es im August 2019 bereits 30 Anträge, die an die entsprechende Behörde (die MA 35, Referat für Einwanderung und Staatsbürgerschaft) übermittelt worden sind. In den seltenen Fällen, wenn der Wohnsitz außerhalb Wiens liegt, erfolgt die Übermittlung der Antragsunterlagen an die zuständige Behörde des jeweiligen Bundeslandes. Tendenziell steigt im Unternehmen der Anteil an nicht-österreichischen bzw. nicht EU-Bürgerinnen und -Bürgern. Diese Tendenz wird vom Unternehmen begrüßt, weil die dadurch entstehende größere Diversität als bereichernd wahrgenommen wird.

Rekrutierung

Pro Jahr erreichen uns ca. 20.000 Bewerbungen. 70% dieser Bewerbungen werden bereits nach erster Durchsicht ausgeschieden. Die etwa 6.000 verbleibenden Kandidatinnen und Kandidaten kommen in eine engere Auswahl, aus der jährlich an die 2.000 offene Positionen besetzt werden.

Die Suche nach diesen Personen mit speziellen Ausbildungen und bereits praktisch erworbenen Kenntnissen findet – wie bereits erwähnt – großflächig statt, national und international, intern und extern. Intern bedeutet in unserem Fall über eine Jobplattform, auf die alle Mitarbeiterinnen und Mitarbeiter aller Tochterunternehmen im In- und Ausland Zugriff haben. Somit ist Mobilität innerhalb des Unternehmens möglich. Alle offenen Positionen werden zuerst auf dieser Plattform ausgeschrieben, bevor sie extern veröffentlicht werden.

Externe Inserate werden über verschiedene Medien geschalten. Das Unternehmen bedient sich hier auch verstärkt Social-Media-Kanäle. Top Positionen oder offenen Stellen, denen ein bestimmtes Anforderungsprofil zugrunde liegt, das nicht von vielen Personen erfüllt werden kann, werden vorrangig über Netzwerke besetzt, in Ausnahmefällen auch über Headhunter.

Sobald eine Shortlist der möglichen Kandidatinnen und Kandidaten erstellt ist, beginnt der eigentliche Rekrutierungsprozess. Mehrstufige Auswahlverfahren ermöglichen einen tiefen Einblick in die Fähigkeiten, professionelle als auch persönliche. Bei der Personalauswahl muss das Gesamtbild stimmig sein. Die zukünftige Mitarbeiterin bzw. der zukünftige Mitarbeiter soll die fachlichen Anforderungen erfüllen, in das Team passen und sich mit dem Unternehmen identifizieren können.

Wenn die Bewerberin bzw. der Bewerber eine lange Anreise zurücklegen müsste, werden erste Bewerbungsgespräche oft via Telefon oder Videokonferenz abgehalten, um die Reisekosten und den persönlichen Aufwand zu minimieren. Erst in den weiteren Runden werden dann persönliche Treffen arrangiert, die eventuell schon ein Visum bedingen und somit zeitintensiver in der Vorbereitung sind.

Kooperationen mit Universitäten erweitern die Such- und Auswahlmöglichkeiten. Auch viele interne Programme zur Weiterbildung bieten die Möglichkeit, sich innerhalb der Gruppe zu bewegen. Das Recruiting Team wird auch hier für die Suche nach den richtigen Kandidatinnen und Kandidaten herangezogen.

Employer Branding ist ein wichtiger Teil des Recruitings. Es ist uns bewusst, dass wir als international agierender Arbeitgeber attraktive Rahmenbedingungen schaffen müssen, um bestausgebildete Mitarbeiterinnen und Mitarbeiter für unser Unternehmen begeistern zu können und um sie möglichst langfristig an das Unternehmen binden zu können.

Das bekannte Problem des Fachkräftemangels, vor allem in der IT, ist auch für unser Unternehmen eine große Herausforderung bei der Besetzung von entsprechenden Positionen. Die am österreichischen Arbeitsmarkt vorgemerkten Arbeitssuchenden können hier nur in sehr geringem Maße für die Besetzung von vakanten Positionen herangezogen werden. Temporäre Projektmitarbeiterinnen und Projektmitarbeiter im IT-Bereich, die sich bewähren, versuchen wir für uns zu gewinnen. Hier handelt es sich oftmals um indische Staatsbürgerinnen und Staatsbürger.

Integration

Die Integration am Arbeitsplatz beginnt in unserem Unternehmen bereits während des Auswahlverfahrens. Zukünftige Mitarbeiterinnen und Mitarbeiter, für die wir den Zugang zum österreichischen Arbeitsmarkt erst erschließen müssen, erhalten alle dafür nötigen Informationen bereits während der Hearings. Nach Endauswahl werden diese Kandidatinnen und Kandidaten an den Integration Manager vermittelt, damit der Prozess zur Erlangung der Aufenthalts- bzw. Beschäftigungsbewilligung zeitnah beginnen kann. Die Vorbereitung aller Antragsunterlagen werden durch den Integration Manager vorgenommen, auch die Abgabe erfolgt durch ihn, wenn die zukünftige Mitarbeiterin bzw. der zukünftige Mitarbeiter nicht Vorort ist oder auch wenn die Erfahrung mit Behördengängen fehlt und die Hemmschwelle groß ist. Die Einreichgebühren übernimmt die Bank.

Bei mitübersiedelnden Familienangehörigen unterstützt das Unternehmen ebenfalls bei der Antragstellung, aber auch bei weiteren Bedarfen, wie etwa Wohnungssuche und Schul- und Kindergartensuche.

Während der Prozess zur Erlangung des Aufenthaltstitels bzw. der Beschäftigungsbewilligung läuft, steht der Integration Manager nach Möglichkeit mit den Behörden im Kontakt, um eventuell nachgeforderte Unterlagen möglichst schnell nachreichen zu können, aber auch um den Kandidatinnen und Kandidaten und den zukünftigen Führungskräften jederzeit den „Status Quo" nennen zu können.

Hier möchte ich ansetzen, um im Detail auf die Probleme bei der Erlangung der Aufenthaltstitel und Beschäftigungsbewilligungen einzugehen. Bei Beantragung einer Beschäftigungsbewilligung, welche bis Juni 2020 noch für kroatische Staatsbürgerinnen und -bürger bzw. für Studentinnen und Studenten mit kroatischer Staatsbürgerschaft oder Drittstaatenangehörigkeit benötigt wird, besteht bereits seit längerer Zeit die Möglichkeit, diese über „AMS eServices" online durchzuführen. Ebenso verhält es sich bei anderen Anträgen, wie etwa das Ansuchen auf „Aus- und Weiterbildung im Konzern", eine Bewilligung, die wir in unserem Unternehmen aufgrund von Potentialentwicklungen innerhalb der Gruppe immer wieder benötigen.

Ist der Antrag abgegeben, verliert sich leider jegliche Transparenz des Prozesses. Die Möglichkeit, seitens des AMS die Vergabe eines jeweiligen Status zu setzen, welcher vom antragstellenden Unternehmen eingesehen werden kann, scheint nicht wirklich genutzt zu werden. Eine Empfangsbestätigung folgt prompt, jedoch keine weitere Information, bis der Antrag bearbeitet wird, oftmals zeitgleich die Information, dass der Antrag nun bearbeitet wurde und somit abgeschlossen ist. Diese Informationslücke kann bis zu sechs Wochen dauern. Trotz der Abgabe über „AMS eServices" werden nachzufordernde Unterlagen vom AMS meist nicht online gestellt, sondern oftmals über den Postweg an das Unternehmen gerichtet. Das zieht eine weitere Verzögerung mit sich. Die direkte telefonische Erreichbarkeit der jeweiligen Referentinnen und Referenten des AMS ist seit kurzem nicht gegeben, da die Telefonvermittlung des AMS Anweisung hat, keine Telefonate durchzustellen. Eine schriftliche Anfrage muss an das allgemeine Postfach des AMS gerichtet werden. Hier erfolgt zwar eine automatische Bestätigung über das Einlangen der E-Mail, die Beantwortung der jeweiligen Frage kann jedoch wieder einige Tage dauern. Somit verzögert sich die Vorlage des Antrages beim Beirat des AMS, der für die Befürwortung oder Ablehnung der Anträge endverantwortlich ist. Beiratssitzungen finden in der Regel einmal wöchentlich statt.

Die Beantragung eines Aufenthaltstitels für Drittstaatenangehörige gestaltet sich wesentlich aufwendiger, zeitintensiver und schwieriger, da der gesamte Antrag bei der jeweiligen Behörde, in Wien ist das die MA35, Referat für Einwanderung und Staatsbürgerschaft, eingebracht werden muss, wobei der Teil, der den Zugang zum österreichischen Arbeitsmarkt betrifft, an das AMS weitergeleitet wird. Bei Abgabe des Antrages erhält man eine Einreichbestätigung, die eventuell fehlende bzw. nachzureichende Unterlagen aufweist, aber danach verliert sich auch hier jegliche Transparenz des Prozesses. Man erfährt nicht, wann der Akt beim AMS einlangt, wann die Bearbeitung des Antrages aufgenommen wird bzw. welche Referentin oder welcher Referent für die Bearbeitung zuständig ist. Meist unterliegt der beantragte Aufenthaltstitel einem Punktesystem und man kann sich im Vorfeld ausrechnen, ob der Antrag entspricht und positiv beschieden werden kann. Überraschungen kann es dennoch geben. Vordienstzeiten, die nicht anrechenbar sind, Sprachzertifikate, die zu alt sind oder als Nachweis nicht akzeptiert werden können und anderes mehr. Die Verständigung über derartiges Fehlen von Dokumenten oder erforderlicher Nachreichung erfolgt in der Regel auf dem Postweg, oft Wochen nach Einbringung des Antrages bei der Erstantragstelle, der MA35. Auch die Verständigung über ein eingeleitetes Ersatzarbeitskräfteverfahren kann bis zu 6 Wochen dauern, dazu kommen nochmals einige Wochen, während denen das Ersatzarbeitskräfteverfahren abgewickelt wird.

Somit müssen wir den Prozess zur Erlangung einer Beschäftigungsbewilligung mit mindestens sechs Wochen ansetzen, gerechnet ab dem Zeitpunkt der online-Übermittlung an das AMS. Bei Erlangung eines Aufenthaltstitels wie einer „Rot-Weiß-Rot Karte" oder einer „Blauen Karte EU" setzen wir zumindest drei bis vier Monate an, bevor wir die Kandidatin bzw. den Kandidaten als Mitarbeiterin bzw. Mitarbeiter bei uns begrüßen können. Dieser Zeitraum muss meist nochmals verlängert werden, da die Kandidatinnen und Kandidaten oft erst nach Vorliegen eines positiven Bescheides seitens der Behörde das momentan noch aufrechte Beschäftigungsverhältnis im Ausland kündigen. Im schlimmsten Fall kann die Kandidatin bzw. der Kandidat erst nach sechs oder mehr Monaten die Beschäftigung in unserem Unternehmen aufnehmen. Ein beinahe unzumutbar langer Zeitraum, in dem die Mitarbeiterin bzw. der Mitarbeiter bereits dringend gebraucht werden würde. Manchmal ist das Wissen um diesen langwierigen Prozess ein Grund, dass sich Führungskräfte nicht für die Topkandidatin oder den Topkandidaten entscheiden, um diesen oftmals langwierigen Prozess zu vermeiden.

Die Erlangung einer Beschäftigungsbewilligung bzw. eines Aufenthaltstitels ist für alle Beteiligte mühsam, für das Unternehmen und die jeweiligen Führungskräfte, vor allem aber für die Kandidatinnen und Kandidaten, die nicht wirklich genau abwiegen können, wann der Umzug in das Gastland bzw. in die neue Heimat stattfinden wird können. Gilt es doch in vielen Fällen, die Zelte in der Heimat komplett abzubrechen. Ein derartiger Umzug ist ein Lebenseinschnitt, der gut geplant werden muss, umso mehr, wenn es sich etwa um die Übersiedlung von einer mehrköpfigen Familie handelt.

Weitere Probleme ergeben sich auch aufgrund diverser Anforderungen üblichsten Aufenthaltstitel für Hochqualifizieren, der Rot-Weiß-Rot Karte in ihren unterschiedlichen Varianten. So ist der Nachweis einer ortsüblichen Unterkunft erforderlich, gültig für zumindest vierundzwanzig Monate. Was als ortsüblich zu verstehen ist wird jedoch nicht näher erläutert. Natürlich darf es sich hierbei nicht um ein Massenquartier handeln, aber die Angabe einer Mindestgröße in Quadratmeter pro Person wäre sehr hilfreich. Unser hervorragendes Netzwerk und die Kooperation mit Anbietern von Business Apartments lassen uns das Problem der nachgewiesenen Unterkunft zumeist sehr gut und rasch lösen, dennoch ist es für die Kandidatin bzw. den Kandidaten oft sehr verwunderlich, wie ein Mietvertrag geschlossen werden soll, wenn sie sich selbst noch tausende Kilometer entfernt befinden. Hier würden wir es sehr begrüßen, wenn die geplante Gesetzesänderung in Kraft tritt, die vom Nachweis einer gesicherten Unterkunft absieht.

Zu berücksichtigen ist auch, dass Kandidatinnen und Kandidaten aus nicht liberalen Ländern oftmals Berührungsängste im Umgang mit Behörden haben. Sie fürchten die Abgabe falscher Unterlagen und damit verbundener Repressalien. Das führt manchmal zu einem erhöhten Zeitaufwand, bis die Abgabe des Antrages mit den erforderlichen Unterlagen erfolgen kann. Die Angst vor Fehlern hemmt den Tatendrang und verursacht Verzögerungen.

Kandidatinnen und Kandidaten, die sichtvermerkfrei nach Österreich einreisen können, haben die Möglichkeit, den Antrag persönlich bei der österreichischen Behörde im Inland abzugeben bzw. während des Verfahrens zur Erlangung des beantragten Aufenthaltstitels die erforderlichen Fingerprints bei der Behörde in Österreich abzugeben, ohne dass dafür die ausländische Vertretungsbehörde zur Ausstellung eines Visa D eingeschaltet werden muss.

Kandidatinnen und Kandidaten, die nicht sichtvermerkfrei nach Österreich einreisen dürfen, sind nicht berechtigt, eine Antragsstellung bei der Inlandsbehörde durchzuführen und benötigen für die Einreise ein Visum, welches die österreichische Auslandsbehörde, die Botschaft, ausstellt. Bei der Beantragung eines derartigen Visums werden Fingerprints genommen und seit geraumer Zeit besteht aufgrund einer Verordnung des Bundesministeriums für Inneres die Möglichkeit, diese abgenommenen Fingerprints an die Inlandsbehörde, in Wien die MA35, weiterzuleiten, um diese auch für den jeweils beantragten Aufenthaltstitel zu verwenden. Leider wird das in der Praxis nicht oder noch nicht so gehandhabt. Dadurch ergibt sich eine weitere Verzögerung von etwa vier bis sechs Wochen in der Ausfolgung des Aufenthaltstitels für Antragstellerinnen und Antragsteller, die zur Einreise nach Österreich ein Visum benötigen.

All diese Probleme, mit denen wir bei der Antragstellung bzw. während des Antragsverfahrens konfrontiert sind, erhöhen den Druck auf die Kandidatinnen und Kandidaten, aber auch auf die Führungskräfte des Unternehmens und den für die Ausländerbeschäftigung Verantwortlichen im HR enorm. Ungewissheit über die Dauer des Verfahrens bzw. den Ausgang des Verfahrens erschweren die Planung im Personalbereich sehr. Daher plädieren wir für ein erleichtertes und schnelleres Verfahren bei der Erlangung des Zugangs zum österreichischen Arbeitsmarkt, vor allem für Staatsbürgerinnen und Staatsbürger aus Drittstaaten. Wir wünschen uns transparente Verfahren und rasche Mitteilung betreffend nachzureichender Unterlagen. Eine online-Abgabe der Anträge wäre auch für Aufenthaltstitel bei der zuständigen Behörde wünschenswert. Eventuell sogar mit der Möglichkeit, die das AMS betreffende Unterlagen direkt an das AMS zu übermitteln. Ich denke, dass das das Verfahren beschleunigen könnte. Unsere Kandidatinnen und Kandidaten und deren Unterlagen sind nach mehrstufigen Hearings und internen Kontrollen derart geprüft, dass wir einen weiteren Vorschlag zur Beschleunigung der Beschäftigungsaufnahme machen möchten: Eine vorübergehend gültige Aufenthaltsbescheinigung, die es unseren Kandidatinnen und Kandidaten erlaubt, die Beschäftigung relativ zügig aufzunehmen, obwohl das eigentliche Verfahren noch im Laufen ist. Die Gültigkeit einer solchen vorübergehenden Aufenthaltsbescheinigung könnte z.B. mit sechs Monaten befristet werden, da dies erfahrungsgemäß der Zeitraum ist, zu dem der Aufenthaltstitel spätestens ausgehändigt wird. In den letzten zwölf Jahren wurden unsere Anträge alle positiv beschieden, auch das ist ein Zeichen, dass unsere Kandidatinnen und Kandidaten den Anforderungen der Behörden im Grunde entsprechen.

Wichtig erscheint es mir in diesem Zusammenhang, darauf hinzuweisen, dass wir an und für sich ein sehr gutes Einvernehmen mit den Behörden haben und Unterstützung seitens der jeweiligen Referentinnen und Referenten erfahren, wenn es zu Unklarheiten oder Problemen kommt.

An diesem Punkt möchte ich betonen, dass wir in unserem Unternehmen eine Willkommenskultur leben, die den zukünftigen Mitarbeiterinnen und Mitarbeitern hohe Wertschätzung entgegenbringt. Das würden wir uns auch noch mehr von den Behörden erwarten. Deswegen legen wir Wert darauf, dass eine eventuelle Sprachbarriere keine Schlechterstellung nach sich zieht. Sei es im Kontakt mit den Behörden, Bildungseinrichtungen oder potentiellen Vermietern. Hier übernehmen wir gerne den Erstkontakt und/oder Terminvereinbarungen. Deswegen begrüßen wir die Möglichkeit, dass die Einreichung der Antragsunterlagen für Aufenthaltstitel und Beschäftigungsbewilligungen vom Arbeitgeber durchgeführt werden kann.

Nach Erlangung der Aufenthalts- bzw. Beschäftigungsbewilligung kümmern wir uns weiter um die Mitarbeiterin bzw. den Mitarbeiter und gegebenenfalls auch um ihre bzw. seine Angehörigen. Das Unternehmen hilft bei Anträgen aller Art, wie Mitversicherung, Familienbeihilfe oder Fahrzeugimport. Wenn sich Lebenssituationen ändern oder Verlängerungen von Aufenthalts- bzw. Beschäftigungsbewilligungen anfallen, steht das Unternehmen weiterhin unterstützend zur Seite.

Alle Fragen und Probleme werden ernst genommen und nach Möglichkeit taggleich erledigt bzw. mit der Mitarbeiterin oder dem Mitarbeiter Kontakt aufgenommen, um zu signalisieren, dass ihr bzw. sein Anliegen eingelangt ist und bearbeitet wird.

Die Konzernsprache in der Erste Group Bank AG ist Englisch. Das Unternehmen stellt Plattformen zur Vernetzung zur Verfügung, es organisiert Sprachkurse und es werden sogenannte „International Dinner" organisiert. Der Integration Manager stellt Kontakte zwischen den Mitarbeiter her, um den Erfahrungsaustausch zu forcieren. Alle diese Maßnahmen erfolgen in der Absicht einer für beide Seiten zufriedenstellende Integration.

Schlussworte

Ich bin stolz ein Teil der Erste Group Bank AG sein zu dürfen und meinen Teil zum Erfolg des Unternehmens beitragen zu können. Aus meiner Sicht ist unser Unternehmen ein hervorragendes Beispiel für eine Good Practice im Umgang mit Mitarbeiterinnen und Mitarbeitern, die aus dem Ausland rekrutiert und in das Unternehmen aufgenommen werden, weil sie auch die Unterstützung der Bank erfahren, wenn es um die Integration in die neue Heimat und den eventuell anderen Kulturkreis geht.

Die Good Practice besteht darin, dass alle Prozesse bankintern abgewickelt werden. Die zukünftige Mitarbeiterin bzw. der zukünftige Mitarbeiter steht in ständigem Kontakt mit betriebsinternen Personen, die das Unternehmen präsentieren und vertreten. Damit ist gewährleistet, dass jedes Problem sofort aufgegriffen und gelöst werden kann. Es gibt für jeden Prozessschritt einen Single Point of Contact und diese Ansprechperson ist wiederum stark vernetzt mit den vorhergehenden bzw. nachfolgenden Prozessverantwortlichen. Es entstehen keine Informationslücken und alle beteiligten Personen haben den gleichen Wissensstand.

Good Practice auch deshalb, weil wir uns nicht nur auf die Bewilligung zum Zugang auf den österreichischen Arbeitsmarkt beschränken, sondern weil wir darüber hinaus jede neue Mitarbeiterin bzw. jeden neuen Mitarbeiter aus dem Ausland begleiten und bestmöglich unterstützen. Diese Unterstützung endet nicht, wann immer eine Situation eintritt, die Betreuung erfordert, wird diese gegeben.

Obwohl sich die Anzahl der Mitarbeiterinnen und Mitarbeiter aus dem Ausland kontinuierlich erhöht und sich somit auch die Anträge auf Aufenthalts- und Beschäftigungsbewilligung vervielfacht haben, ist es unserem Unternehmen das dauerhafte Unterstützungsangebot wichtig. Wir sind der Meinung, dass sich diese Mitarbeiterinnen und Mitarbeiter durch dieses Angebot auf ihre Aufgaben konzentrieren können, was sowohl im individuellen, als auch im unternehmerischen Interesse ist, ein Mehrwert für beide Seiten.

Wir sind stets bestrebt, uns und unsere Leistungen nach Vorgaben der Möglichkeit weiterzuentwickeln, nicht nur den Trends, sondern auch den Bedarfen der Zielgruppen anzupassen. Wir legen großen Wert auf das Feedback und die damit verbundenen Anregungen und Wünsche, aber auch auf Kritik, die uns hilft, manches überdenken und zu verbessern. Eine ähnliche Haltung wünsche ich mir auch ganz persönlich von Behörden und deren Mitarbeiterinnen und Mitarbeitern, sowie von jenen, für die Vorgaben dort verantwortlich zeichnen: Mehr auf die Bedarfe einzugehen, einen Dialog zu führen und gemeinsame Lösungen entsprechend den Gesetzesvorgaben zu finden.

Anmerken möchte ich hier noch, dass Umstellungen bei den Behörden in Wien im Gange sind und diese vielversprechend wirken. Ob diese jedoch wirklich mehr Transparenz bringen und eine Beschleunigung der Verfahren mit sich ziehen werden, wird sich erst erweisen. Auch das Feedback von unseren zukünftigen Mitarbeiterinnen und Mitarbeitern nach deren persönlicher Vorsprache bei den Ämtern können wir mit Spannung erwarten.

Verzeichnis der AutorInnen

Friedrich **Altenburg**, Mag. MSc, studierte Geschichte und Kommunikationswissenschaften an der Universität Salzburg. Nach 19 Jahren in der internationalen Entwicklungszusammenarbeit und Humanitären Hilfe an der Schnittstelle von Migration und Entwicklung wechselte er 2011 als wissenschaftlicher Mitarbeiter und Lehrgangsleiter an das Department Migration und Globalisierung der Donau-Universität Krems.

Rainer **Bauböck**, Univ.-Prof. Dr., ist derzeit Teilzeitprofessor am Robert Schuman Centre des Europäischen Hochschulinstituts in Florenz und Obmann der Kommission für Migrations- und Integrationsforschung der Österreichischen Akademie der Wissenschaften. Er unterrichtet an der Central European University in Wien. Von 2007-2018 hatte er den Lehrstuhl für soziale und politische Theorie am Europäischen Hochschulinstitut inne. Er forscht über Staatsbürgerschaft, Migration und Demokratietheorie.

Gudrun **Biffl**, Univ.-Prof.[in] Mag.[a] Dr.[in], ist Emeritus Professorin der Donau-Universität Krems und war von 2008 bis 2017 Inhaberin des Lehrstuhls für Migrationsforschung und Leiterin des Departments für Migration und Globalisierung der Donau-Universität Krems. Zwischen 2010 und 2015 war sie außerdem Dekanin der Fakultät Wirtschaft und Globalisierung. Bevor sie an die Donau-Universität gekommen ist, war sie als Wirtschaftsforscherin am Österreichischen Institut für Wirtschaftsforschung tätig. Ihre Forschungsschwerpunkte umfassen Migrationsforschung im Bereich Arbeitsmarkt, Bildung, Gender, industrielle Arbeitsbeziehungen und Institutionenwandel und arbeitsbedingte Krankheiten.

Özge **Bilgili** is an assistant professor of interdisciplinary social science at Utrecht University where she is a member of the European Research Centre on Migration and Ethnic Relations (ERCOMER). Since 2016, Özge Bilgili is the chair of Dutch Association for Migration Research (DAMR). Her research interests include a wide range of issues related to migration, social cohesion and relevant policy approaches across the globe.

Mathias **Czaika**, Univ.-Prof. Dr., ist Professor für Migration und Integration und Leiter des Departments für Migration und Globalisierung an der Donau-Universität Krems, sowie Research Associate am Department for International Development an der Universität Oxford. Er forscht zu internationalen Migrationsprozessen und der Rolle von Migrationspolitik.

Sonja **Fransen** is a post-doctoral researcher at the Political Sociology Department of University of Amsterdam working on Migration as Development Project.

Sonja Fransen is an expert of the Great Lakes region has written extensively on forced migration, return migration and remittances.

Margarita **Fourer** is a PhD Candidate in Migration Studies at the Danube University Krems. Having worked in refugee resettlement Kenya and relocation (family reunification and Canadian sponsorship) in Israel, her current research topic is on bilateral arrangements between states to process and settle refugees offshore. In particular, the research focuses on the effect of these arrangements on the hosting state and communities.

Ernst **Fürlinger,** Dr. habil., hat sein Studium der katholischen Fachtheologie in Salzburg und Religionswissenschaft in Wien absolviert. Von 2001-2006 verbrachte er einen Forschungsaufenthalt in Nordindien zum nichtdualistischen Shivaismus von Kaschmir. Seit 2006 ist Ernst Fürlinger als Religionswissenschaftler an der Universität Wien und an der Donau-Universität Krems tätig. Er habilitierte 2013 im Fach Religionswissenschaft an der Universität Wien. Von 2011 bis 2019 leitete er das Zentrum Religion und Globalisierung an der Donau-Universität Krems. Seine gegenwärtigen Arbeitsschwerpunkte umfassen Klimagerechtigkeit, Ethik und Spiritualität der Nachhaltigkeit.

Amparo **González-Ferrer** is Senior Research Fellow at the Spanish National Re-search Council (CSIC). She worked on family-linked migration, political integration of migrants and determinants of international migration. She coordinated the TEMPER project - Temporary versus Permanent Migration and was main investigator of the Spanish team of MAFE-Migration between Africa and Europe, both funded by the VII Framework Program of the EU Commission. In 2019 she was on leave from CSIC and on a temporary assignment at the High Commissioner for Child Poverty of the Spanish government.

Andrea **Götzelmann-Rosado** has been working for the International Organization for Migration (IOM) since 2008. Currently she is responsible for knowledge management and liaison in the IOM Country Office for Austria. Prior to that, she headed the AVRR Unit for eight years. She studied Political Science and English at the Universities of Vienna and Edinburgh and worked in Public Relations for a few years before starting to work with IOM.

Washika **Haak-Saheem**, Dr., Masterstudium der Angewandten Kulturwissenschaften (2003), Promotion im Fachbereich Betriebswirtschaftslehre an der Leuphana Universität in Lüneburg. Von 2009-2016 Assistent Professorin an der University of Dubai, 2016-2018 Assoziierte Professorin und Direktorin des BA Programms an der University of Dubai. Seit August 2018 Assoziierte Professorin an der Henley Business School (University of Reading, UK) im Bereich Internationales Management und Strategie mit Forschungsschwerpunkten auf Internationales Personalmanagement, Transnationale Mobilität sowie Wissensmanagement und -transfer in den arabischen Golfstaaten.

Hakan **Kilic** is working since 2017 as a researcher at the Department for Migration and Globalization of the Danube University Krems while also being a PhD student in Migration Studies. He studied political science at the University of Vienna and lectured between 2013-2017 at the University of Gaziantep/Turkey. His research focuses on highly qualified migration, return migration and integration.

Sascha **Krannich**, Dr., ist Research Associate am Institut für Geschichte der Medizin an der Justus-Liebig-Universität Gießen mit den Schwerpunkten Migration, Migrationspolitik, Entwicklung, Menschenrechte und Global Health. Zudem ist er Lehrbeauftragter an der Hochschule Fulda. Forschungsaufenthalte unternahm er u.a. an der Princeton University und an der University of California, Los Angeles.

Ave **Lauren** is currently National Coordinator for Estonia at the European Migration Network (EMN). She holds a Ph.D. in Economic Geography from the University of Cambridge, where her work focused on highly-skilled immigration to the United States, particularly Silicon Valley. Prior to joining the EMN, Ave worked in a number of research positions internationally, including a Fellowship at the John W. Kluge Center at the Library of Congress in Washington, DC. Her expertise includes highly-skilled migration, labour market integration, identity politics, global cities, technopoles and global mobility.

Thomas **Pfeffer,** Dr., ist wissenschaftlicher Mitarbeiter am Department für Migration und Globalisierung. Als Soziologe mit Fokus auf Systemtheorie, Bildungs- und Organisationssoziologie beschäftigt er sich mit dem internationalen Transfer von Qualifikationen und Kompetenzen, mit institutionellen Formen des Umgangs mit Migration und Diversität und mit Anwendungen der Systemtheorie in der empirischen Migrationsforschung.

Monder **Ram,** OBE, Prof., is the Director of the Centre for Research in Ethnic Minority Entrepreneurship (CREME). He is a leading authority on small business and ethnic minority entrepreneurship research and has published widely on the subject, and has extensive experience of working in and acting as a consultant to small and ethnic minority businesses. He acts as advisor the government on the importance and value of ethnic minority businesses through his position on the APPG for BAME Business Owners. Monder also holds visiting positions at Warwick University and the University of Turku.

Lydia **Rössl**, Dr.[in], hat an der Universität Wien in der Kultur- und Sozialanthropologie promoviert. Sie ist seit 2010 wissenschaftliche Mitarbeiterin am Department für Migration und Globalisierung der Donau-Universität Krems und in der Forschung und Lehre tätig. Ihre Arbeitsschwerpunkte umfassen u.a. Integration und Diversität im Gesundheitssystem, medizinischer Pluralismus und qualitative Netzwerkforschung.

Ali Ahmad **Safi** is a PhD student in the Department of Migration and Globalization at Danube University Krems (DUK). He obtained his MA in Peace and Conflict Studies from European Peace University. Ali has worked for VIDC since 2015 as consultant and has authored research papers on Afghan refugee and diaspora communities in Europe. Trained as physician, he has extensively published on political, security and social topics in Afghanistan in various international research and media organizations. His research areas are migration, diaspora, labor market and non-state security actors.

Christiane **Schnetzer**, Dipl. Ing.[in] MA, ist Unternehmensberaterin für Organisationsentwicklung und Umweltmanagement und als diplomierte Trainerin der Erwachsenenbildung für Global Mobility, interkulturelle Themen und Vielfalt tätig. Sie ist Co-Vorstandsvorsitzende des Clubs der Angehörigen der Bediensteten des österreichischen Außenministeriums. Sie studierte in Deutschland an der Technischen Universität Bergakademie Freiberg Grundstoffverfahrenstechnik, an der Hochschule für Wirtschaft und Recht Berlin Umwelt- und Qualitätsmanagement und an der Donau-Universität Krems Interkulturelle Kompetenz.

Inmaculada **Serrano** is a Senior Researcher at the University Institute for the Study of Migrations (IUEM) of Comillas Pontifical University. She is a PhD on Political Science by the Autonomous University of Madrid and her research focuses on international migration and forced migration. She has worked at UNHCR Geneva and several international research projects, including MAFE/MESE - Migration between Africa and Europe/Spain – and TEMPER - Temporary versus Permanent Migration. Currently, she is the Research Coordinator of the H2020 IMMERSE project – Mapping the Integration of Refugee and Migrant Children in Europe – at IUEM.

Franziska **Simader-Schober**, MSc, ist als Migrationsexpertin für die Ausländerbeschäftigung in der Erste Group Bank AG tätig. Hier beschäftigt sie sich im Speziellen mit der Erlangung des Zugangs zum österreichischen Arbeitsmarkt für nicht EU-Bürgerinnen und EU-Bürger. In Folge kümmert sie sich um die Integration dieser Mitarbeiterinnen und Mitarbeiter in das Unternehmen, unterstützt darüber hinaus auch bei alltägliche Anforderungen, vorwiegend bei Behördenangelegenheiten.

Alexander **Spiegelfeld** is a Research and Communications Associate at the IOM Country Office for Austria. He studied Social Policy and Development at the London School of Economics and Political Science, as well as Nonprofit, Social and Healthcare management at the Management Centre Innsbruck. Prior to his assignment with the IOM, Alexander worked as a program manager for the Directorate-General Employment, Social Affairs and Inclusion of the European Commission.

Adrien **Vandenbunder** is a PhD candidate in economics at the University of Paris-Dauphine (LEDa-DIAL) and the French Institute for Demographic Studies (INED). His thesis focuses on the definitions, determinants and effects of repeated and circular migrations, with the case study of Senegal. He was previously data manager on the TEMPER project.

Marieke **van Houte**, Dr.[in], is a postdoctoral researcher at the Department of Public Administration and Sociology at Erasmus University Rotterdam. Her research is on the relationship between migration, change, conflict and development. Key themes are migration from (post-) conflict countries, return migration, transnational engagement of migrants, and processes of structure and agency in mobility. She completed the PhD on return migration after conflict at Maastricht University. Before joining Erasmus University, she worked as a Marie Curie Research Fellow at the International Migration Institute (University of Oxford), and at Vrije Universiteit Amsterdam.